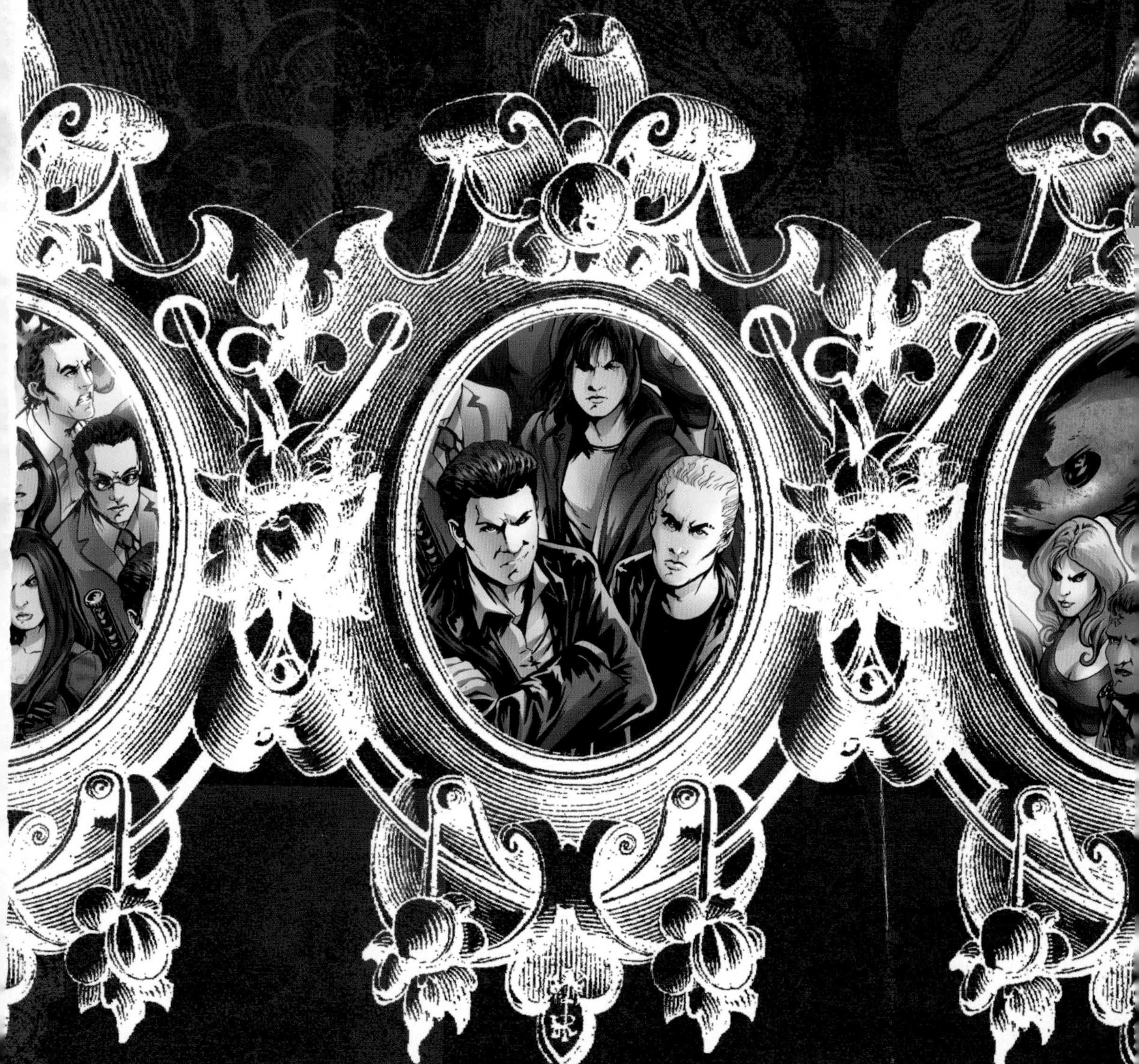

ANGEL™

—AFTER THE FALL—

VOLUME 1

PLOTTED BY
JOSS WHEDON AND BRIAN LYNCH

SCRIPTED BY BRIAN LYNCH
ILLUSTRATED BY FRANCO URRU

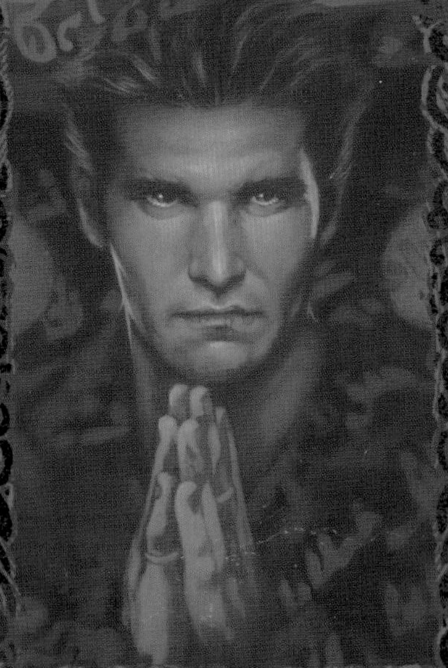

COLORED BY
JASON JENSEN, ART LYON, AND ILARIA TRAVERSI

COVER ART BY ALEX GARNER

LETTERED BY ROBBIE ROBBINS

ORIGINAL SERIES EDITED BY CHRIS RYALL

COLLECTION EDITED BY JUSTIN EISINGER

COLLECTION DESIGNED BY ROBBIE ROBBINS

ISBN: 978-1-60010-181-6

11 10 09 08   01 02 03 04

www.IDWPUBLISHING.com

Angel created by Joss Whedon and David Greenwalt.
Special thanks to our Watcher, Joss Whedon, and Fox Worldwide Publishing's
Debbie Olshan for their invaluable assistance.

IDW Publishing
Operations:
Moshe Berger, Chairman
Ted Adams, President
Clifford Meth, EVP of Strategies
Matthew Ruzicka, CPA, Controller
Alan Payne, VP of Sales
Lorelei Bunjes, Dir. of Digital Services
Marci Kahn, Executive Assistant
Alonzo Simon, Shipping Manager

Editorial:
Chris Ryall, Publisher/Editor-in-Chief
Scott Dunbier, Editor, Special Projects
Justin Eisinger, Editor
Kris Oprisko, Editor/Foreign Lic.
Denton J. Tipton, Editor
Tom Waltz, Editor

Design:
Robbie Robbins, EVP/Sr. Graphic Artist
Ben Templesmith, Artist/Designer
Neil Uyetake, Art Director
Chris Mowry, Graphic Artist
Amauri Osorio, Graphic Artist

It was a weekly ritual. I'd go over to my friend's house, or my friends piled into my apartment, and we'd watch the new episode of *Angel*. It began with the very first episode, with my then–girlfriend. The girl and I broke up (I got custody of the DVDs), but the ritual continued with other friends.

And one night (the Internet tells me it was March 4, 2002 to be exact… ooooh, beware the, um, 4th of March…), an episode of *Angel* out-and-out ruined me. To recap, Angel had a newborn son, Wesley discovered prophecies that Angel was going to kill said newborn son, and the forces of Wolfram & Hart and every demon in the city wanted a piece of said newborn son.

And Holtz. Oh, don't get me started on Holtz.

This arc wasn't without its laugh-out-loud moments. Sure, the Drive-Thru Hamburger being a conduit for a higher power was hilarious, and Demon Skip had the best deadpan delivery on television, but they were mere blips of relief from the stress. As per usual, Mr. Whedon and Mr. Greenwalt were throwing everything at our heroes. How on Earth was Angel going to save his son? I mean, even Wesley was working against him. This was going to be something, but surely everything would be okay, they wouldn't—

—oh wait, they *would* steal the baby and toss 'im into a hell dimension. Angel's on the ground, defeated (Wolfram & Hart even kinda took pity on him), the baby went to Hell in the care of Angel's then-greatest enemy, Wesley is dying… what other show attempts these kinds of things? It was truly one of the best hours of television I had ever seen, and I couldn't wait until next week.

But then the show went away for a *month*. Reruns until April 15th. Those cold-hearted bastards made me wait a month to see if everything was okay.

Of course, this being *Angel*, everything was not okay, nor would it ever be okay. Sure, the baby came back, but he had a big ol' chip on his shoulder and an attraction for Angel's ladyfriend. Wesley and Angel worked out their problems, but then Wesley had to go and die.

And Fred. Oh, don't get me started on Fred.

That month-long wait, though, was nothing in comparison to the three long years I had to endure before finding out what happened after Angel, Spike, Gunn and Illyria stood in that alleyway, ready to face down hordes of evil.

But this time, I had a say in what happened. Beyond my usual shouting at the television, I am now helping steer the ship. I get to be a cold-hearted bastard! Life, sometimes, can be quite awesome.

The wait is over. They're back.

And I'm so sorry about the month-long wait between issues. I've been there.

Brian Lynch
04/08/08

introduction

chapter
one

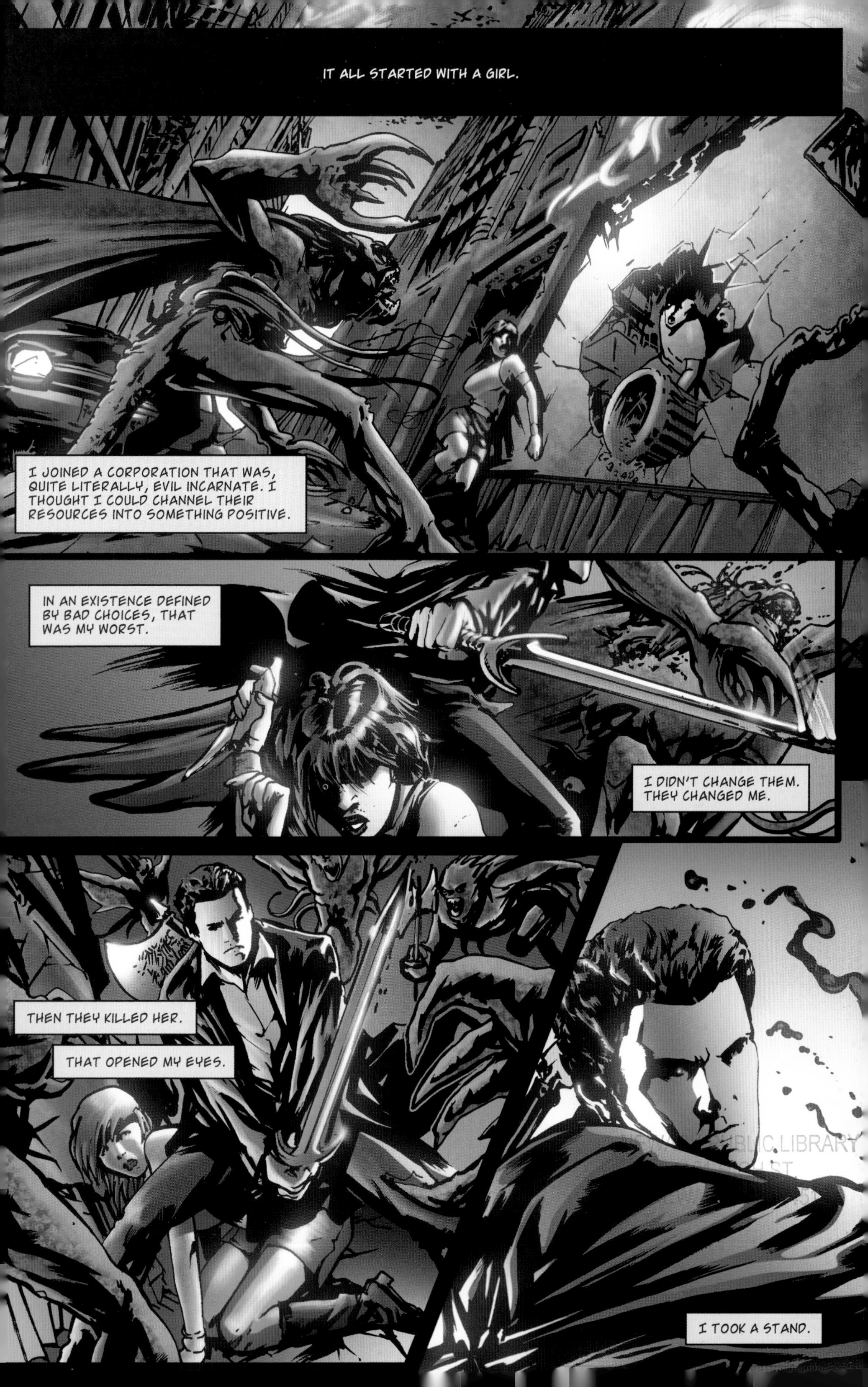
IT ALL STARTED WITH A GIRL.
I JOINED A CORPORATION THAT WAS, QUITE LITERALLY, EVIL INCARNATE. I THOUGHT I COULD CHANNEL THEIR RESOURCES INTO SOMETHING POSITIVE.
IN AN EXISTENCE DEFINED BY BAD CHOICES, THAT WAS MY WORST.
I DIDN'T CHANGE THEM. THEY CHANGED ME.
THEN THEY KILLED HER.
THAT OPENED MY EYES.
I TOOK A STAND.

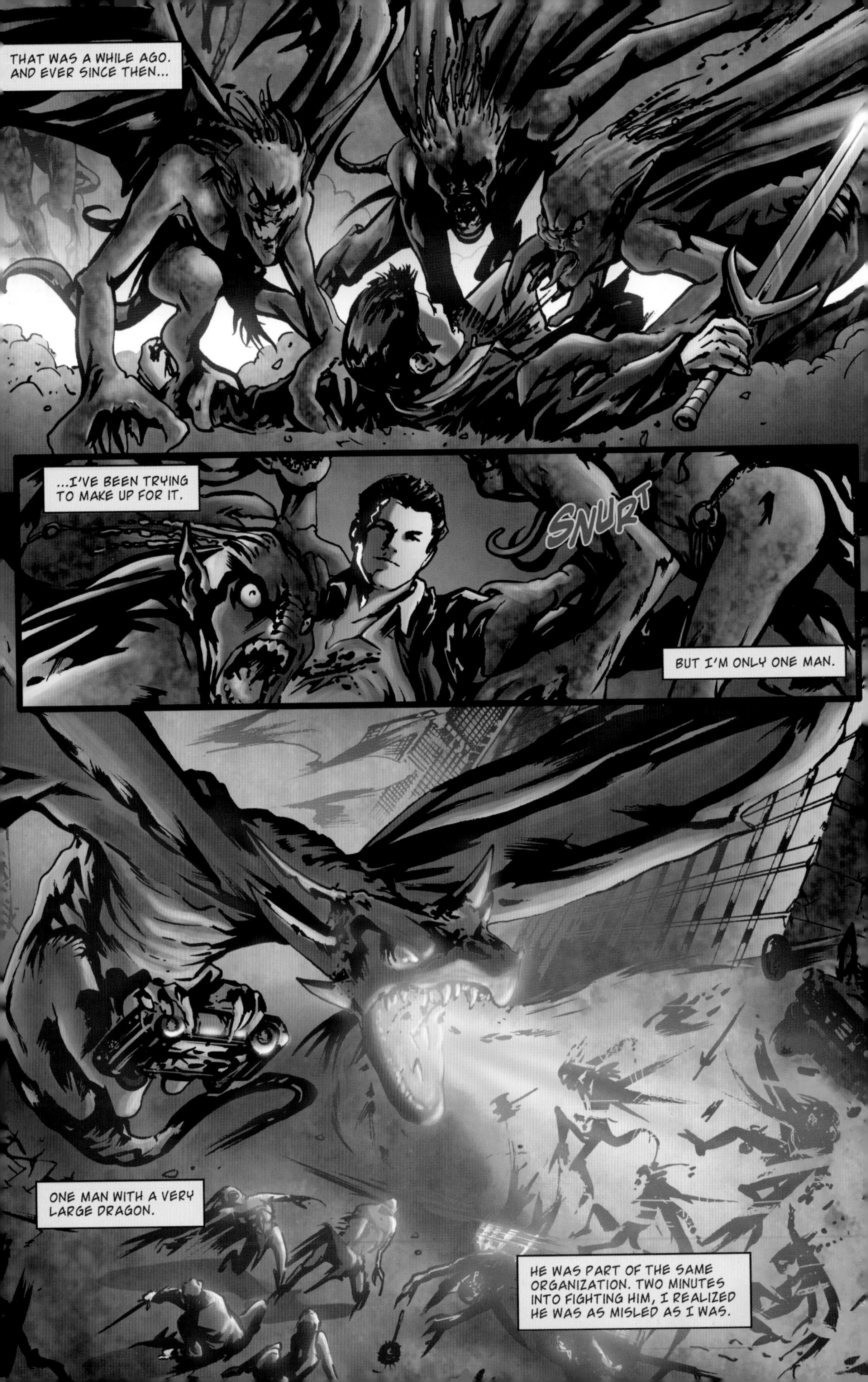
THAT WAS A WHILE AGO. AND EVER SINCE THEN...
...I'VE BEEN TRYING TO MAKE UP FOR IT.
SNURT
BUT I'M ONLY ONE MAN.
ONE MAN WITH A VERY LARGE DRAGON.
HE WAS PART OF THE SAME ORGANIZATION. TWO MINUTES INTO FIGHTING HIM, I REALIZED HE WAS AS MISLED AS I WAS.

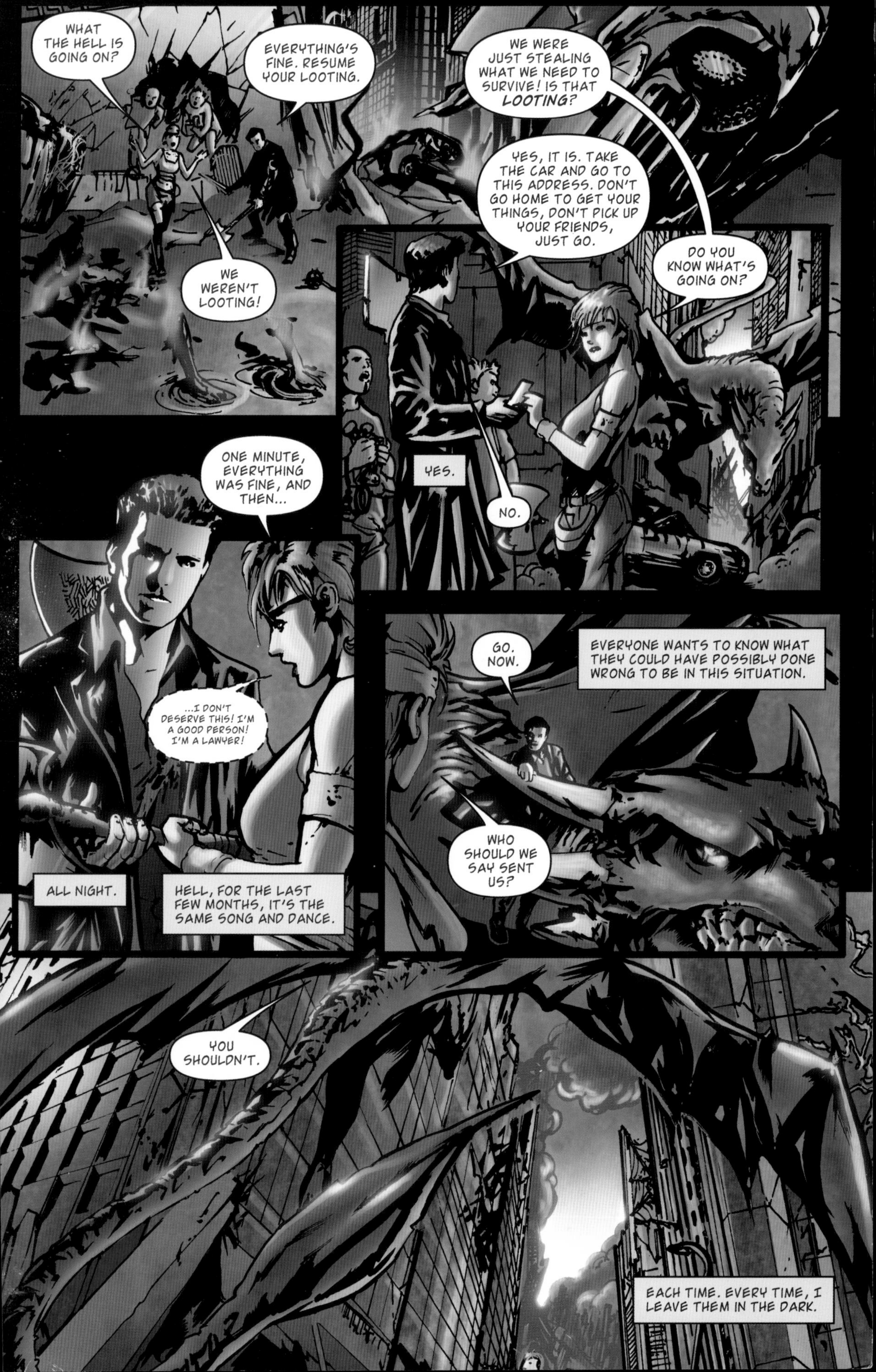
WHAT THE HELL IS GOING ON?
EVERYTHING'S FINE. RESUME YOUR LOOTING.
WE WEREN'T LOOTING!
WE WERE JUST STEALING WHAT WE NEED TO SURVIVE! IS THAT LOOTING?
YES, IT IS. TAKE THE CAR AND GO TO THIS ADDRESS. DON'T GO HOME TO GET YOUR THINGS, DON'T PICK UP YOUR FRIENDS, JUST GO.
DO YOU KNOW WHAT'S GOING ON?
YES.
NO.
ONE MINUTE, EVERYTHING WAS FINE, AND THEN...
...I DON'T DESERVE THIS! I'M A GOOD PERSON! I'M A LAWYER!
ALL NIGHT.
HELL, FOR THE LAST FEW MONTHS, IT'S THE SAME SONG AND DANCE.
GO. NOW.
EVERYONE WANTS TO KNOW WHAT THEY COULD HAVE POSSIBLY DONE WRONG TO BE IN THIS SITUATION.
WHO SHOULD WE SAY SENT US?
YOU SHOULDN'T.
EACH TIME. EVERY TIME, I LEAVE THEM IN THE DARK.

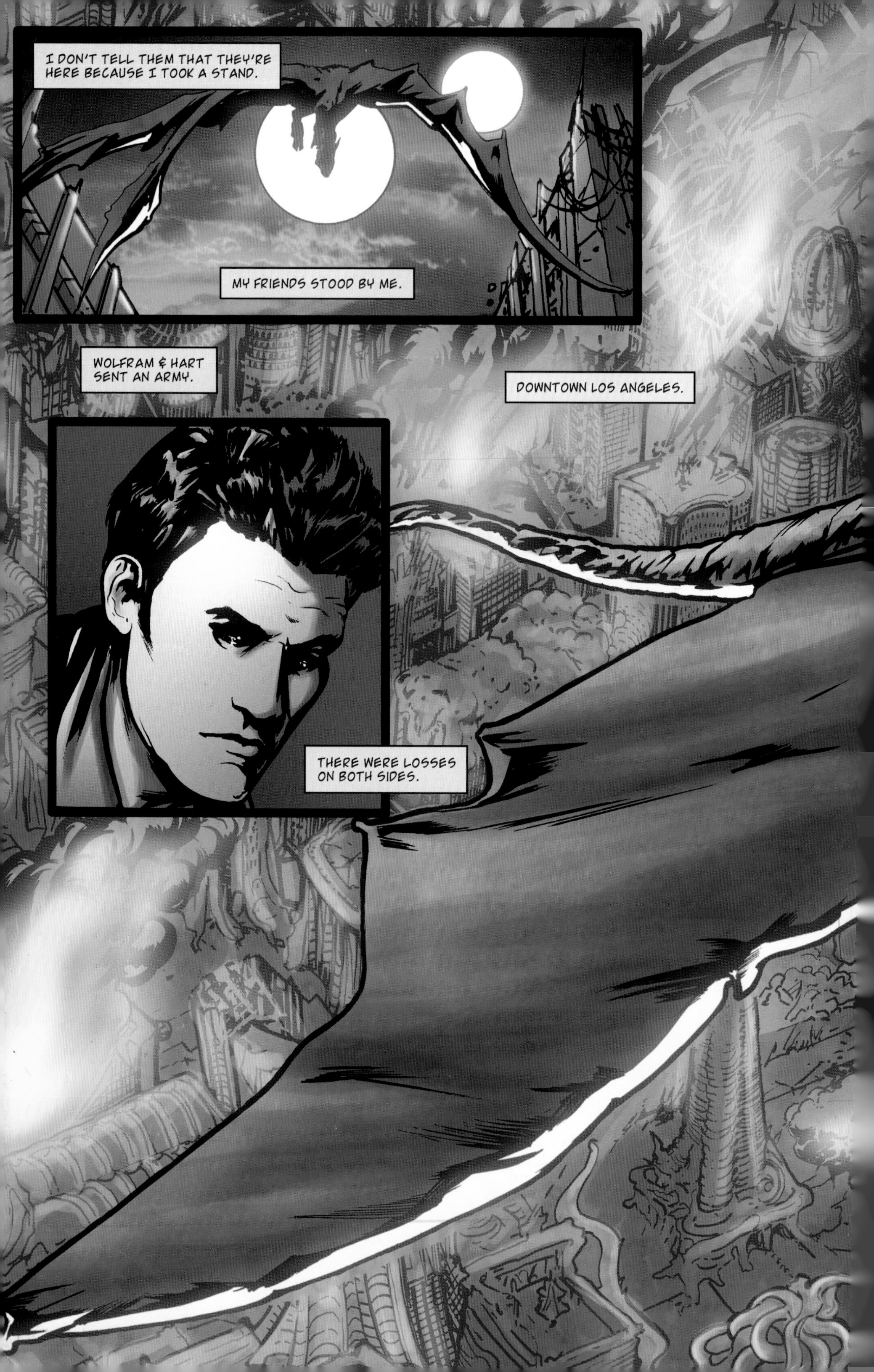
I DON'T TELL THEM THAT THEY'RE HERE BECAUSE I TOOK A STAND.
MY FRIENDS STOOD BY ME.
WOLFRAM & HART SENT AN ARMY.
DOWNTOWN LOS ANGELES.
THERE WERE LOSSES ON BOTH SIDES.

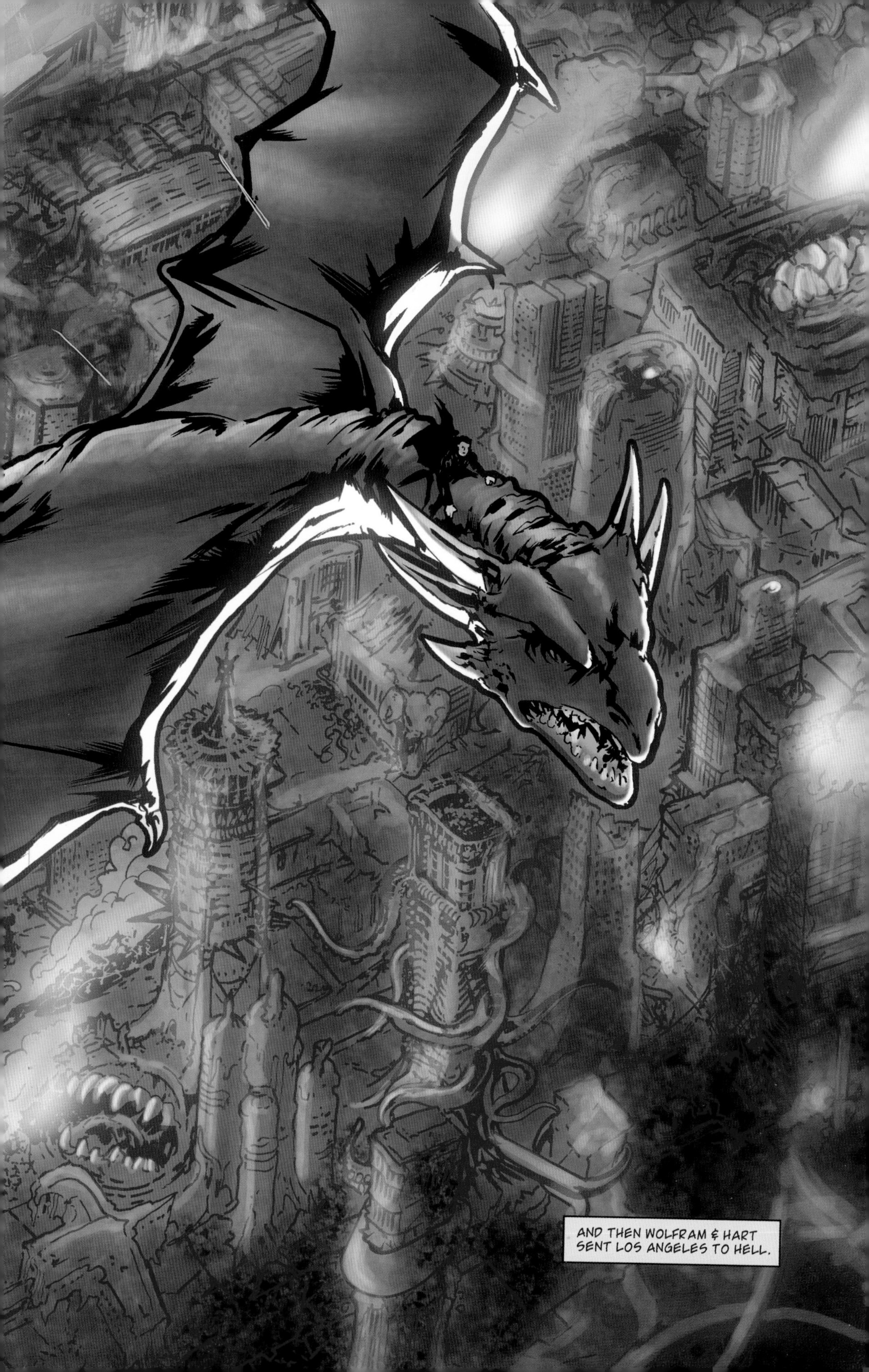
AND THEN WOLFRAM & HART SENT LOS ANGELES TO HELL.

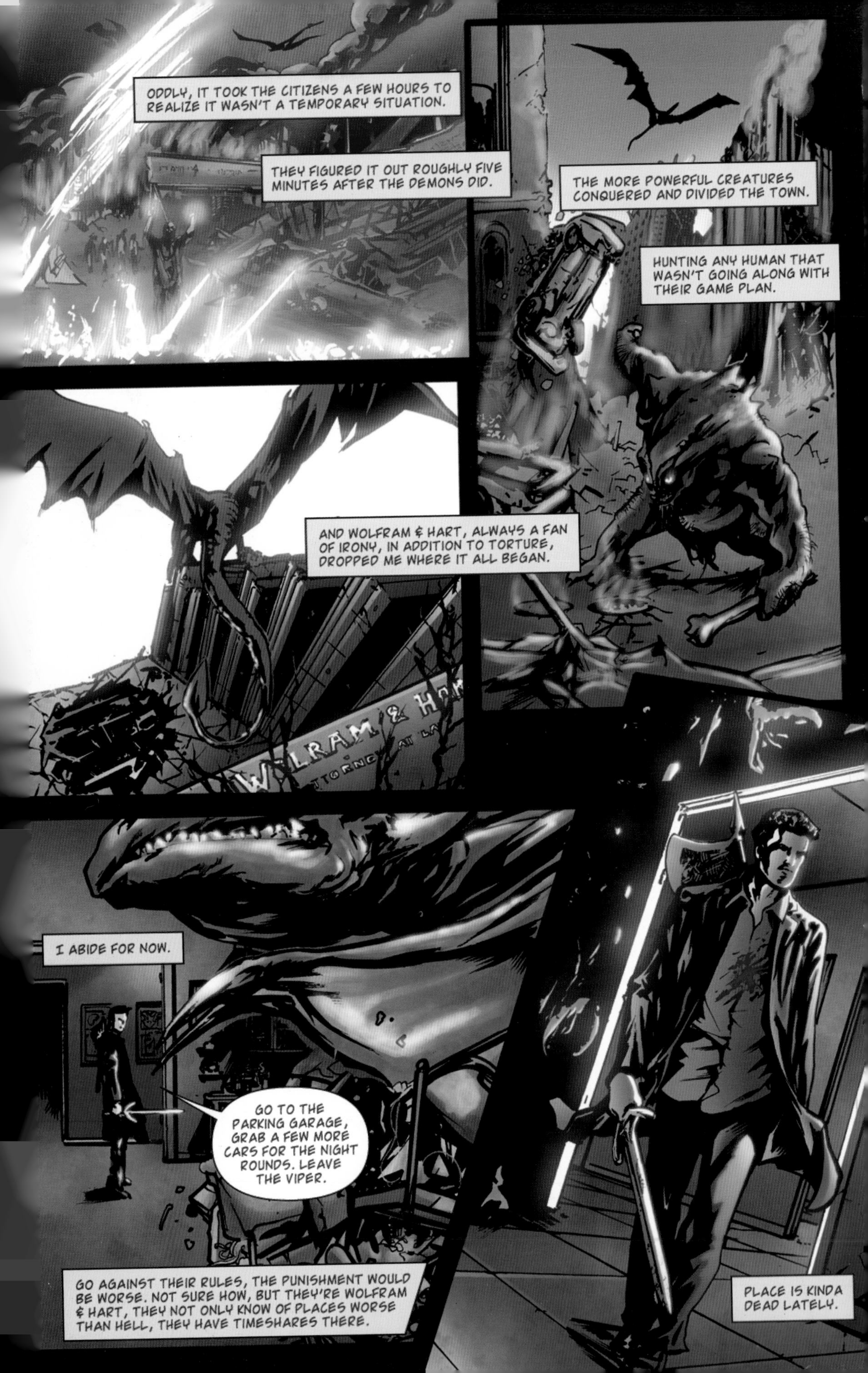
ODDLY, IT TOOK THE CITIZENS A FEW HOURS TO REALIZE IT WASN'T A TEMPORARY SITUATION.
THEY FIGURED IT OUT ROUGHLY FIVE MINUTES AFTER THE DEMONS DID.
THE MORE POWERFUL CREATURES CONQUERED AND DIVIDED THE TOWN.
HUNTING ANY HUMAN THAT WASN'T GOING ALONG WITH THEIR GAME PLAN.
AND WOLFRAM & HART, ALWAYS A FAN OF IRONY, IN ADDITION TO TORTURE, DROPPED ME WHERE IT ALL BEGAN.
I ABIDE FOR NOW.
GO TO THE PARKING GARAGE, GRAB A FEW MORE CARS FOR THE NIGHT ROUNDS. LEAVE THE VIPER.
GO AGAINST THEIR RULES, THE PUNISHMENT WOULD BE WORSE. NOT SURE HOW, BUT THEY'RE WOLFRAM & HART, THEY NOT ONLY KNOW OF PLACES WORSE THAN HELL, THEY HAVE TIMESHARES THERE.
PLACE IS KINDA DEAD LATELY.

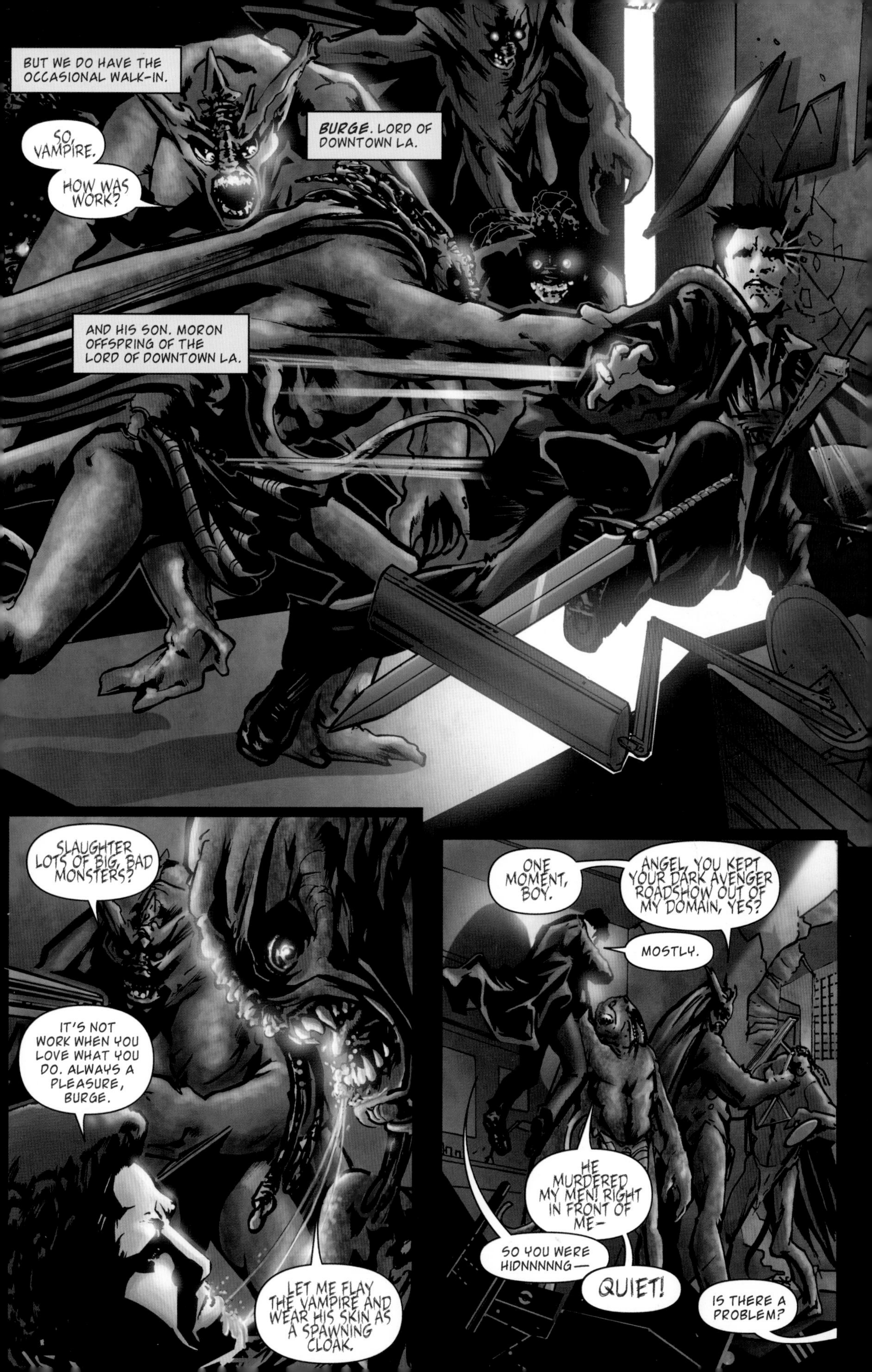
BUT WE DO HAVE THE OCCASIONAL WALK-IN.
SO, VAMPIRE.
HOW WAS WORK?
BURGE. LORD OF DOWNTOWN LA.
AND HIS SON. MORON OFFSPRING OF THE LORD OF DOWNTOWN LA.
SLAUGHTER LOTS OF BIG, BAD MONSTERS?
IT'S NOT WORK WHEN YOU LOVE WHAT YOU DO. ALWAYS A PLEASURE, BURGE.
LET ME FLAY THE VAMPIRE AND WEAR HIS SKIN AS A SPAWNING CLOAK.
ONE MOMENT, BOY.
ANGEL, YOU KEPT YOUR DARK AVENGER ROADSHOW OUT OF MY DOMAIN, YES?
MOSTLY.
HE MURDERED MY MEN! RIGHT IN FRONT OF ME—
SO YOU WERE HIDNNNNNG—
QUIET!
IS THERE A PROBLEM?

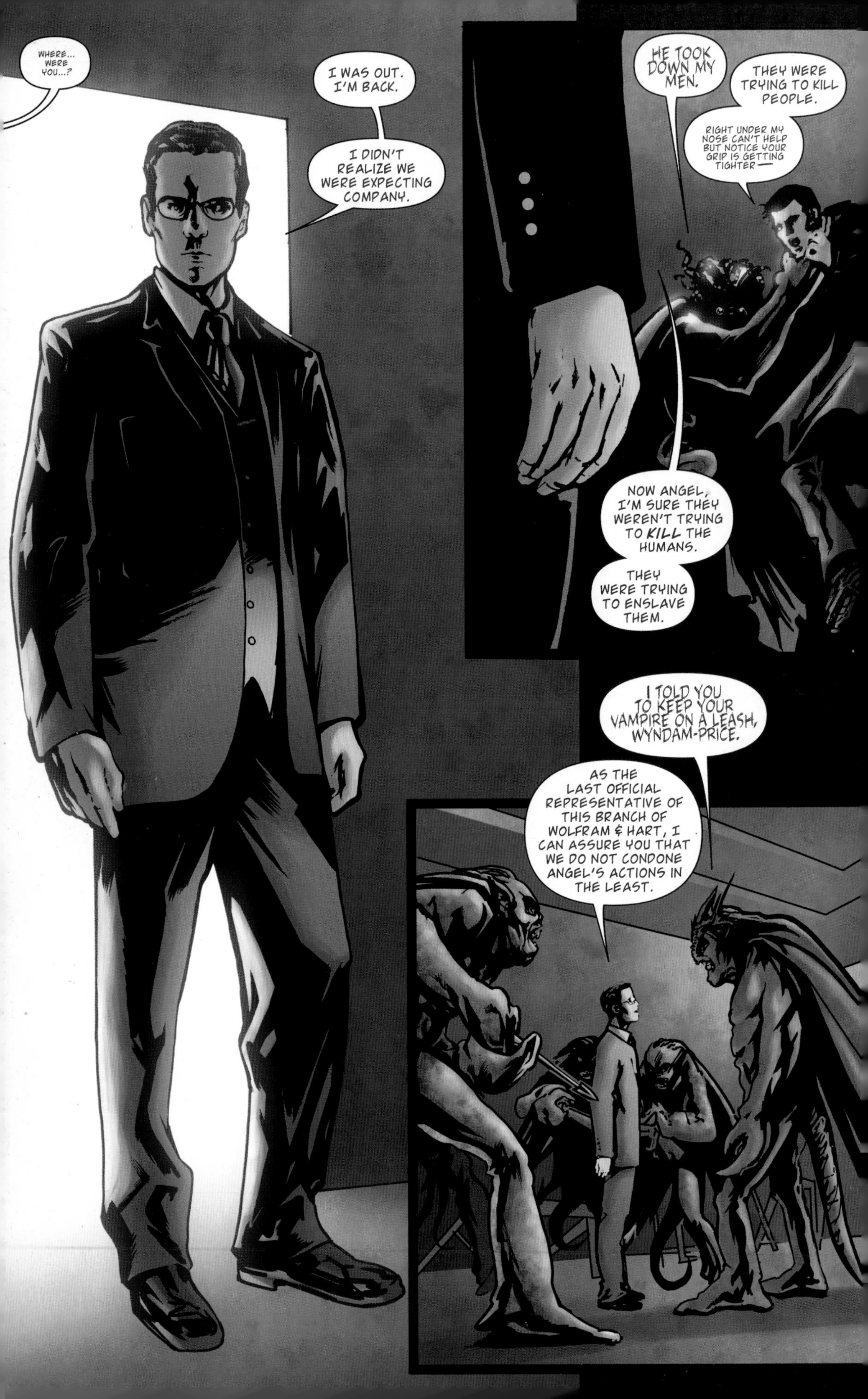
WHERE... WERE YOU...?
I WAS OUT. I'M BACK.
I DIDN'T REALIZE WE WERE EXPECTING COMPANY.
HE TOOK DOWN MY MEN.
THEY WERE TRYING TO KILL PEOPLE.
RIGHT UNDER MY NOSE CAN'T HELP BUT NOTICE YOUR GRIP IS GETTING TIGHTER—
NOW ANGEL, I'M SURE THEY WEREN'T TRYING TO KILL THE HUMANS.
THEY WERE TRYING TO ENSLAVE THEM.
I TOLD YOU TO KEEP YOUR VAMPIRE ON A LEASH, WYNDAM-PRICE.
AS THE LAST OFFICIAL REPRESENTATIVE OF THIS BRANCH OF WOLFRAM & HART, I CAN ASSURE YOU THAT WE DO NOT CONDONE ANGEL'S ACTIONS IN THE LEAST.

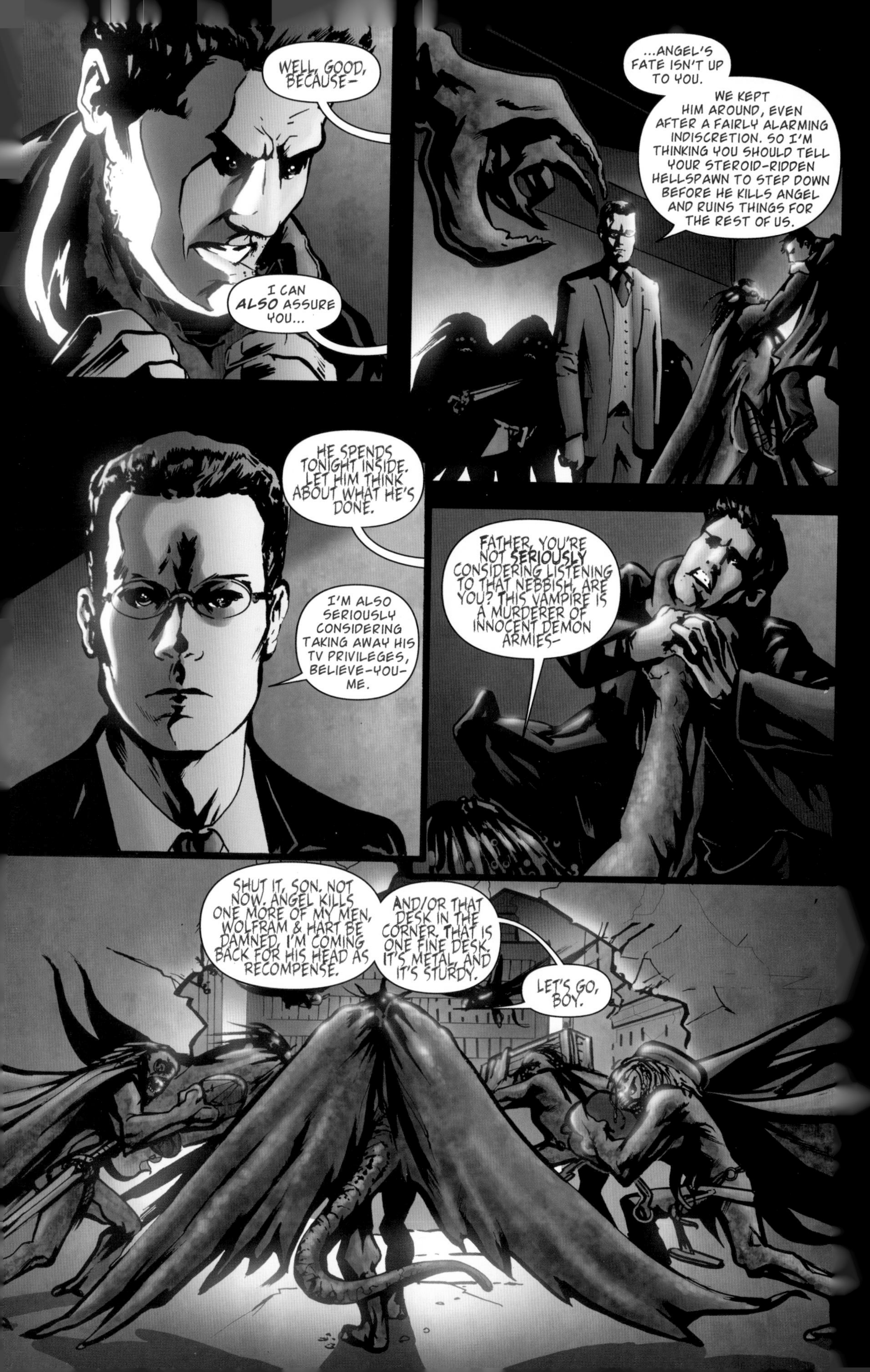
WELL, GOOD, BECAUSE–
I CAN ALSO ASSURE YOU...
...ANGEL'S FATE ISN'T UP TO YOU.
WE KEPT HIM AROUND, EVEN AFTER A FAIRLY ALARMING INDISCRETION. SO I'M THINKING YOU SHOULD TELL YOUR STEROID-RIDDEN HELLSPAWN TO STEP DOWN BEFORE HE KILLS ANGEL AND RUINS THINGS FOR THE REST OF US.
HE SPENDS TONIGHT INSIDE. LET HIM THINK ABOUT WHAT HE'S DONE.
I'M ALSO SERIOUSLY CONSIDERING TAKING AWAY HIS TV PRIVILEGES, BELIEVE-YOU-ME.
FATHER, YOU'RE NOT SERIOUSLY CONSIDERING LISTENING TO THAT NEBBISH, ARE YOU? THIS VAMPIRE IS A MURDERER OF INNOCENT DEMON ARMIES–
SHUT IT, SON. NOT NOW. ANGEL KILLS ONE MORE OF MY MEN, WOLFRAM & HART BE DAMNED, I'M COMING BACK FOR HIS HEAD AS RECOMPENSE.
AND/OR THAT DESK IN THE CORNER. THAT IS ONE FINE DESK. IT'S METAL, AND IT'S STURDY.
LET'S GO, BOY.

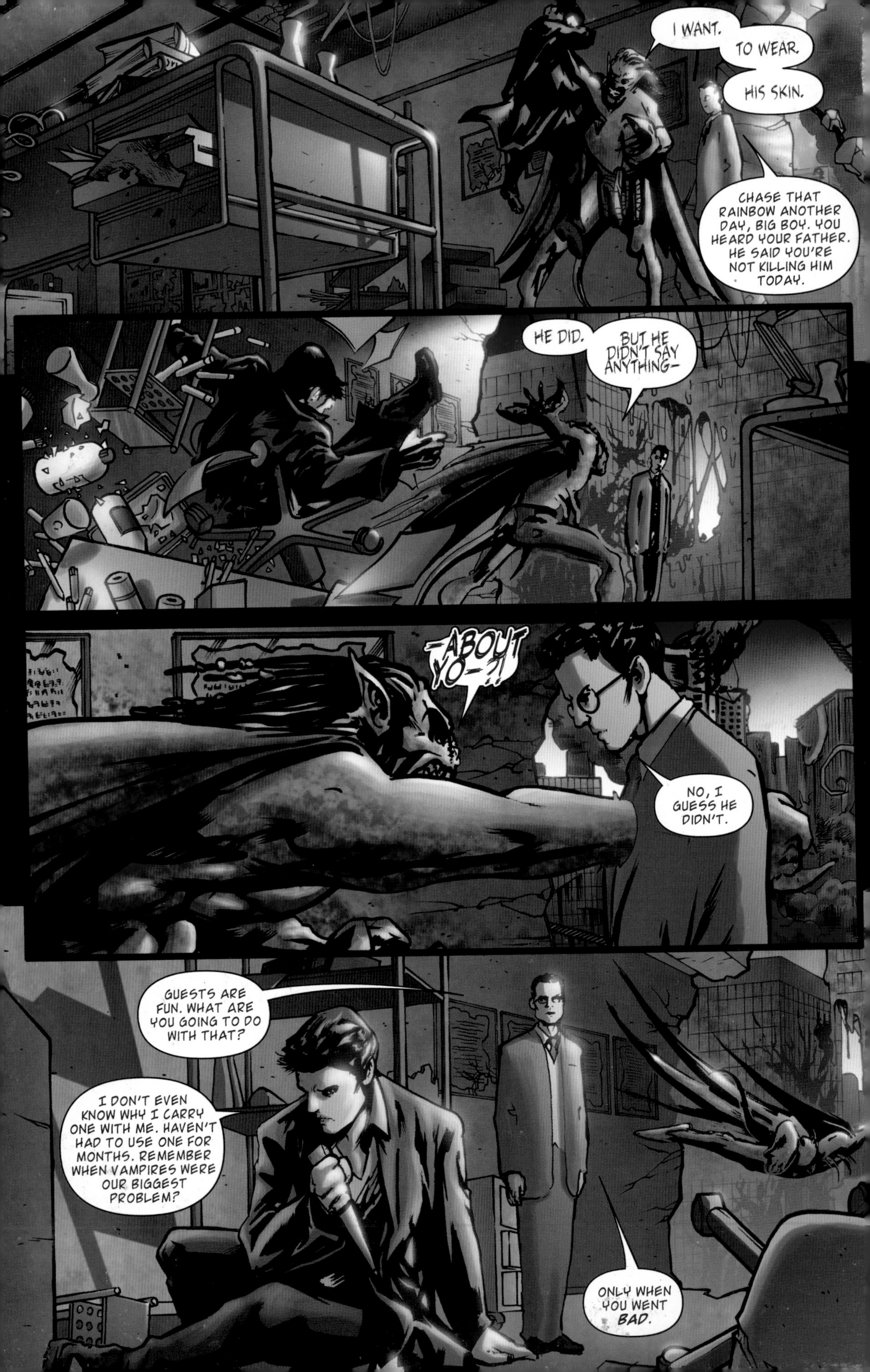
I WANT.
TO WEAR.
HIS SKIN.
CHASE THAT RAINBOW ANOTHER DAY, BIG BOY. YOU HEARD YOUR FATHER. HE SAID YOU'RE NOT KILLING HIM TODAY.
HE DID.
BUT HE DIDN'T SAY ANYTHING—
—ABOUT YO—?!
NO, I GUESS HE DIDN'T.
GUESTS ARE FUN. WHAT ARE YOU GOING TO DO WITH THAT?
I DON'T EVEN KNOW WHY I CARRY ONE WITH ME. HAVEN'T HAD TO USE ONE FOR MONTHS. REMEMBER WHEN VAMPIRES WERE OUR BIGGEST PROBLEM?
ONLY WHEN YOU WENT BAD.

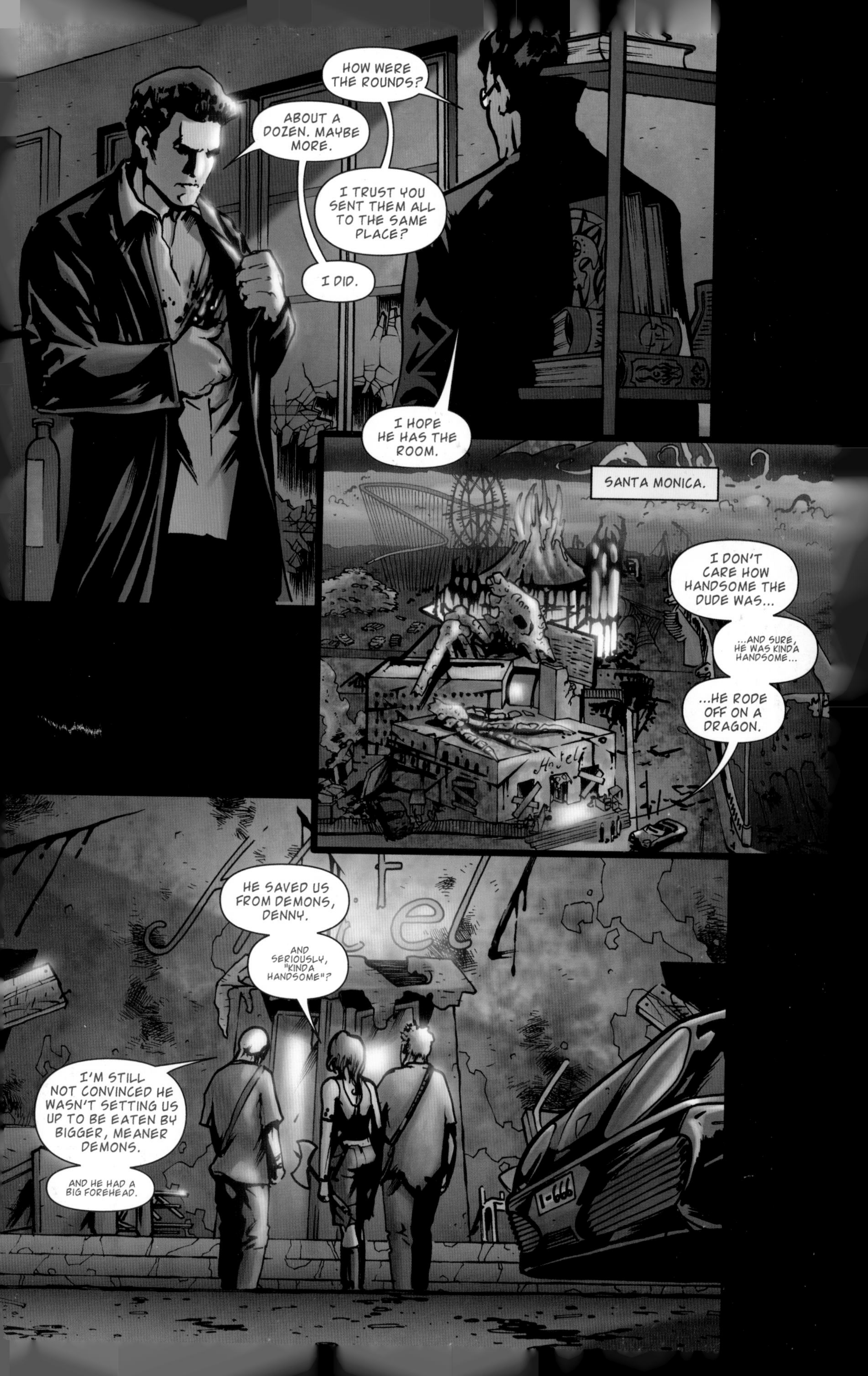
HOW WERE THE ROUNDS?
ABOUT A DOZEN. MAYBE MORE.
I TRUST YOU SENT THEM ALL TO THE SAME PLACE?
I DID.
I HOPE HE HAS THE ROOM.
SANTA MONICA.
I DON'T CARE HOW HANDSOME THE DUDE WAS...
...AND SURE, HE WAS KINDA HANDSOME...
...HE RODE OFF ON A DRAGON.
HE SAVED US FROM DEMONS, DENNY.
AND SERIOUSLY, "KINDA HANDSOME"?
I'M STILL NOT CONVINCED HE WASN'T SETTING US UP TO BE EATEN BY BIGGER, MEANER DEMONS.
AND HE HAD A BIG FOREHEAD.
I-666

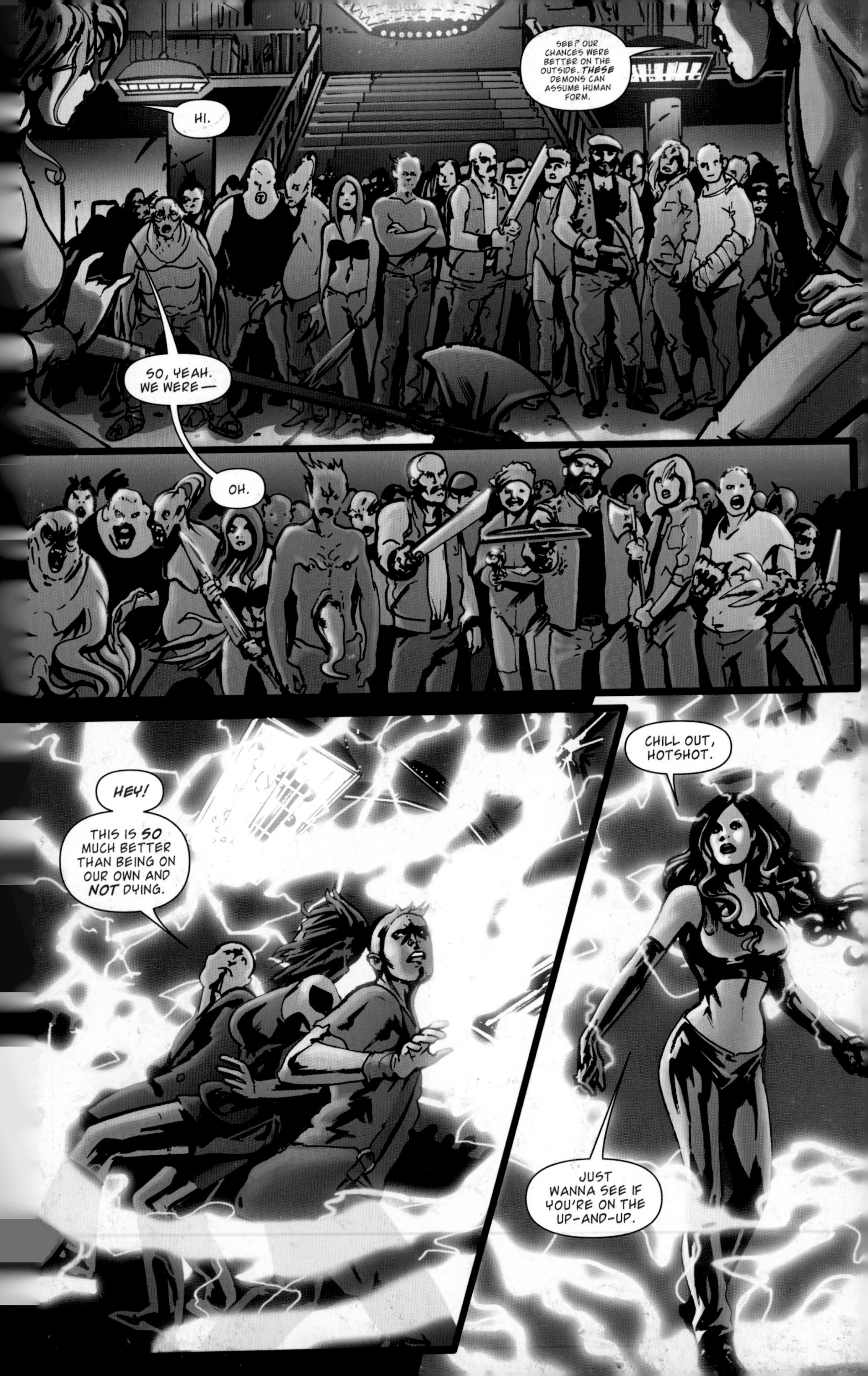
HI.
SEE? OUR CHANCES WERE BETTER ON THE OUTSIDE. THESE DEMONS CAN ASSUME HUMAN FORM.
SO, YEAH. WE WERE—
OH.
HEY!
THIS IS SO MUCH BETTER THAN BEING ON OUR OWN AND NOT DYING.
CHILL OUT, HOTSHOT.
JUST WANNA SEE IF YOU'RE ON THE UP-AND-UP.

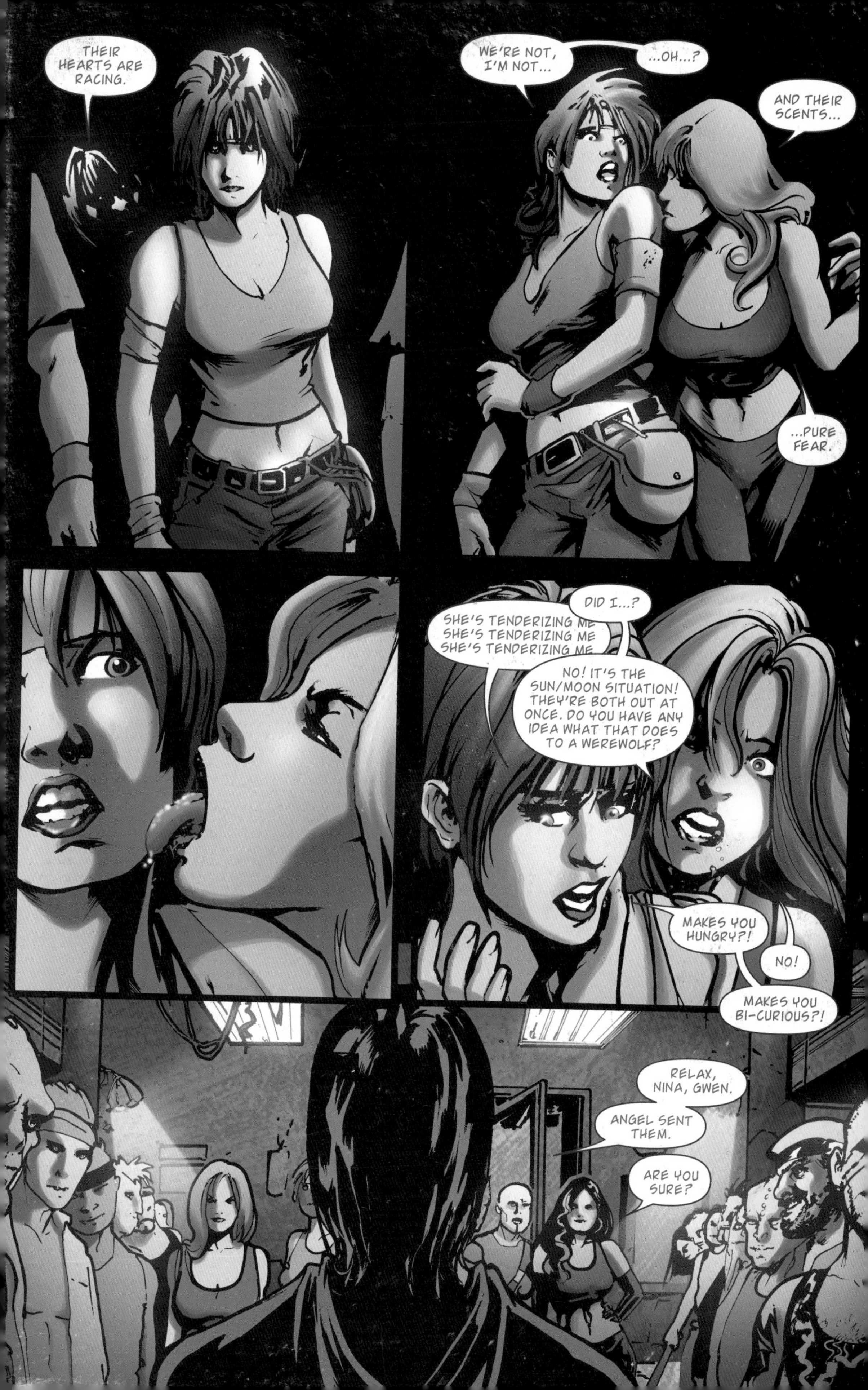
THEIR HEARTS ARE RACING.
WE'RE NOT, I'M NOT...
...OH...?
AND THEIR SCENTS...
...PURE FEAR.
SHE'S TENDERIZING ME SHE'S TENDERIZING ME SHE'S TENDERIZING ME
DID I...?
NO! IT'S THE SUN/MOON SITUATION! THEY'RE BOTH OUT AT ONCE. DO YOU HAVE ANY IDEA WHAT THAT DOES TO A WEREWOLF?
MAKES YOU HUNGRY?!
NO!
MAKES YOU BI-CURIOUS?!
RELAX, NINA, GWEN.
ANGEL SENT THEM.
ARE YOU SURE?

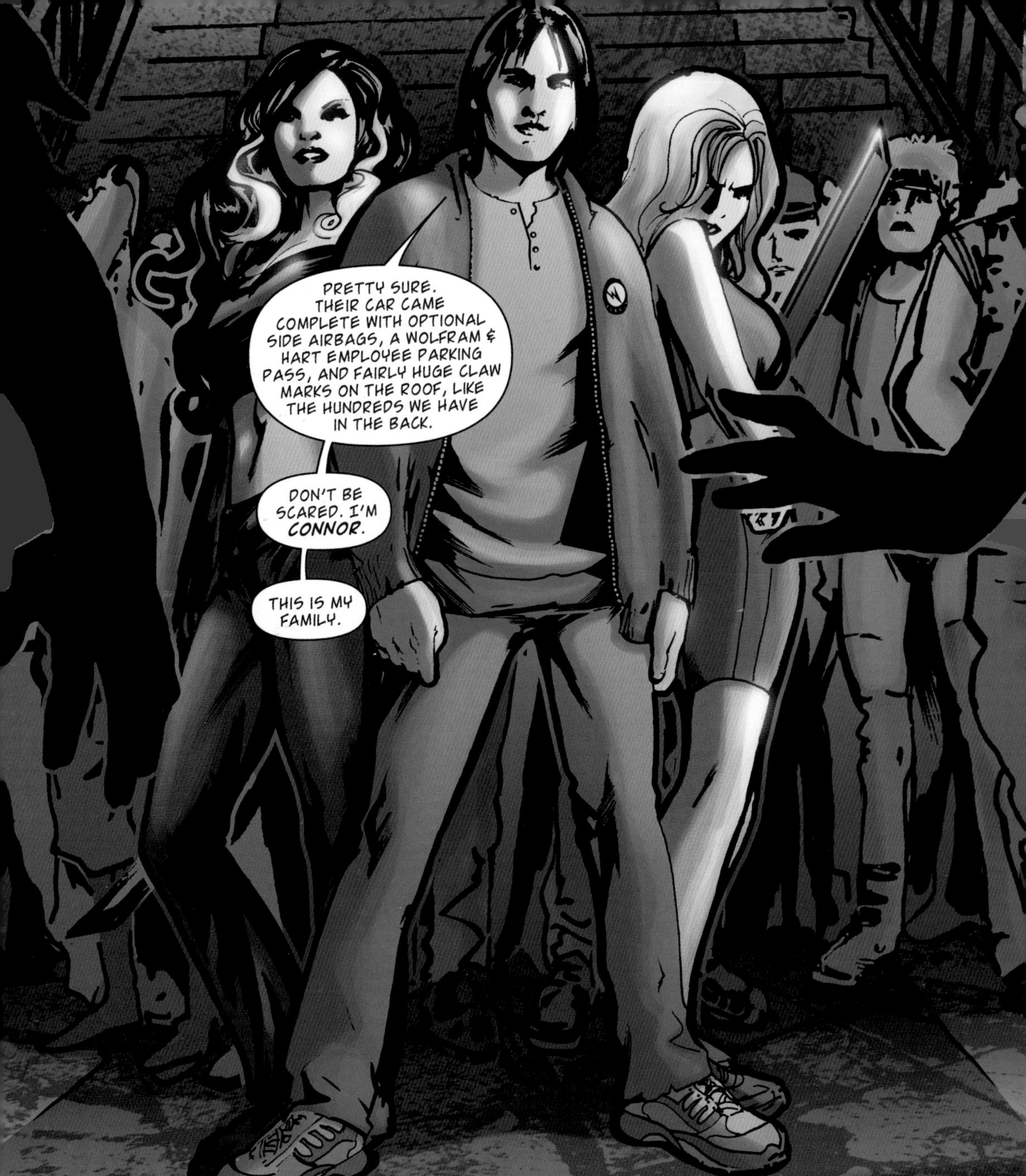
PRETTY SURE. THEIR CAR CAME COMPLETE WITH OPTIONAL SIDE AIRBAGS, A WOLFRAM & HART EMPLOYEE PARKING PASS, AND FAIRLY HUGE CLAW MARKS ON THE ROOF, LIKE THE HUNDREDS WE HAVE IN THE BACK.
DON'T BE SCARED. I'M CONNOR.
THIS IS MY FAMILY.

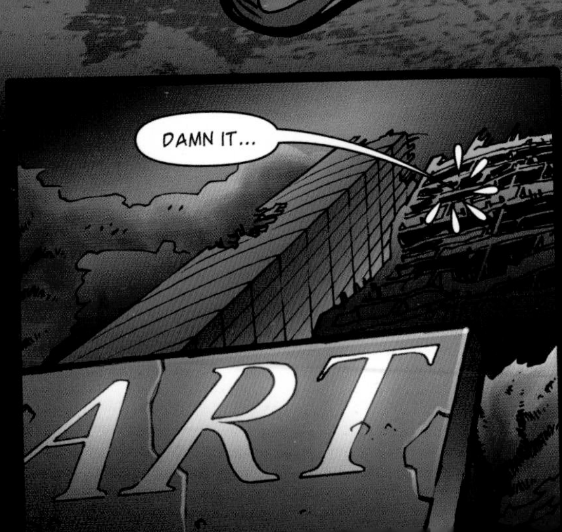
DAMN IT...
ART

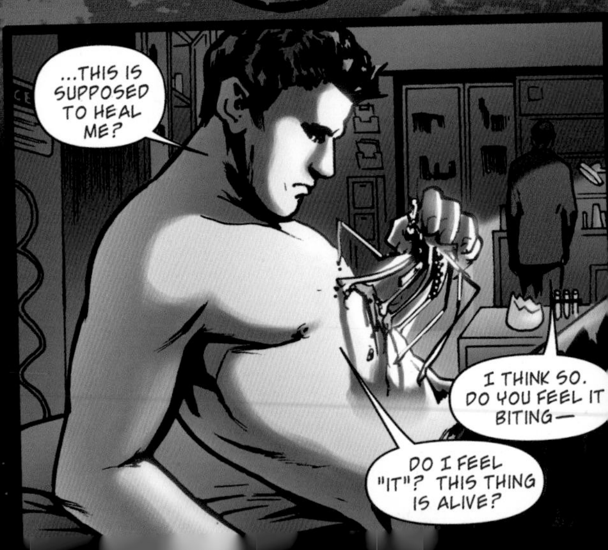
...THIS IS SUPPOSED TO HEAL ME?
I THINK SO. DO YOU FEEL IT BITING—
DO I FEEL "IT"? THIS THING IS ALIVE?

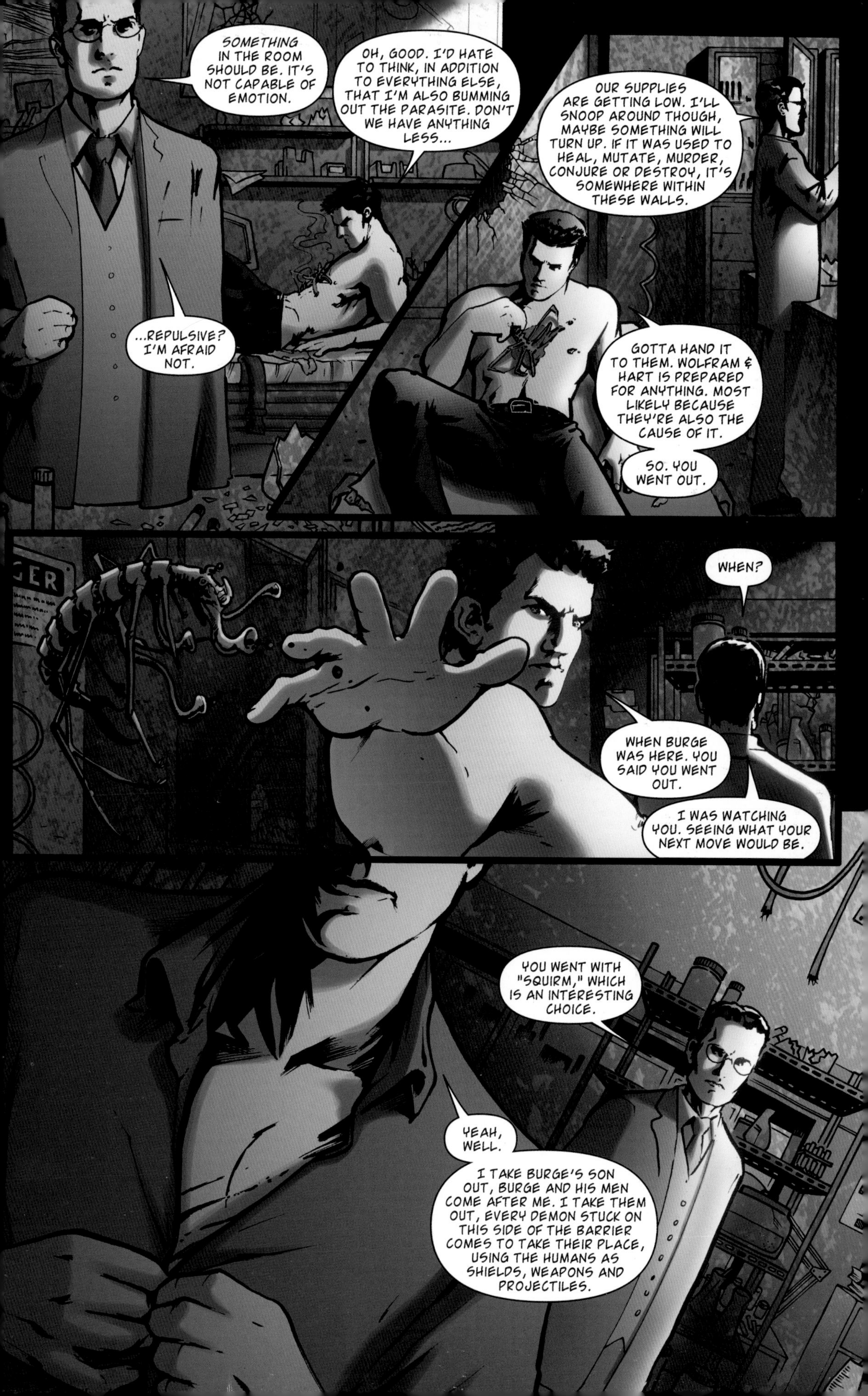
SOMETHING IN THE ROOM SHOULD BE. IT'S NOT CAPABLE OF EMOTION.
OH, GOOD. I'D HATE TO THINK, IN ADDITION TO EVERYTHING ELSE, THAT I'M ALSO BUMMING OUT THE PARASITE. DON'T WE HAVE ANYTHING LESS...
...REPULSIVE? I'M AFRAID NOT.
OUR SUPPLIES ARE GETTING LOW. I'LL SNOOP AROUND THOUGH, MAYBE SOMETHING WILL TURN UP. IF IT WAS USED TO HEAL, MUTATE, MURDER, CONJURE OR DESTROY, IT'S SOMEWHERE WITHIN THESE WALLS.
GOTTA HAND IT TO THEM. WOLFRAM & HART IS PREPARED FOR ANYTHING. MOST LIKELY BECAUSE THEY'RE ALSO THE CAUSE OF IT.
SO. YOU WENT OUT.
WHEN?
WHEN BURGE WAS HERE. YOU SAID YOU WENT OUT.
I WAS WATCHING YOU. SEEING WHAT YOUR NEXT MOVE WOULD BE.
YOU WENT WITH "SQUIRM," WHICH IS AN INTERESTING CHOICE.
YEAH, WELL.
I TAKE BURGE'S SON OUT, BURGE AND HIS MEN COME AFTER ME. I TAKE THEM OUT, EVERY DEMON STUCK ON THIS SIDE OF THE BARRIER COMES TO TAKE THEIR PLACE, USING THE HUMANS AS SHIELDS, WEAPONS AND PROJECTILES.

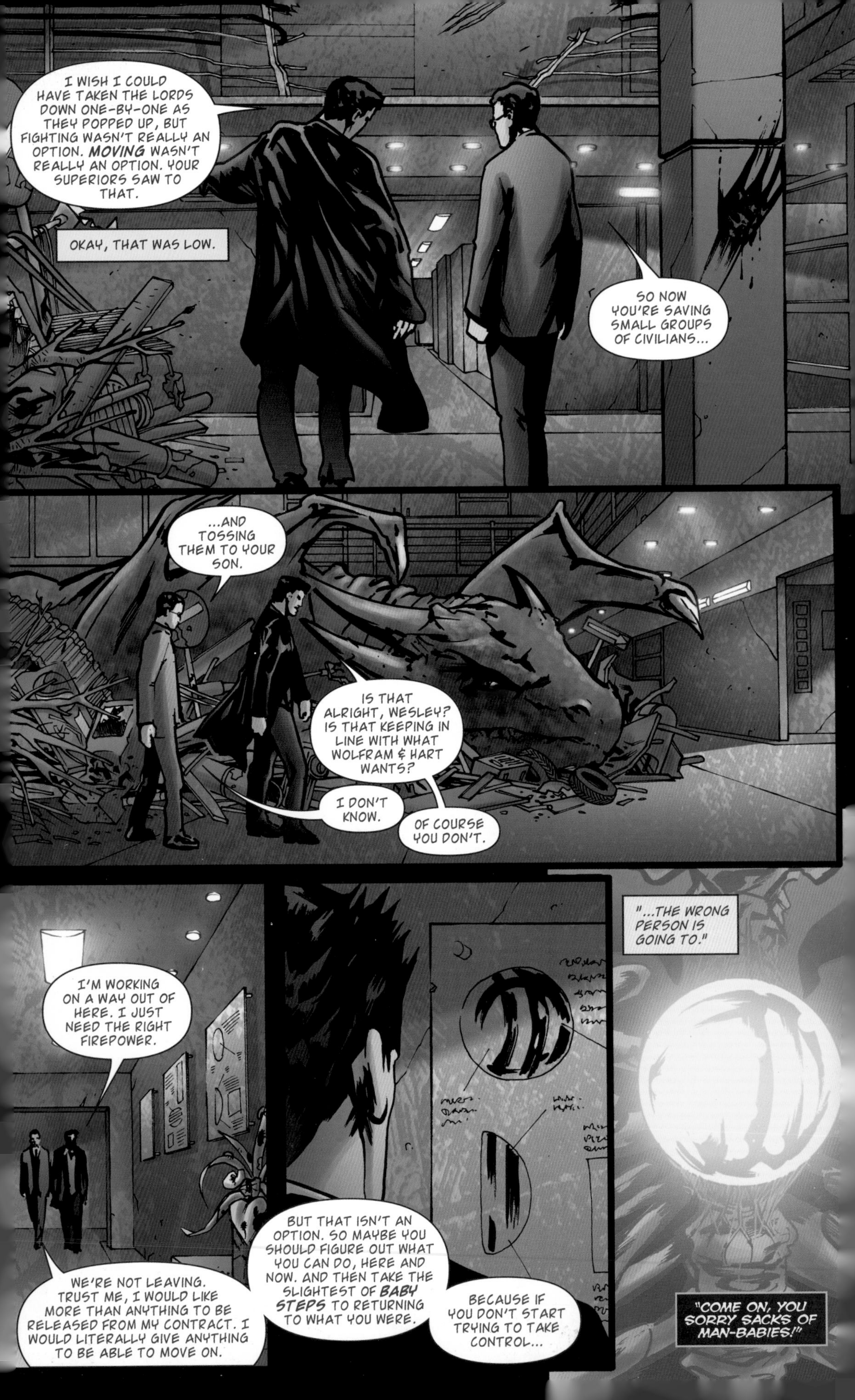
I WISH I COULD HAVE TAKEN THE LORDS DOWN ONE-BY-ONE AS THEY POPPED UP, BUT FIGHTING WASN'T REALLY AN OPTION. MOVING WASN'T REALLY AN OPTION. YOUR SUPERIORS SAW TO THAT.
OKAY, THAT WAS LOW.
SO NOW YOU'RE SAVING SMALL GROUPS OF CIVILIANS...
...AND TOSSING THEM TO YOUR SON.
IS THAT ALRIGHT, WESLEY? IS THAT KEEPING IN LINE WITH WHAT WOLFRAM & HART WANTS?
I DON'T KNOW.
OF COURSE YOU DON'T.
I'M WORKING ON A WAY OUT OF HERE. I JUST NEED THE RIGHT FIREPOWER.
WE'RE NOT LEAVING. TRUST ME, I WOULD LIKE MORE THAN ANYTHING TO BE RELEASED FROM MY CONTRACT. I WOULD LITERALLY GIVE ANYTHING TO BE ABLE TO MOVE ON.
BUT THAT ISN'T AN OPTION. SO MAYBE YOU SHOULD FIGURE OUT WHAT YOU CAN DO, HERE AND NOW. AND THEN TAKE THE SLIGHTEST OF BABY STEPS TO RETURNING TO WHAT YOU WERE.
BECAUSE IF YOU DON'T START TRYING TO TAKE CONTROL...
"...THE WRONG PERSON IS GOING TO."
"COME ON, YOU SORRY SACKS OF MAN-BABIES!"

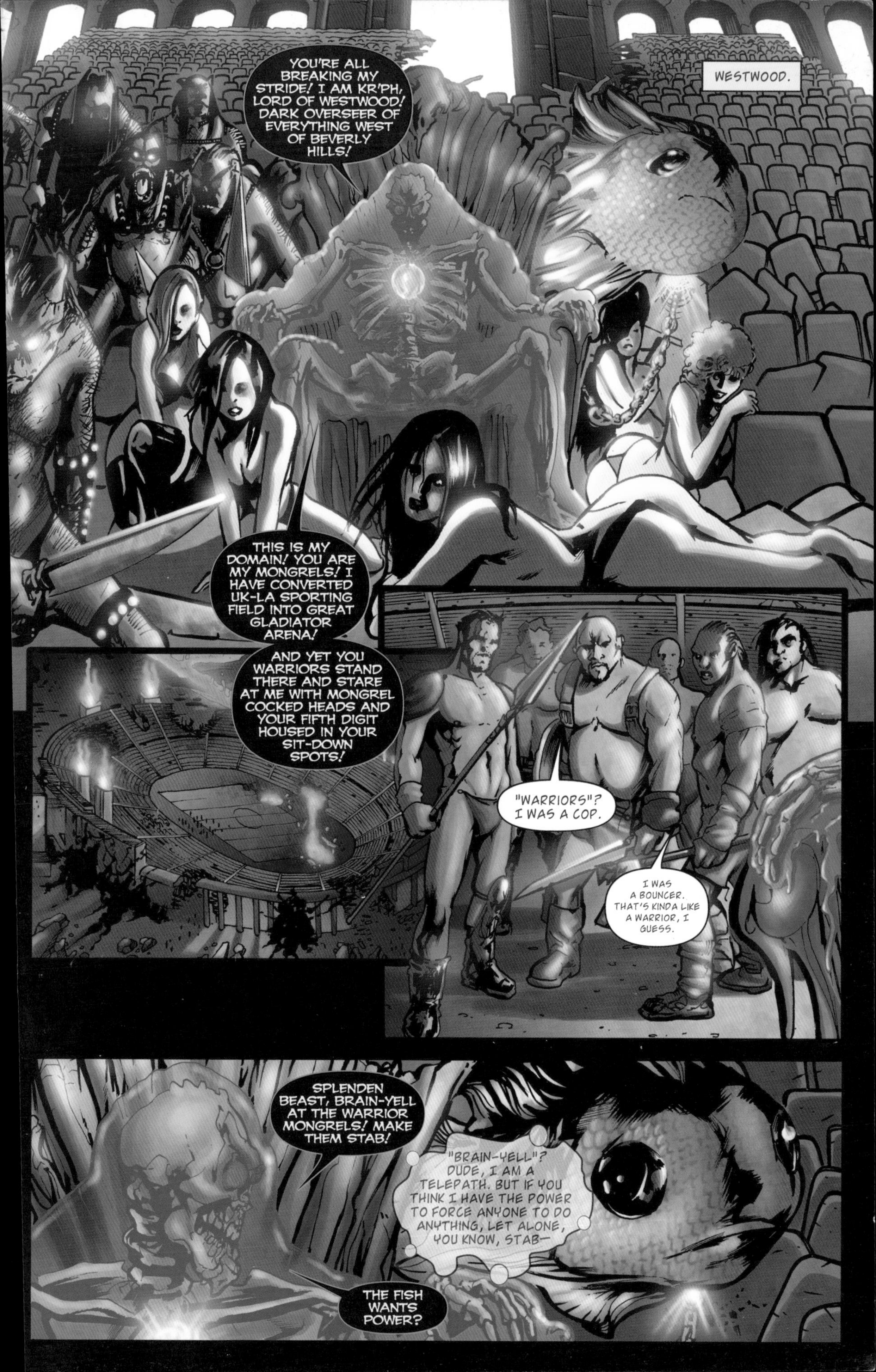
WESTWOOD.
YOU'RE ALL BREAKING MY STRIDE! I AM KR'PH, LORD OF WESTWOOD! DARK OVERSEER OF EVERYTHING WEST OF BEVERLY HILLS!
THIS IS MY DOMAIN! YOU ARE MY MONGRELS! I HAVE CONVERTED UK-LA SPORTING FIELD INTO GREAT GLADIATOR ARENA!
AND YET YOU WARRIORS STAND THERE AND STARE AT ME WITH MONGREL COCKED HEADS AND YOUR FIFTH DIGIT HOUSED IN YOUR SIT-DOWN SPOTS!
"WARRIORS"? I WAS A COP.
I WAS A BOUNCER. THAT'S KINDA LIKE A WARRIOR, I GUESS.
SPLENDEN BEAST, BRAIN-YELL AT THE WARRIOR MONGRELS! MAKE THEM STAB!
"BRAIN-YELL"? DUDE, I AM A TELEPATH. BUT IF YOU THINK I HAVE THE POWER TO FORCE ANYONE TO DO ANYTHING, LET ALONE, YOU KNOW, STAB—
THE FISH WANTS POWER?

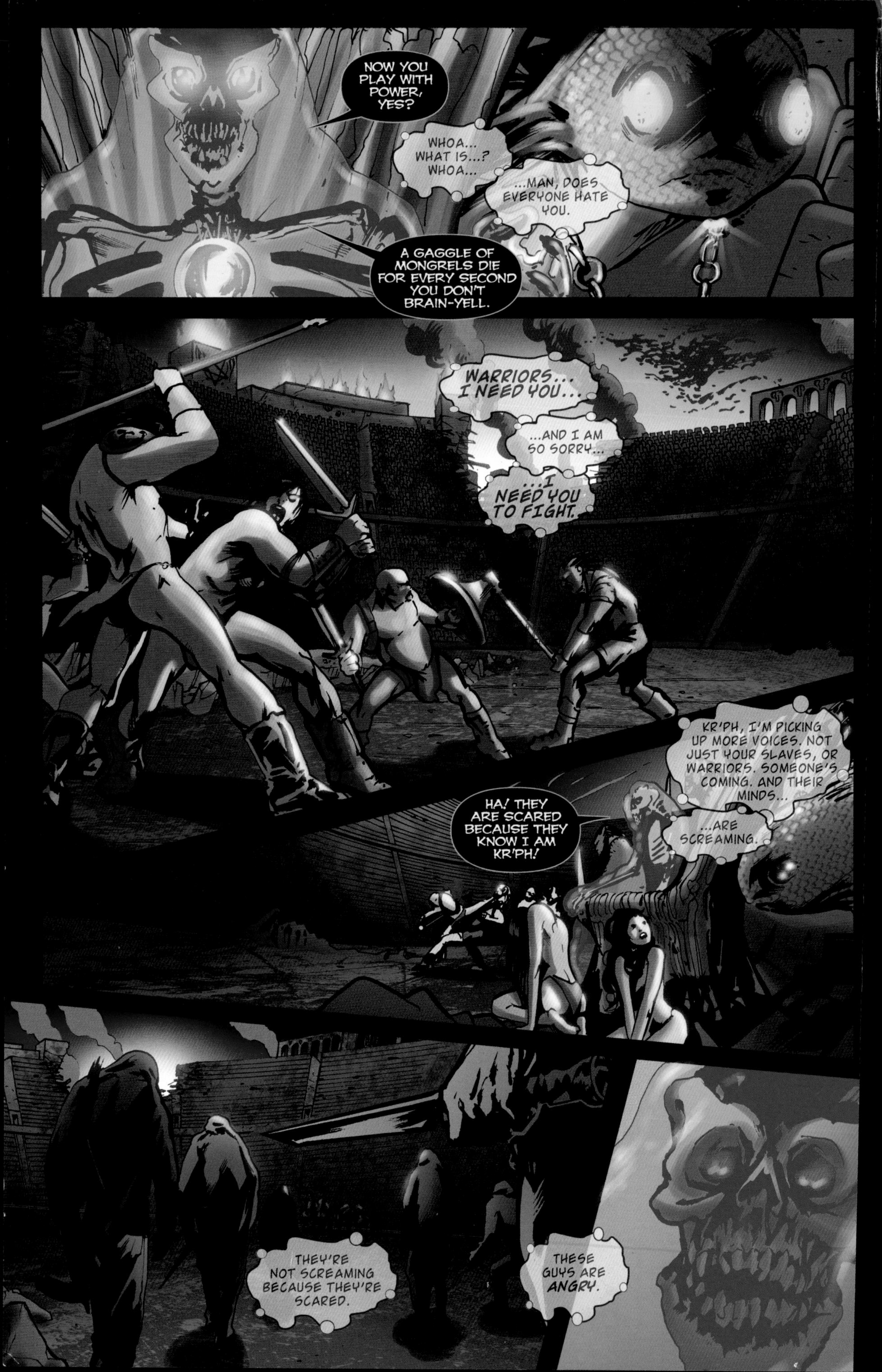
NOW YOU PLAY WITH POWER, YES?
WHOA... WHAT IS...? WHOA...
...MAN, DOES EVERYONE HATE YOU.
A GAGGLE OF MONGRELS DIE FOR EVERY SECOND YOU DON'T BRAIN-YELL.
WARRIORS... I NEED YOU...
...AND I AM SO SORRY...
...I NEED YOU TO FIGHT.
KR'PH, I'M PICKING UP MORE VOICES. NOT JUST YOUR SLAVES, OR WARRIORS. SOMEONE'S COMING. AND THEIR MINDS...
HA! THEY ARE SCARED BECAUSE THEY KNOW I AM KR'PH!
...ARE SCREAMING.
THEY'RE NOT SCREAMING BECAUSE THEY'RE SCARED.
THESE GUYS ARE ANGRY.

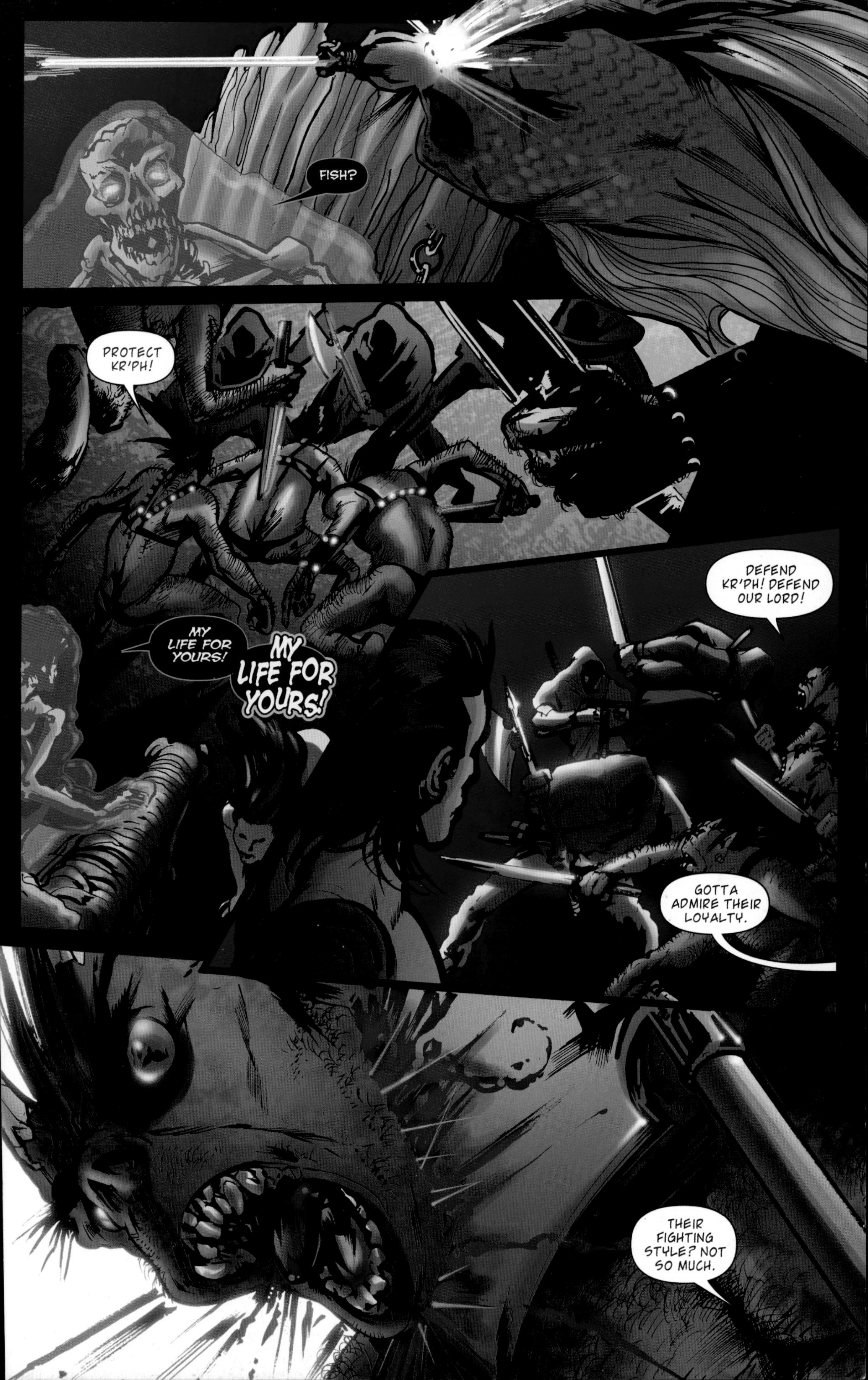
FISH?
PROTECT KR'PH!
DEFEND KR'PH! DEFEND OUR LORD!
MY LIFE FOR YOURS!
MY LIFE FOR YOURS!
GOTTA ADMIRE THEIR LOYALTY.
THEIR FIGHTING STYLE? NOT SO MUCH.

LAZY FISH! WAKE UP AND YELL AT THEIR HEADS TO GO! FIGHT WELL, GUARDS! YOUR LOVE FOR ME IS UNBOUNDFUL!
...
WHOEVER THIS IS, I AM ANGERED BUT NOT TURNING A BACKSIDE TO BARGAINING!
YOU ARE MIGHTY AND NOBLE MONGRELS! A HANDSHAKING CAN HAPPEN!
TELL ME WHAT YOU WANT! I CAN HELP YOU GET IT!

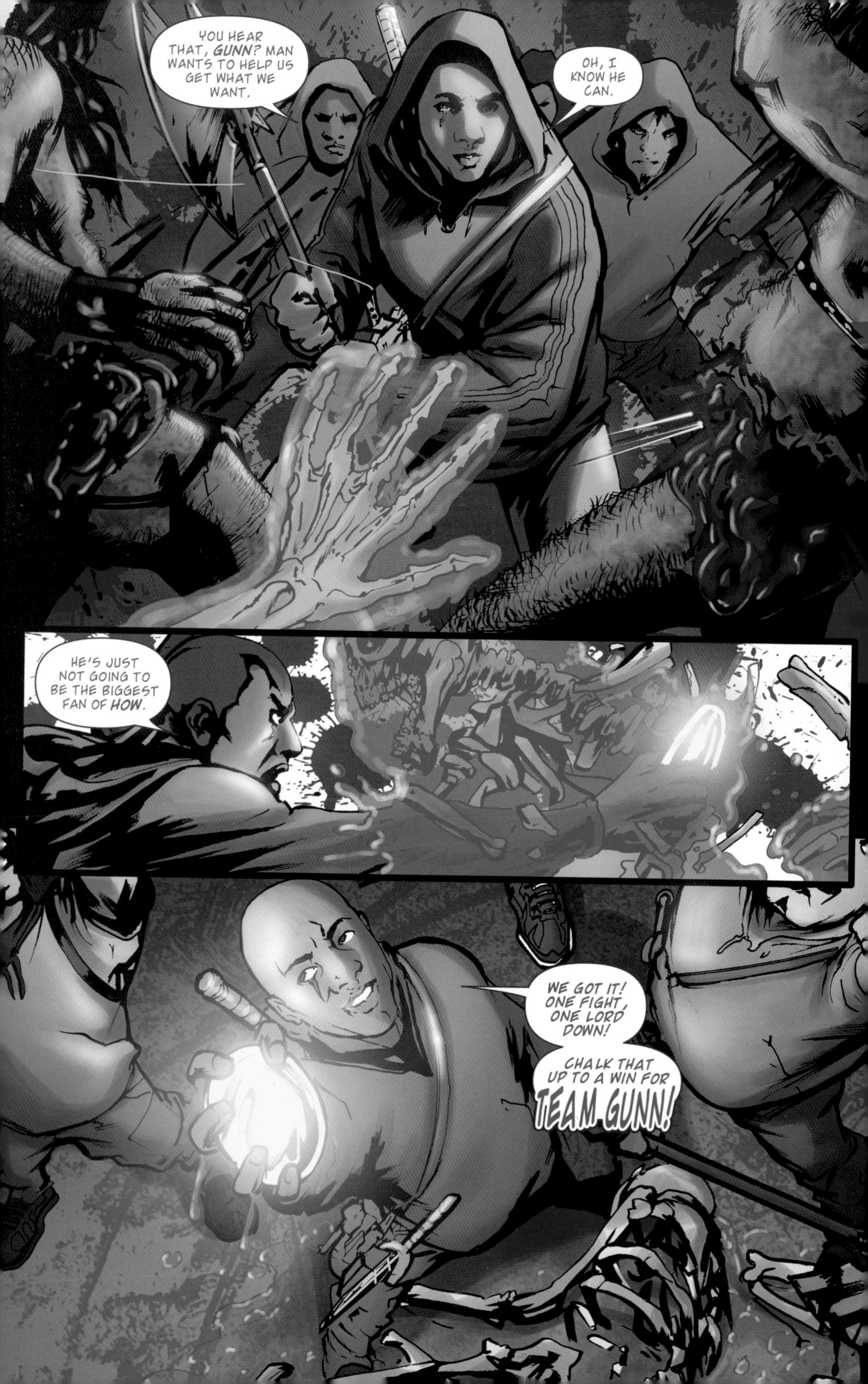
YOU HEAR THAT, GUNN? MAN WANTS TO HELP US GET WHAT WE WANT.
OH, I KNOW HE CAN.
HE'S JUST NOT GOING TO BE THE BIGGEST FAN OF HOW.
WE GOT IT! ONE FIGHT, ONE LORD DOWN!
CHALK THAT UP TO A WIN FOR TEAM GUNN!

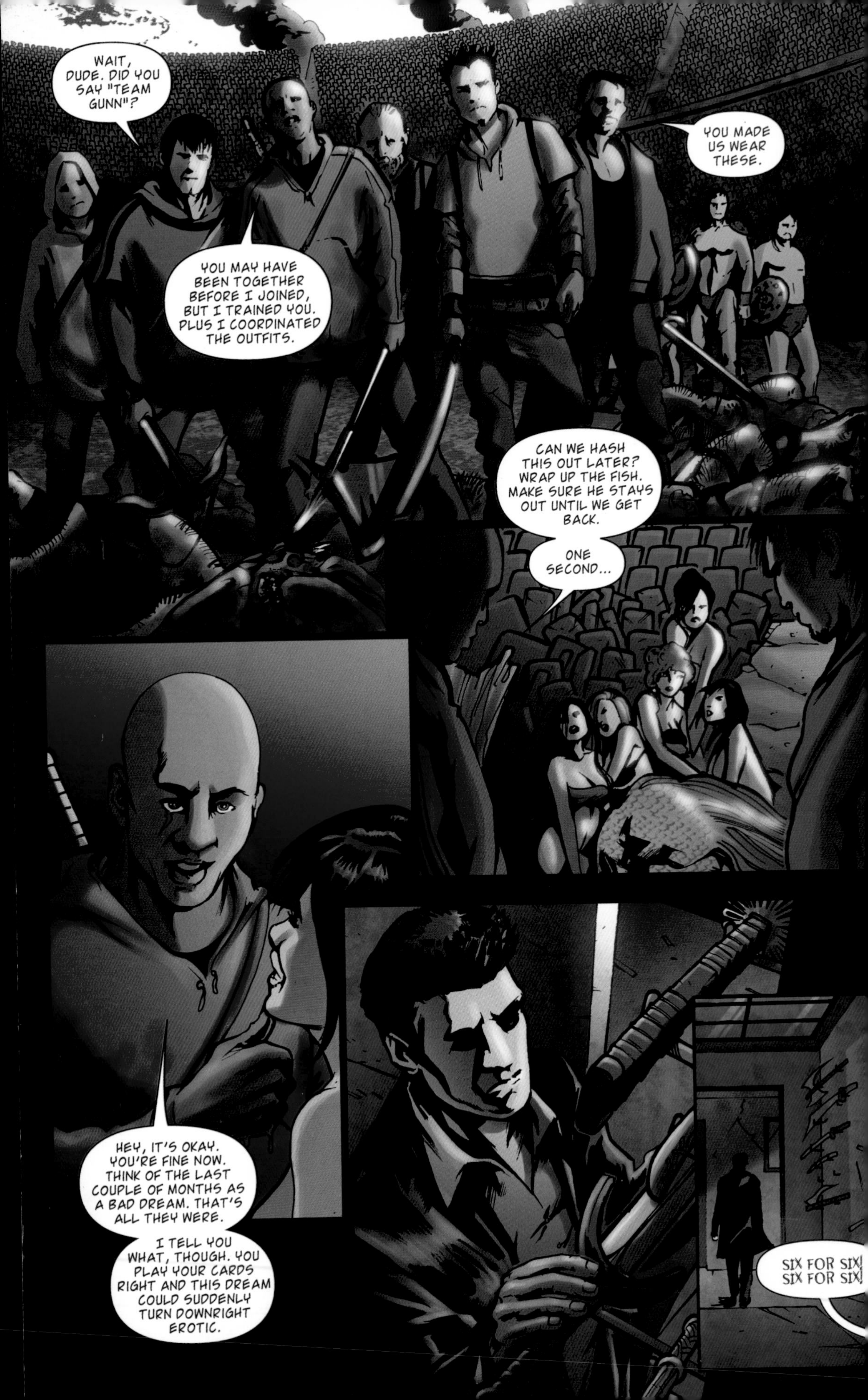
WAIT, DUDE. DID YOU SAY "TEAM GUNN"?
YOU MADE US WEAR THESE.
YOU MAY HAVE BEEN TOGETHER BEFORE I JOINED, BUT I TRAINED YOU. PLUS I COORDINATED THE OUTFITS.
CAN WE HASH THIS OUT LATER? WRAP UP THE FISH. MAKE SURE HE STAYS OUT UNTIL WE GET BACK.
ONE SECOND...
HEY, IT'S OKAY. YOU'RE FINE NOW. THINK OF THE LAST COUPLE OF MONTHS AS A BAD DREAM. THAT'S ALL THEY WERE.
I TELL YOU WHAT, THOUGH. YOU PLAY YOUR CARDS RIGHT AND THIS DREAM COULD SUDDENLY TURN DOWNRIGHT EROTIC.
SIX FOR SIX! SIX FOR SIX!

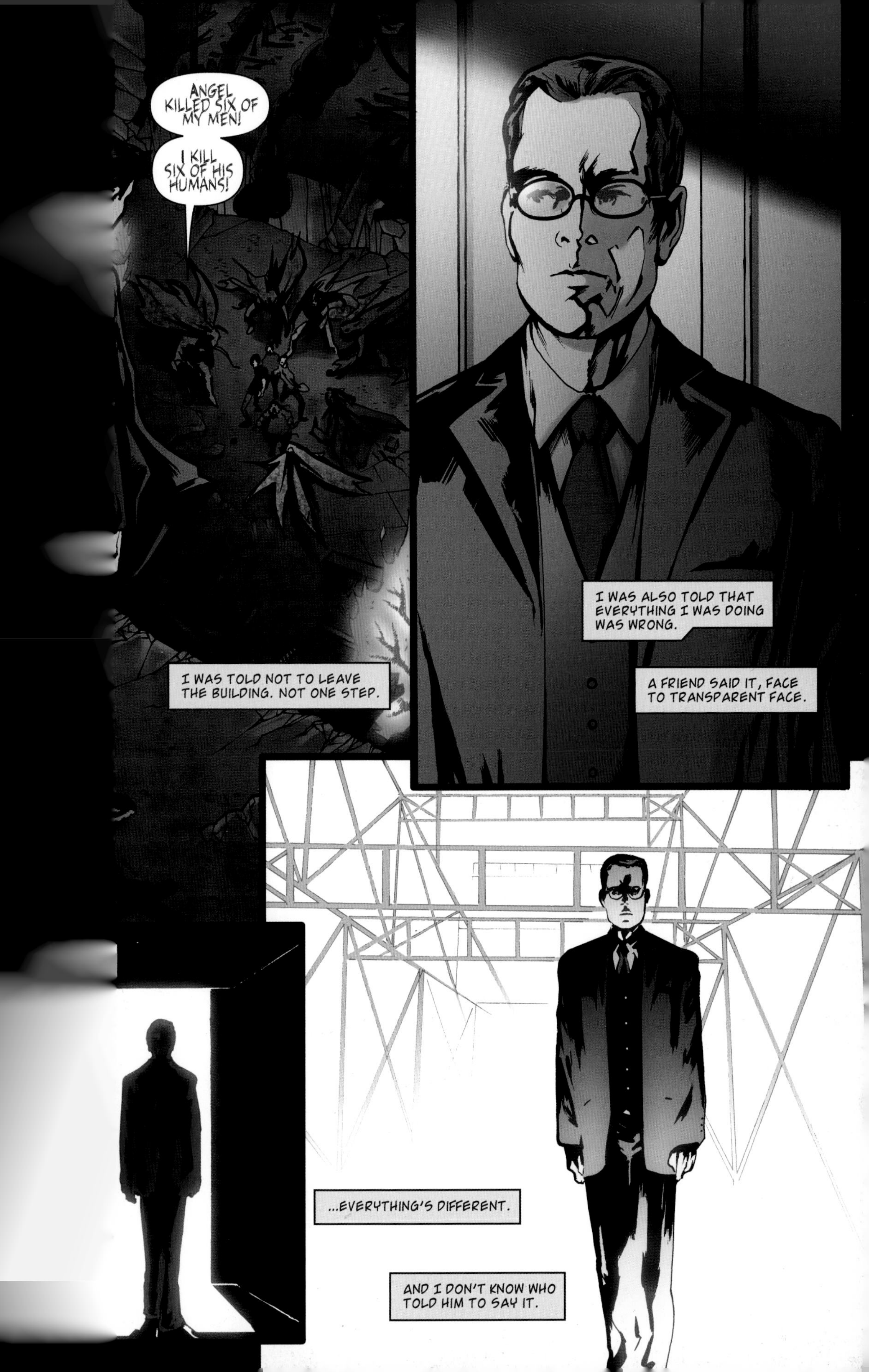
ANGEL KILLED SIX OF MY MEN!
I KILL SIX OF HIS HUMANS!
I WAS TOLD NOT TO LEAVE THE BUILDING. NOT ONE STEP.
I WAS ALSO TOLD THAT EVERYTHING I WAS DOING WAS WRONG.
A FRIEND SAID IT, FACE TO TRANSPARENT FACE.
...EVERYTHING'S DIFFERENT.
AND I DON'T KNOW WHO TOLD HIM TO SAY IT.

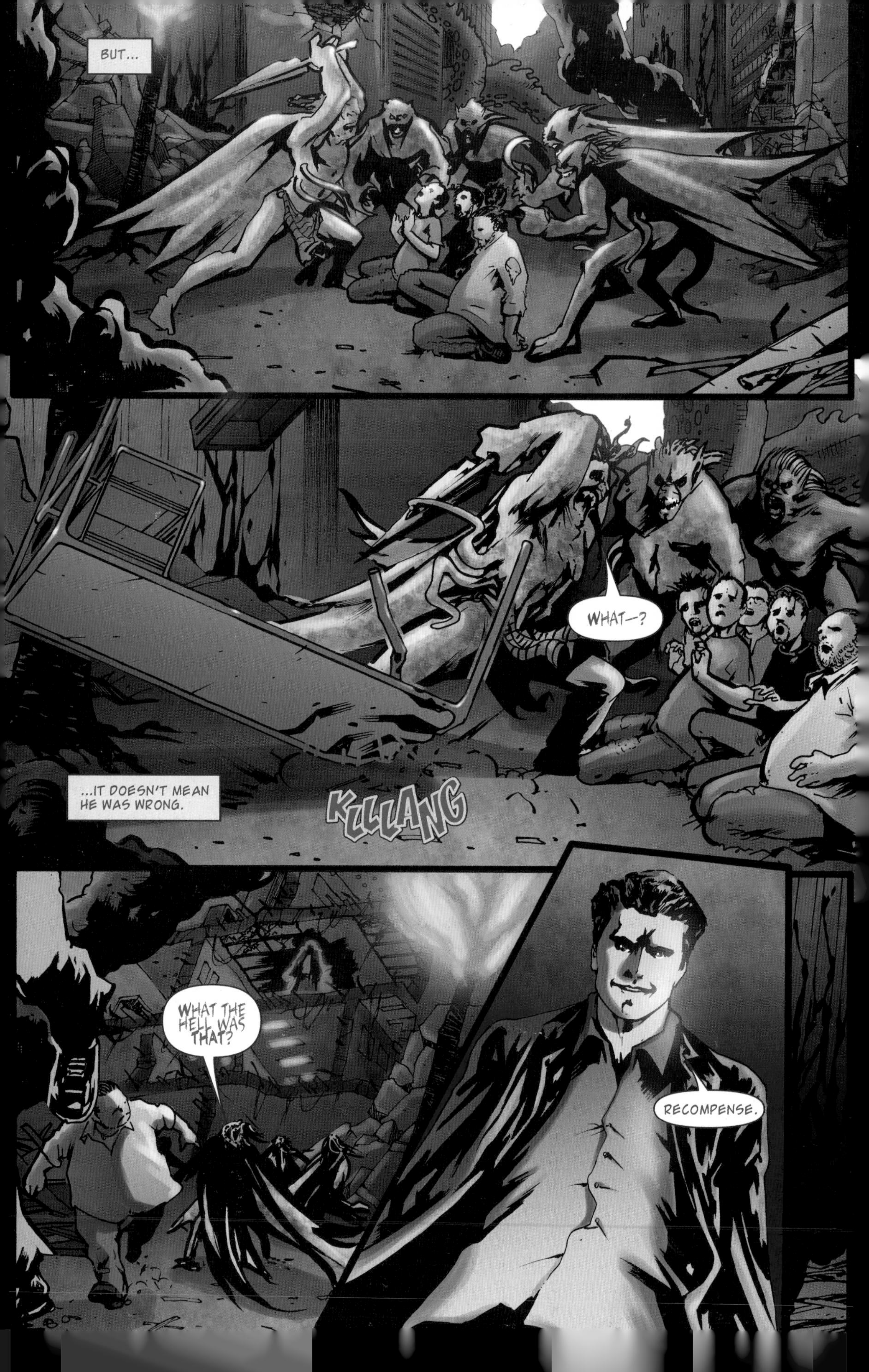
BUT...
WHAT—?
...IT DOESN'T MEAN HE WAS WRONG.
KLLANG
WHAT THE HELL WAS THAT?
RECOMPENSE.

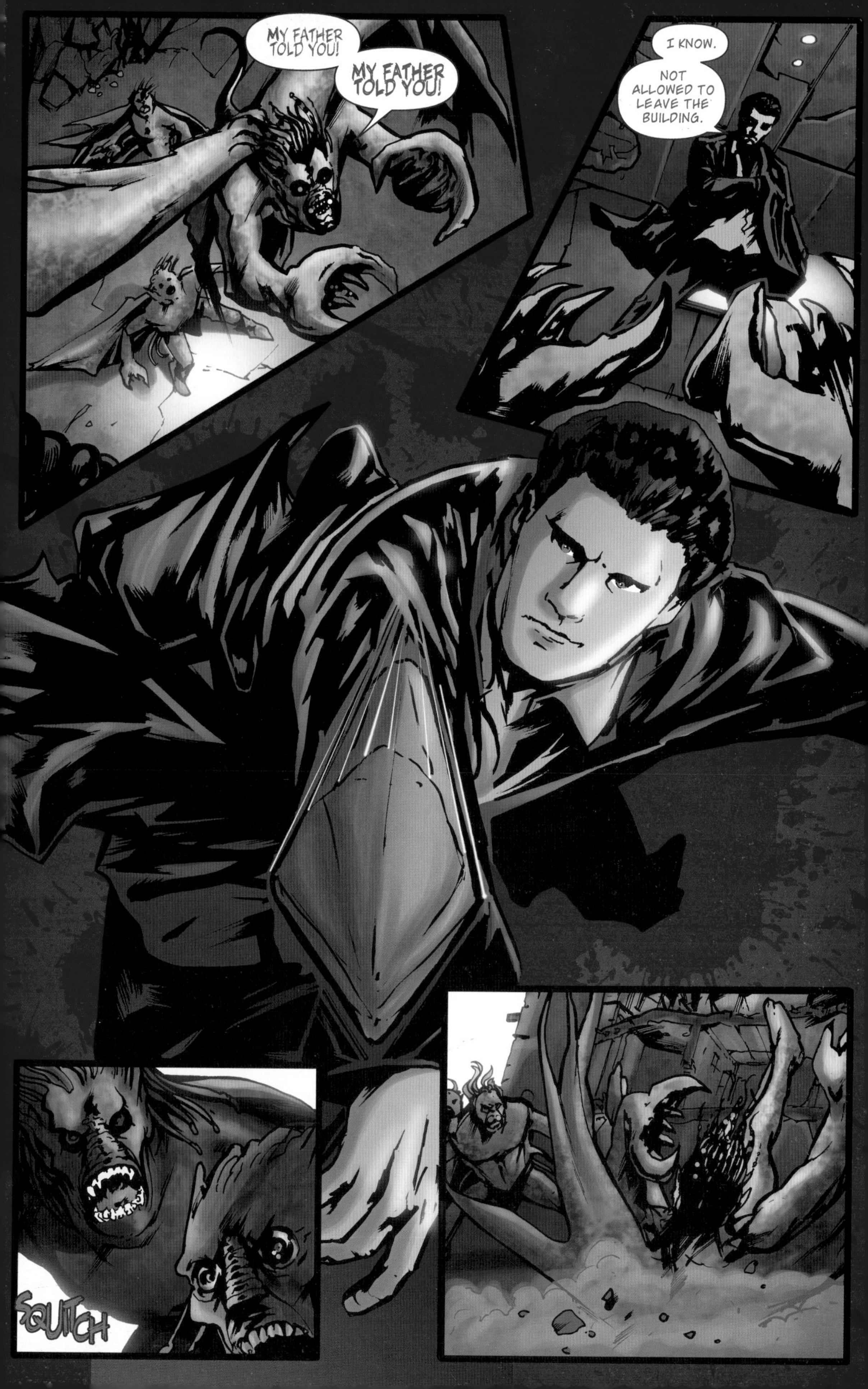
MY FATHER TOLD YOU!
MY FATHER TOLD YOU!
I KNOW.
NOT ALLOWED TO LEAVE THE BUILDING.
SQUITCH

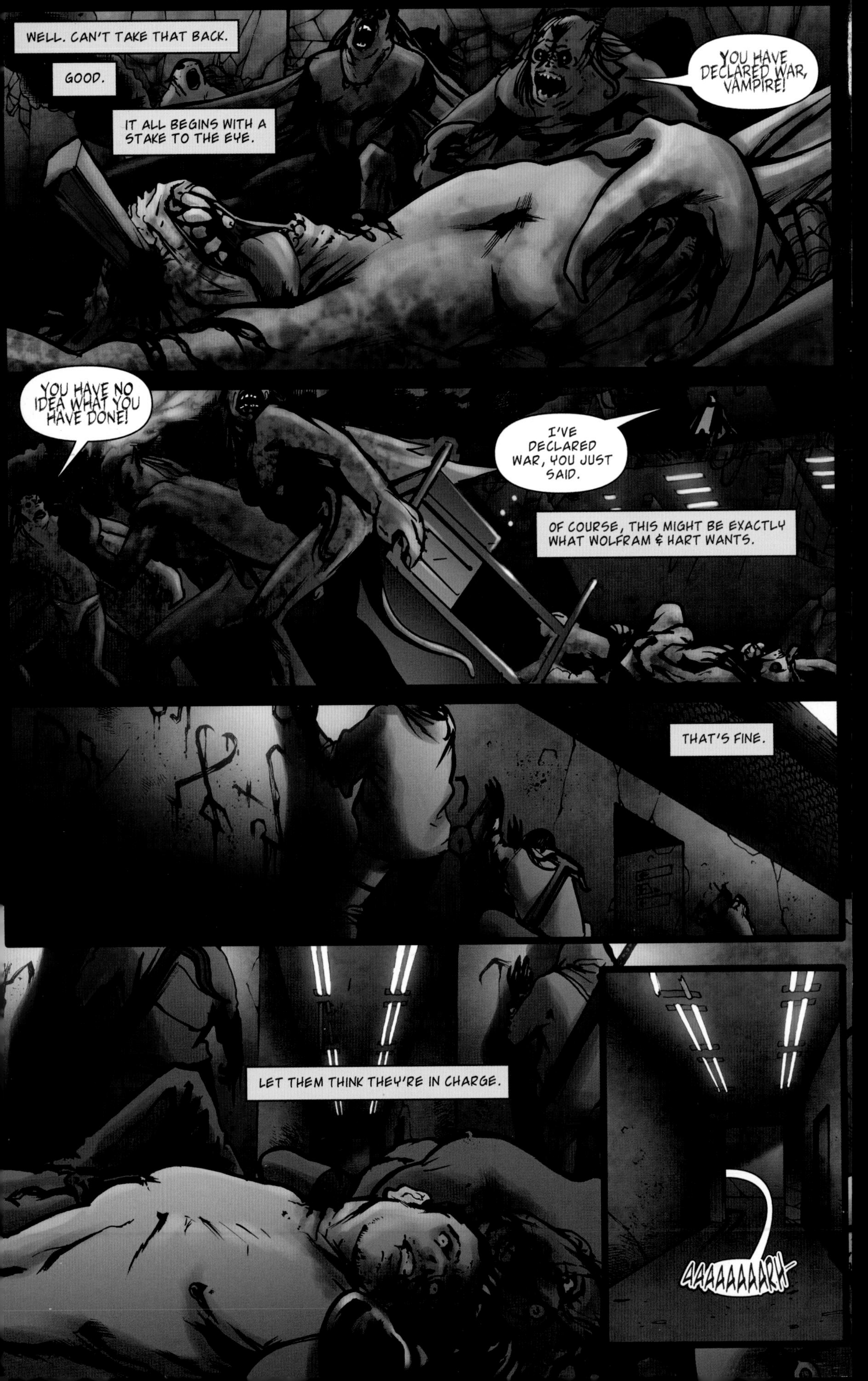
WELL. CAN'T TAKE THAT BACK.
GOOD.
IT ALL BEGINS WITH A STAKE TO THE EYE.
YOU HAVE DECLARED WAR, VAMPIRE!
YOU HAVE NO IDEA WHAT YOU HAVE DONE!
I'VE DECLARED WAR, YOU JUST SAID.
OF COURSE, THIS MIGHT BE EXACTLY WHAT WOLFRAM & HART WANTS.
THAT'S FINE.
LET THEM THINK THEY'RE IN CHARGE.
AAAAAAAARH

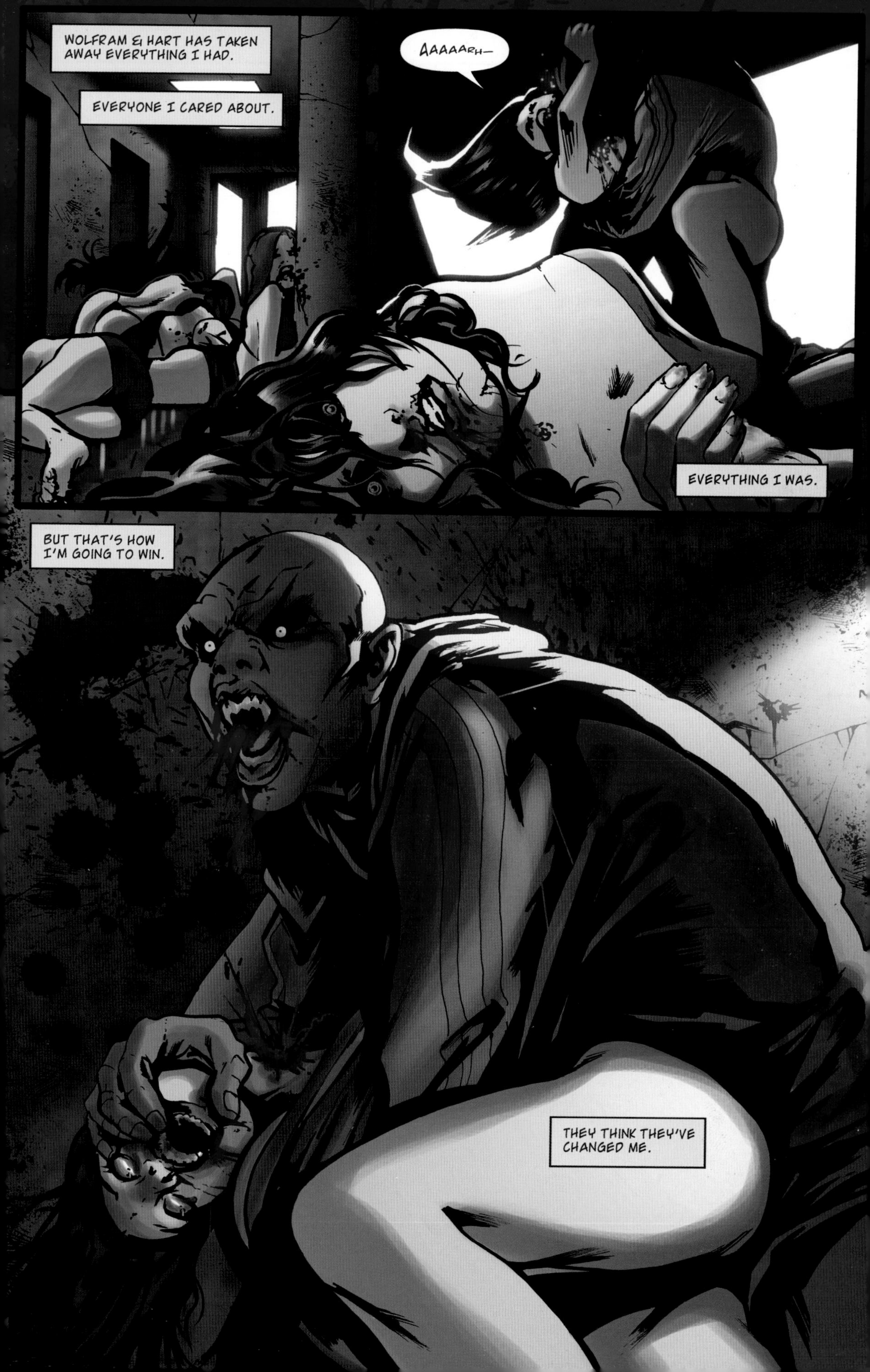
WOLFRAM & HART HAS TAKEN AWAY EVERYTHING I HAD.
EVERYONE I CARED ABOUT.
AAAAARH—
EVERYTHING I WAS.
BUT THAT'S HOW I'M GOING TO WIN.
THEY THINK THEY'VE CHANGED ME.

chapter
two

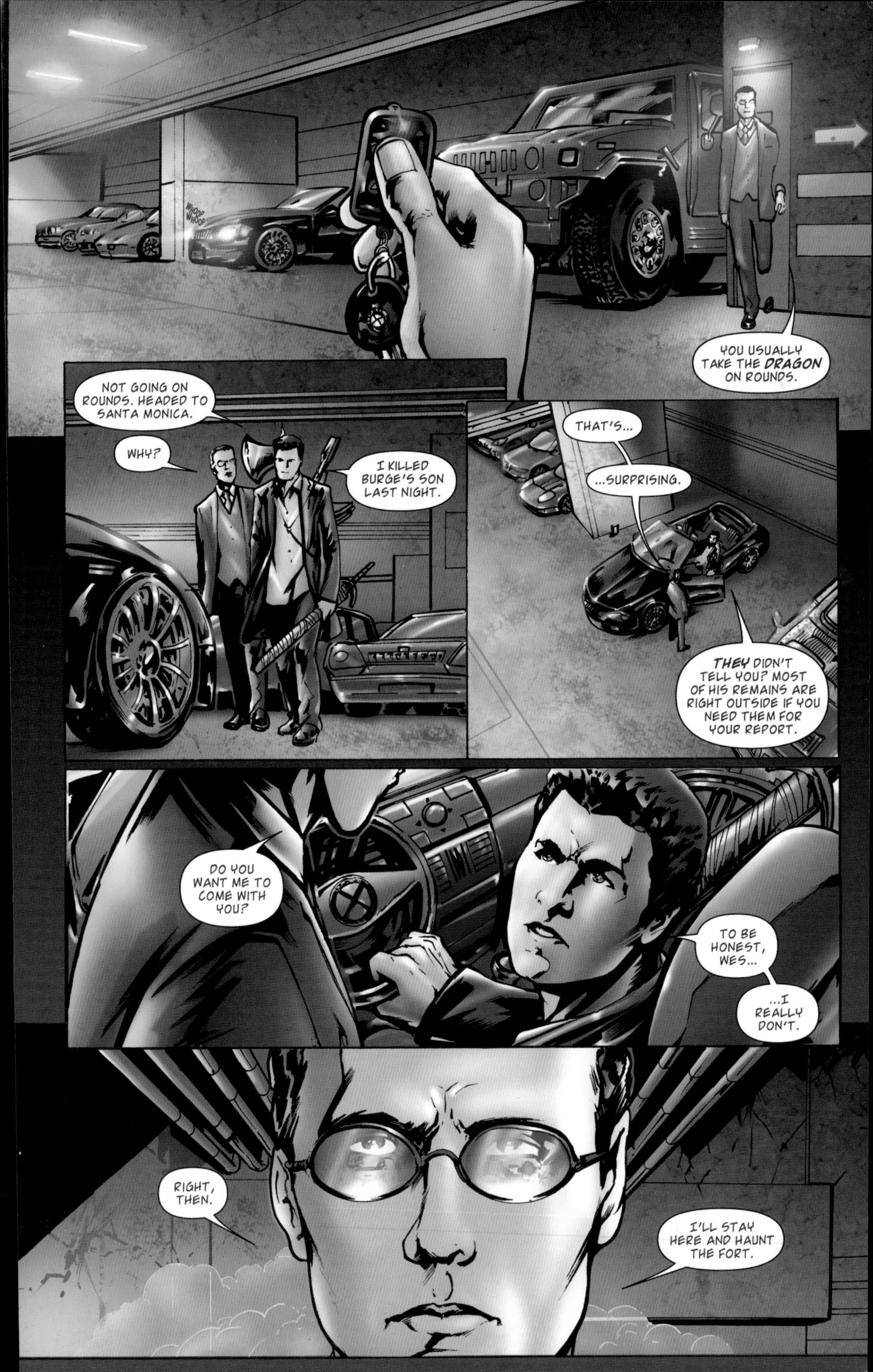
WHOOP WHOOP
YOU USUALLY TAKE THE DRAGON ON ROUNDS.
NOT GOING ON ROUNDS. HEADED TO SANTA MONICA.
WHY?
I KILLED BURGE'S SON LAST NIGHT.
THAT'S...
...SURPRISING.
THEY DIDN'T TELL YOU? MOST OF HIS REMAINS ARE RIGHT OUTSIDE IF YOU NEED THEM FOR YOUR REPORT.
DO YOU WANT ME TO COME WITH YOU?
TO BE HONEST, WES...
...I REALLY DON'T.
RIGHT, THEN.
I'LL STAY HERE AND HAUNT THE FORT.

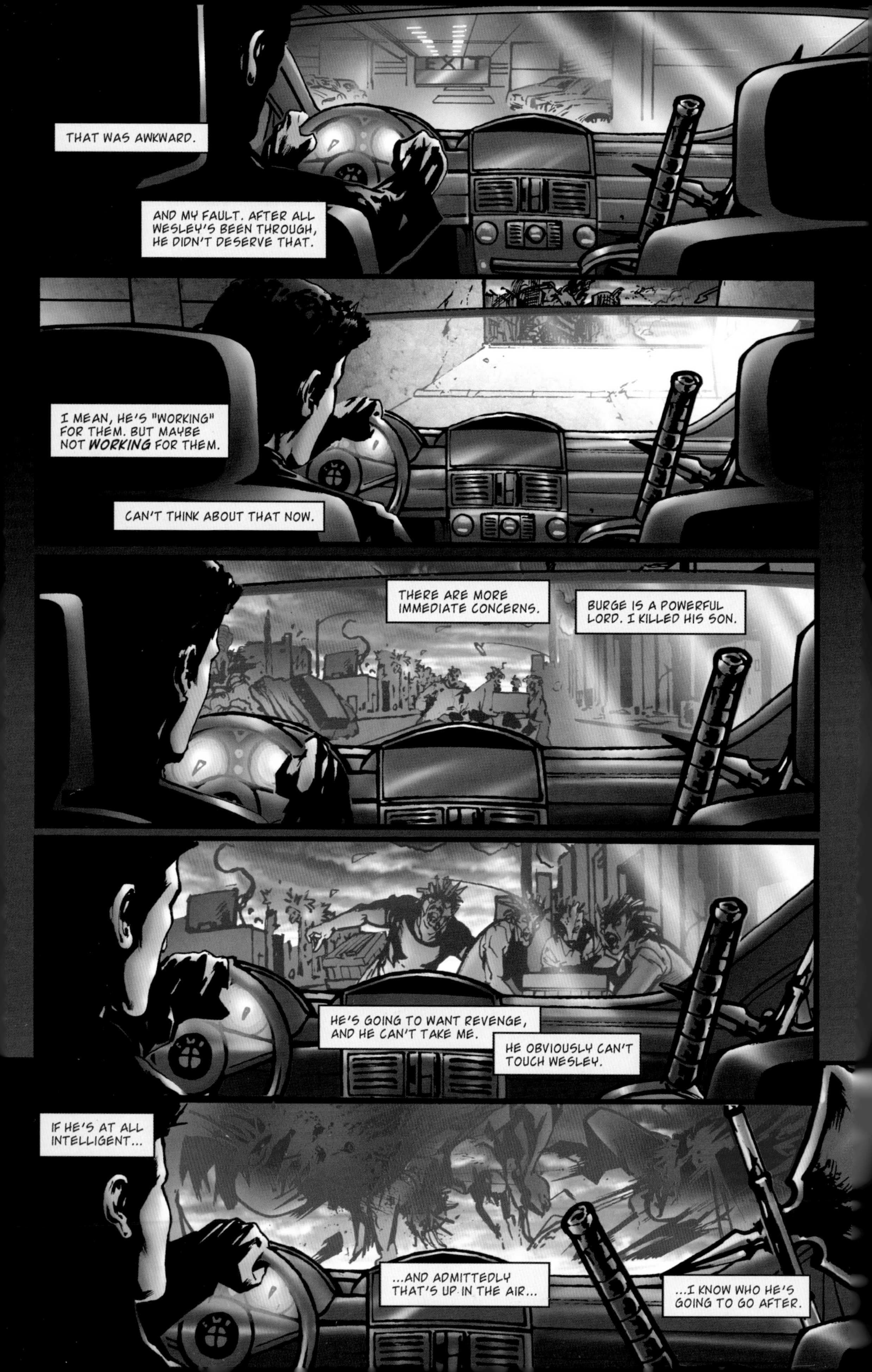
EXIT
THAT WAS AWKWARD.
AND MY FAULT. AFTER ALL WESLEY'S BEEN THROUGH, HE DIDN'T DESERVE THAT.
I MEAN, HE'S "WORKING" FOR THEM. BUT MAYBE NOT WORKING FOR THEM.
CAN'T THINK ABOUT THAT NOW.
THERE ARE MORE IMMEDIATE CONCERNS.
BURGE IS A POWERFUL LORD. I KILLED HIS SON.
HE'S GOING TO WANT REVENGE, AND HE CAN'T TAKE ME.
HE OBVIOUSLY CAN'T TOUCH WESLEY.
IF HE'S AT ALL INTELLIGENT...
...AND ADMITTEDLY THAT'S UP IN THE AIR...
...I KNOW WHO HE'S GOING TO GO AFTER.

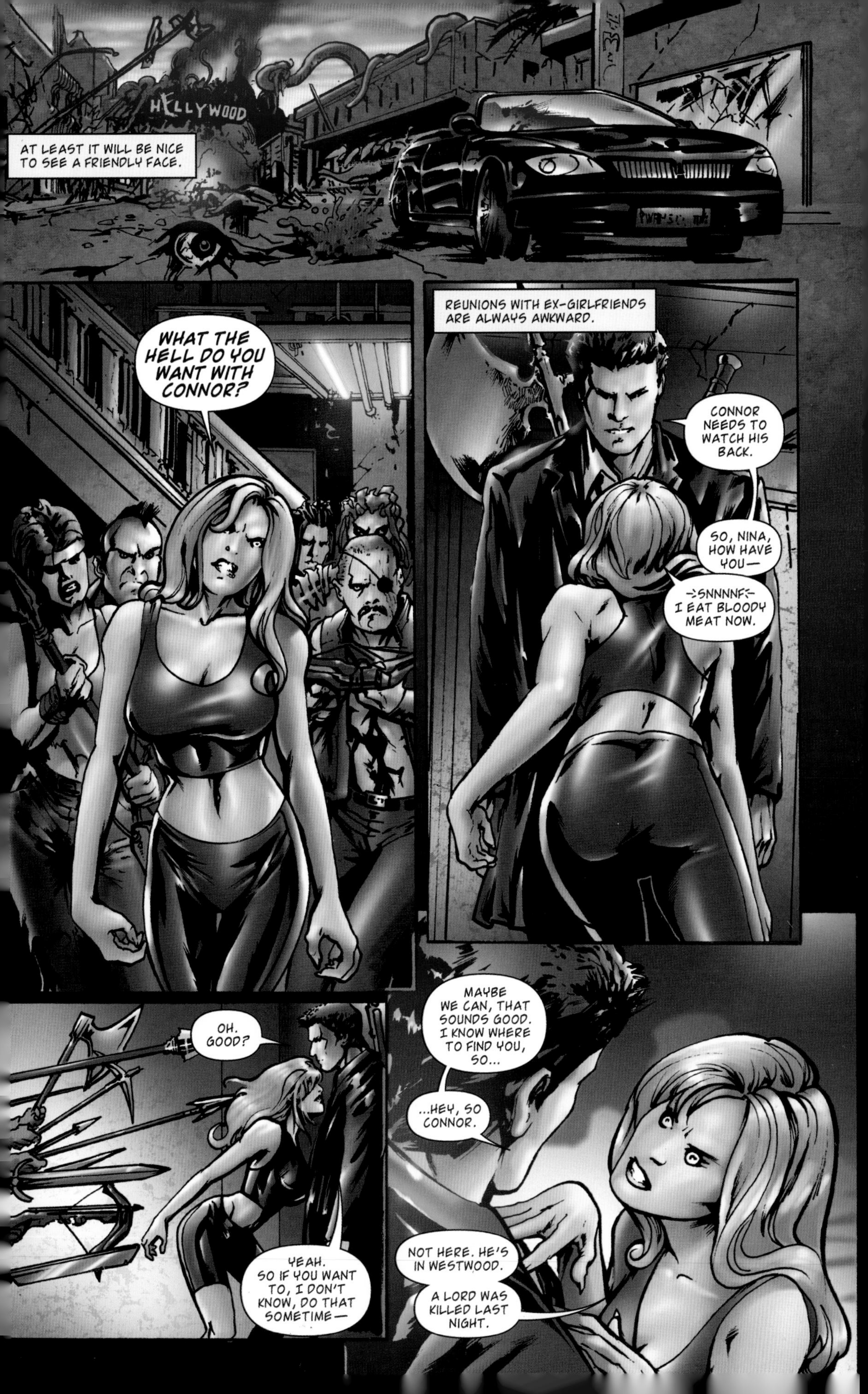
HELLYWOOD
AT LEAST IT WILL BE NICE TO SEE A FRIENDLY FACE.
WHAT THE HELL DO YOU WANT WITH CONNOR?
REUNIONS WITH EX-GIRLFRIENDS ARE ALWAYS AWKWARD.
CONNOR NEEDS TO WATCH HIS BACK.
SO, NINA, HOW HAVE YOU—
–SNNNNF– I EAT BLOODY MEAT NOW.
OH. GOOD?
YEAH. SO IF YOU WANT TO, I DON'T KNOW, DO THAT SOMETIME—
MAYBE WE CAN, THAT SOUNDS GOOD. I KNOW WHERE TO FIND YOU, SO...
...HEY, SO CONNOR.
NOT HERE. HE'S IN WESTWOOD.
A LORD WAS KILLED LAST NIGHT.

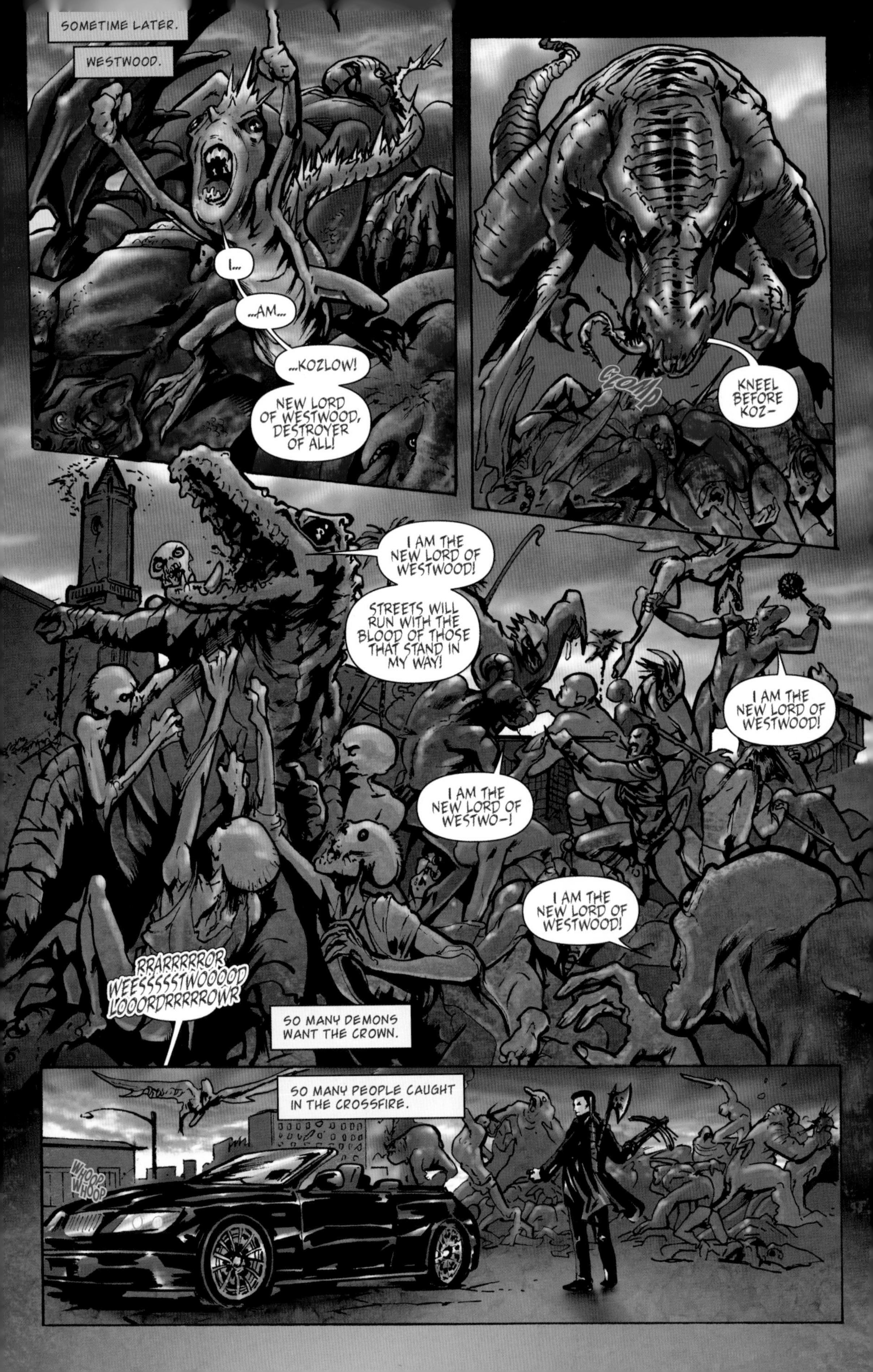
SOMETIME LATER.
WESTWOOD.
I...
...AM...
...KOZLOW!
NEW LORD OF WESTWOOD, DESTROYER OF ALL!
CROMP
KNEEL BEFORE KOZ–
I AM THE NEW LORD OF WESTWOOD!
STREETS WILL RUN WITH THE BLOOD OF THOSE THAT STAND IN MY WAY!
I AM THE NEW LORD OF WESTWOOD!
I AM THE NEW LORD OF WESTWO–!
I AM THE NEW LORD OF WESTWOOD!
RRARRRRROR WEESSSSSTWOOOOD LOOORDRRRRROWR
SO MANY DEMONS WANT THE CROWN.
SO MANY PEOPLE CAUGHT IN THE CROSSFIRE.
WHOOP WHOOP

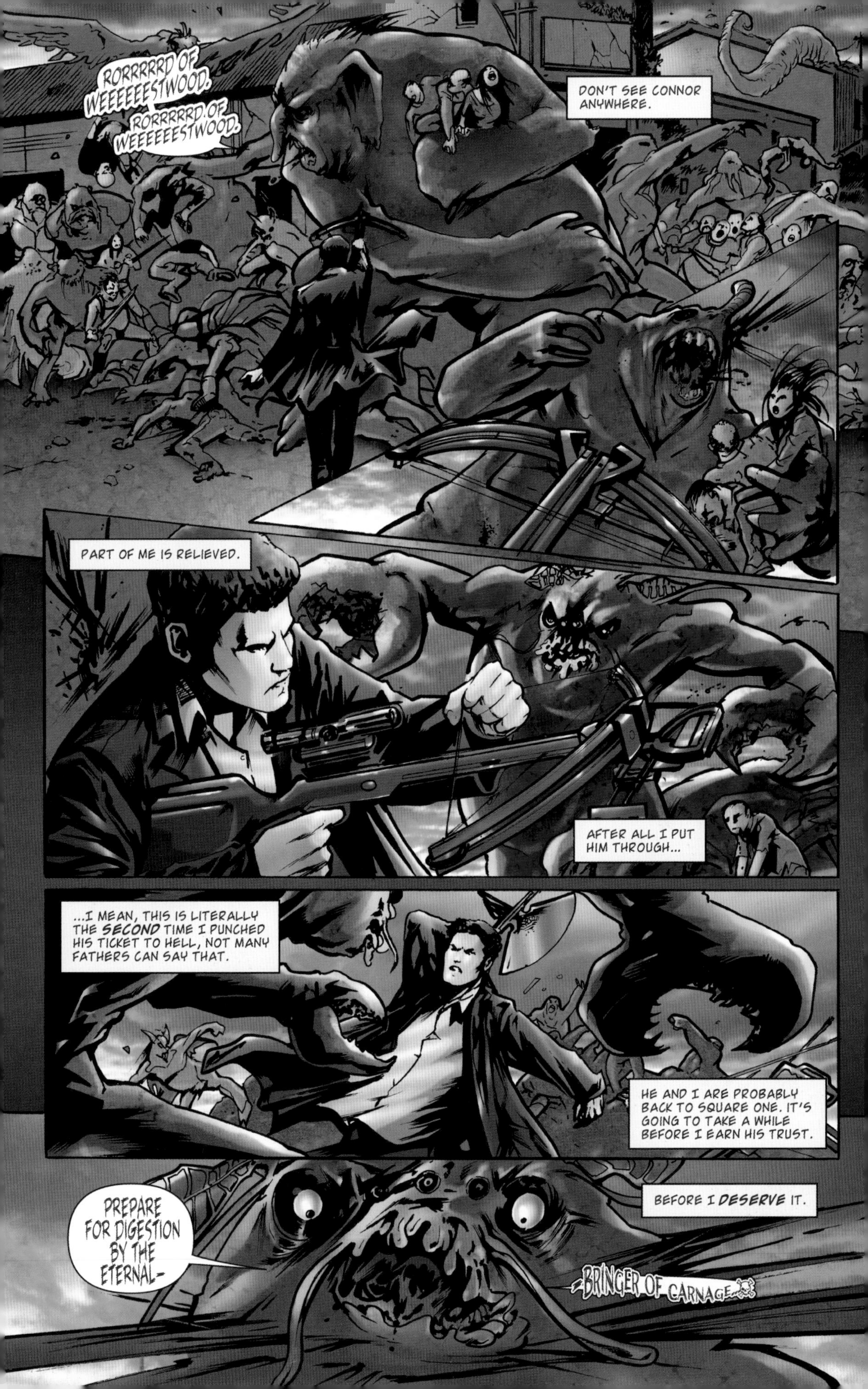
RORRRRRD OF WEEEEEEESTWOOD.
RORRRRRD OF WEEEEEEESTWOOD.
DON'T SEE CONNOR ANYWHERE.
PART OF ME IS RELIEVED.
AFTER ALL I PUT HIM THROUGH...
...I MEAN, THIS IS LITERALLY THE SECOND TIME I PUNCHED HIS TICKET TO HELL, NOT MANY FATHERS CAN SAY THAT.
HE AND I ARE PROBABLY BACK TO SQUARE ONE. IT'S GOING TO TAKE A WHILE BEFORE I EARN HIS TRUST.
BEFORE I DESERVE IT.
PREPARE FOR DIGESTION BY THE ETERNAL-
BRINGER OF CARNAGE

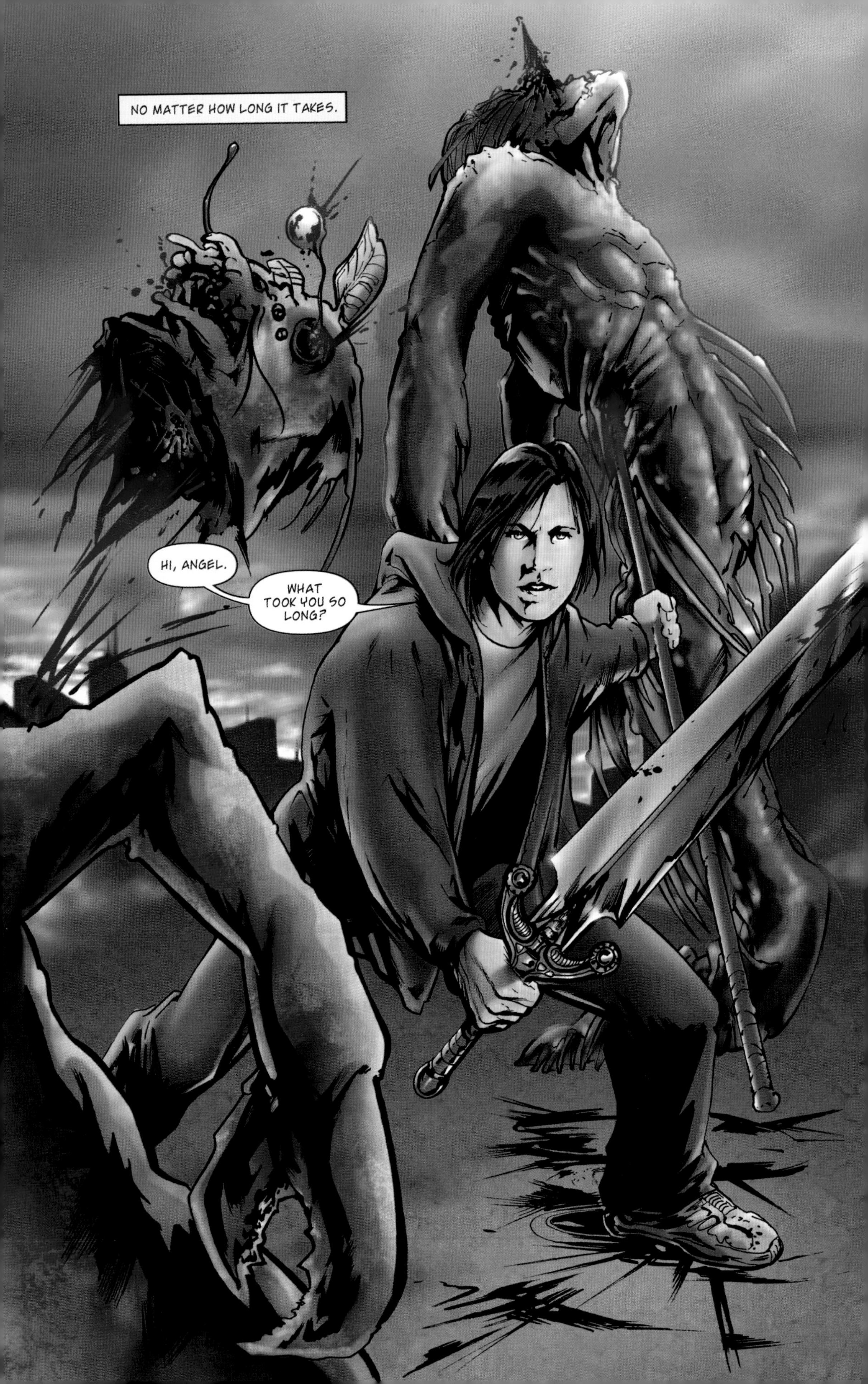
NO MATTER HOW LONG IT TAKES.
HI, ANGEL.
WHAT TOOK YOU SO LONG?

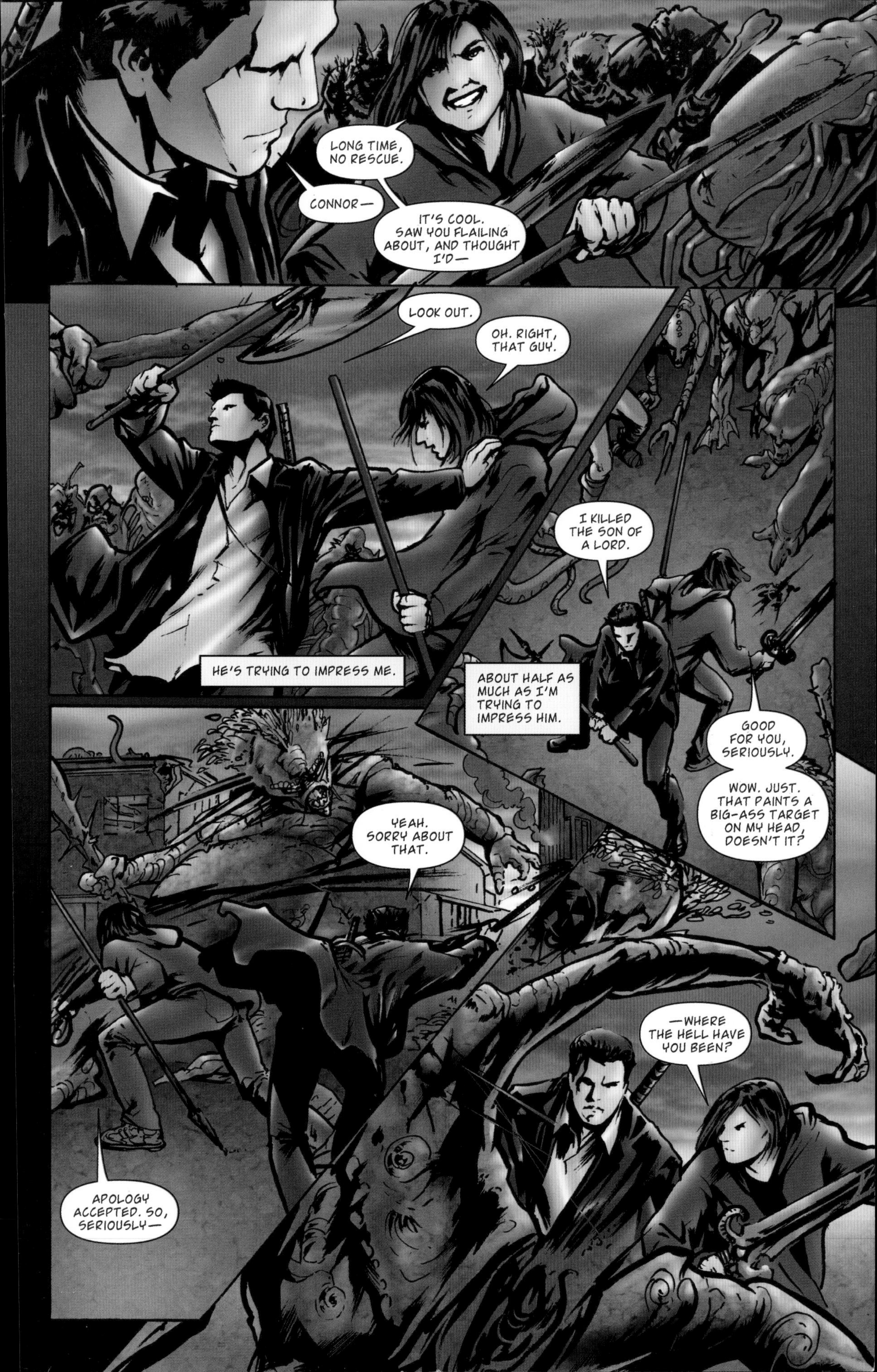
LONG TIME, NO RESCUE.
CONNOR—
IT'S COOL. SAW YOU FLAILING ABOUT, AND THOUGHT I'D—
LOOK OUT.
OH. RIGHT, THAT GUY.
HE'S TRYING TO IMPRESS ME.
I KILLED THE SON OF A LORD.
ABOUT HALF AS MUCH AS I'M TRYING TO IMPRESS HIM.
GOOD FOR YOU, SERIOUSLY.
WOW. JUST. THAT PAINTS A BIG-ASS TARGET ON MY HEAD, DOESN'T IT?
YEAH. SORRY ABOUT THAT.
APOLOGY ACCEPTED. SO, SERIOUSLY—
—WHERE THE HELL HAVE YOU BEEN?

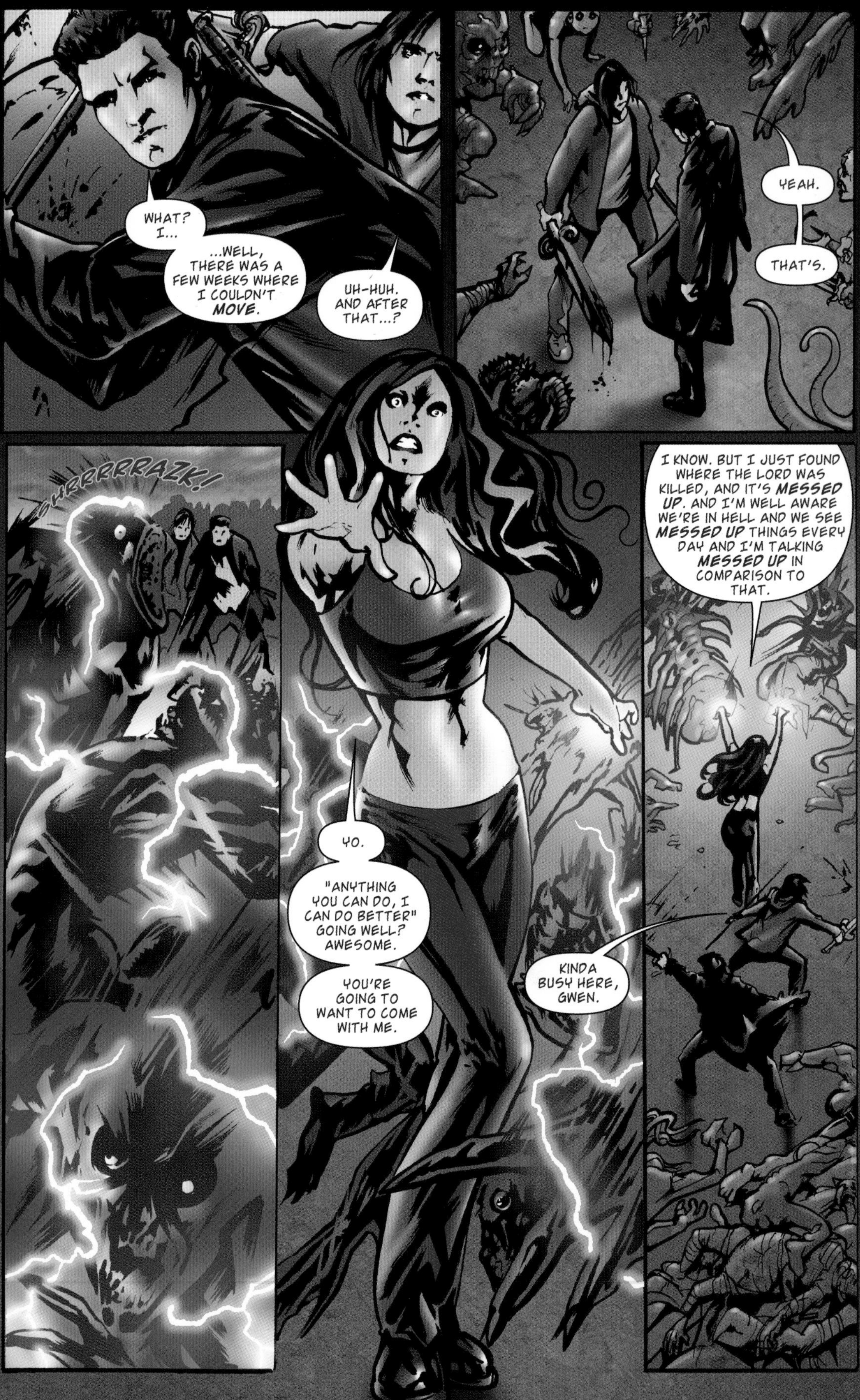
WHAT? I...
...WELL, THERE WAS A FEW WEEKS WHERE I COULDN'T MOVE.
UH-HUH. AND AFTER THAT...?
YEAH.
THAT'S.
SHRRRRRAZK!
YO.
KINDA BUSY HERE, GWEN.
"ANYTHING YOU CAN DO, I CAN DO BETTER" GOING WELL? AWESOME.
I KNOW. BUT I JUST FOUND WHERE THE LORD WAS KILLED, AND IT'S MESSED UP. AND I'M WELL AWARE WE'RE IN HELL AND WE SEE MESSED UP THINGS EVERY DAY AND I'M TALKING MESSED UP IN COMPARISON TO THAT.
YOU'RE GOING TO WANT TO COME WITH ME.

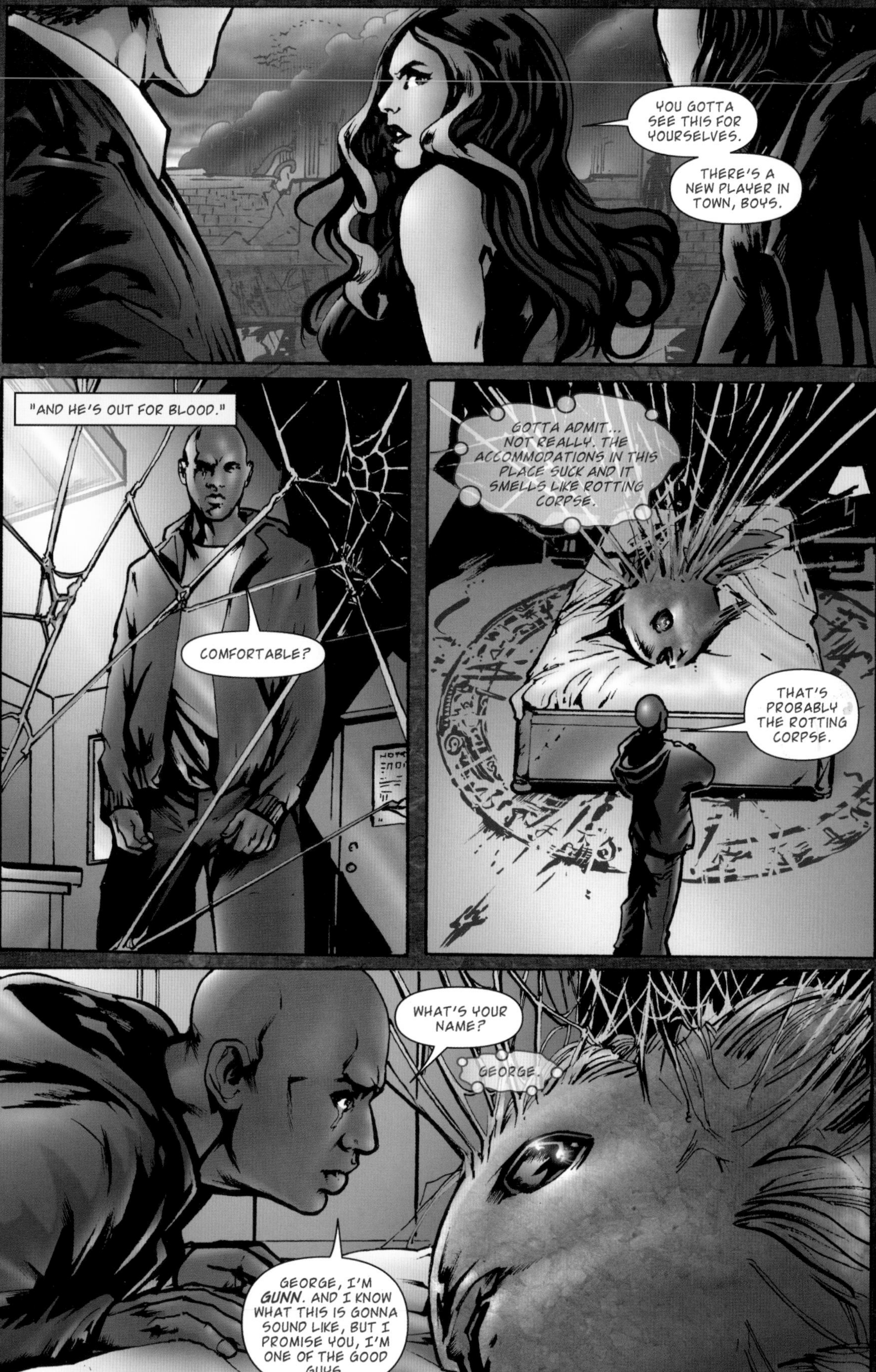
YOU GOTTA SEE THIS FOR YOURSELVES.
THERE'S A NEW PLAYER IN TOWN, BOYS.
"AND HE'S OUT FOR BLOOD."
COMFORTABLE?
GOTTA ADMIT... NOT REALLY. THE ACCOMMODATIONS IN THIS PLACE SUCK AND IT SMELLS LIKE ROTTING CORPSE.
THAT'S PROBABLY THE ROTTING CORPSE.
WHAT'S YOUR NAME?
GEORGE.
GEORGE, I'M GUNN. AND I KNOW WHAT THIS IS GONNA SOUND LIKE, BUT I PROMISE YOU, I'M ONE OF THE GOOD GUYS.

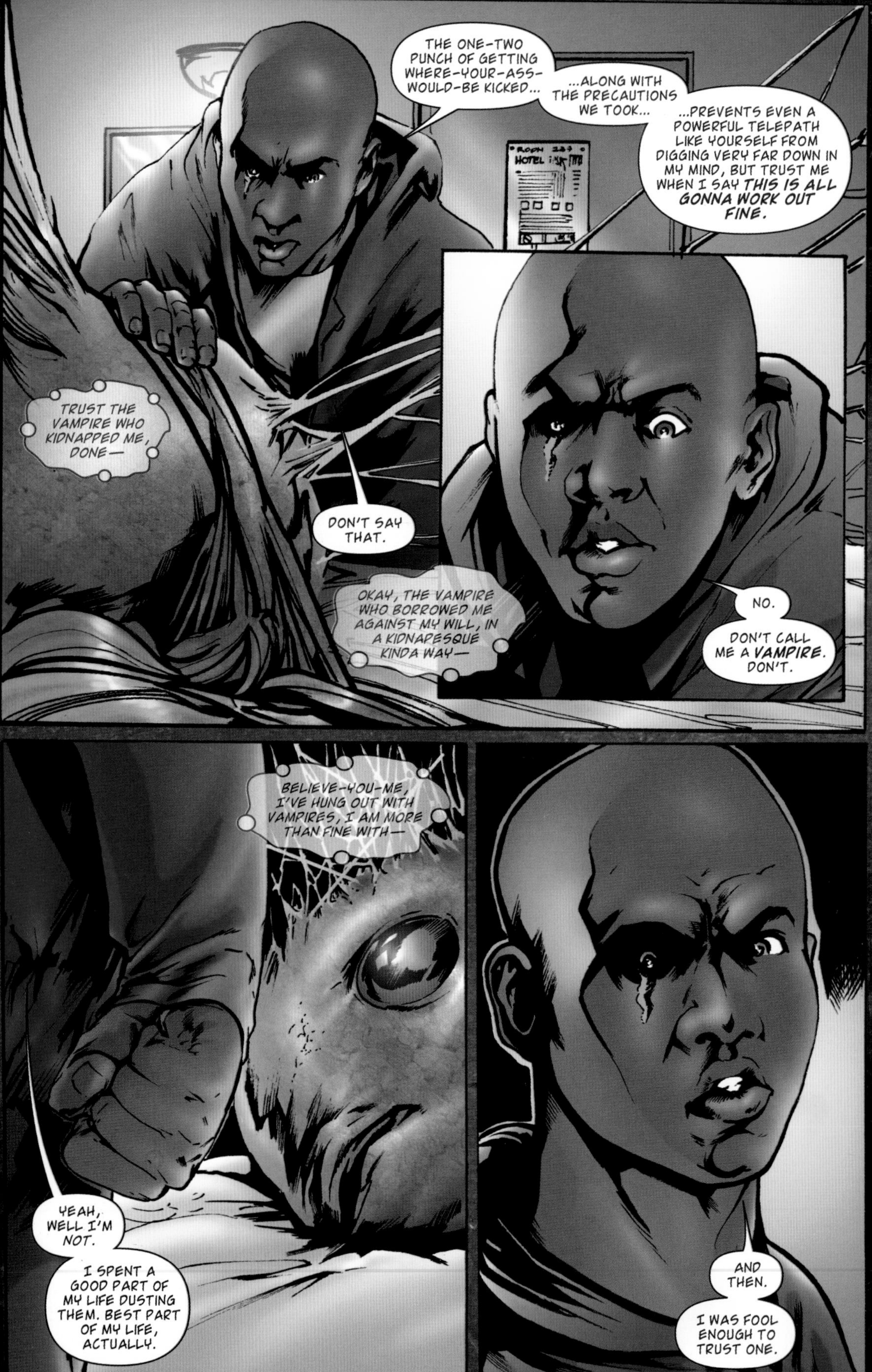
THE ONE-TWO PUNCH OF GETTING WHERE-YOUR-ASS-WOULD-BE KICKED...
...ALONG WITH THE PRECAUTIONS WE TOOK...
...PREVENTS EVEN A POWERFUL TELEPATH LIKE YOURSELF FROM DIGGING VERY FAR DOWN IN MY MIND, BUT TRUST ME WHEN I SAY THIS IS ALL GONNA WORK OUT FINE.
TRUST THE VAMPIRE WHO KIDNAPPED ME, DONE—
DON'T SAY THAT.
OKAY, THE VAMPIRE WHO BORROWED ME AGAINST MY WILL, IN A KIDNAPESQUE KINDA WAY—
NO.
DON'T CALL ME A VAMPIRE. DON'T.
BELIEVE-YOU-ME, I'VE HUNG OUT WITH VAMPIRES, I AM MORE THAN FINE WITH—
YEAH, WELL I'M NOT.
I SPENT A GOOD PART OF MY LIFE DUSTING THEM. BEST PART OF MY LIFE, ACTUALLY.
AND THEN.
I WAS FOOL ENOUGH TO TRUST ONE.

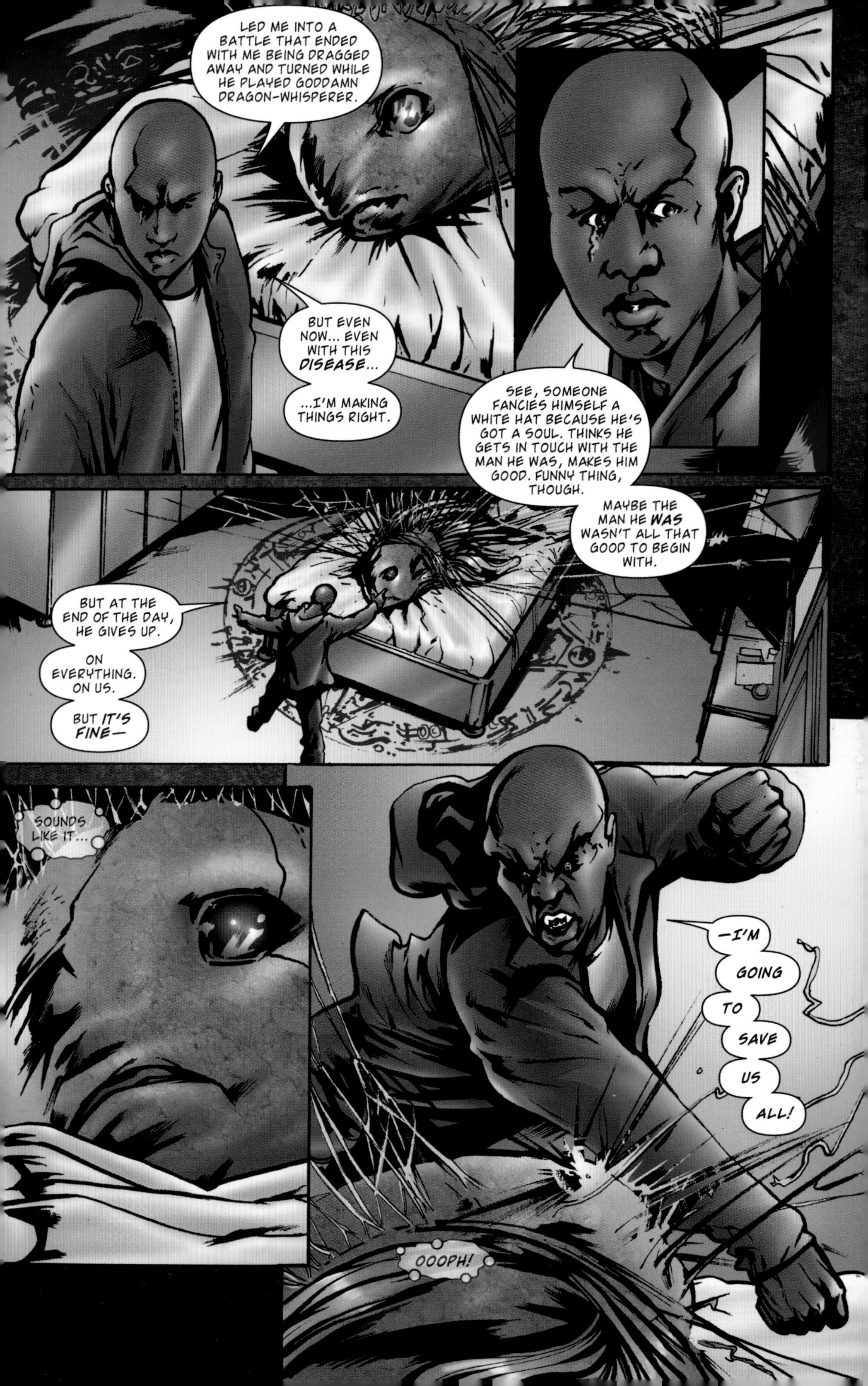
LED ME INTO A BATTLE THAT ENDED WITH ME BEING DRAGGED AWAY AND TURNED WHILE HE PLAYED GODDAMN DRAGON-WHISPERER.
BUT EVEN NOW... EVEN WITH THIS DISEASE...
...I'M MAKING THINGS RIGHT.
SEE, SOMEONE FANCIES HIMSELF A WHITE HAT BECAUSE HE'S GOT A SOUL. THINKS HE GETS IN TOUCH WITH THE MAN HE WAS, MAKES HIM GOOD. FUNNY THING, THOUGH.
MAYBE THE MAN HE WAS WASN'T ALL THAT GOOD TO BEGIN WITH.
BUT AT THE END OF THE DAY, HE GIVES UP.
ON EVERYTHING. ON US.
BUT IT'S FINE—
SOUNDS LIKE IT...
—I'M
GOING
TO
SAVE
US
ALL!
OOOPH!

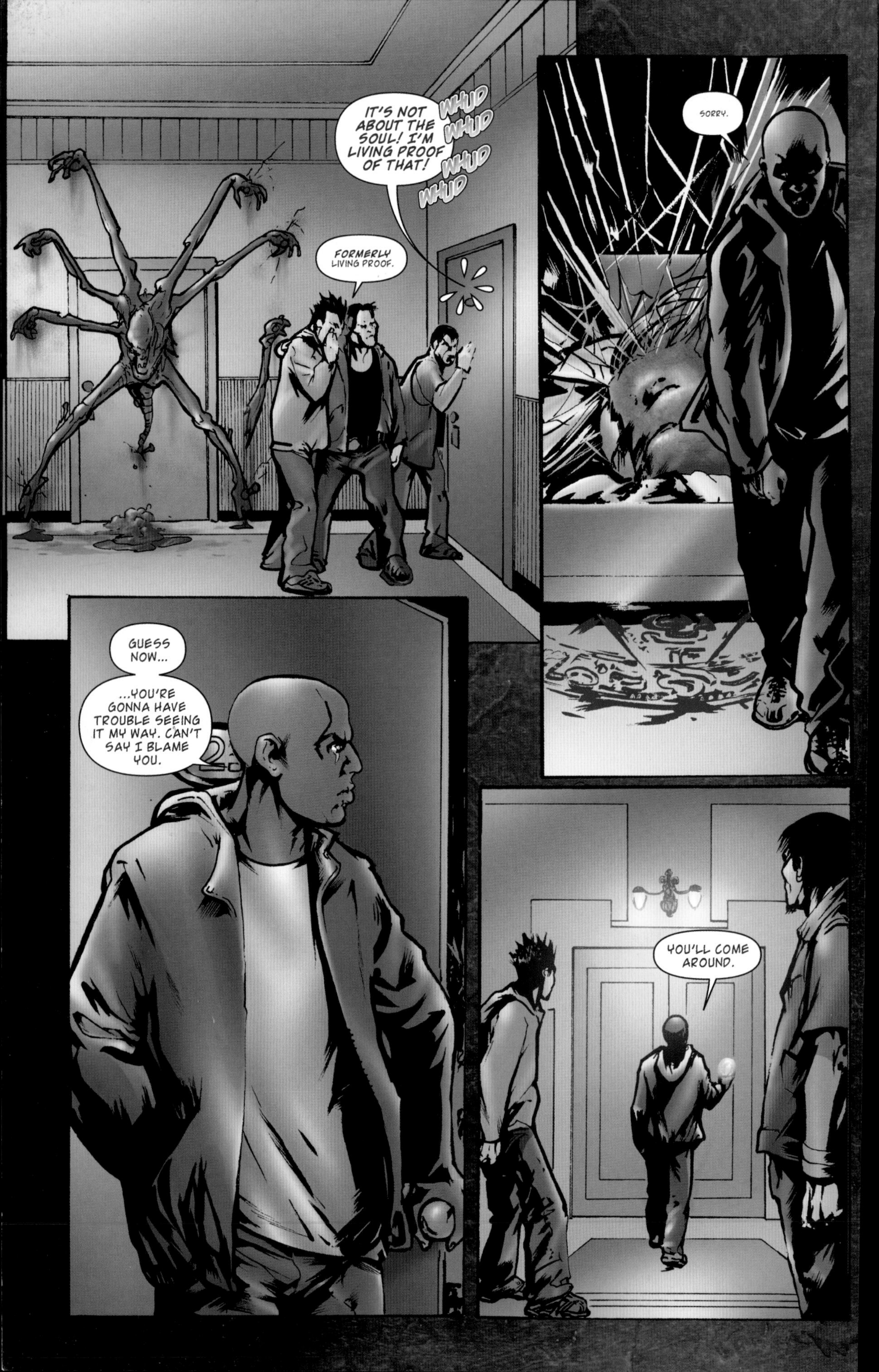
IT'S NOT ABOUT THE SOUL! I'M LIVING PROOF OF THAT!
WHUD
WHUD
WHUD
WHUD
FORMERLY LIVING PROOF.
SORRY.
GUESS NOW...
...YOU'RE GONNA HAVE TROUBLE SEEING IT MY WAY. CAN'T SAY I BLAME YOU.
YOU'LL COME AROUND.

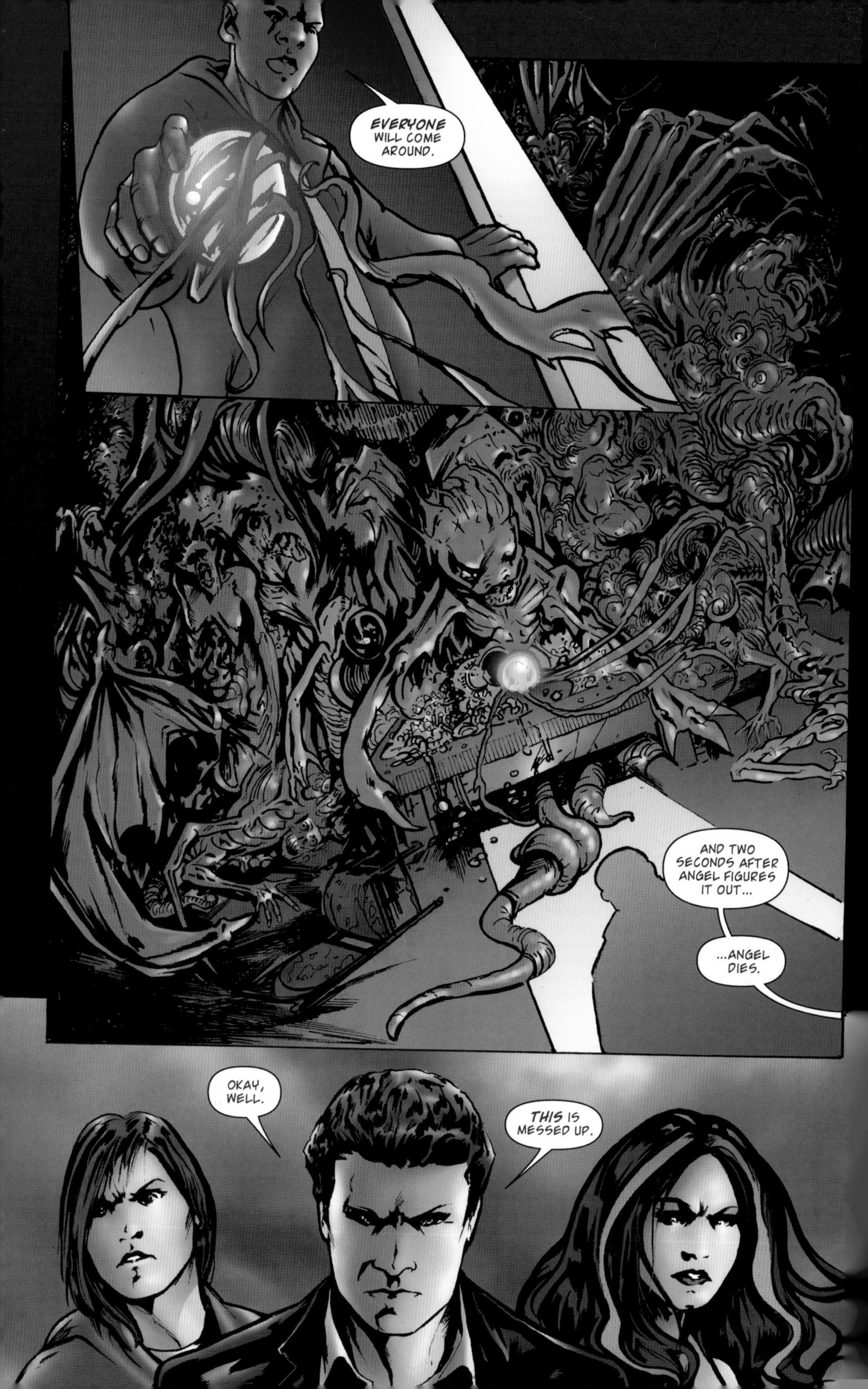
EVERYONE WILL COME AROUND.
AND TWO SECONDS AFTER ANGEL FIGURES IT OUT...
...ANGEL DIES.
OKAY, WELL.
THIS IS MESSED UP.

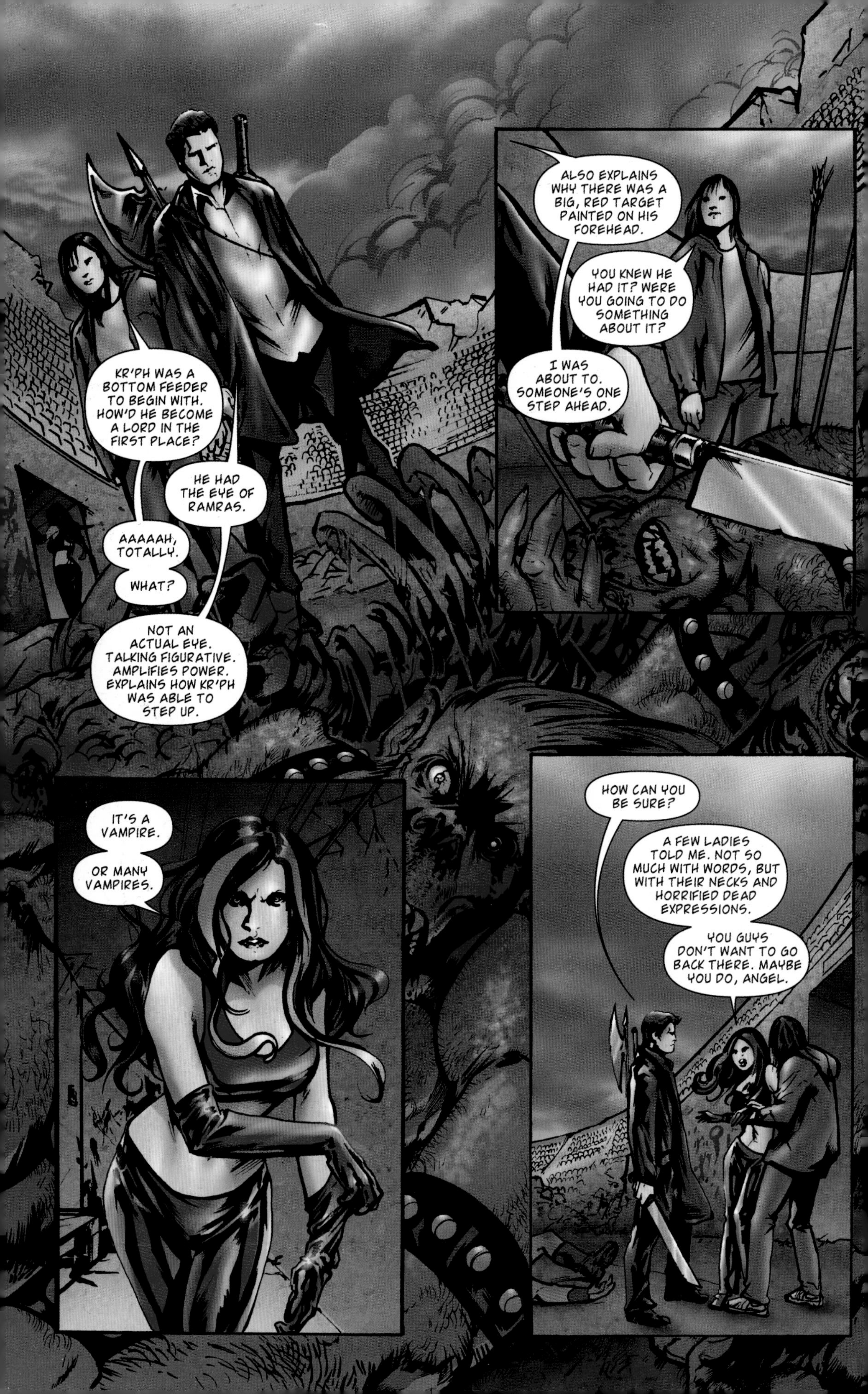
KR'PH WAS A BOTTOM FEEDER TO BEGIN WITH. HOW'D HE BECOME A LORD IN THE FIRST PLACE?
HE HAD THE EYE OF RAMRAS.
AAAAAH, TOTALLY.
WHAT?
NOT AN ACTUAL EYE. TALKING FIGURATIVE. AMPLIFIES POWER. EXPLAINS HOW KR'PH WAS ABLE TO STEP UP.
ALSO EXPLAINS WHY THERE WAS A BIG, RED TARGET PAINTED ON HIS FOREHEAD.
YOU KNEW HE HAD IT? WERE YOU GOING TO DO SOMETHING ABOUT IT?
I WAS ABOUT TO. SOMEONE'S ONE STEP AHEAD.
IT'S A VAMPIRE.
OR MANY VAMPIRES.
HOW CAN YOU BE SURE?
A FEW LADIES TOLD ME. NOT SO MUCH WITH WORDS, BUT WITH THEIR NECKS AND HORRIFIED DEAD EXPRESSIONS.
YOU GUYS DON'T WANT TO GO BACK THERE. MAYBE YOU DO, ANGEL.

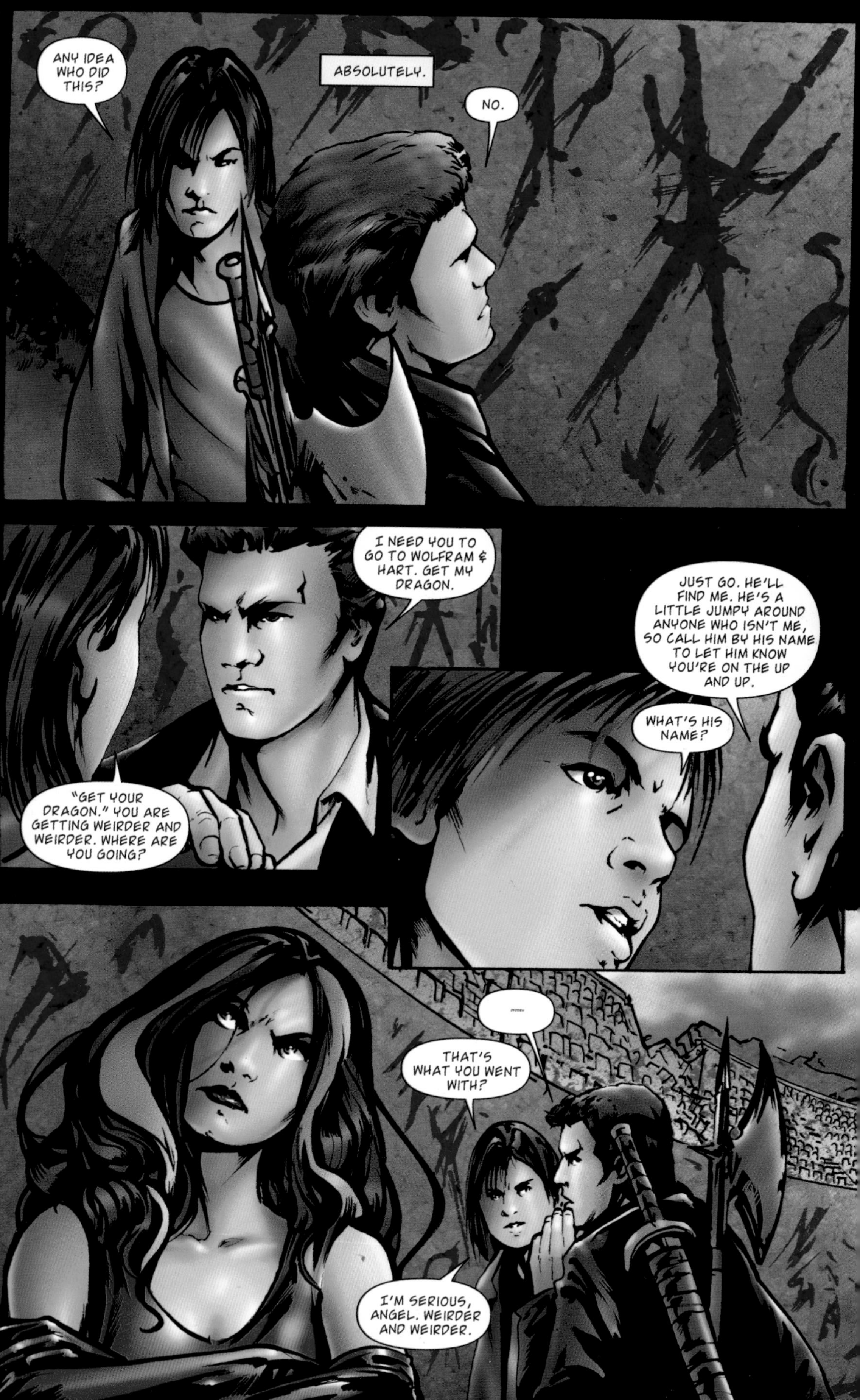
ANY IDEA WHO DID THIS?
ABSOLUTELY.
NO.
I NEED YOU TO GO TO WOLFRAM & HART. GET MY DRAGON.
"GET YOUR DRAGON." YOU ARE GETTING WEIRDER AND WEIRDER. WHERE ARE YOU GOING?
JUST GO. HE'LL FIND ME. HE'S A LITTLE JUMPY AROUND ANYONE WHO ISN'T ME, SO CALL HIM BY HIS NAME TO LET HIM KNOW YOU'RE ON THE UP AND UP.
WHAT'S HIS NAME?
THAT'S WHAT YOU WENT WITH?
I'M SERIOUS, ANGEL. WEIRDER AND WEIRDER.

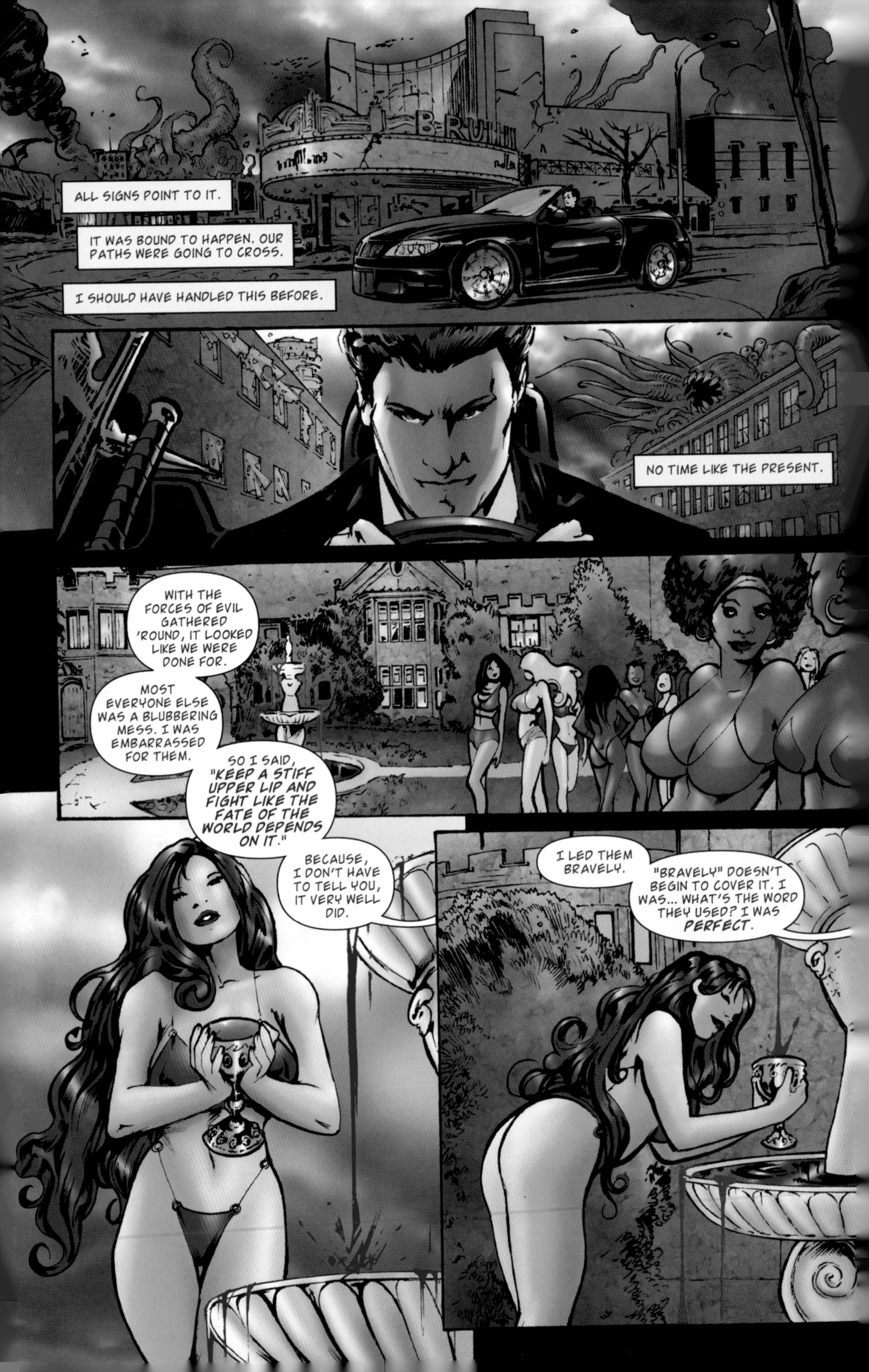
ALL SIGNS POINT TO IT.
IT WAS BOUND TO HAPPEN. OUR PATHS WERE GOING TO CROSS.
I SHOULD HAVE HANDLED THIS BEFORE.
NO TIME LIKE THE PRESENT.
WITH THE FORCES OF EVIL GATHERED 'ROUND, IT LOOKED LIKE WE WERE DONE FOR.
MOST EVERYONE ELSE WAS A BLUBBERING MESS. I WAS EMBARRASSED FOR THEM.
SO I SAID, "KEEP A STIFF UPPER LIP AND FIGHT LIKE THE FATE OF THE WORLD DEPENDS ON IT."
BECAUSE, I DON'T HAVE TO TELL YOU, IT VERY WELL DID.
I LED THEM BRAVELY.
"BRAVELY" DOESN'T BEGIN TO COVER IT. I WAS... WHAT'S THE WORD THEY USED? I WAS PERFECT.

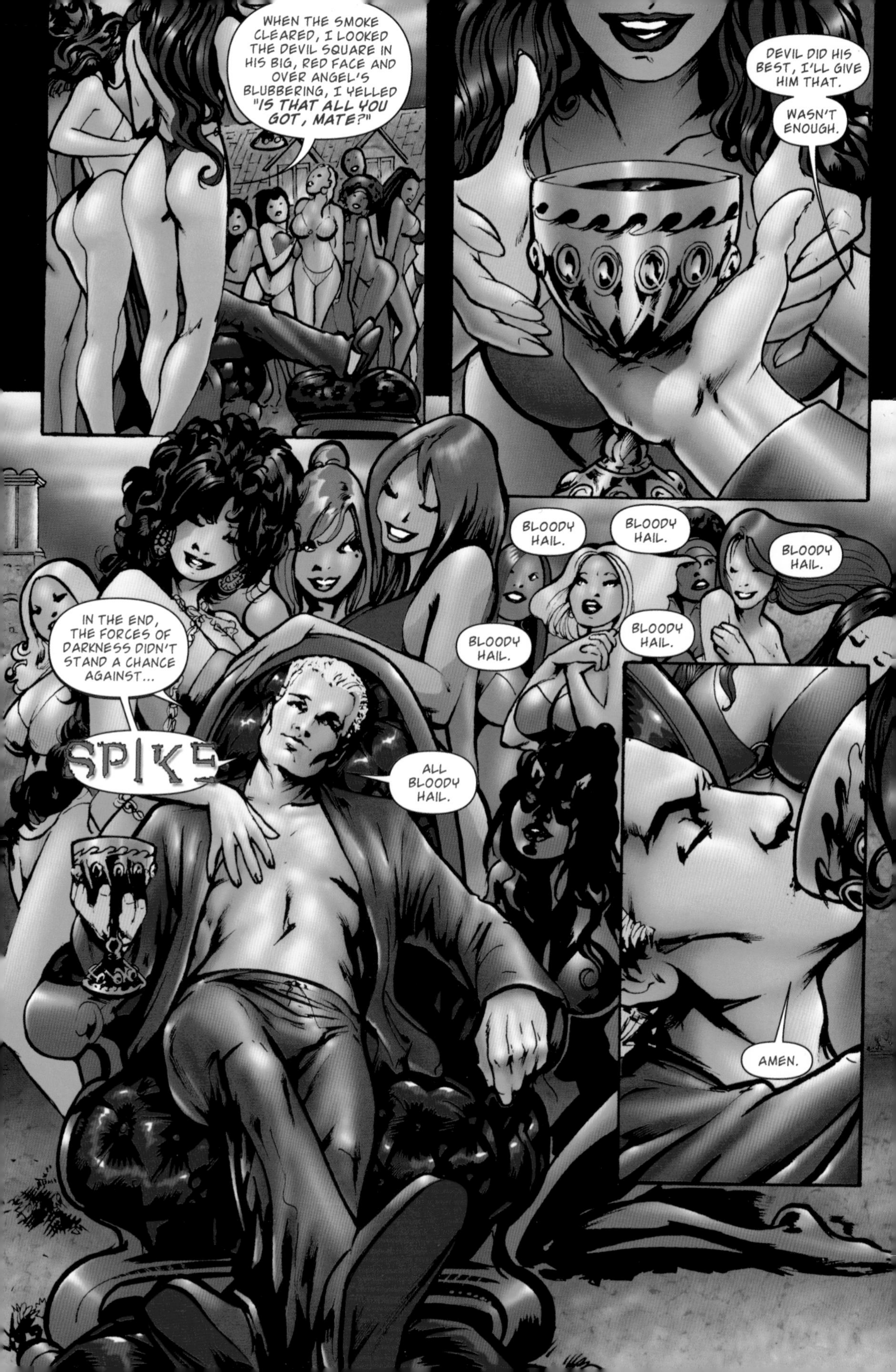
WHEN THE SMOKE CLEARED, I LOOKED THE DEVIL SQUARE IN HIS BIG, RED FACE AND OVER ANGEL'S BLUBBERING, I YELLED "IS THAT ALL YOU GOT, MATE?"
DEVIL DID HIS BEST, I'LL GIVE HIM THAT.
WASN'T ENOUGH.
IN THE END, THE FORCES OF DARKNESS DIDN'T STAND A CHANCE AGAINST...
SPIKE
BLOODY HAIL.
BLOODY HAIL.
BLOODY HAIL.
BLOODY HAIL.
BLOODY HAIL.
ALL BLOODY HAIL.
AMEN.

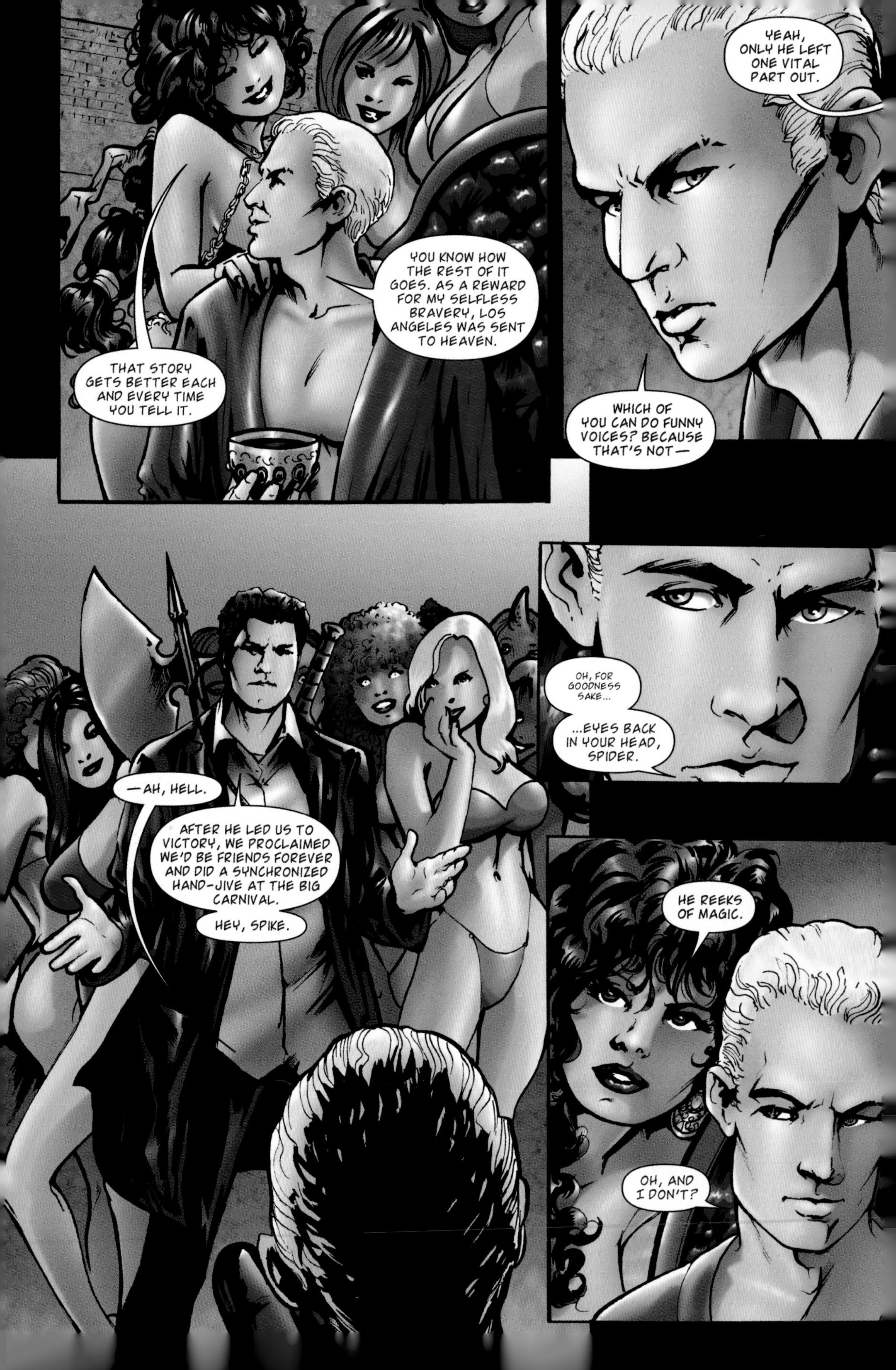
YOU KNOW HOW THE REST OF IT GOES. AS A REWARD FOR MY SELFLESS BRAVERY, LOS ANGELES WAS SENT TO HEAVEN.
THAT STORY GETS BETTER EACH AND EVERY TIME YOU TELL IT.
YEAH, ONLY HE LEFT ONE VITAL PART OUT.
WHICH OF YOU CAN DO FUNNY VOICES? BECAUSE THAT'S NOT—
—AH, HELL.
AFTER HE LED US TO VICTORY, WE PROCLAIMED WE'D BE FRIENDS FOREVER AND DID A SYNCHRONIZED HAND-JIVE AT THE BIG CARNIVAL.
HEY, SPIKE.
OH, FOR GOODNESS SAKE...
...EYES BACK IN YOUR HEAD, SPIDER.
HE REEKS OF MAGIC.
OH, AND I DON'T?

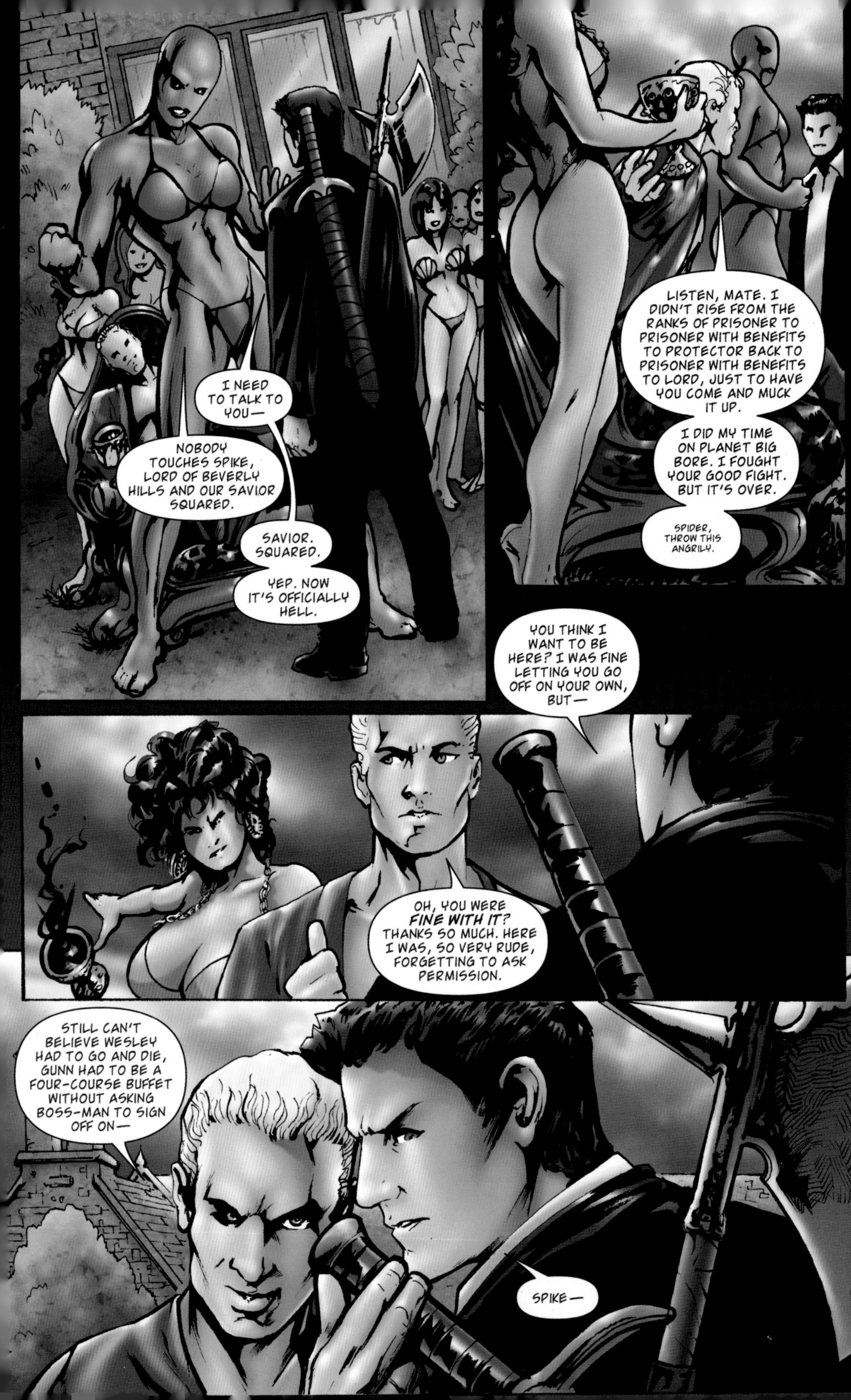
NOBODY TOUCHES SPIKE, LORD OF BEVERLY HILLS AND OUR SAVIOR SQUARED.
I NEED TO TALK TO YOU—
SAVIOR. SQUARED.
YEP. NOW IT'S OFFICIALLY HELL.
LISTEN, MATE. I DIDN'T RISE FROM THE RANKS OF PRISONER TO PRISONER WITH BENEFITS TO PROTECTOR BACK TO PRISONER WITH BENEFITS TO LORD, JUST TO HAVE YOU COME AND MUCK IT UP.
I DID MY TIME ON PLANET BIG BORE. I FOUGHT YOUR GOOD FIGHT. BUT IT'S OVER.
SPIDER, THROW THIS ANGRILY.
YOU THINK I WANT TO BE HERE? I WAS FINE LETTING YOU GO OFF ON YOUR OWN, BUT—
OH, YOU WERE ***FINE WITH IT***? THANKS SO MUCH. HERE I WAS, SO VERY RUDE, FORGETTING TO ASK PERMISSION.
STILL CAN'T BELIEVE WESLEY HAD TO GO AND DIE, GUNN HAD TO BE A FOUR-COURSE BUFFET WITHOUT ASKING BOSS-MAN TO SIGN OFF ON—
SPIKE—

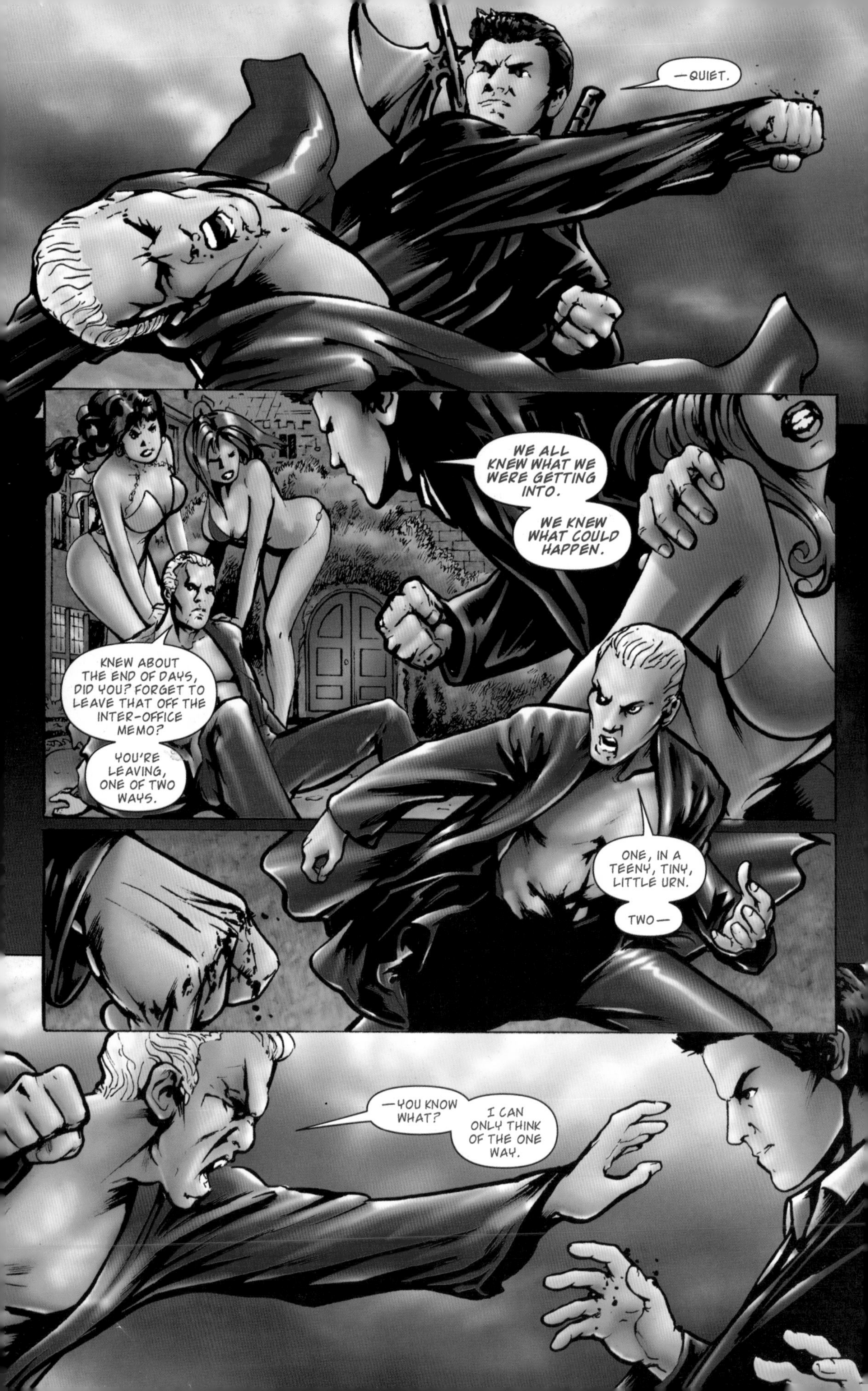
—QUIET.
WE ALL KNEW WHAT WE WERE GETTING INTO.
WE KNEW WHAT COULD HAPPEN.
KNEW ABOUT THE END OF DAYS, DID YOU? FORGET TO LEAVE THAT OFF THE INTER-OFFICE MEMO?
YOU'RE LEAVING, ONE OF TWO WAYS.
ONE, IN A TEENY, TINY, LITTLE URN.
TWO—
—YOU KNOW WHAT?
I CAN ONLY THINK OF THE ONE WAY.

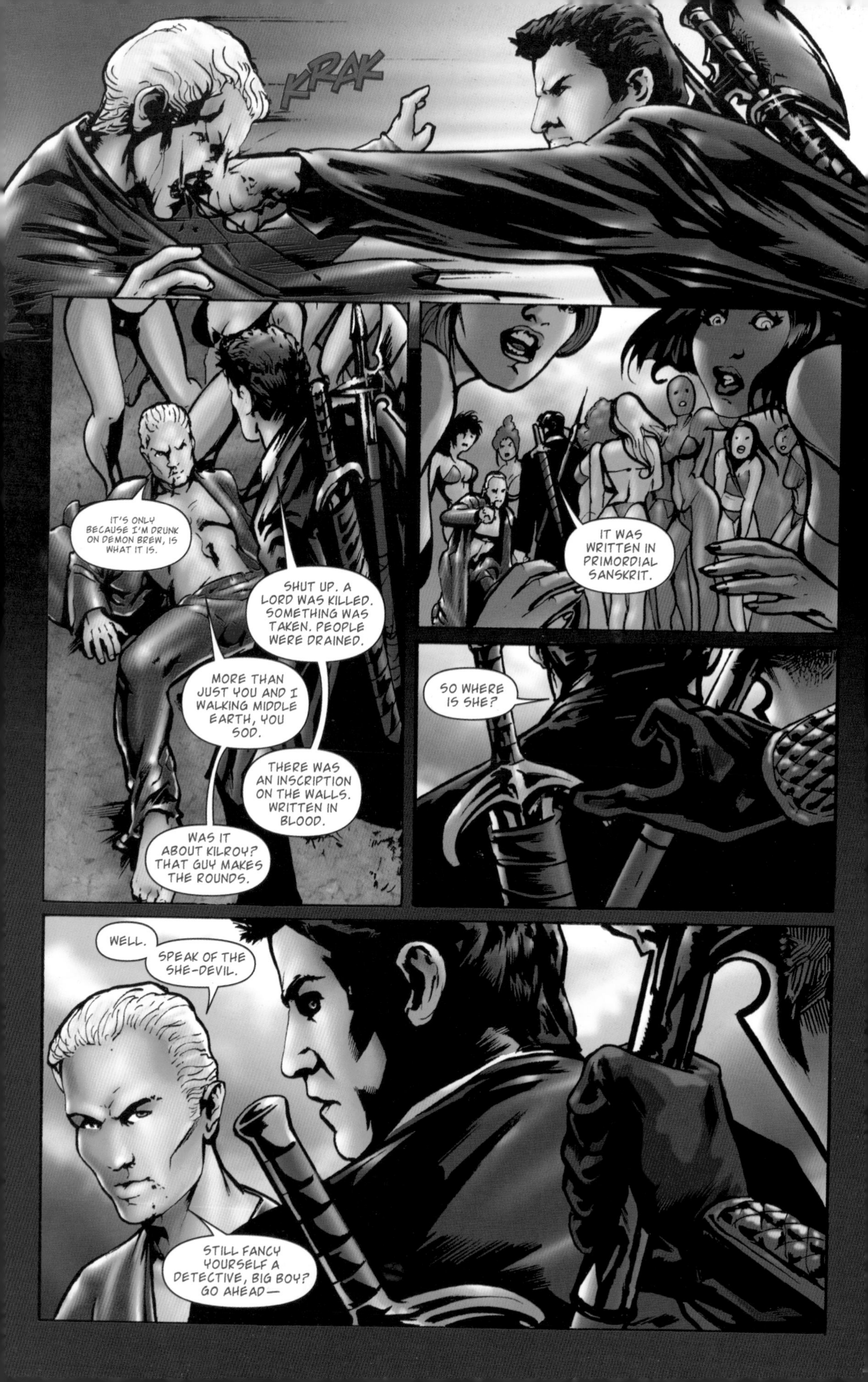
KRAK
IT'S ONLY BECAUSE I'M DRUNK ON DEMON BREW, IS WHAT IT IS.
SHUT UP. A LORD WAS KILLED. SOMETHING WAS TAKEN. PEOPLE WERE DRAINED.
MORE THAN JUST YOU AND I WALKING MIDDLE EARTH, YOU SOD.
THERE WAS AN INSCRIPTION ON THE WALLS. WRITTEN IN BLOOD.
WAS IT ABOUT KILROY? THAT GUY MAKES THE ROUNDS.
IT WAS WRITTEN IN PRIMORDIAL SANSKRIT.
SO WHERE IS SHE?
WELL.
SPEAK OF THE SHE-DEVIL.
STILL FANCY YOURSELF A DETECTIVE, BIG BOY? GO AHEAD—

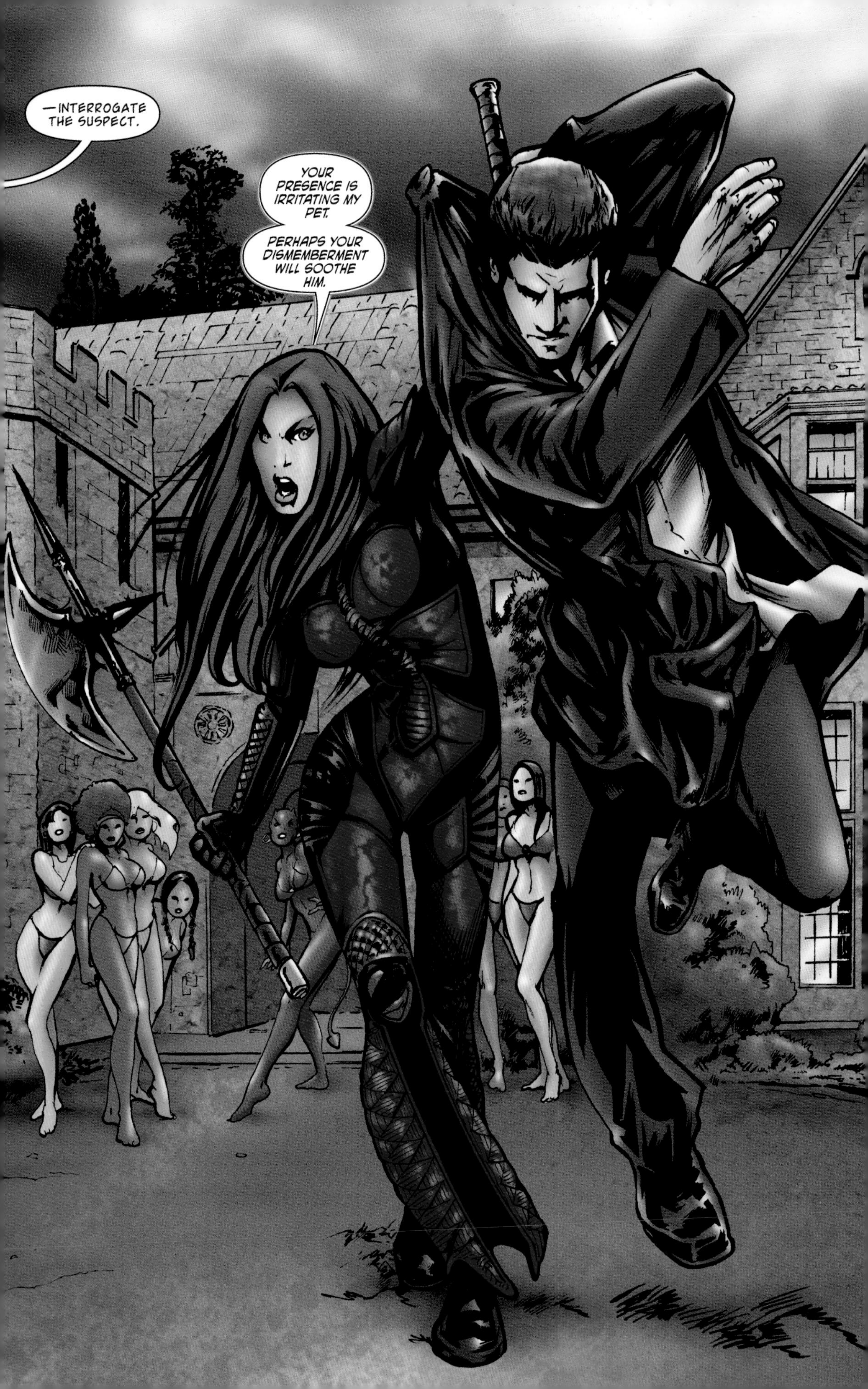
—INTERROGATE THE SUSPECT.
YOUR PRESENCE IS IRRITATING MY PET.
PERHAPS YOUR DISMEMBERMENT WILL SOOTHE HIM.

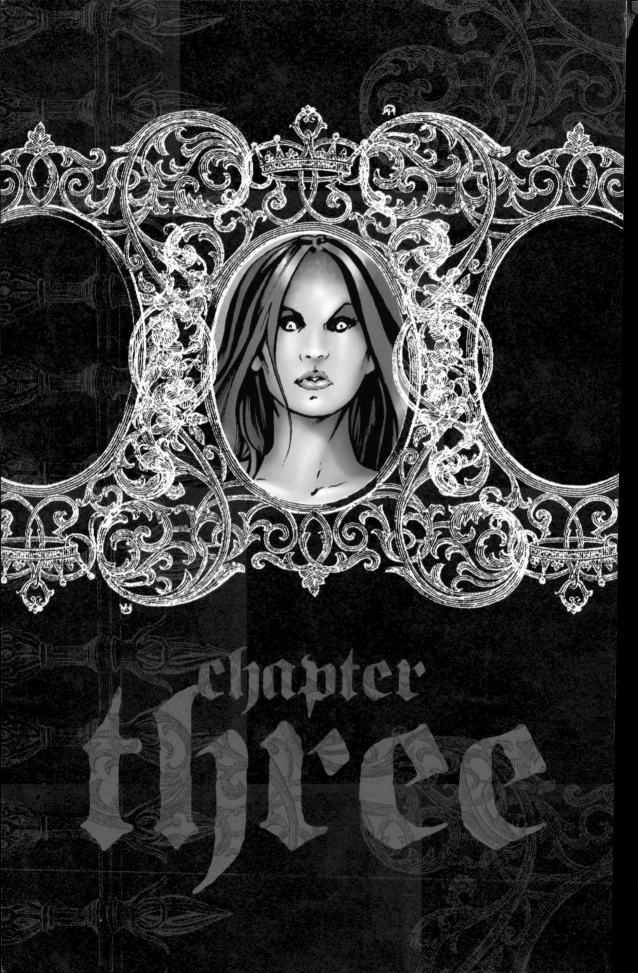

chapter
three

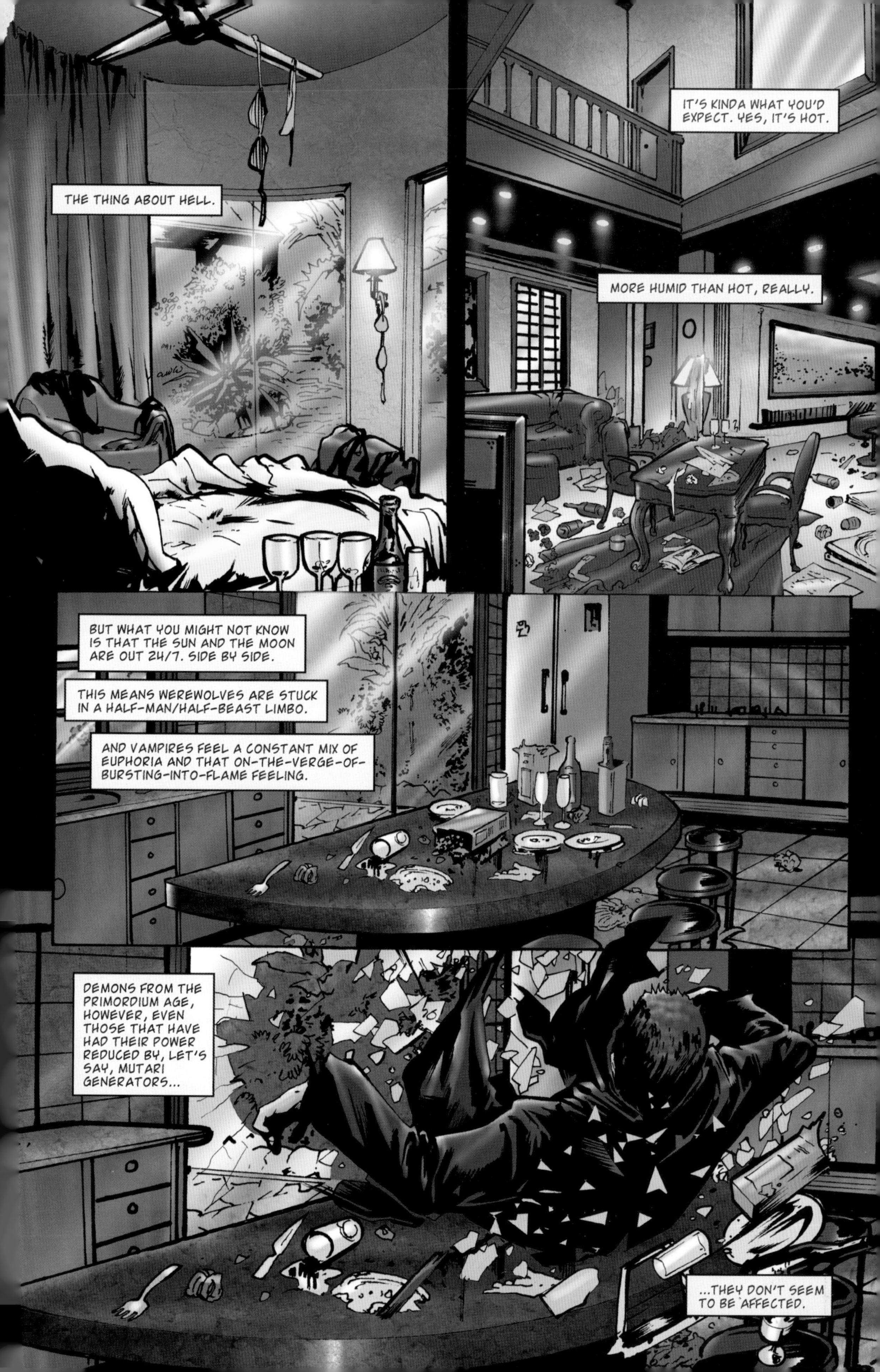
THE THING ABOUT HELL.
IT'S KINDA WHAT YOU'D EXPECT. YES, IT'S HOT.
MORE HUMID THAN HOT, REALLY.
BUT WHAT YOU MIGHT NOT KNOW IS THAT THE SUN AND THE MOON ARE OUT 24/7. SIDE BY SIDE.
THIS MEANS WEREWOLVES ARE STUCK IN A HALF-MAN/HALF-BEAST LIMBO.
AND VAMPIRES FEEL A CONSTANT MIX OF EUPHORIA AND THAT ON-THE-VERGE-OF-BURSTING-INTO-FLAME FEELING.
DEMONS FROM THE PRIMORDIUM AGE, HOWEVER, EVEN THOSE THAT HAVE HAD THEIR POWER REDUCED BY, LET'S SAY, MUTARI GENERATORS...
...THEY DON'T SEEM TO BE AFFECTED.

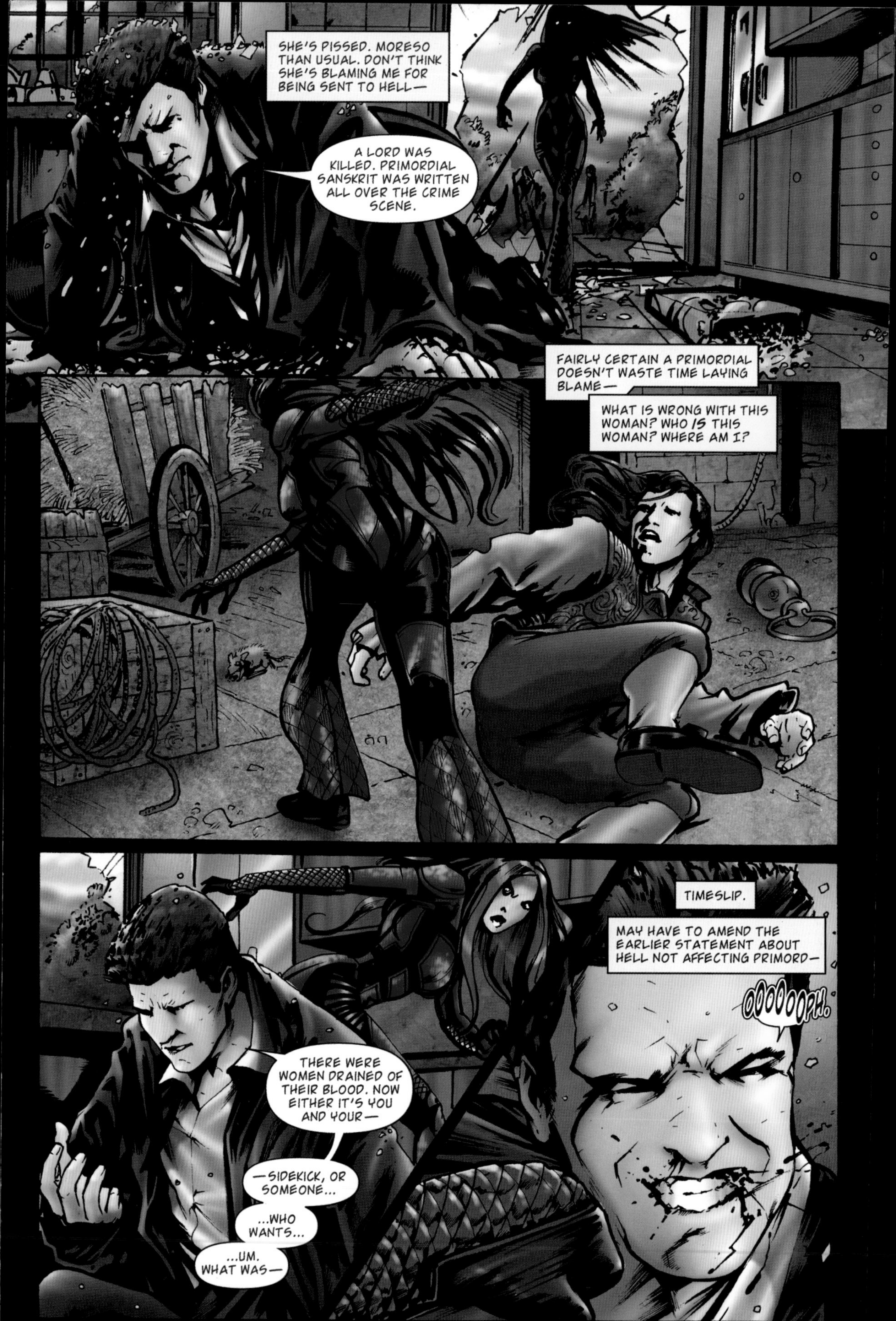
SHE'S PISSED. MORESO THAN USUAL. DON'T THINK SHE'S BLAMING ME FOR BEING SENT TO HELL—
A LORD WAS KILLED. PRIMORDIAL SANSKRIT WAS WRITTEN ALL OVER THE CRIME SCENE.
FAIRLY CERTAIN A PRIMORDIAL DOESN'T WASTE TIME LAYING BLAME—
WHAT IS WRONG WITH THIS WOMAN? WHO *IS* THIS WOMAN? WHERE AM I?
TIMESLIP.
MAY HAVE TO AMEND THE EARLIER STATEMENT ABOUT HELL NOT AFFECTING PRIMORD—
OOOOOOPH.
THERE WERE WOMEN DRAINED OF THEIR BLOOD. NOW EITHER IT'S YOU AND YOUR—
—SIDEKICK, OR SOMEONE...
...WHO WANTS...
...UM. WHAT WAS—

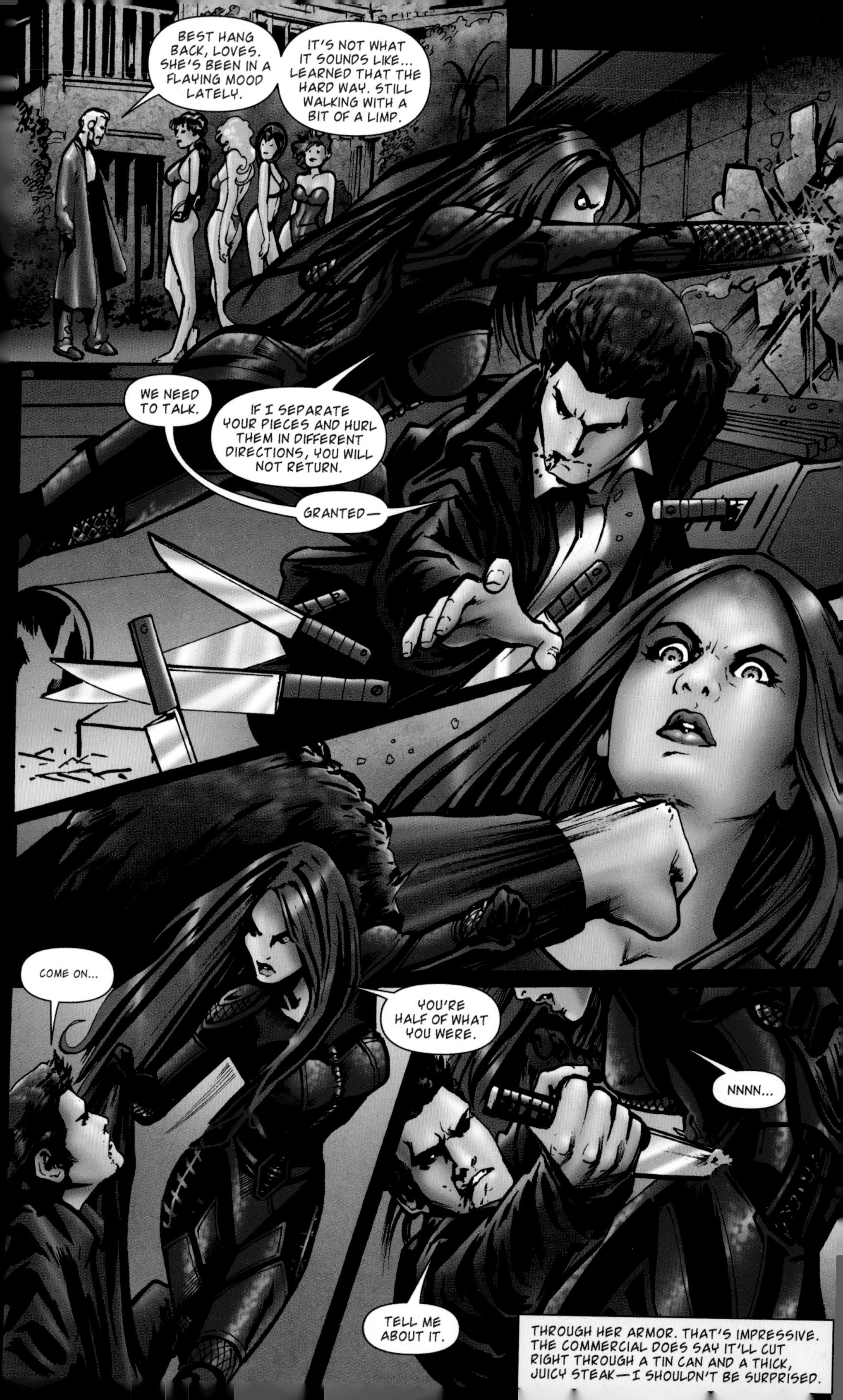
BEST HANG BACK, LOVES. SHE'S BEEN IN A FLAYING MOOD LATELY.
IT'S NOT WHAT IT SOUNDS LIKE... LEARNED THAT THE HARD WAY. STILL WALKING WITH A BIT OF A LIMP.
WE NEED TO TALK.
IF I SEPARATE YOUR PIECES AND HURL THEM IN DIFFERENT DIRECTIONS, YOU WILL NOT RETURN.
GRANTED—
COME ON...
YOU'RE HALF OF WHAT YOU WERE.
NNNN...
TELL ME ABOUT IT.
THROUGH HER ARMOR. THAT'S IMPRESSIVE. THE COMMERCIAL DOES SAY IT'LL CUT RIGHT THROUGH A TIN CAN AND A THICK, JUICY STEAK—I SHOULDN'T BE SURPRISED.

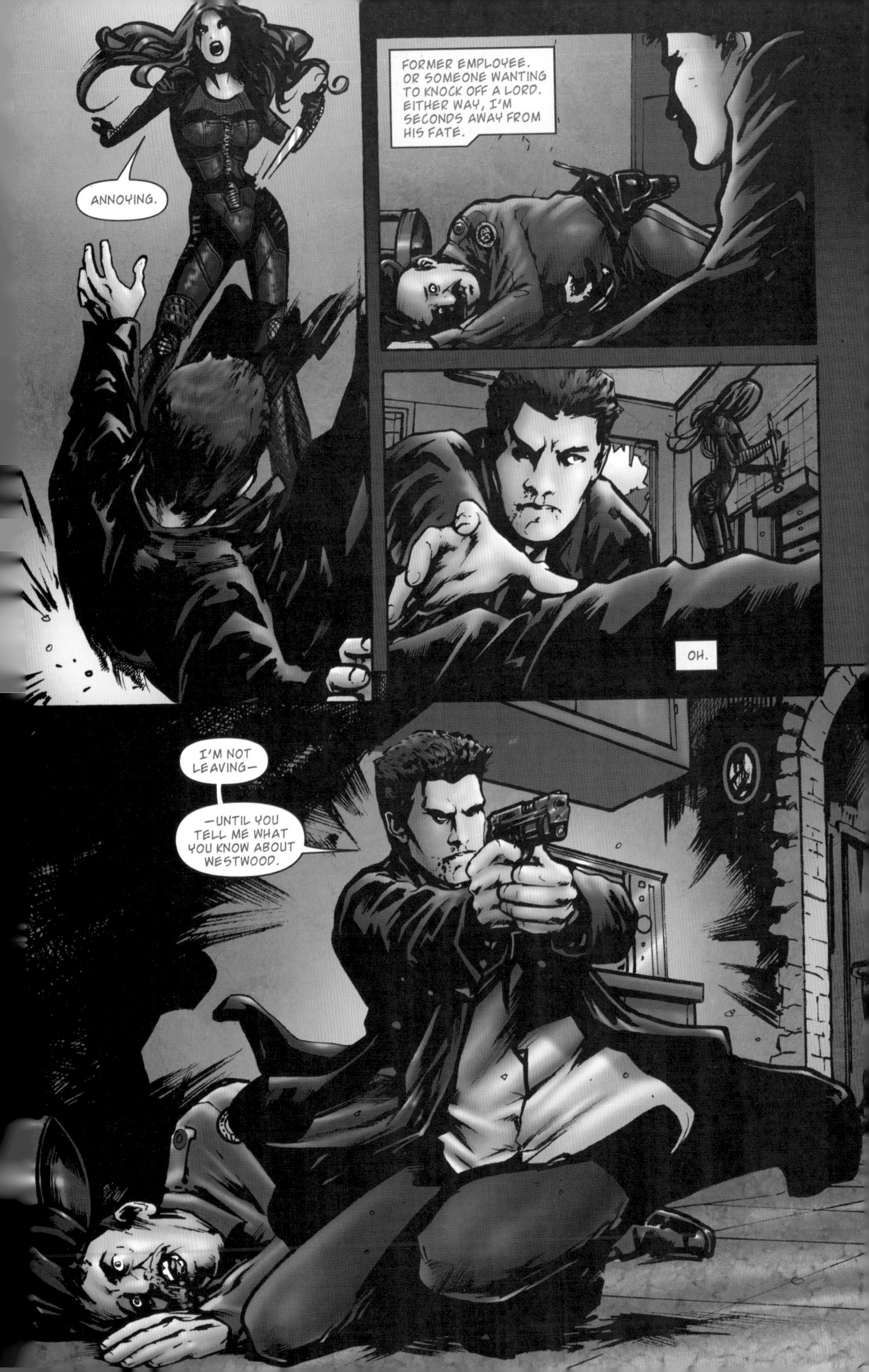
ANNOYING.
FORMER EMPLOYEE. OR SOMEONE WANTING TO KNOCK OFF A LORD. EITHER WAY, I'M SECONDS AWAY FROM HIS FATE.
OH.
I'M NOT LEAVING—
—UNTIL YOU TELL ME WHAT YOU KNOW ABOUT WESTWOOD.

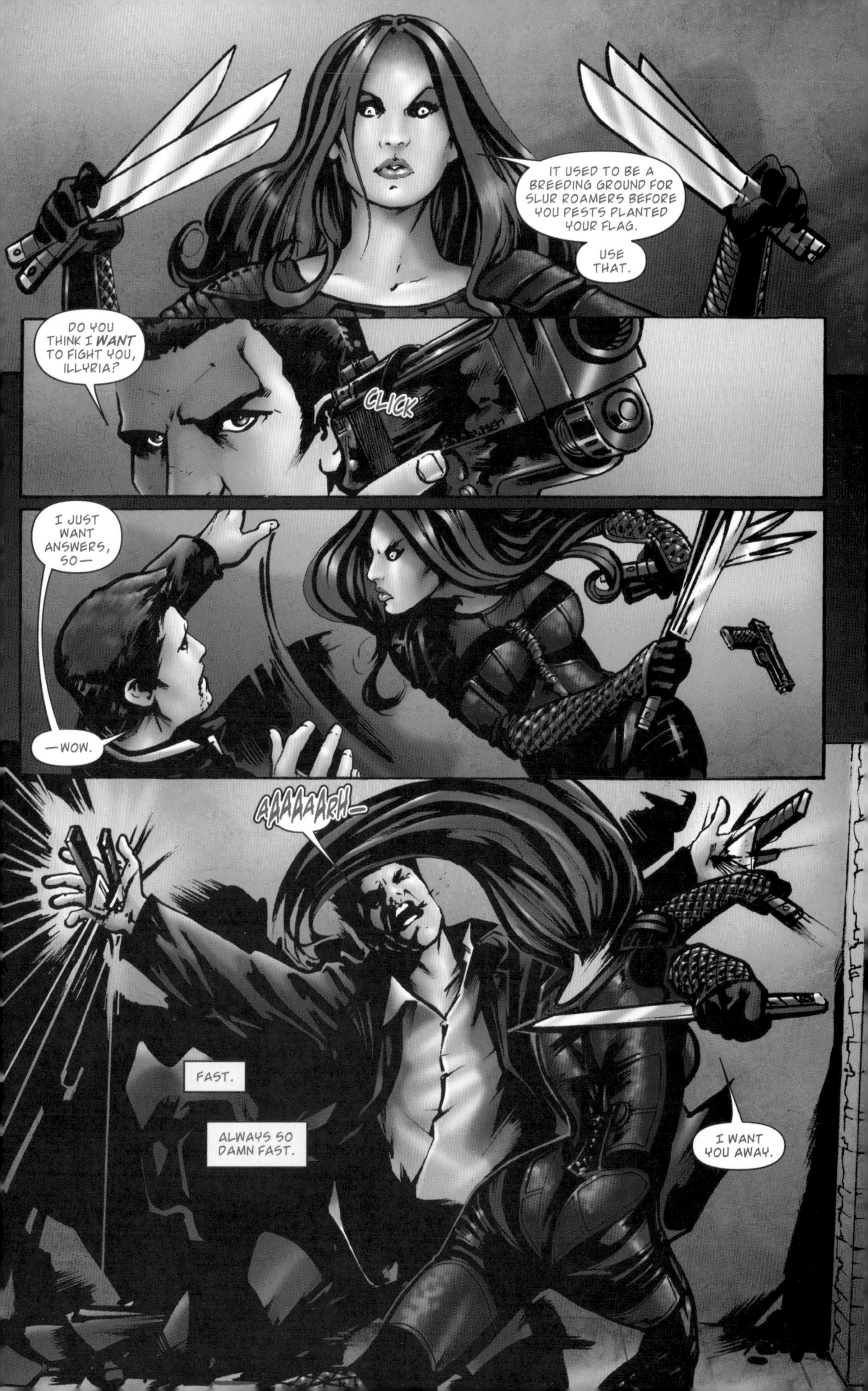
IT USED TO BE A BREEDING GROUND FOR SLUR ROAMERS BEFORE YOU PESTS PLANTED YOUR FLAG.
USE THAT.
DO YOU THINK I *WANT* TO FIGHT YOU, ILLYRIA?
CLICK
I JUST WANT ANSWERS, SO—
—WOW.
AAAAAARH—
FAST.
ALWAYS SO DAMN FAST.
I WANT YOU AWAY.

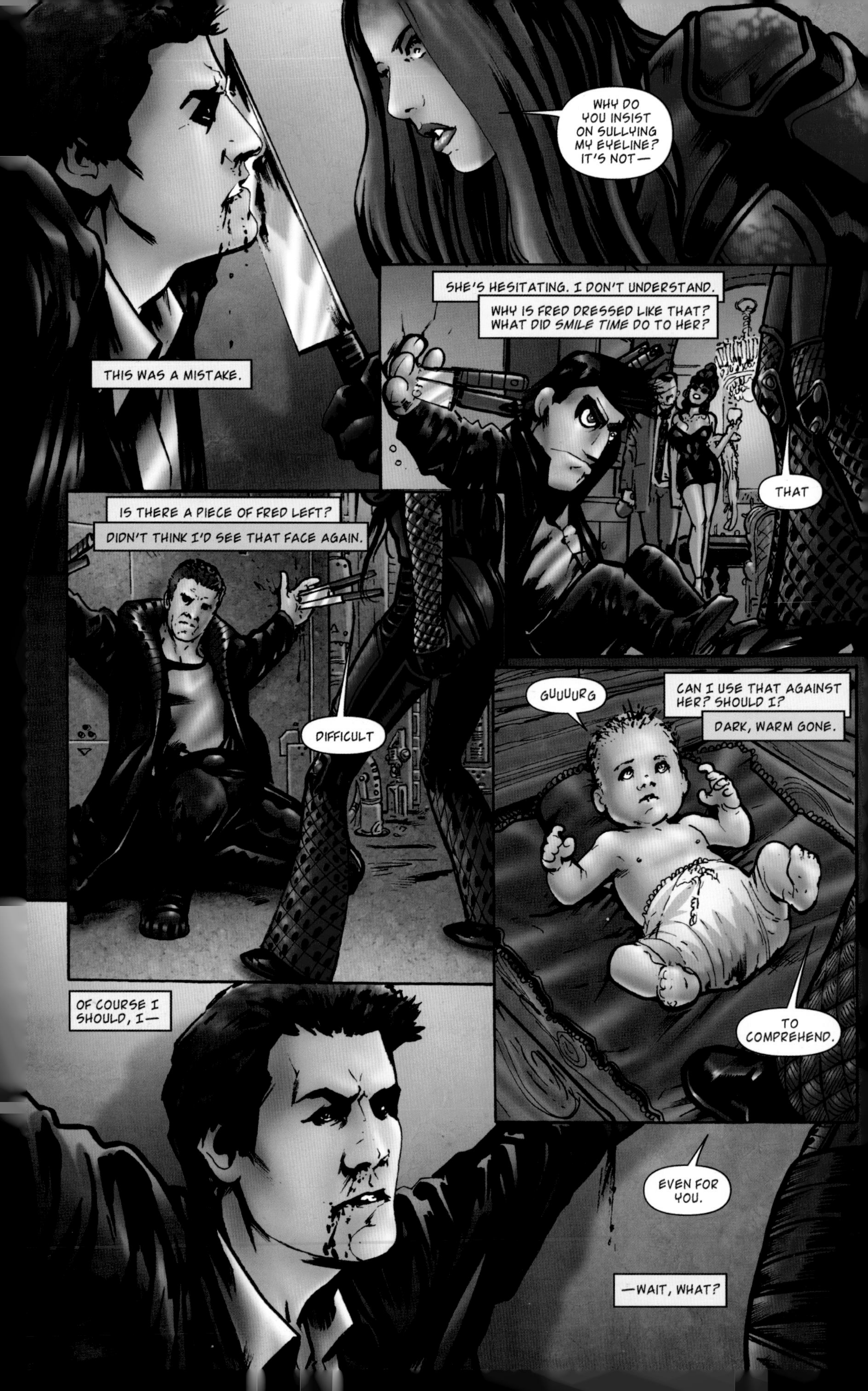
WHY DO YOU INSIST ON SULLYING MY EYELINE? IT'S NOT—
THIS WAS A MISTAKE.
SHE'S HESITATING. I DON'T UNDERSTAND.
WHY IS FRED DRESSED LIKE THAT? WHAT DID SMILE TIME DO TO HER?
THAT
IS THERE A PIECE OF FRED LEFT?
DIDN'T THINK I'D SEE THAT FACE AGAIN.
DIFFICULT
GUUUURG
CAN I USE THAT AGAINST HER? SHOULD I?
DARK, WARM GONE.
TO COMPREHEND.
OF COURSE I SHOULD, I—
EVEN FOR YOU.
—WAIT, WHAT?

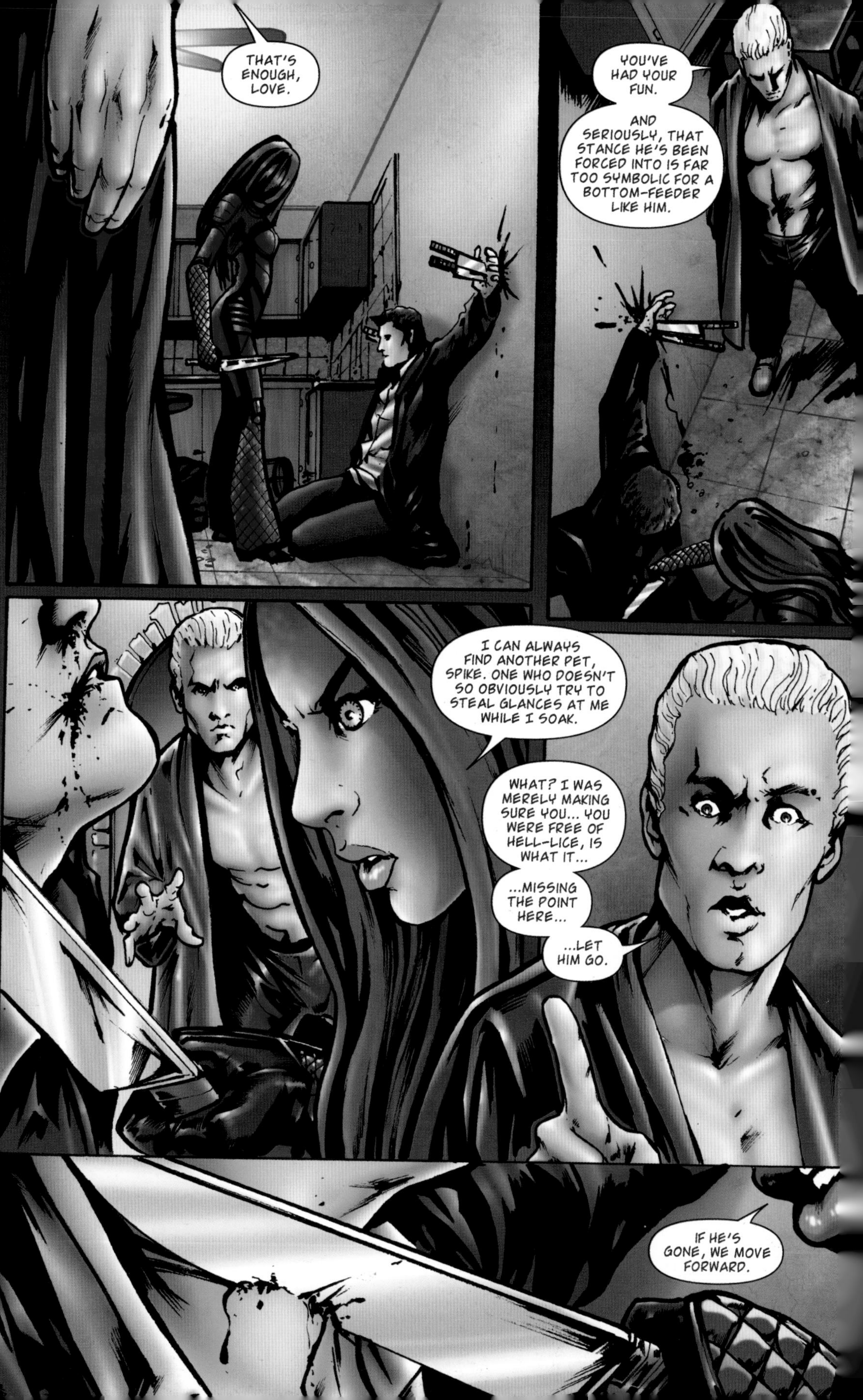
THAT'S ENOUGH, LOVE.
YOU'VE HAD YOUR FUN.
AND SERIOUSLY, THAT STANCE HE'S BEEN FORCED INTO IS FAR TOO SYMBOLIC FOR A BOTTOM-FEEDER LIKE HIM.
I CAN ALWAYS FIND ANOTHER PET, SPIKE. ONE WHO DOESN'T SO OBVIOUSLY TRY TO STEAL GLANCES AT ME WHILE I SOAK.
WHAT? I WAS MERELY MAKING SURE YOU... YOU WERE FREE OF HELL-LICE, IS WHAT IT...
...MISSING THE POINT HERE...
...LET HIM GO.
IF HE'S GONE, WE MOVE FORWARD.

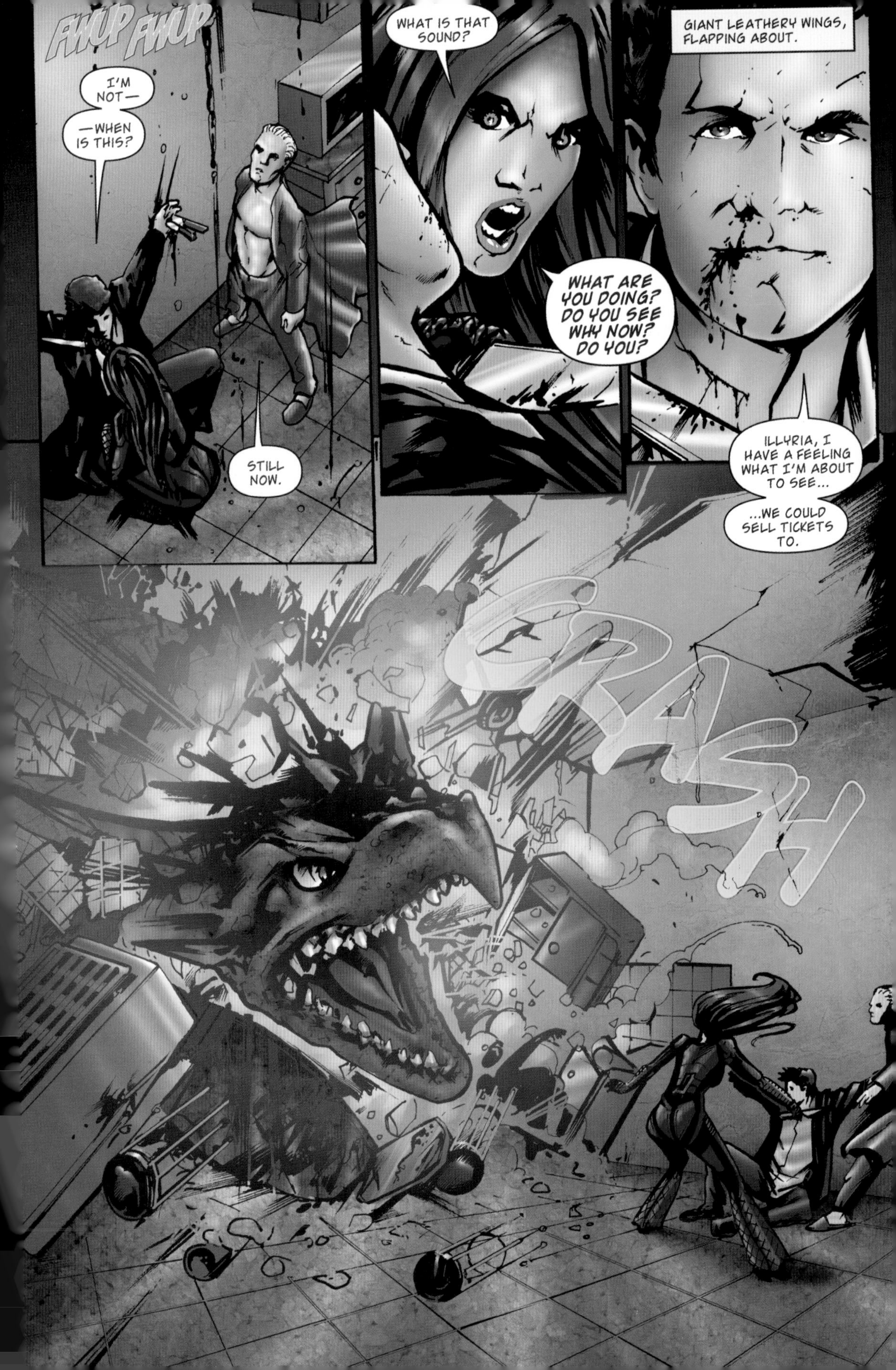
FWUP FWUP
I'M NOT—
—WHEN IS THIS?
STILL NOW.
WHAT IS THAT SOUND?
GIANT LEATHERY WINGS, FLAPPING ABOUT.
WHAT ARE YOU DOING? DO YOU SEE WHY NOW? DO YOU?
ILLYRIA, I HAVE A FEELING WHAT I'M ABOUT TO SEE...
...WE COULD SELL TICKETS TO.
CRASH

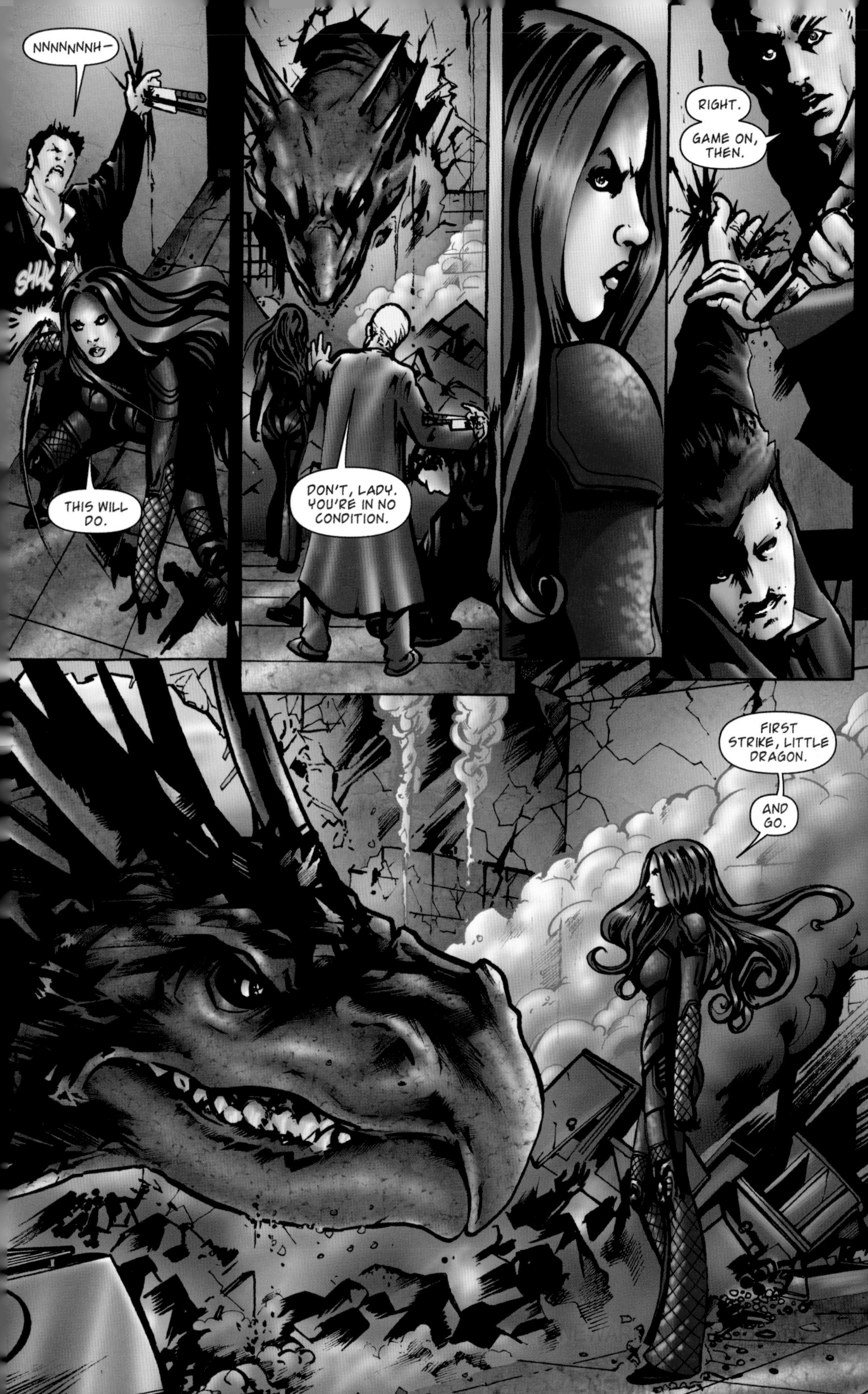
NNNNNNNH—
SHUK
THIS WILL DO.
DON'T, LADY. YOU'RE IN NO CONDITION.
RIGHT.
GAME ON, THEN.
FIRST STRIKE, LITTLE DRAGON.
AND GO.

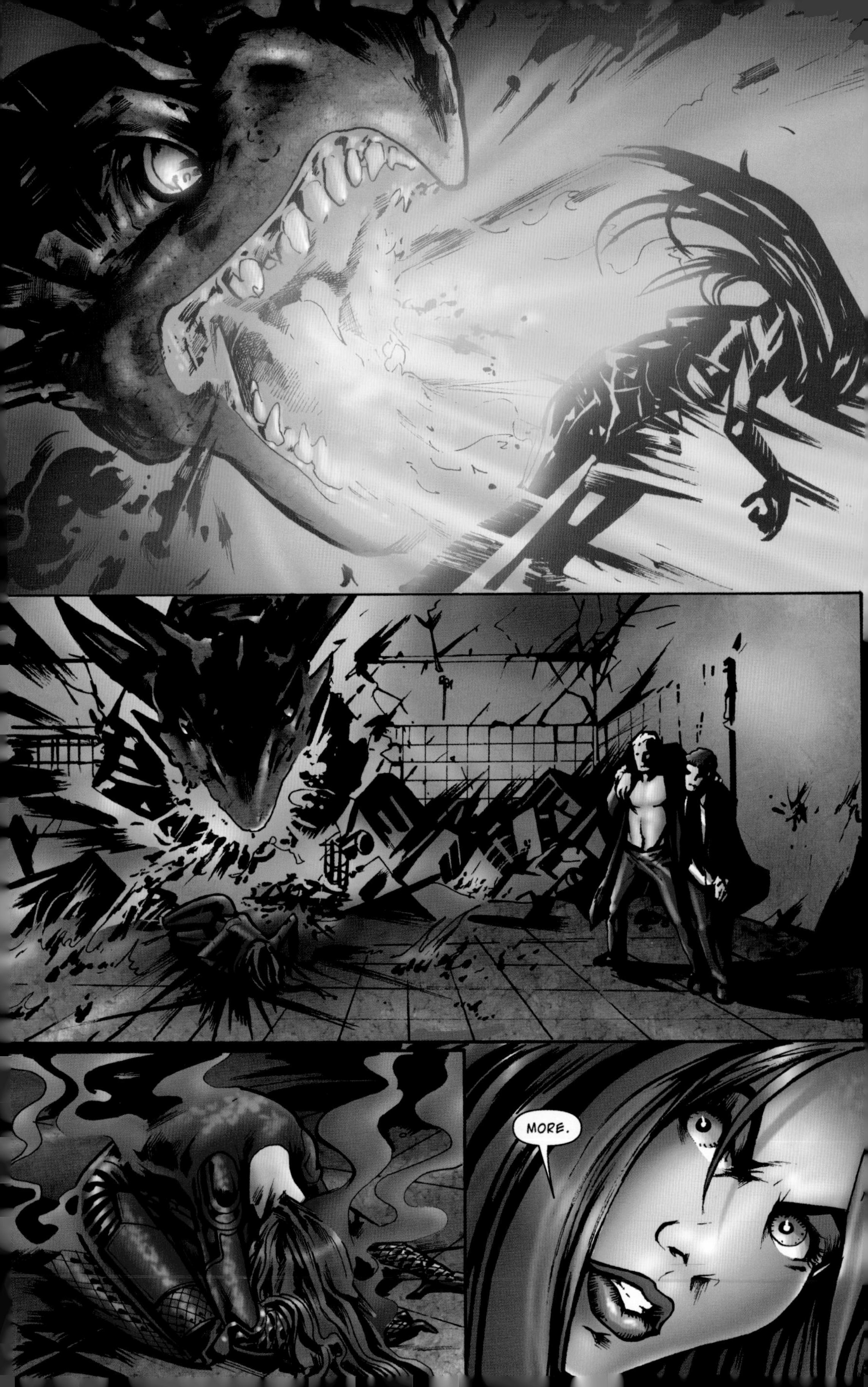
MORE.

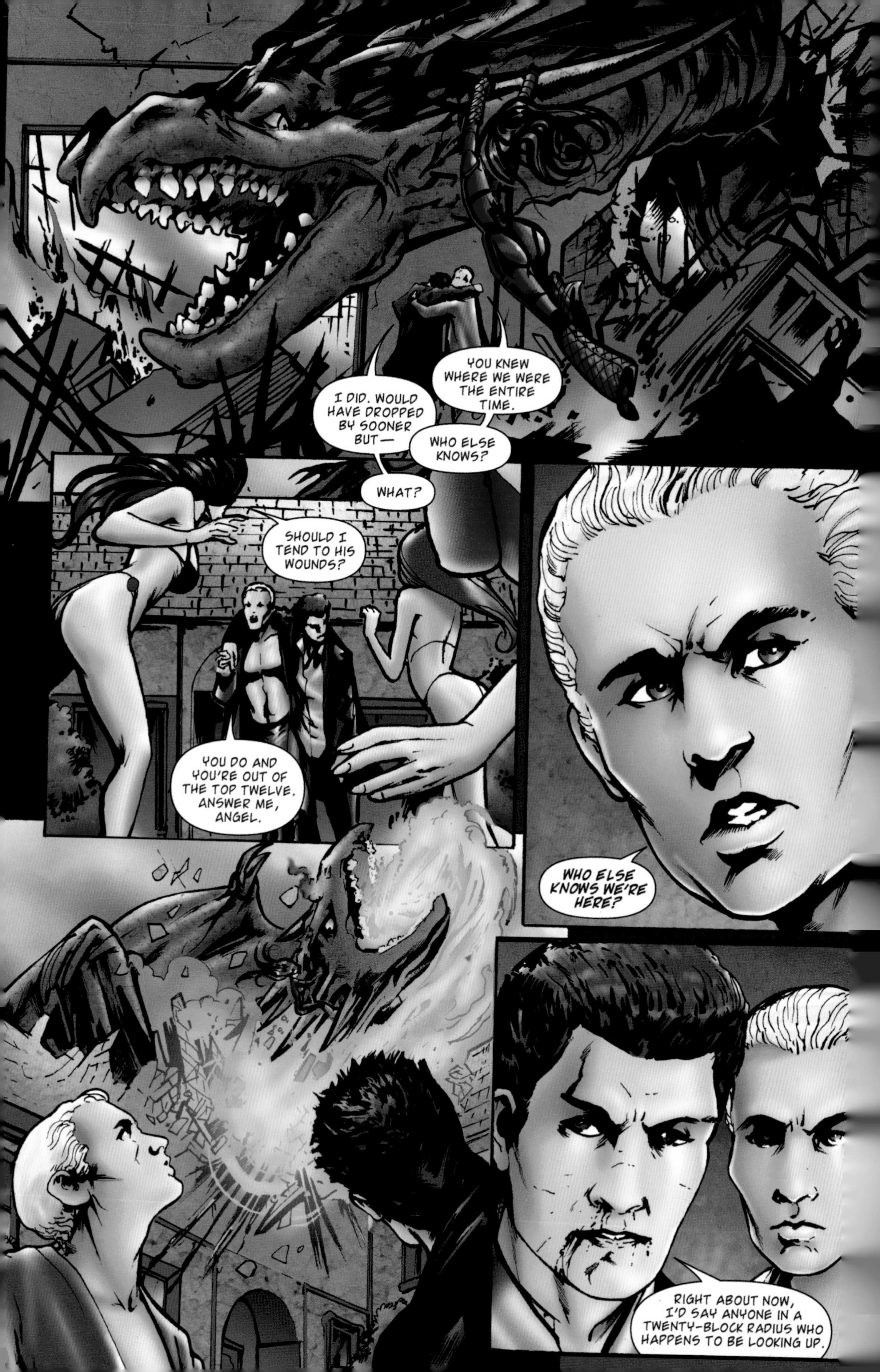
YOU KNEW WHERE WE WERE THE ENTIRE TIME.
I DID. WOULD HAVE DROPPED BY SOONER BUT—
WHO ELSE KNOWS?
WHAT?
SHOULD I TEND TO HIS WOUNDS?
YOU DO AND YOU'RE OUT OF THE TOP TWELVE. ANSWER ME, ANGEL.
WHO ELSE KNOWS WE'RE HERE?
RIGHT ABOUT NOW, I'D SAY ANYONE IN A TWENTY-BLOCK RADIUS WHO HAPPENS TO BE LOOKING UP.

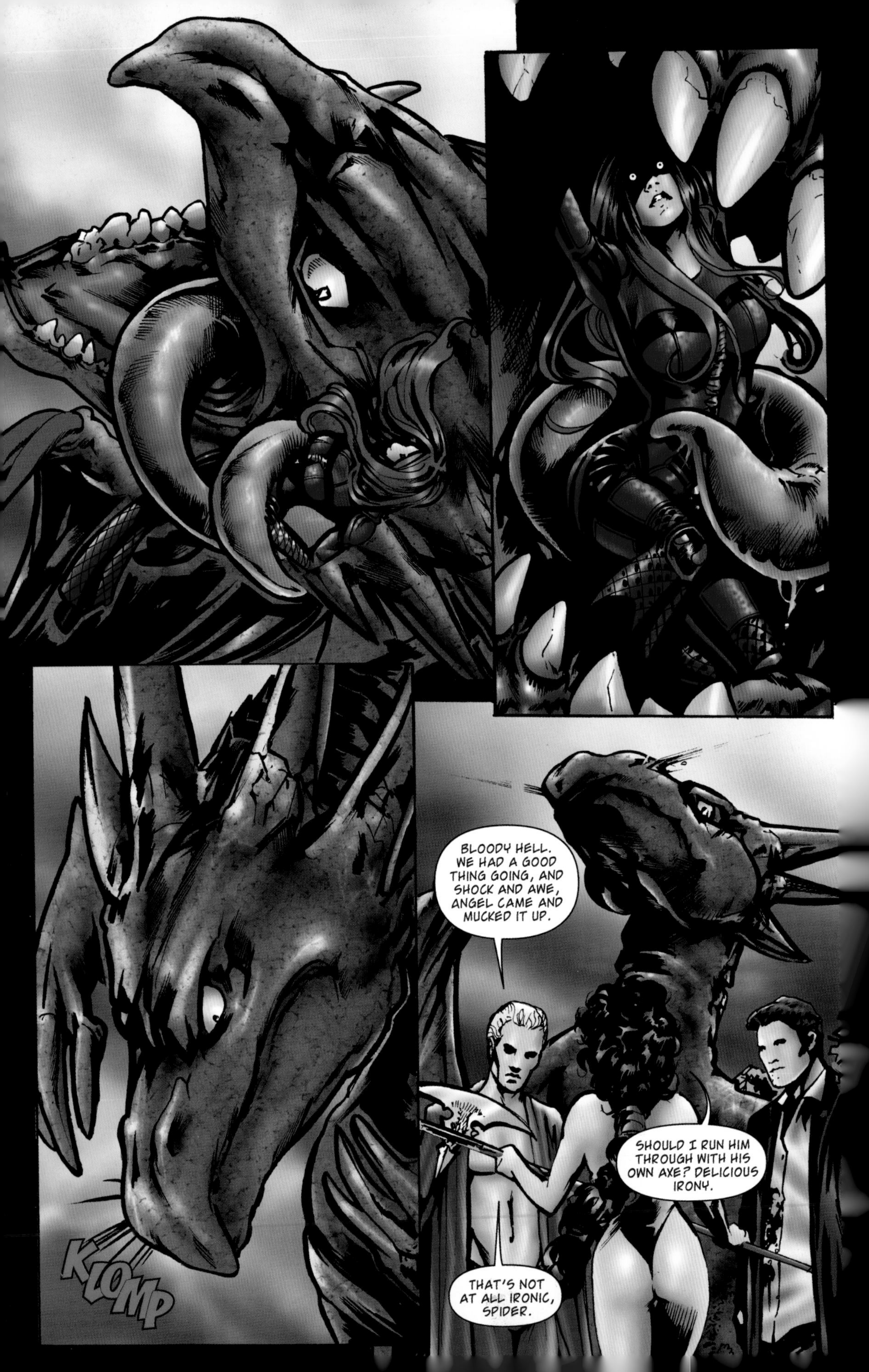
KLOMP
BLOODY HELL. WE HAD A GOOD THING GOING, AND SHOCK AND AWE, ANGEL CAME AND MUCKED IT UP.
SHOULD I RUN HIM THROUGH WITH HIS OWN AXE? DELICIOUS IRONY.
THAT'S NOT AT ALL IRONIC, SPIDER.

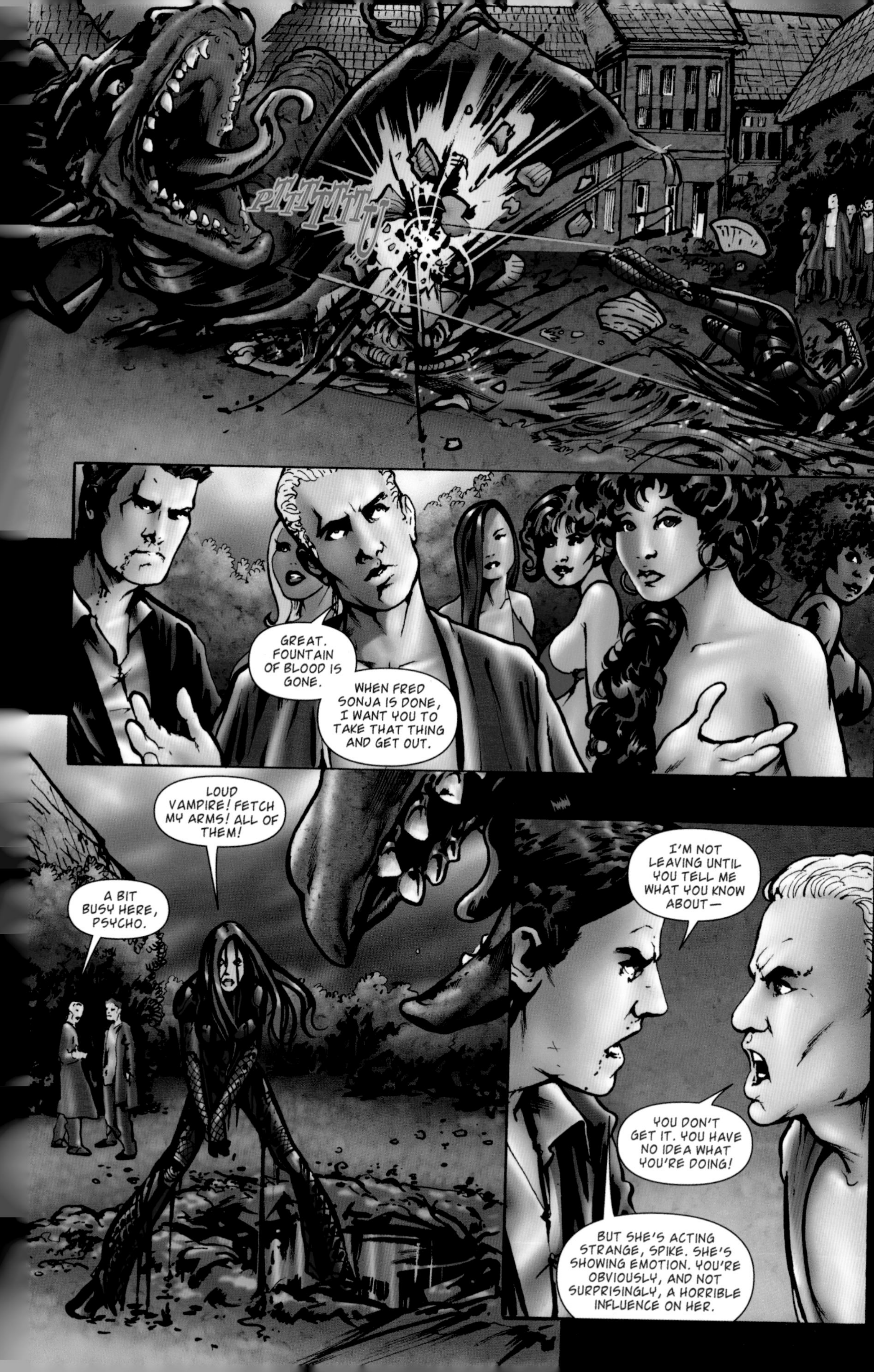
PTTTTTU
GREAT. FOUNTAIN OF BLOOD IS GONE.
WHEN FRED SONJA IS DONE, I WANT YOU TO TAKE THAT THING AND GET OUT.
LOUD VAMPIRE! FETCH MY ARMS! ALL OF THEM!
A BIT BUSY HERE, PSYCHO.
I'M NOT LEAVING UNTIL YOU TELL ME WHAT YOU KNOW ABOUT—
YOU DON'T GET IT. YOU HAVE NO IDEA WHAT YOU'RE DOING!
BUT SHE'S ACTING STRANGE, SPIKE. SHE'S SHOWING EMOTION. YOU'RE OBVIOUSLY, AND NOT SURPRISINGLY, A HORRIBLE INFLUENCE ON HER.

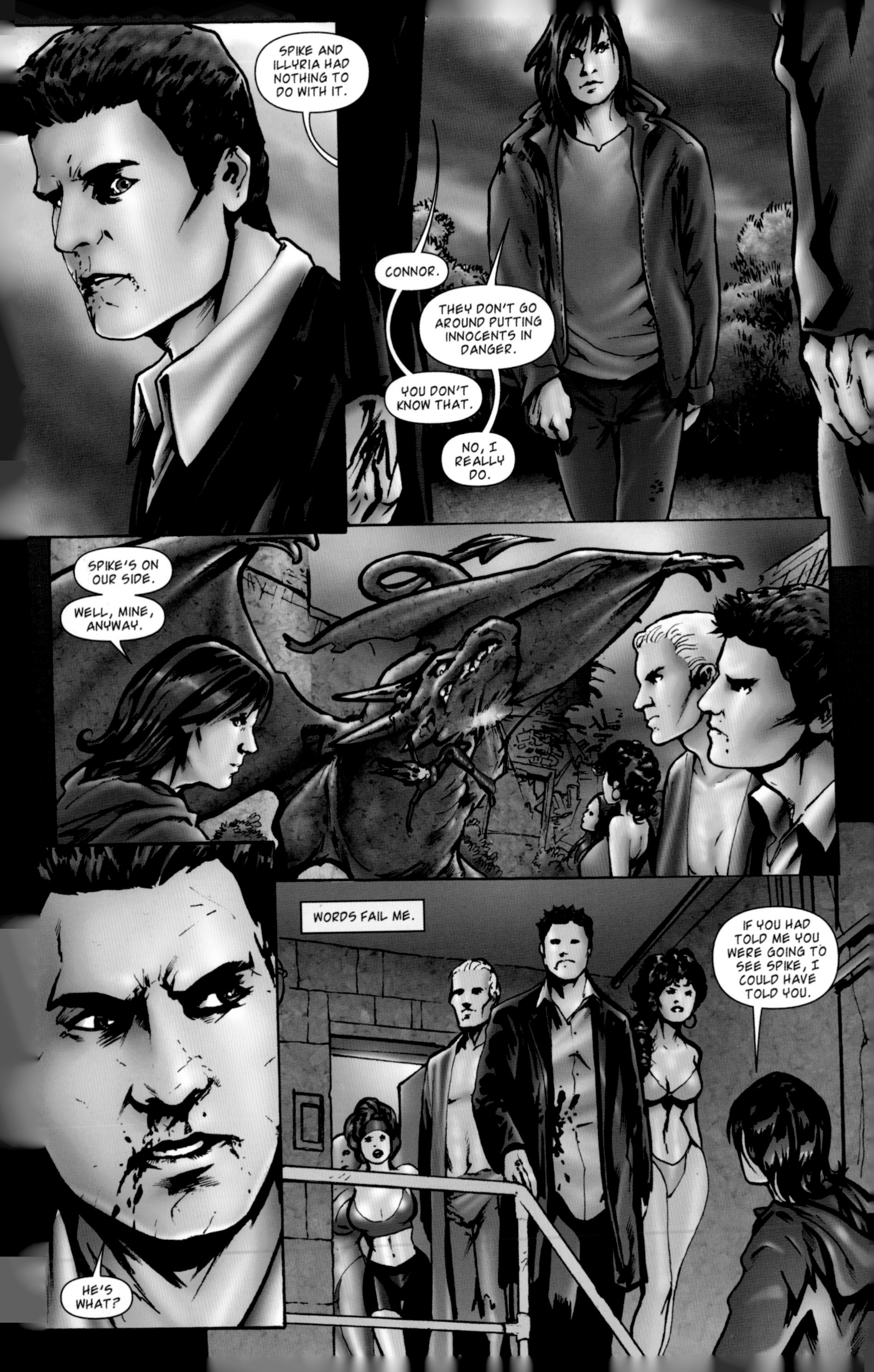
SPIKE AND ILLYRIA HAD NOTHING TO DO WITH IT.
CONNOR.
THEY DON'T GO AROUND PUTTING INNOCENTS IN DANGER.
YOU DON'T KNOW THAT.
NO, I REALLY DO.
SPIKE'S ON OUR SIDE.
WELL, MINE, ANYWAY.
HE'S WHAT?
WORDS FAIL ME.
IF YOU HAD TOLD ME YOU WERE GOING TO SEE SPIKE, I COULD HAVE TOLD YOU.

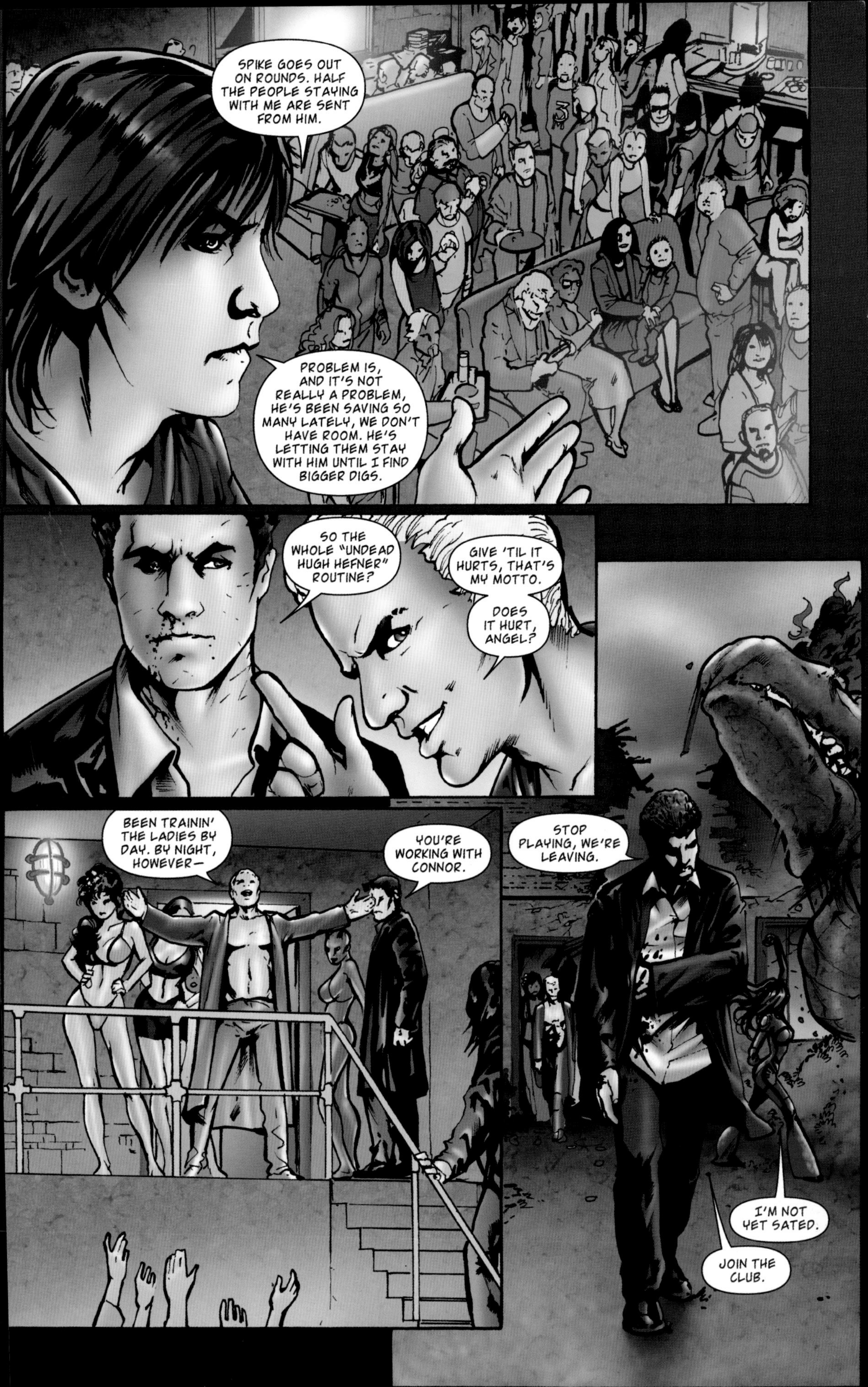
SPIKE GOES OUT ON ROUNDS. HALF THE PEOPLE STAYING WITH ME ARE SENT FROM HIM.
PROBLEM IS, AND IT'S NOT REALLY A PROBLEM, HE'S BEEN SAVING SO MANY LATELY, WE DON'T HAVE ROOM. HE'S LETTING THEM STAY WITH HIM UNTIL I FIND BIGGER DIGS.
SO THE WHOLE "UNDEAD HUGH HEFNER" ROUTINE?
GIVE 'TIL IT HURTS, THAT'S MY MOTTO.
DOES IT HURT, ANGEL?
BEEN TRAININ' THE LADIES BY DAY. BY NIGHT, HOWEVER—
YOU'RE WORKING WITH CONNOR.
STOP PLAYING, WE'RE LEAVING.
I'M NOT YET SATED.
JOIN THE CLUB.

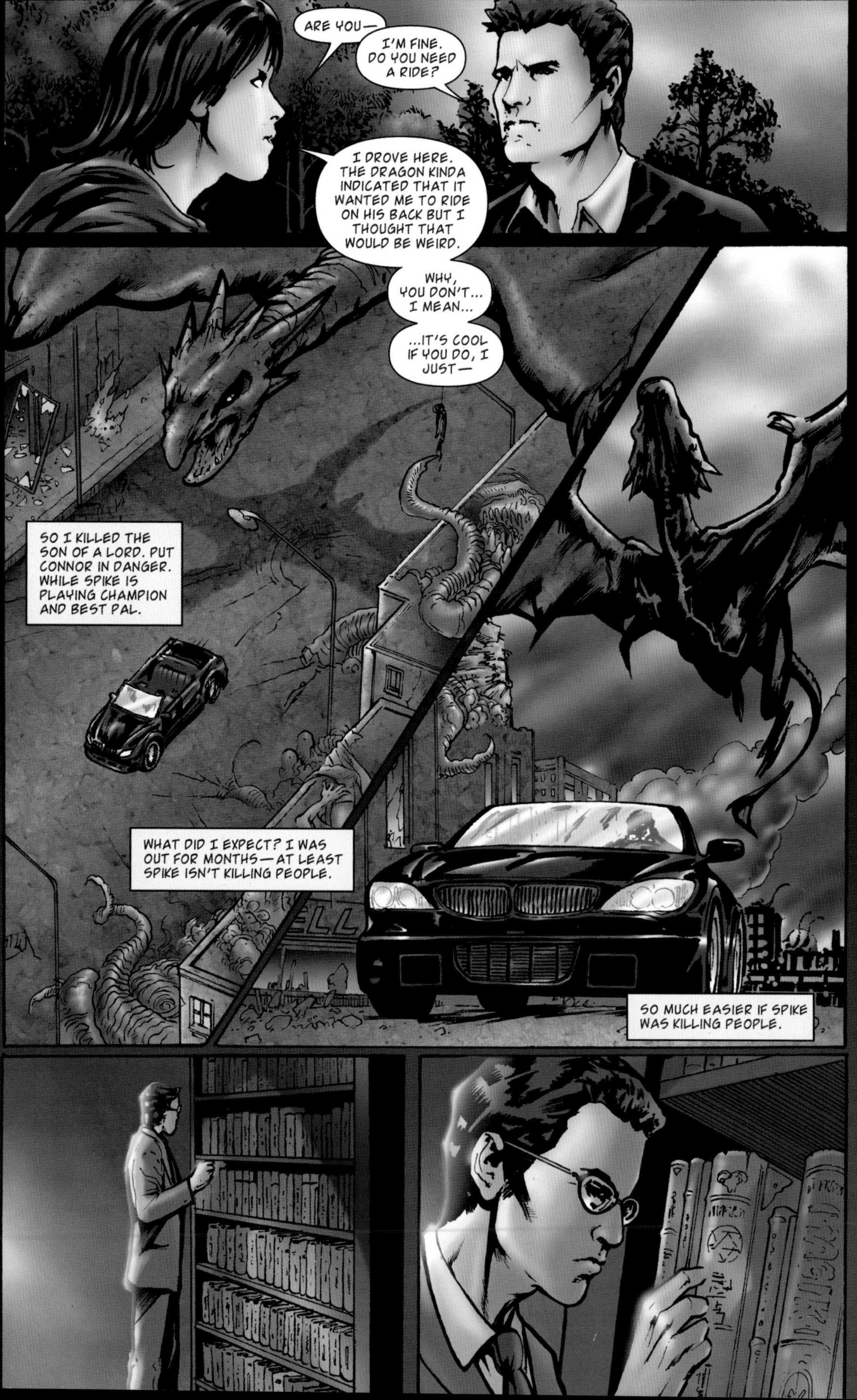
ARE YOU—
I'M FINE. DO YOU NEED A RIDE?
I DROVE HERE. THE DRAGON KINDA INDICATED THAT IT WANTED ME TO RIDE ON HIS BACK BUT I THOUGHT THAT WOULD BE WEIRD.
WHY, YOU DON'T... I MEAN...
...IT'S COOL IF YOU DO, I JUST—
SO I KILLED THE SON OF A LORD. PUT CONNOR IN DANGER. WHILE SPIKE IS PLAYING CHAMPION AND BEST PAL.
WHAT DID I EXPECT? I WAS OUT FOR MONTHS—AT LEAST SPIKE ISN'T KILLING PEOPLE.
SO MUCH EASIER IF SPIKE WAS KILLING PEOPLE.

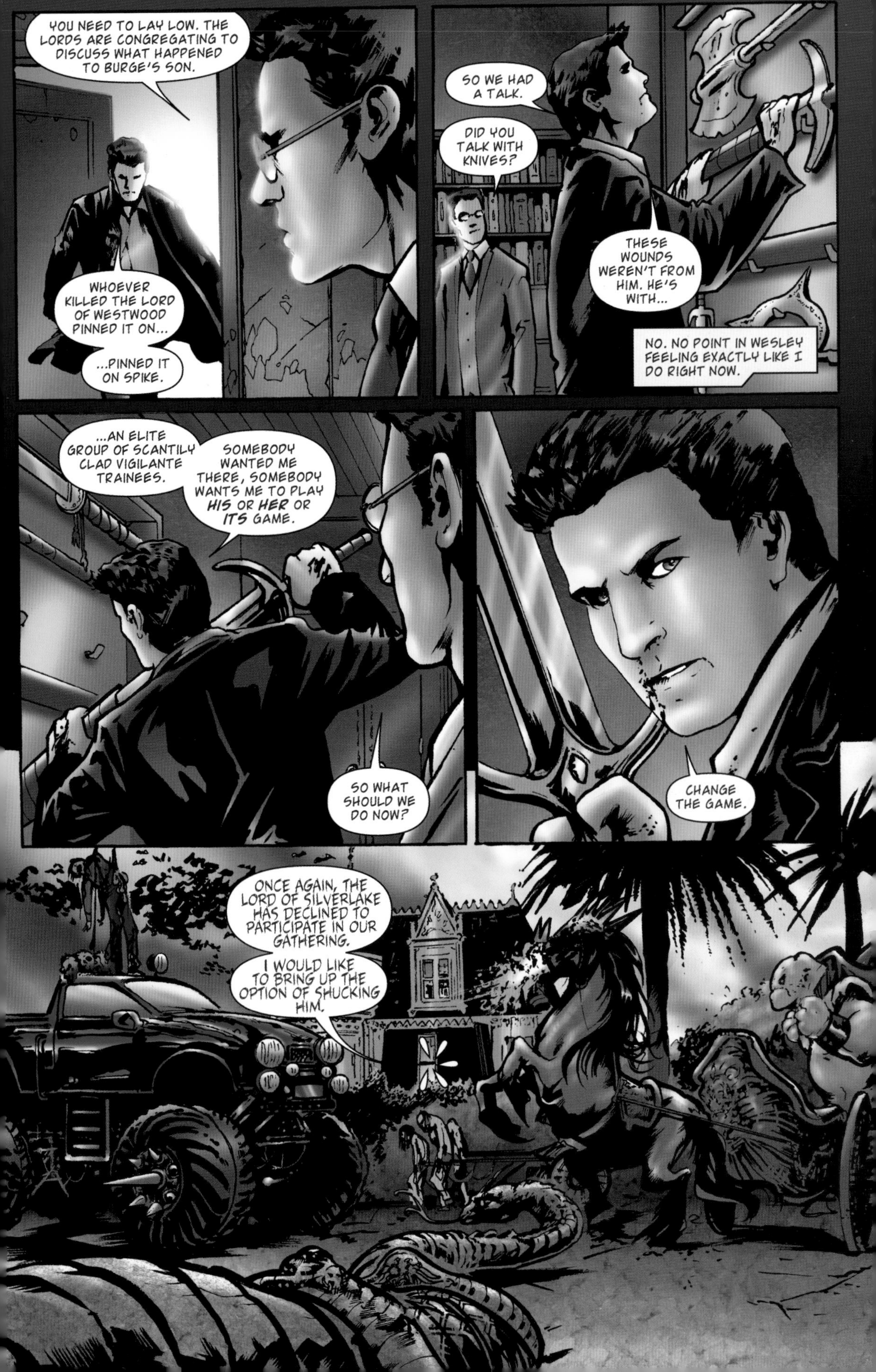
YOU NEED TO LAY LOW. THE LORDS ARE CONGREGATING TO DISCUSS WHAT HAPPENED TO BURGE'S SON.
WHOEVER KILLED THE LORD OF WESTWOOD PINNED IT ON...
...PINNED IT ON SPIKE.
SO WE HAD A TALK.
DID YOU TALK WITH KNIVES?
THESE WOUNDS WEREN'T FROM HIM. HE'S WITH...
NO. NO POINT IN WESLEY FEELING EXACTLY LIKE I DO RIGHT NOW.
...AN ELITE GROUP OF SCANTILY CLAD VIGILANTE TRAINEES.
SOMEBODY WANTED ME THERE, SOMEBODY WANTS ME TO PLAY *HIS* OR *HER* OR *ITS* GAME.
SO WHAT SHOULD WE DO NOW?
CHANGE THE GAME.
ONCE AGAIN, THE LORD OF SILVERLAKE HAS DECLINED TO PARTICIPATE IN OUR GATHERING.
I WOULD LIKE TO BRING UP THE OPTION OF SHUCKING HIM.

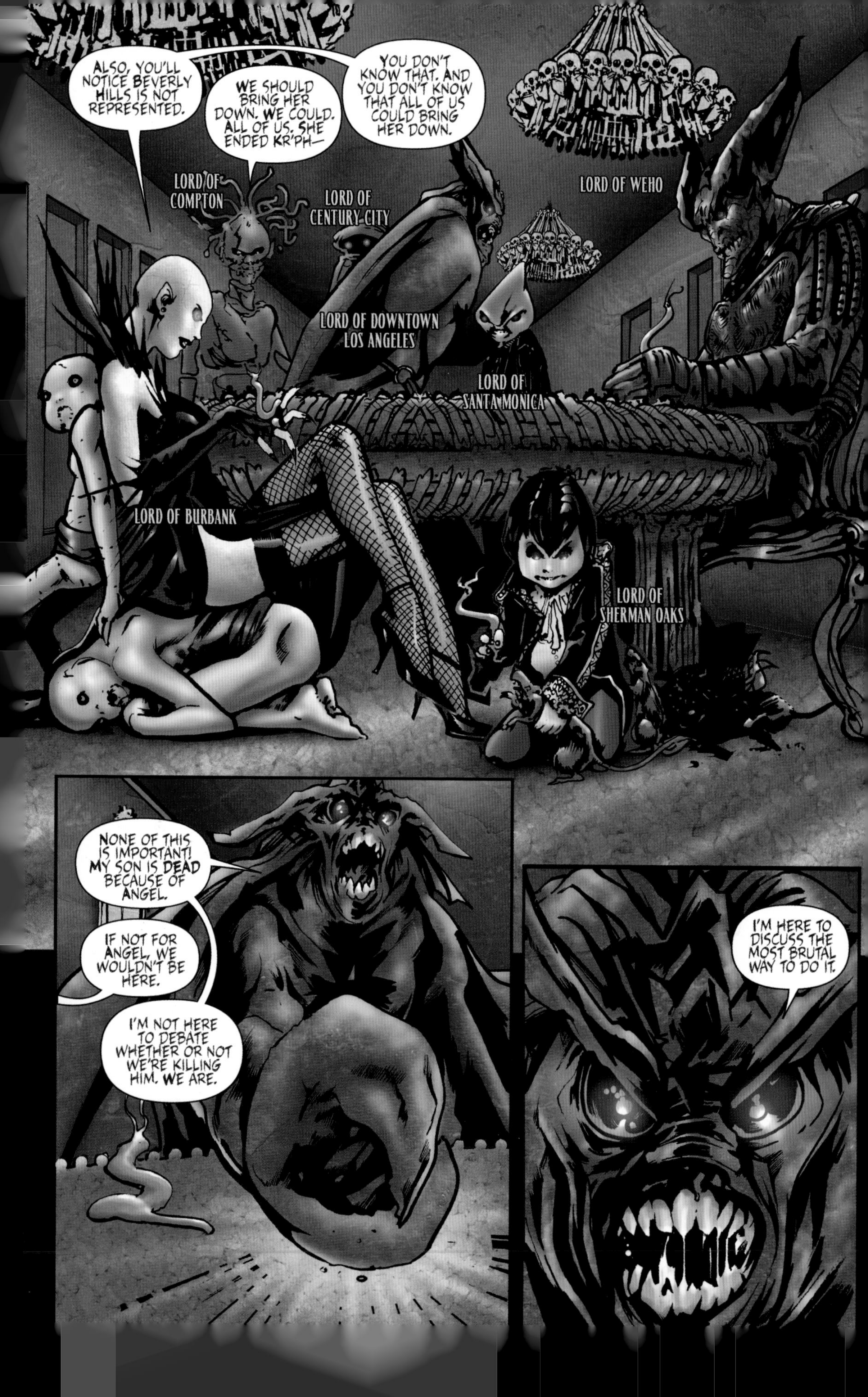
ALSO, YOU'LL NOTICE BEVERLY HILLS IS NOT REPRESENTED.
WE SHOULD BRING HER DOWN. WE COULD. ALL OF US. SHE ENDED KR'PH—
YOU DON'T KNOW THAT. AND YOU DON'T KNOW THAT ALL OF US COULD BRING HER DOWN.
LORD OF COMPTON
LORD OF CENTURY CITY
LORD OF WEHO
LORD OF DOWNTOWN LOS ANGELES
LORD OF SANTA MONICA
LORD OF BURBANK
LORD OF SHERMAN OAKS
NONE OF THIS IS IMPORTANT! MY SON IS DEAD BECAUSE OF ANGEL.
IF NOT FOR ANGEL, WE WOULDN'T BE HERE.
I'M NOT HERE TO DEBATE WHETHER OR NOT WE'RE KILLING HIM. WE ARE.
I'M HERE TO DISCUSS THE MOST BRUTAL WAY TO DO IT.

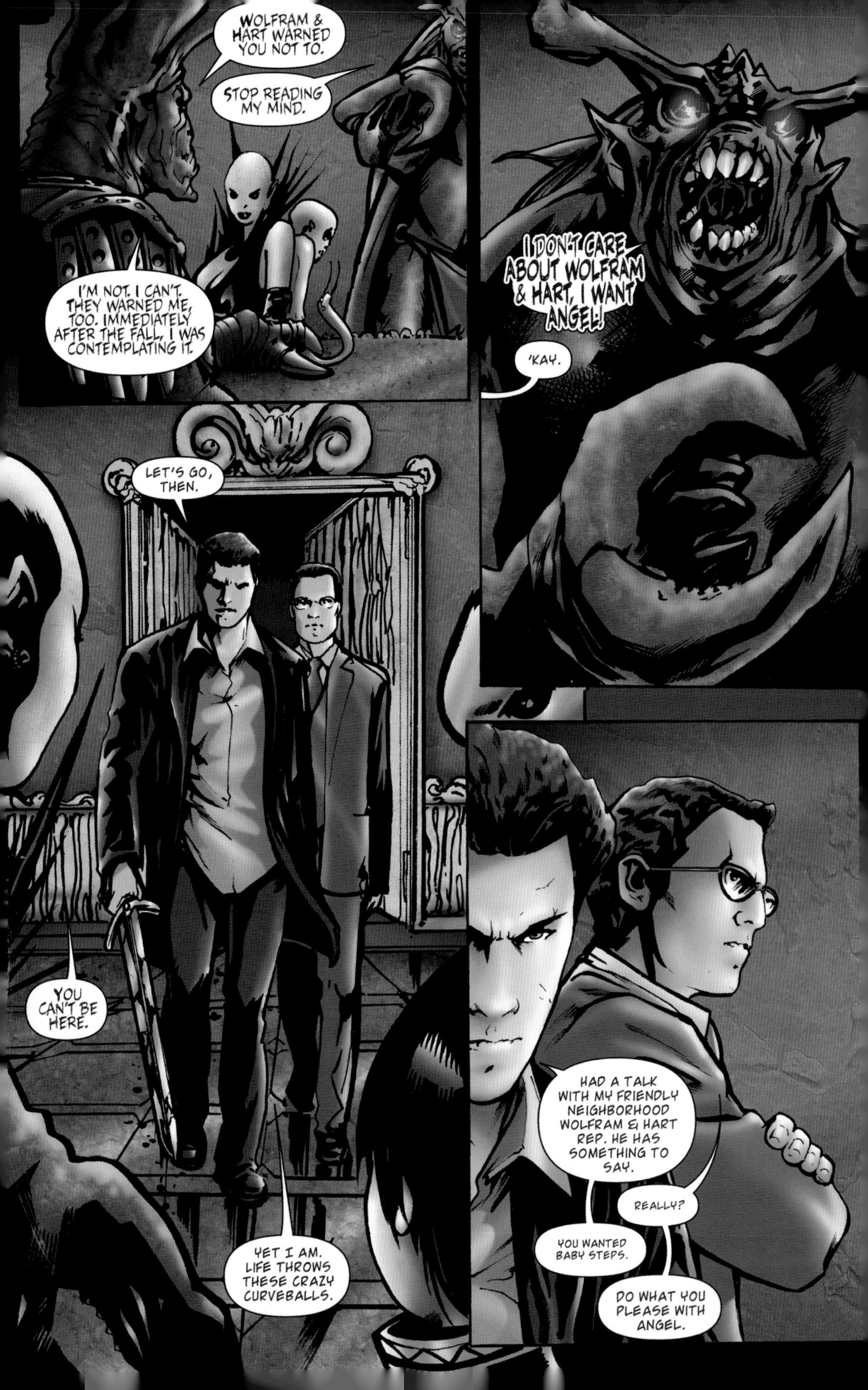
WOLFRAM & HART WARNED YOU NOT TO.
STOP READING MY MIND.
I'M NOT. I CAN'T. THEY WARNED ME, TOO. IMMEDIATELY AFTER THE FALL, I WAS CONTEMPLATING IT.
I DON'T CARE ABOUT WOLFRAM & HART, I WANT ANGEL!
'KAY.
LET'S GO, THEN.
YOU CAN'T BE HERE.
YET I AM. LIFE THROWS THESE CRAZY CURVEBALLS.
HAD A TALK WITH MY FRIENDLY NEIGHBORHOOD WOLFRAM & HART REP. HE HAS SOMETHING TO SAY.
REALLY?
YOU WANTED BABY STEPS.
DO WHAT YOU PLEASE WITH ANGEL.

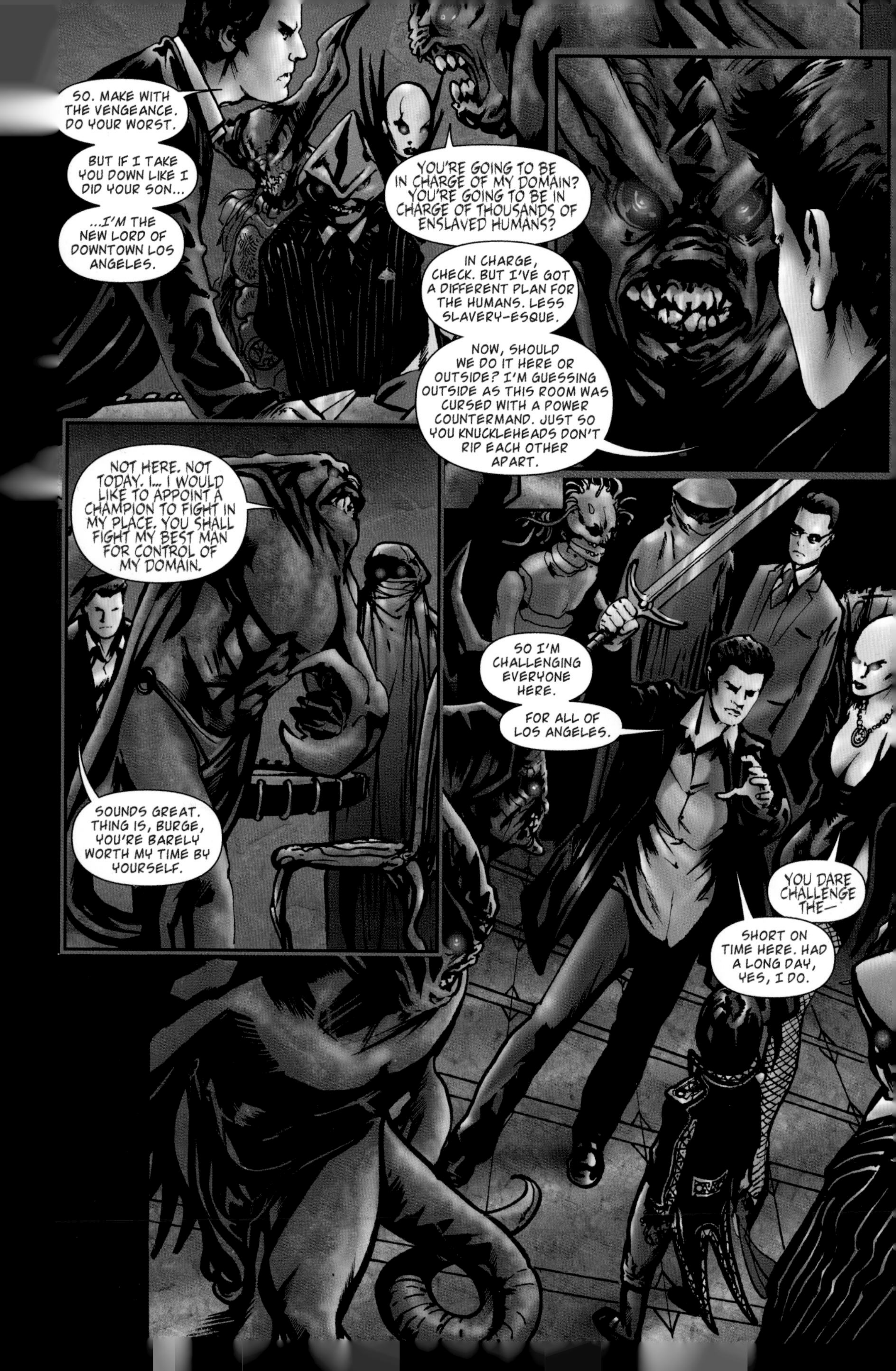
SO. MAKE WITH THE VENGEANCE. DO YOUR WORST.
BUT IF I TAKE YOU DOWN LIKE I DID YOUR SON...
...I'M THE NEW LORD OF DOWNTOWN LOS ANGELES.
YOU'RE GOING TO BE IN CHARGE OF MY DOMAIN? YOU'RE GOING TO BE IN CHARGE OF THOUSANDS OF ENSLAVED HUMANS?
IN CHARGE, CHECK. BUT I'VE GOT A DIFFERENT PLAN FOR THE HUMANS. LESS SLAVERY-ESQUE.
NOW, SHOULD WE DO IT HERE OR OUTSIDE? I'M GUESSING OUTSIDE AS THIS ROOM WAS CURSED WITH A POWER COUNTERMAND. JUST SO YOU KNUCKLEHEADS DON'T RIP EACH OTHER APART.
NOT HERE. NOT TODAY. I... I WOULD LIKE TO APPOINT A CHAMPION TO FIGHT IN MY PLACE. YOU SHALL FIGHT MY BEST MAN FOR CONTROL OF MY DOMAIN.
SOUNDS GREAT. THING IS, BURGE, YOU'RE BARELY WORTH MY TIME BY YOURSELF.
SO I'M CHALLENGING EVERYONE HERE.
FOR ALL OF LOS ANGELES.
YOU DARE CHALLENGE THE—
SHORT ON TIME HERE. HAD A LONG DAY, YES, I DO.

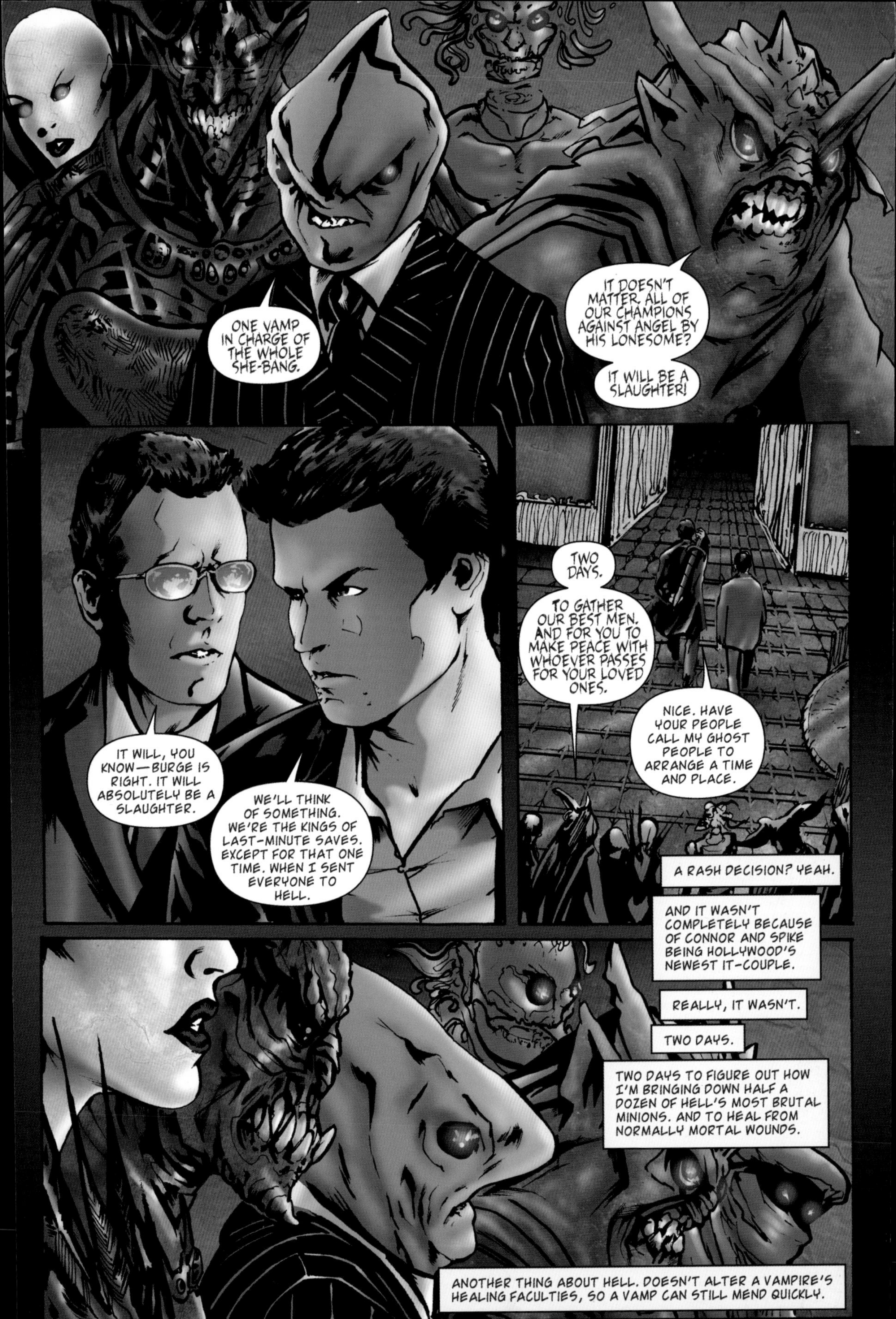

ONE VAMP IN CHARGE OF THE WHOLE SHE-BANG.
IT DOESN'T MATTER. ALL OF OUR CHAMPIONS AGAINST ANGEL BY HIS LONESOME?
IT WILL BE A SLAUGHTER!
IT WILL, YOU KNOW—BURGE IS RIGHT. IT WILL ABSOLUTELY BE A SLAUGHTER.
WE'LL THINK OF SOMETHING. WE'RE THE KINGS OF LAST-MINUTE SAVES. EXCEPT FOR THAT ONE TIME. WHEN I SENT EVERYONE TO HELL.
TWO DAYS.
TO GATHER OUR BEST MEN. AND FOR YOU TO MAKE PEACE WITH WHOEVER PASSES FOR YOUR LOVED ONES.
NICE. HAVE YOUR PEOPLE CALL MY GHOST PEOPLE TO ARRANGE A TIME AND PLACE.
A RASH DECISION? YEAH.
AND IT WASN'T COMPLETELY BECAUSE OF CONNOR AND SPIKE BEING HOLLYWOOD'S NEWEST IT-COUPLE.
REALLY, IT WASN'T.
TWO DAYS.
TWO DAYS TO FIGURE OUT HOW I'M BRINGING DOWN HALF A DOZEN OF HELL'S MOST BRUTAL MINIONS. AND TO HEAL FROM NORMALLY MORTAL WOUNDS.
ANOTHER THING ABOUT HELL. DOESN'T ALTER A VAMPIRE'S HEALING FACULTIES, SO A VAMP CAN STILL MEND QUICKLY.

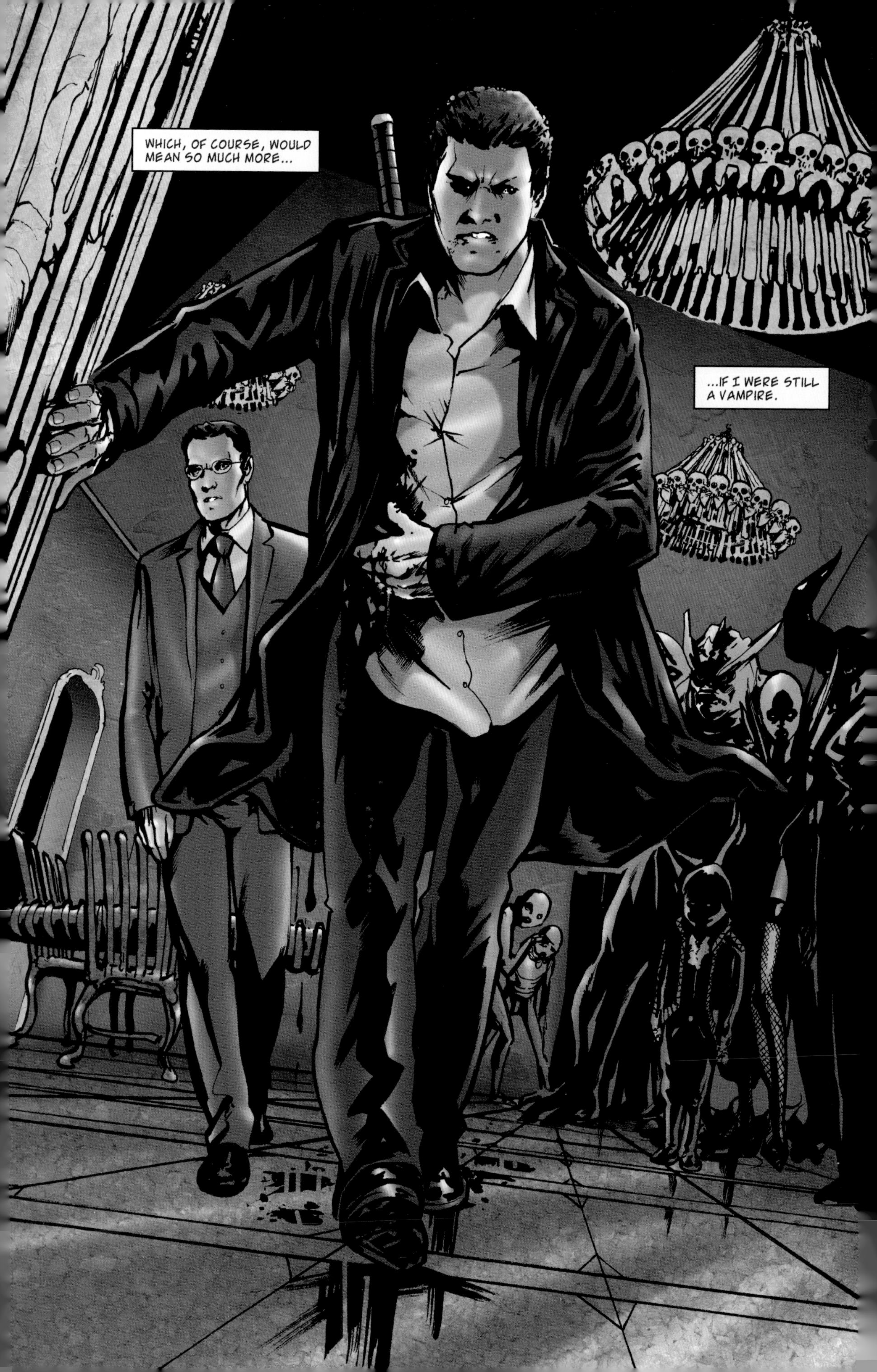
WHICH, OF COURSE, WOULD MEAN SO MUCH MORE...
...IF I WERE STILL A VAMPIRE.

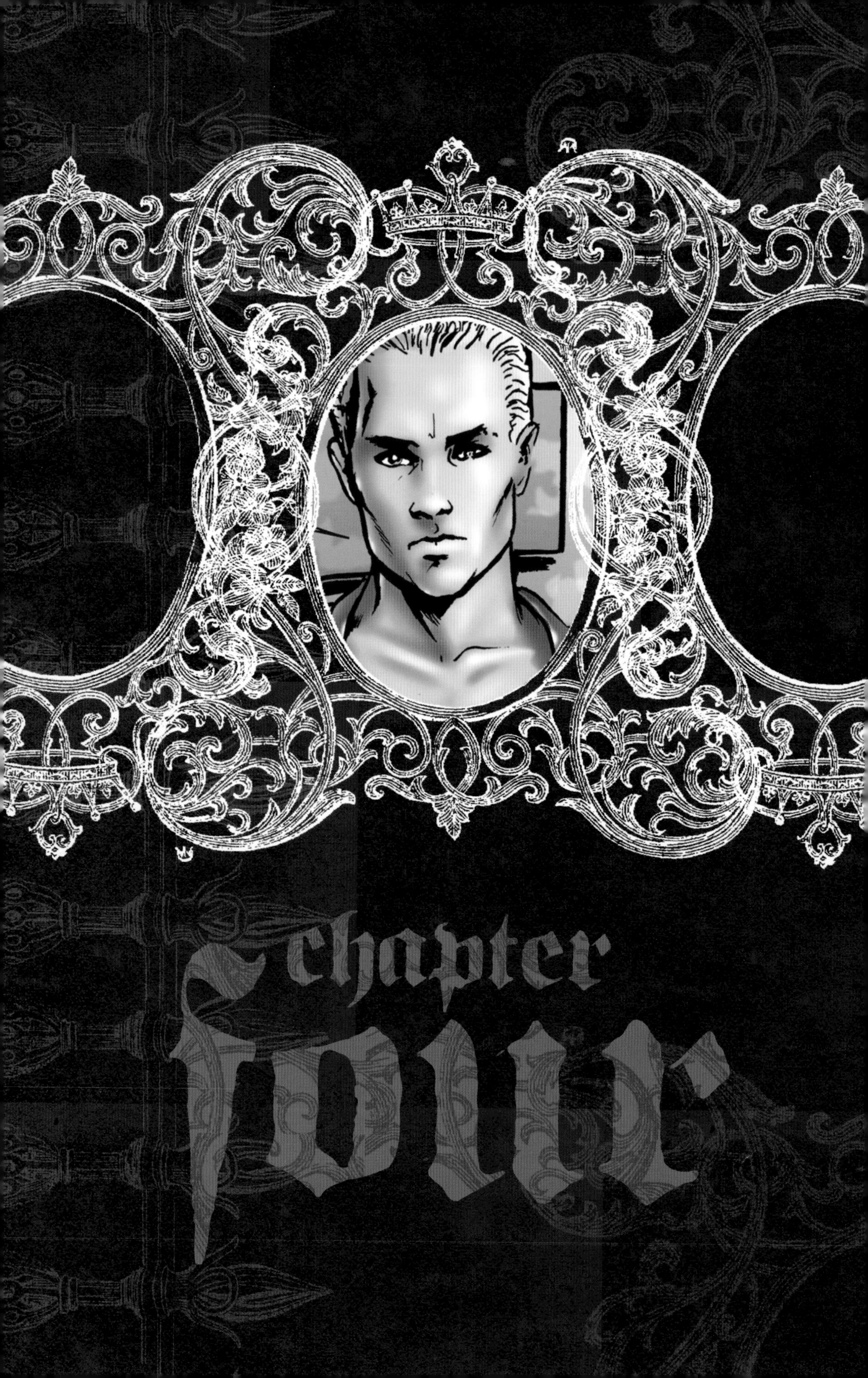

chapter four

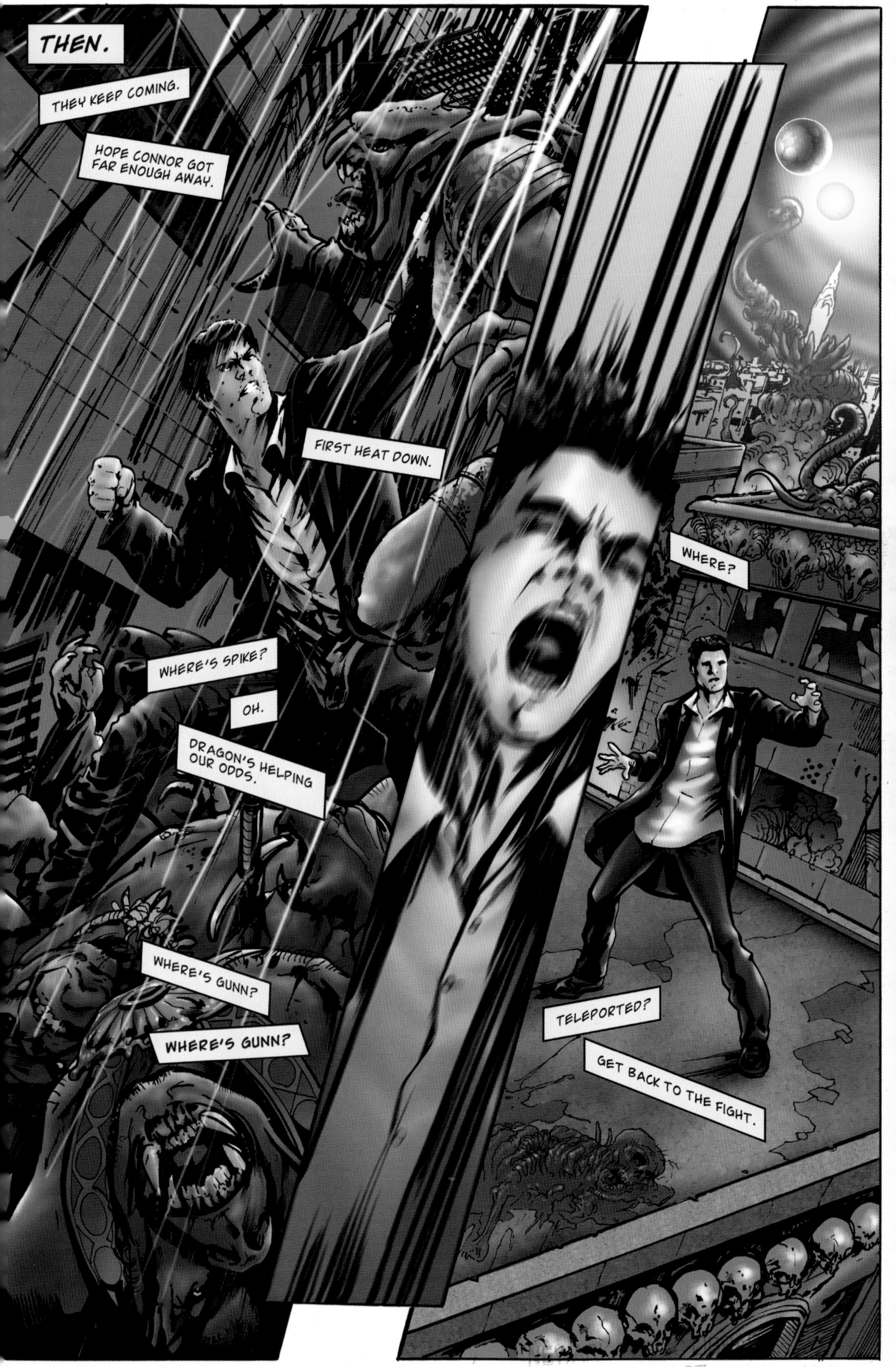
THEN.
THEY KEEP COMING.
HOPE CONNOR GOT FAR ENOUGH AWAY.
FIRST HEAT DOWN.
WHERE'S SPIKE?
OH.
DRAGON'S HELPING OUR ODDS.
WHERE'S GUNN?
WHERE'S GUNN?
WHERE?
TELEPORTED?
GET BACK TO THE FIGHT.

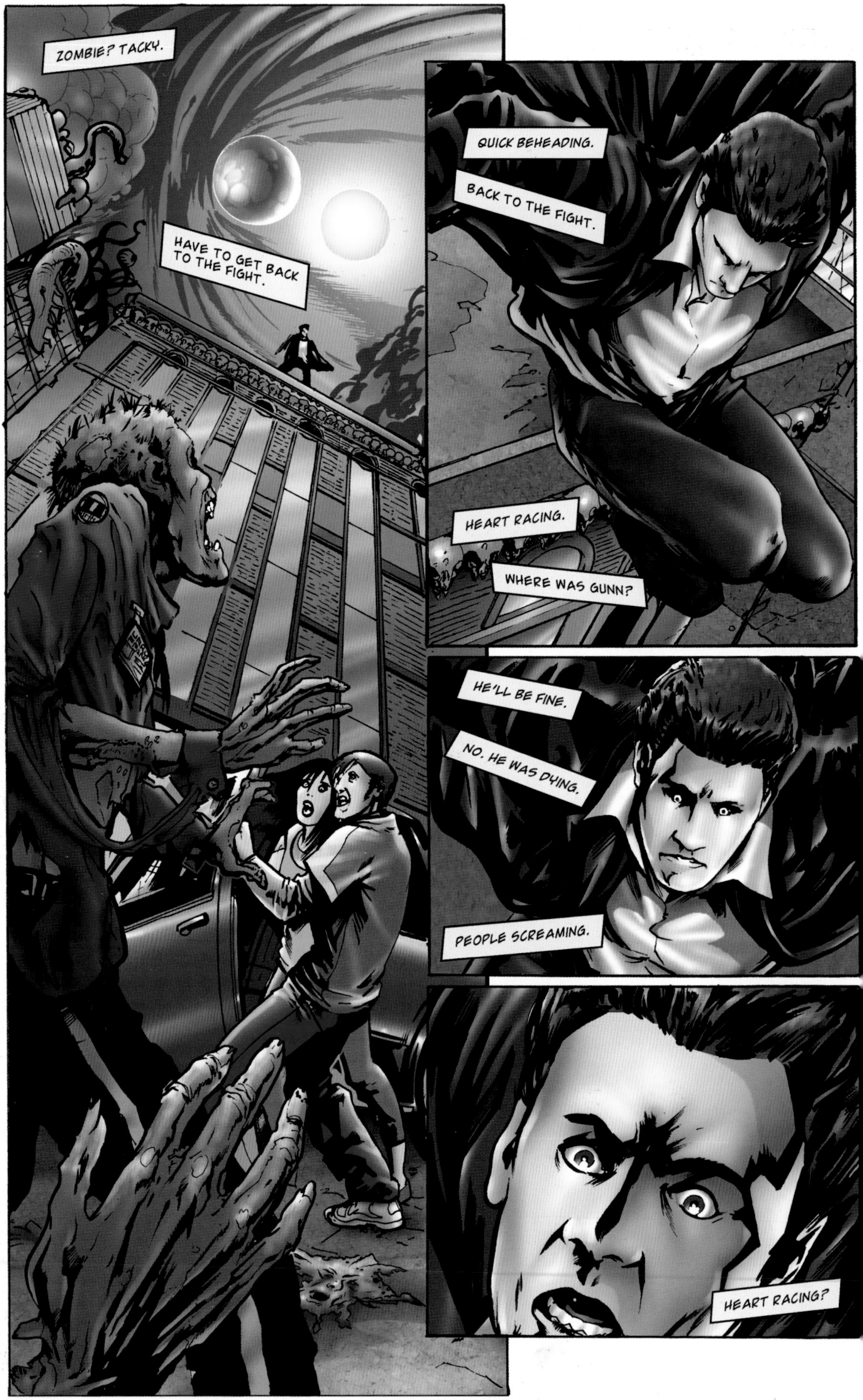
ZOMBIE? TACKY.
HAVE TO GET BACK TO THE FIGHT.
QUICK BEHEADING.
BACK TO THE FIGHT.
HEART RACING.
WHERE WAS GUNN?
HE'LL BE FINE.
NO. HE WAS DYING.
PEOPLE SCREAMING.
HEART RACING?

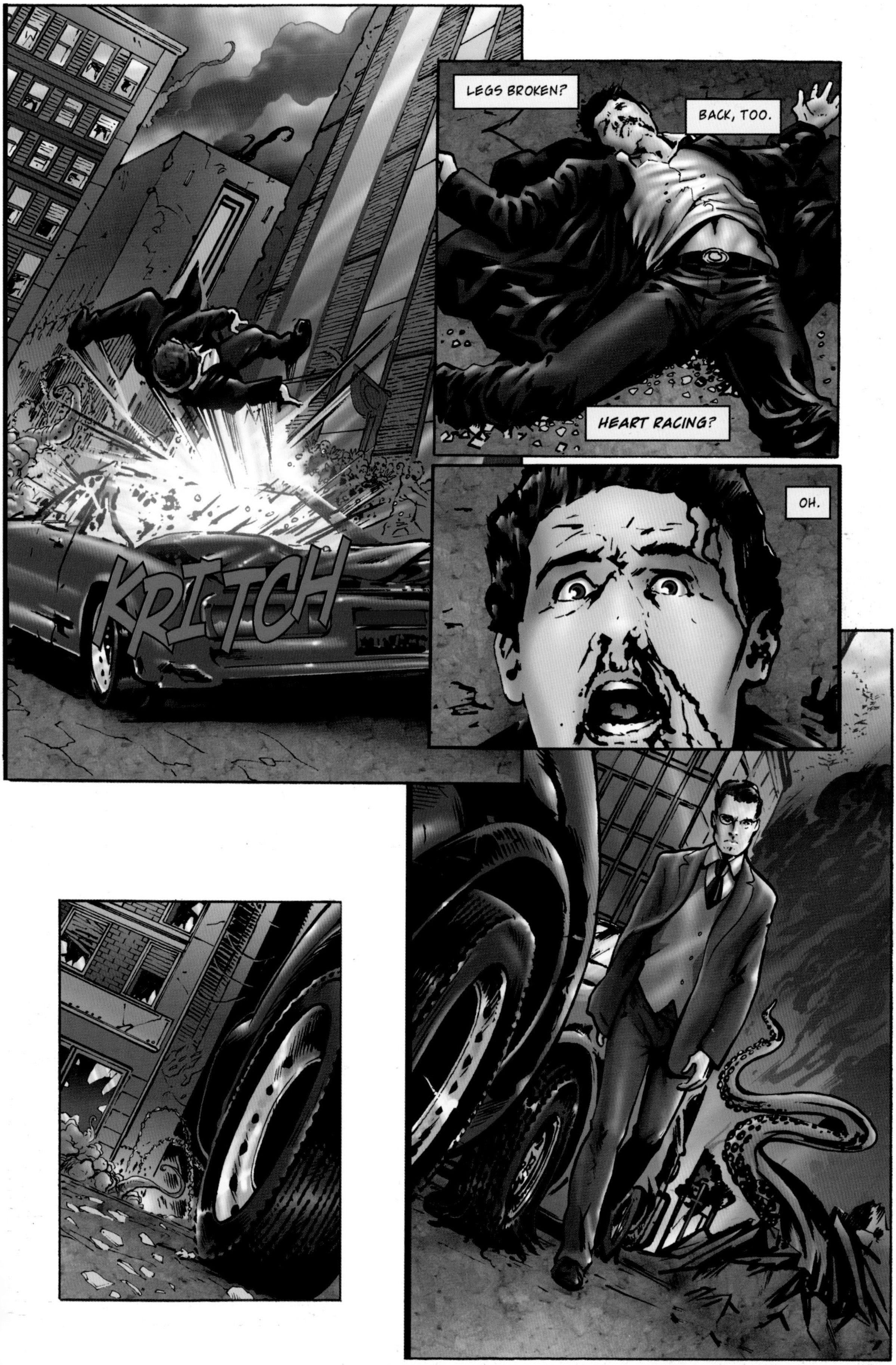
KRITCH
LEGS BROKEN?
BACK, TOO.
HEART RACING?
OH.

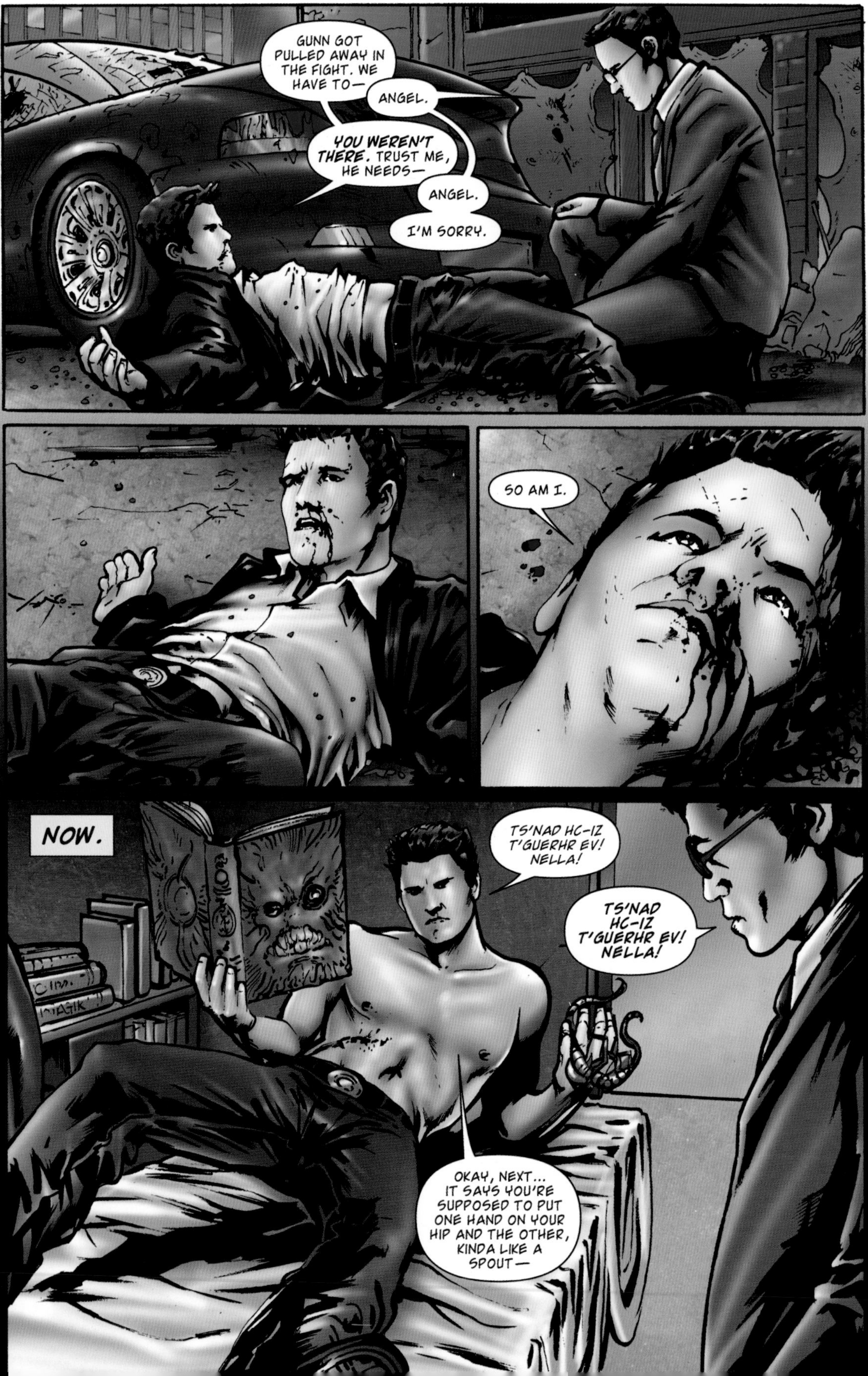
GUNN GOT PULLED AWAY IN THE FIGHT. WE HAVE TO—
ANGEL.
YOU WEREN'T THERE. TRUST ME, HE NEEDS—
ANGEL.
I'M SORRY.
SO AM I.
NOW.
TS'NAD HC-IZ T'GUERHR EV! NELLA!
TS'NAD HC-IZ T'GUERHR EV! NELLA!
OKAY, NEXT... IT SAYS YOU'RE SUPPOSED TO PUT ONE HAND ON YOUR HIP AND THE OTHER, KINDA LIKE A SPOUT—

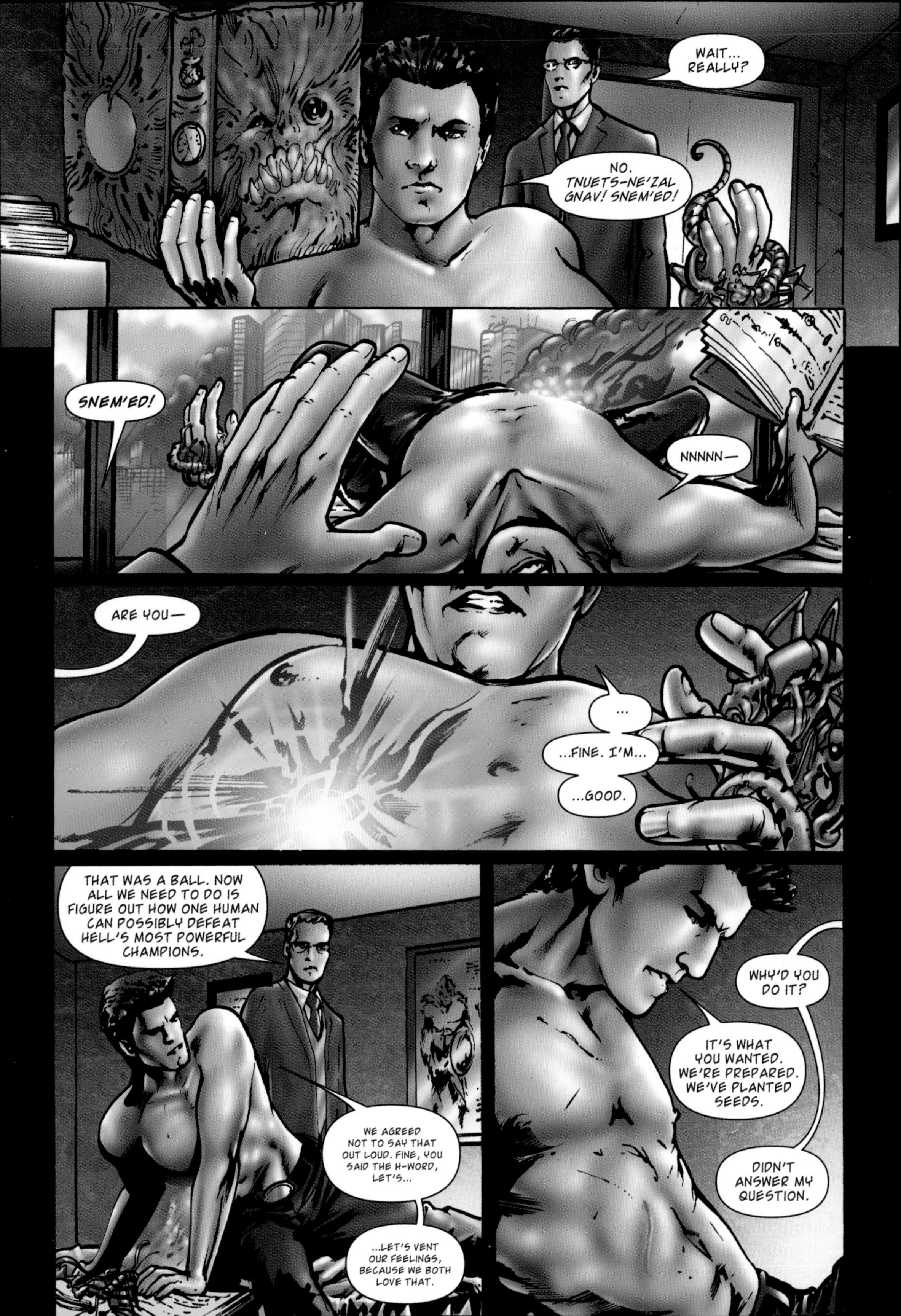

WAIT... REALLY?
NO. TNUETS-NE'ZAL GNAV! SNEM'ED!
SNEM'ED!
NNNNN—
ARE YOU—
...
...FINE. I'M...
...GOOD.
THAT WAS A BALL. NOW ALL WE NEED TO DO IS FIGURE OUT HOW ONE HUMAN CAN POSSIBLY DEFEAT HELL'S MOST POWERFUL CHAMPIONS.
WE AGREED NOT TO SAY THAT OUT LOUD. FINE, YOU SAID THE H-WORD, LET'S...
...LET'S VENT OUR FEELINGS, BECAUSE WE BOTH LOVE THAT.
WHY'D YOU DO IT?
IT'S WHAT YOU WANTED. WE'RE PREPARED. WE'VE PLANTED SEEDS.
DIDN'T ANSWER MY QUESTION.

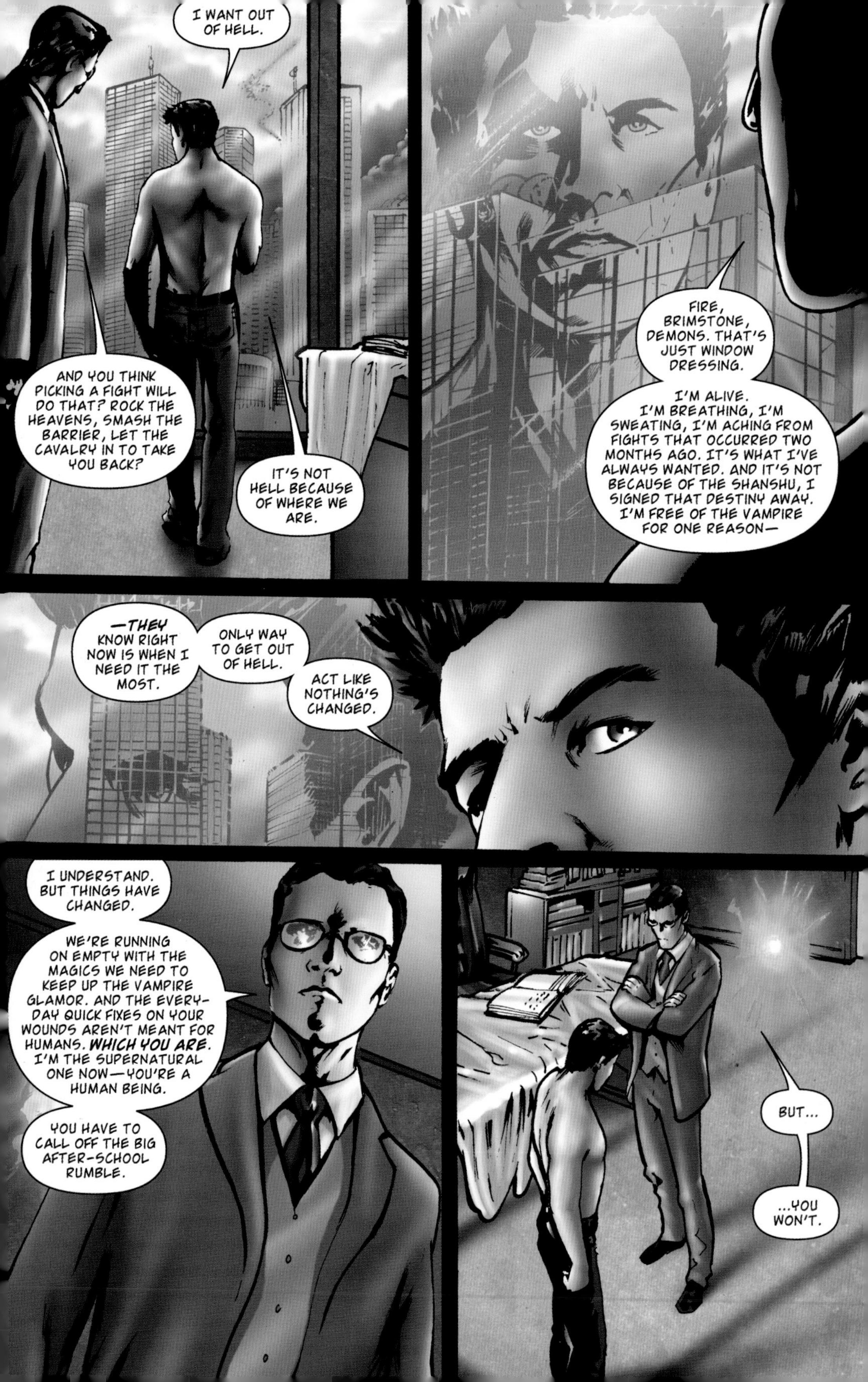
I WANT OUT OF HELL.
AND YOU THINK PICKING A FIGHT WILL DO THAT? ROCK THE HEAVENS, SMASH THE BARRIER, LET THE CAVALRY IN TO TAKE YOU BACK?
IT'S NOT HELL BECAUSE OF WHERE WE ARE.
FIRE, BRIMSTONE, DEMONS. THAT'S JUST WINDOW DRESSING.
I'M ALIVE. I'M BREATHING, I'M SWEATING, I'M ACHING FROM FIGHTS THAT OCCURRED TWO MONTHS AGO. IT'S WHAT I'VE ALWAYS WANTED. AND IT'S NOT BECAUSE OF THE SHANSHU, I SIGNED THAT DESTINY AWAY. I'M FREE OF THE VAMPIRE FOR ONE REASON—
—*THEY* KNOW RIGHT NOW IS WHEN I NEED IT THE MOST.
ONLY WAY TO GET OUT OF HELL.
ACT LIKE NOTHING'S CHANGED.
I UNDERSTAND. BUT THINGS HAVE CHANGED.
WE'RE RUNNING ON EMPTY WITH THE MAGICS WE NEED TO KEEP UP THE VAMPIRE GLAMOR. AND THE EVERY-DAY QUICK FIXES ON YOUR WOUNDS AREN'T MEANT FOR HUMANS. ***WHICH YOU ARE***. I'M THE SUPERNATURAL ONE NOW—YOU'RE A HUMAN BEING.
YOU HAVE TO CALL OFF THE BIG AFTER-SCHOOL RUMBLE.
BUT...
...YOU WON'T.

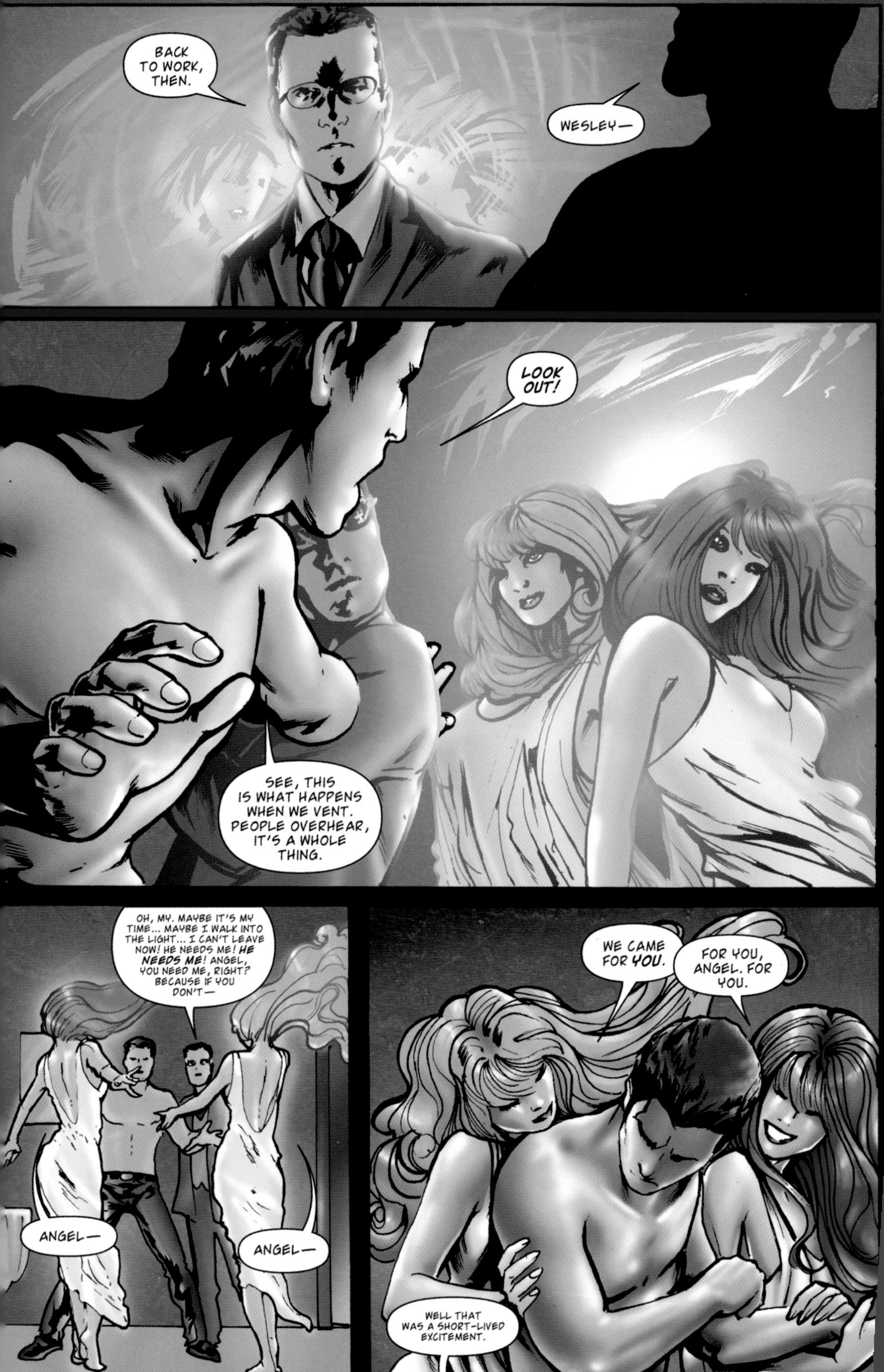
BACK TO WORK, THEN.
WESLEY—
LOOK OUT!
SEE, THIS IS WHAT HAPPENS WHEN WE VENT. PEOPLE OVERHEAR, IT'S A WHOLE THING.
OH, MY. MAYBE IT'S MY TIME... MAYBE I WALK INTO THE LIGHT... I CAN'T LEAVE NOW! HE NEEDS ME! **HE NEEDS ME**! ANGEL, YOU NEED ME, RIGHT? BECAUSE IF YOU DON'T—
ANGEL—
ANGEL—
WE CAME FOR ***YOU***.
FOR YOU, ANGEL. FOR YOU.
WELL THAT WAS A SHORT-LIVED EXCITEMENT.

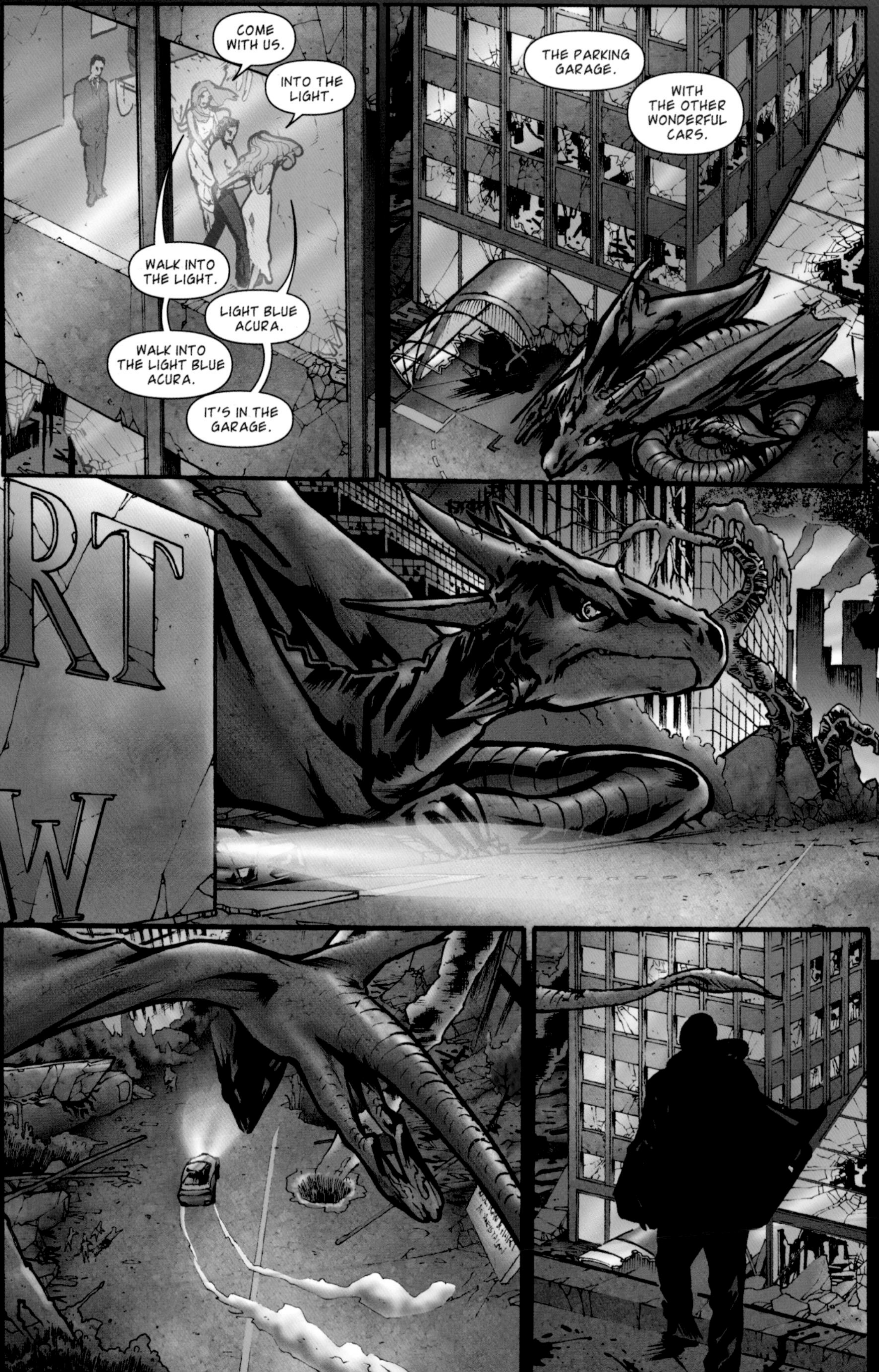
COME WITH US.
INTO THE LIGHT.
WALK INTO THE LIGHT.
LIGHT BLUE ACURA.
WALK INTO THE LIGHT BLUE ACURA.
IT'S IN THE GARAGE.
THE PARKING GARAGE.
WITH THE OTHER WONDERFUL CARS.
RT
W

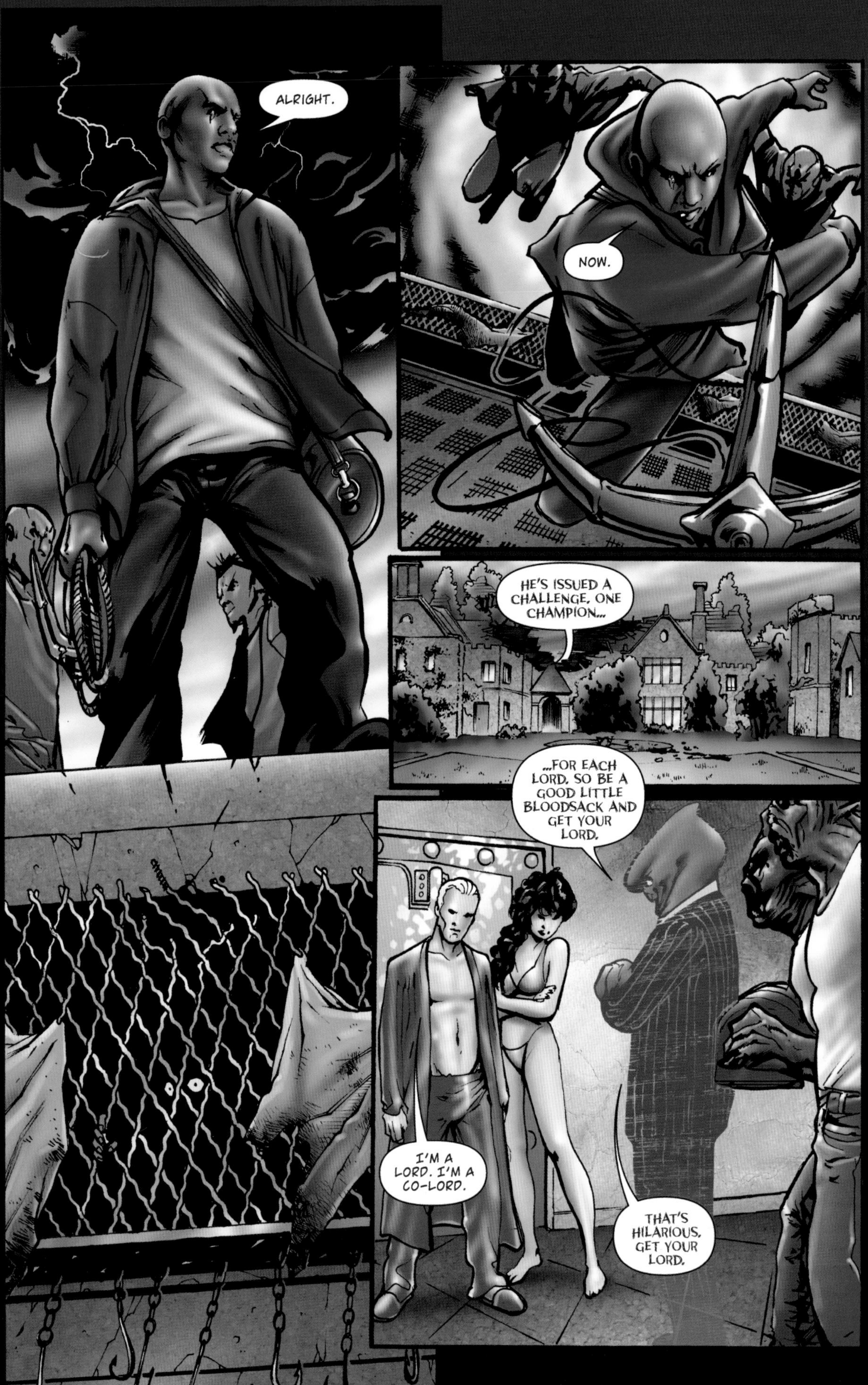
ALRIGHT.
NOW.
HE'S ISSUED A CHALLENGE, ONE CHAMPION...
...FOR EACH LORD. SO BE A GOOD LITTLE BLOODSACK AND GET YOUR LORD.
I'M A LORD. I'M A CO-LORD.
THAT'S HILARIOUS. GET YOUR LORD.

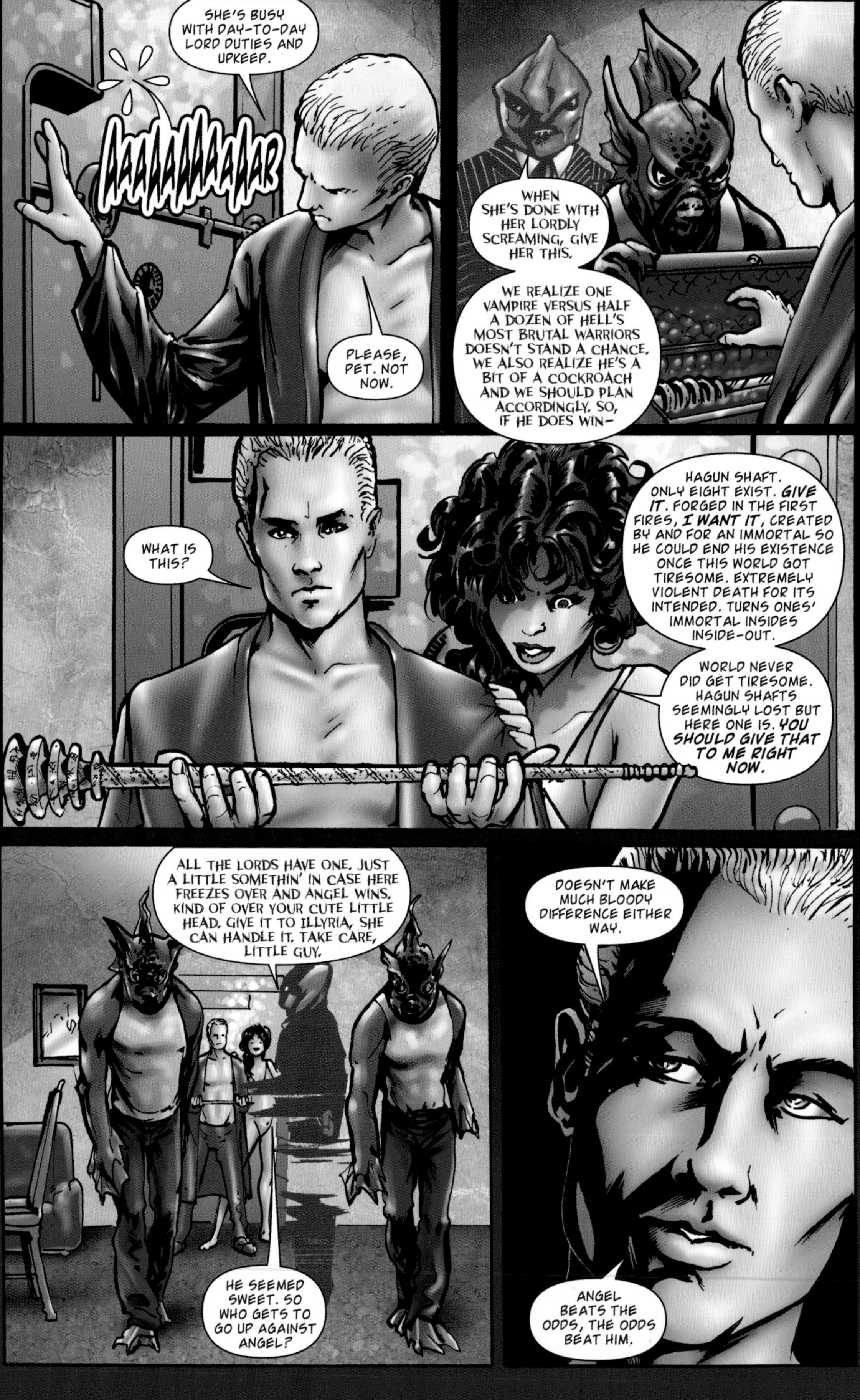
SHE'S BUSY WITH DAY-TO-DAY LORD DUTIES AND UPKEEP.
AAAAAAAAAAAR
PLEASE, PET. NOT NOW.
WHEN SHE'S DONE WITH HER LORDLY SCREAMING, GIVE HER THIS.
WE REALIZE ONE VAMPIRE VERSUS HALF A DOZEN OF HELL'S MOST BRUTAL WARRIORS DOESN'T STAND A CHANCE. WE ALSO REALIZE HE'S A BIT OF A COCKROACH AND WE SHOULD PLAN ACCORDINGLY. SO, IF HE DOES WIN—
WHAT IS THIS?
HAGUN SHAFT. ONLY EIGHT EXIST. GIVE IT. FORGED IN THE FIRST FIRES, I WANT IT, CREATED BY AND FOR AN IMMORTAL SO HE COULD END HIS EXISTENCE ONCE THIS WORLD GOT TIRESOME. EXTREMELY VIOLENT DEATH FOR ITS INTENDED. TURNS ONES' IMMORTAL INSIDES INSIDE-OUT.
WORLD NEVER DID GET TIRESOME. HAGUN SHAFTS SEEMINGLY LOST BUT HERE ONE IS. YOU SHOULD GIVE THAT TO ME RIGHT NOW.
ALL THE LORDS HAVE ONE. JUST A LITTLE SOMETHIN' IN CASE HERE FREEZES OVER AND ANGEL WINS. KIND OF OVER YOUR CUTE LITTLE HEAD. GIVE IT TO ILLYRIA, SHE CAN HANDLE IT. TAKE CARE, LITTLE GUY.
HE SEEMED SWEET. SO WHO GETS TO GO UP AGAINST ANGEL?
DOESN'T MAKE MUCH BLOODY DIFFERENCE EITHER WAY.
ANGEL BEATS THE ODDS, THE ODDS BEAT HIM.

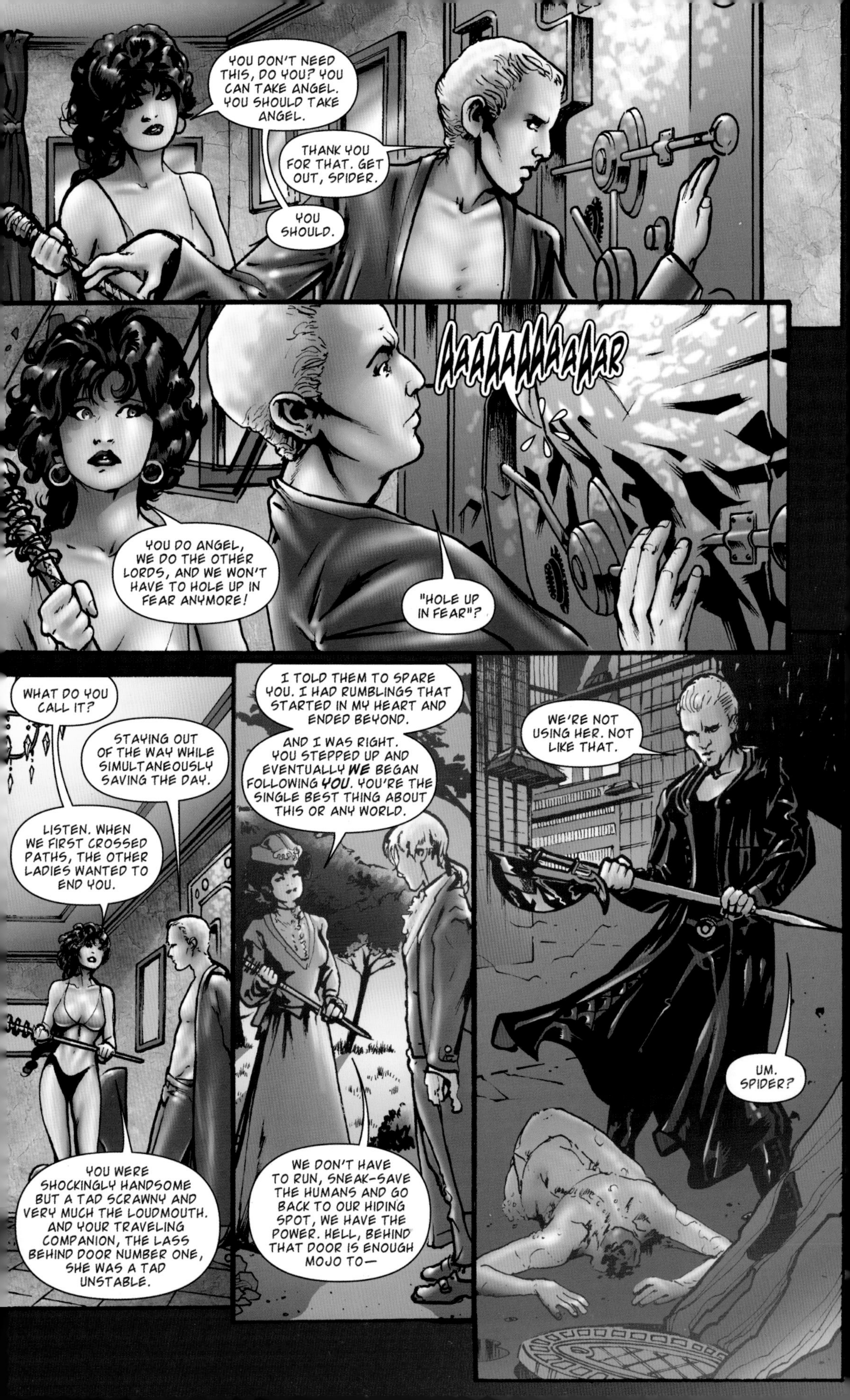
YOU DON'T NEED THIS, DO YOU? YOU CAN TAKE ANGEL. YOU SHOULD TAKE ANGEL.
THANK YOU FOR THAT. GET OUT, SPIDER.
YOU SHOULD.
AAAAAAAAAAR
YOU DO ANGEL, WE DO THE OTHER LORDS, AND WE WON'T HAVE TO HOLE UP IN FEAR ANYMORE!
"HOLE UP IN FEAR"?
WHAT DO YOU CALL IT?
STAYING OUT OF THE WAY WHILE SIMULTANEOUSLY SAVING THE DAY.
LISTEN. WHEN WE FIRST CROSSED PATHS, THE OTHER LADIES WANTED TO END YOU.
YOU WERE SHOCKINGLY HANDSOME BUT A TAD SCRAWNY AND VERY MUCH THE LOUDMOUTH. AND YOUR TRAVELING COMPANION, THE LASS BEHIND DOOR NUMBER ONE, SHE WAS A TAD UNSTABLE.
I TOLD THEM TO SPARE YOU. I HAD RUMBLINGS THAT STARTED IN MY HEART AND ENDED BEYOND.
AND I WAS RIGHT. YOU STEPPED UP AND EVENTUALLY WE BEGAN FOLLOWING YOU. YOU'RE THE SINGLE BEST THING ABOUT THIS OR ANY WORLD.
WE DON'T HAVE TO RUN, SNEAK-SAVE THE HUMANS AND GO BACK TO OUR HIDING SPOT, WE HAVE THE POWER. HELL, BEHIND THAT DOOR IS ENOUGH MOJO TO—
WE'RE NOT USING HER. NOT LIKE THAT.
UM. SPIDER?

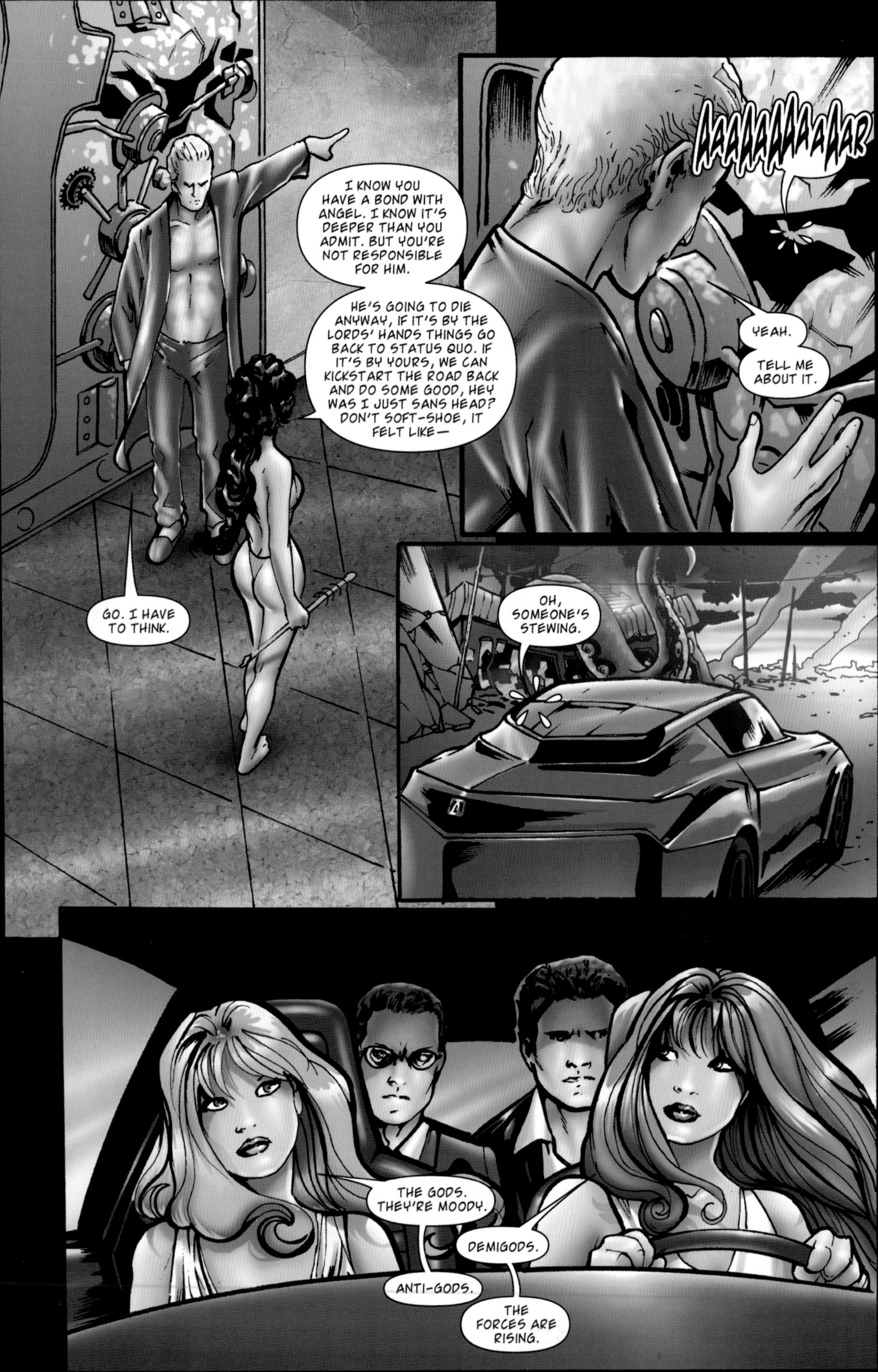
I KNOW YOU HAVE A BOND WITH ANGEL. I KNOW IT'S DEEPER THAN YOU ADMIT. BUT YOU'RE NOT RESPONSIBLE FOR HIM.
HE'S GOING TO DIE ANYWAY, IF IT'S BY THE LORDS' HANDS THINGS GO BACK TO STATUS QUO. IF IT'S BY YOURS, WE CAN KICKSTART THE ROAD BACK AND DO SOME GOOD, HEY WAS I JUST SANS HEAD? DON'T SOFT-SHOE, IT FELT LIKE—
GO. I HAVE TO THINK.
AAAAAAAAAAAR
YEAH.
TELL ME ABOUT IT.
OH, SOMEONE'S STEWING.
THE GODS. THEY'RE MOODY.
DEMIGODS.
ANTI-GODS.
THE FORCES ARE RISING.

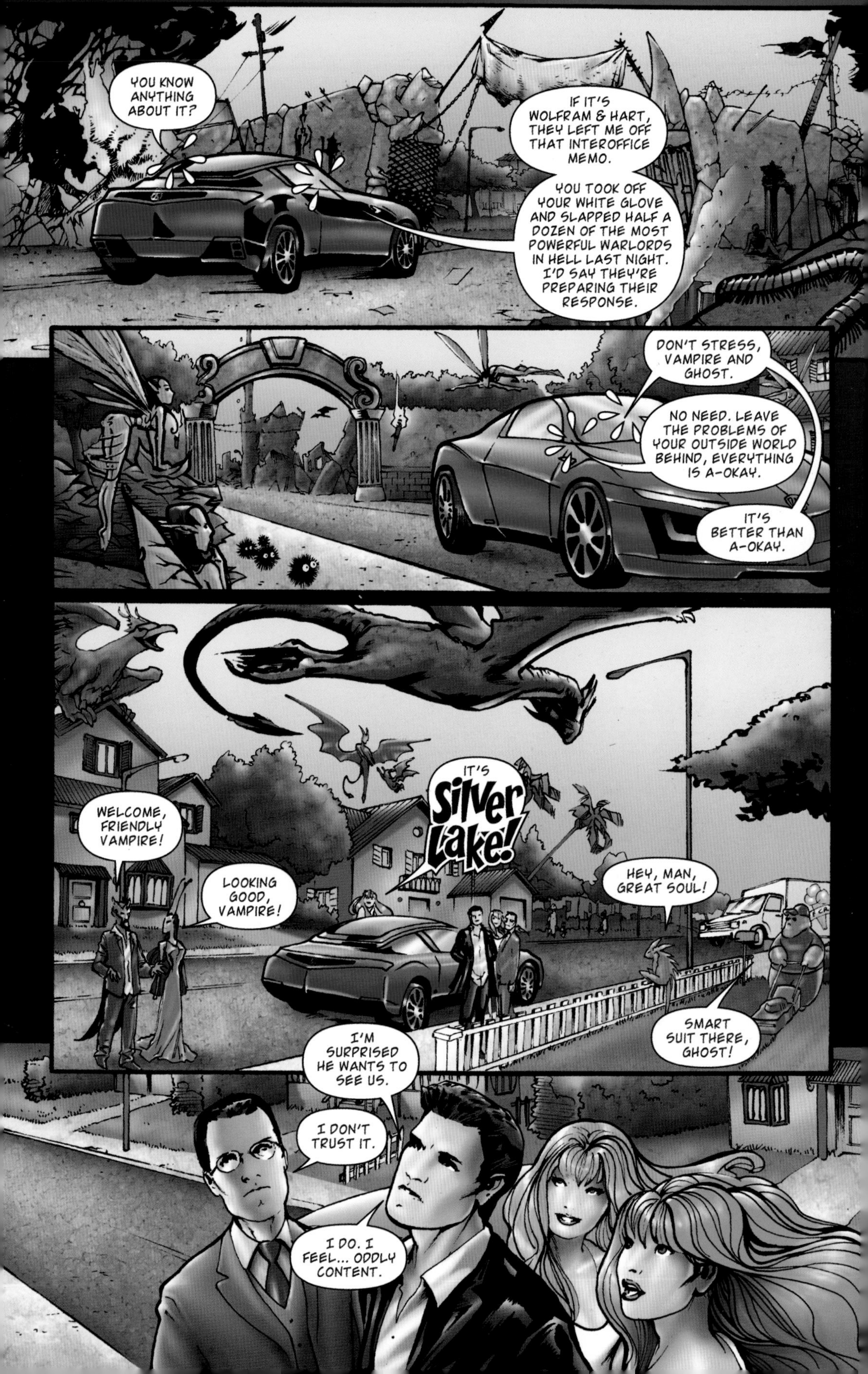
YOU KNOW ANYTHING ABOUT IT?
IF IT'S WOLFRAM & HART, THEY LEFT ME OFF THAT INTEROFFICE MEMO.
YOU TOOK OFF YOUR WHITE GLOVE AND SLAPPED HALF A DOZEN OF THE MOST POWERFUL WARLORDS IN HELL LAST NIGHT. I'D SAY THEY'RE PREPARING THEIR RESPONSE.
DON'T STRESS, VAMPIRE AND GHOST.
NO NEED. LEAVE THE PROBLEMS OF YOUR OUTSIDE WORLD BEHIND, EVERYTHING IS A-OKAY.
IT'S BETTER THAN A-OKAY.
IT'S
Silver Lake!
WELCOME, FRIENDLY VAMPIRE!
LOOKING GOOD, VAMPIRE!
HEY, MAN, GREAT SOUL!
SMART SUIT THERE, GHOST!
I'M SURPRISED HE WANTS TO SEE US.
I DON'T TRUST IT.
I DO. I FEEL... ODDLY CONTENT.

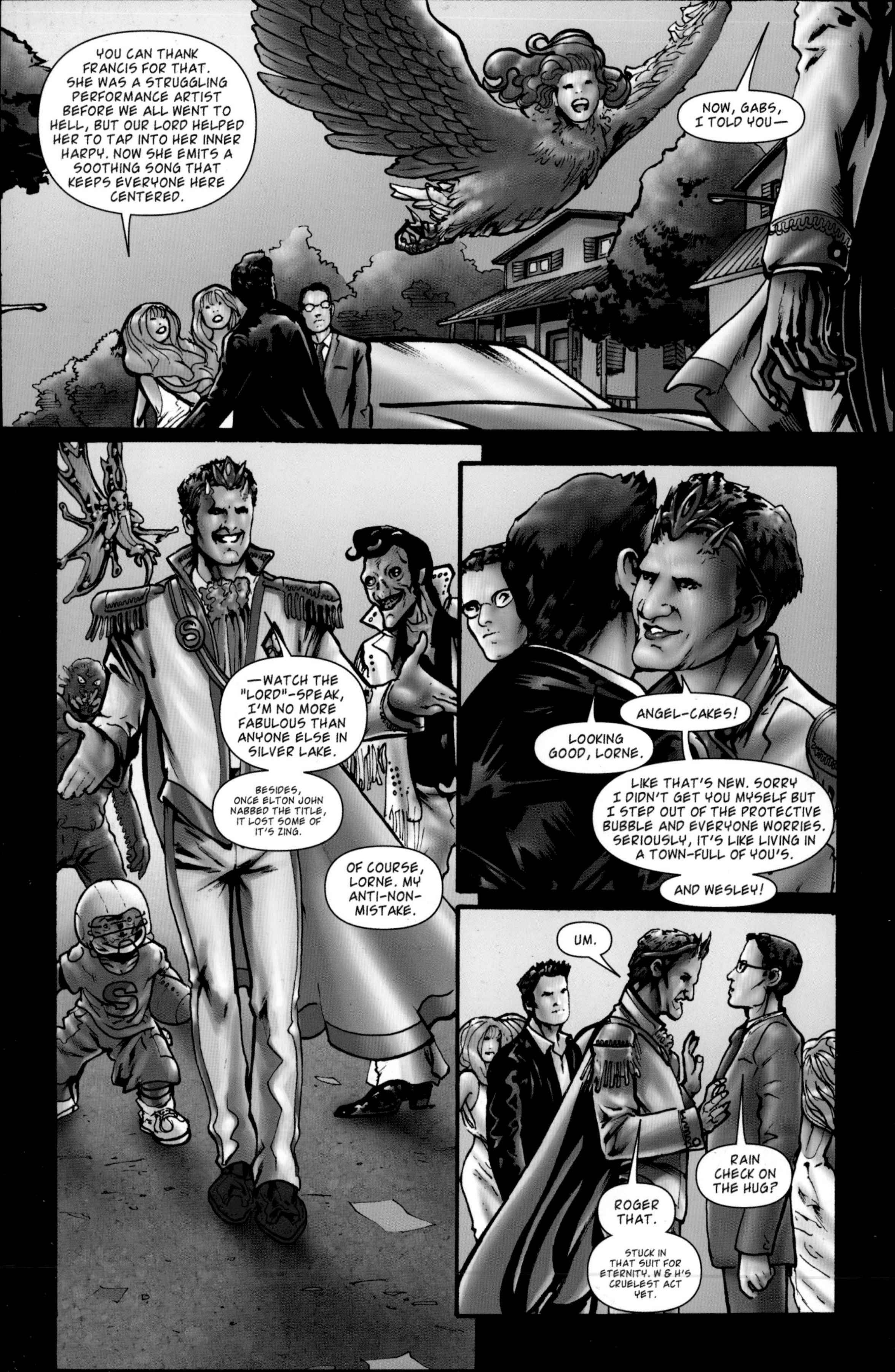
YOU CAN THANK FRANCIS FOR THAT. SHE WAS A STRUGGLING PERFORMANCE ARTIST BEFORE WE ALL WENT TO HELL, BUT OUR LORD HELPED HER TO TAP INTO HER INNER HARPY. NOW SHE EMITS A SOOTHING SONG THAT KEEPS EVERYONE HERE CENTERED.
NOW, GABS, I TOLD YOU—
—WATCH THE "LORD"-SPEAK, I'M NO MORE FABULOUS THAN ANYONE ELSE IN SILVER LAKE.
BESIDES, ONCE ELTON JOHN NABBED THE TITLE, IT LOST SOME OF IT'S ZING.
OF COURSE, LORNE. MY ANTI-NON-MISTAKE.
ANGEL-CAKES!
LOOKING GOOD, LORNE.
LIKE THAT'S NEW. SORRY I DIDN'T GET YOU MYSELF BUT I STEP OUT OF THE PROTECTIVE BUBBLE AND EVERYONE WORRIES. SERIOUSLY, IT'S LIKE LIVING IN A TOWN-FULL OF YOU'S.
AND WESLEY!
UM.
RAIN CHECK ON THE HUG?
ROGER THAT.
STUCK IN THAT SUIT FOR ETERNITY. W & H'S CRUELEST ACT YET.

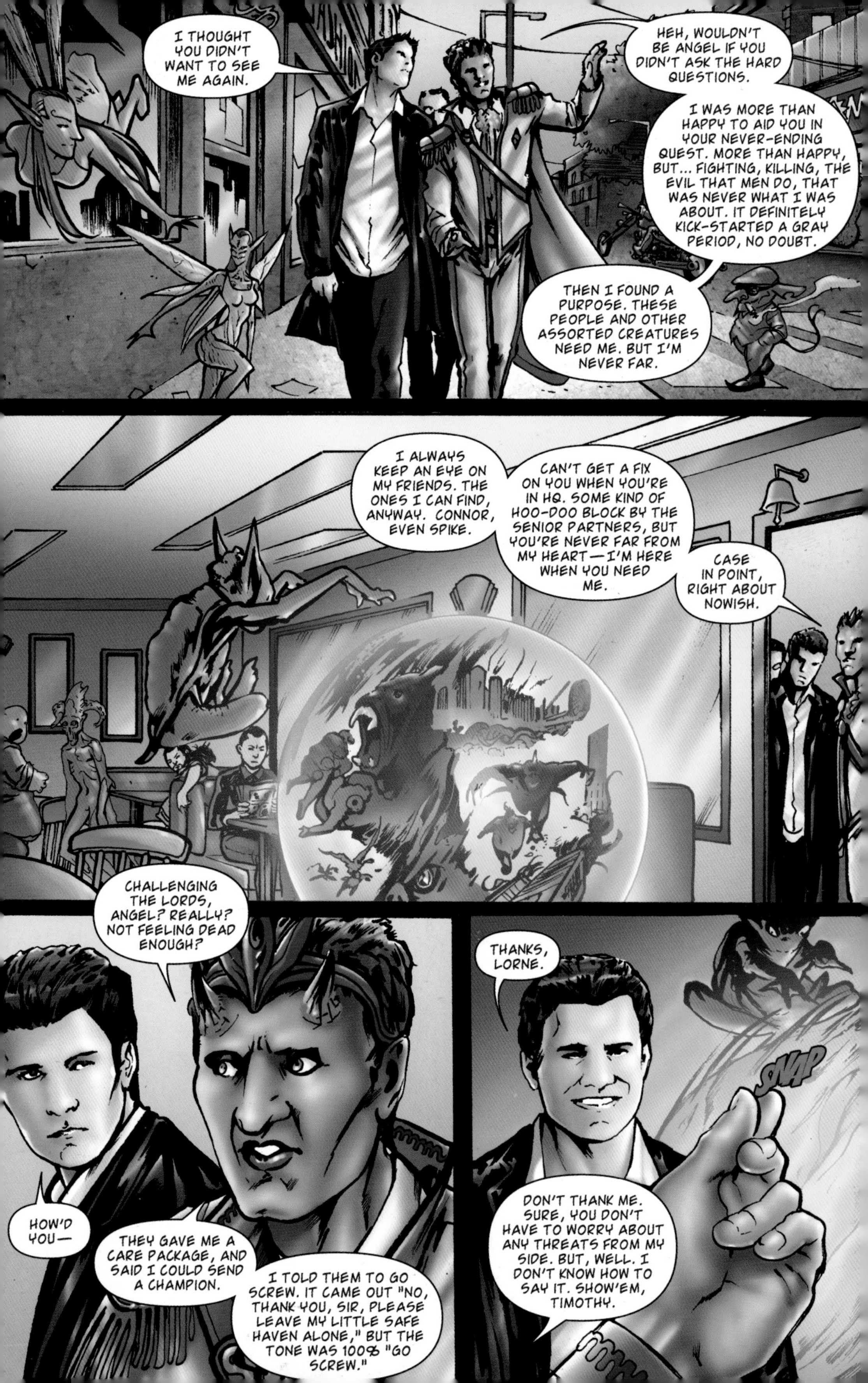
I THOUGHT YOU DIDN'T WANT TO SEE ME AGAIN.
HEH, WOULDN'T BE ANGEL IF YOU DIDN'T ASK THE HARD QUESTIONS.
I WAS MORE THAN HAPPY TO AID YOU IN YOUR NEVER-ENDING QUEST. MORE THAN HAPPY, BUT... FIGHTING, KILLING, THE EVIL THAT MEN DO, THAT WAS NEVER WHAT I WAS ABOUT. IT DEFINITELY KICK-STARTED A GRAY PERIOD, NO DOUBT.
THEN I FOUND A PURPOSE. THESE PEOPLE AND OTHER ASSORTED CREATURES NEED ME. BUT I'M NEVER FAR.
I ALWAYS KEEP AN EYE ON MY FRIENDS. THE ONES I CAN FIND, ANYWAY. CONNOR, EVEN SPIKE.
CAN'T GET A FIX ON YOU WHEN YOU'RE IN HQ. SOME KIND OF HOO-DOO BLOCK BY THE SENIOR PARTNERS, BUT YOU'RE NEVER FAR FROM MY HEART—I'M HERE WHEN YOU NEED ME.
CASE IN POINT, RIGHT ABOUT NOWISH.
CHALLENGING THE LORDS, ANGEL? REALLY? NOT FEELING DEAD ENOUGH?
HOW'D YOU—
THEY GAVE ME A CARE PACKAGE, AND SAID I COULD SEND A CHAMPION.
I TOLD THEM TO GO SCREW. IT CAME OUT "NO, THANK YOU, SIR, PLEASE LEAVE MY LITTLE SAFE HAVEN ALONE," BUT THE TONE WAS 100% "GO SCREW."
THANKS, LORNE.
SNAP
DON'T THANK ME. SURE, YOU DON'T HAVE TO WORRY ABOUT ANY THREATS FROM MY SIDE. BUT, WELL. I DON'T KNOW HOW TO SAY IT. SHOW'EM, TIMOTHY.

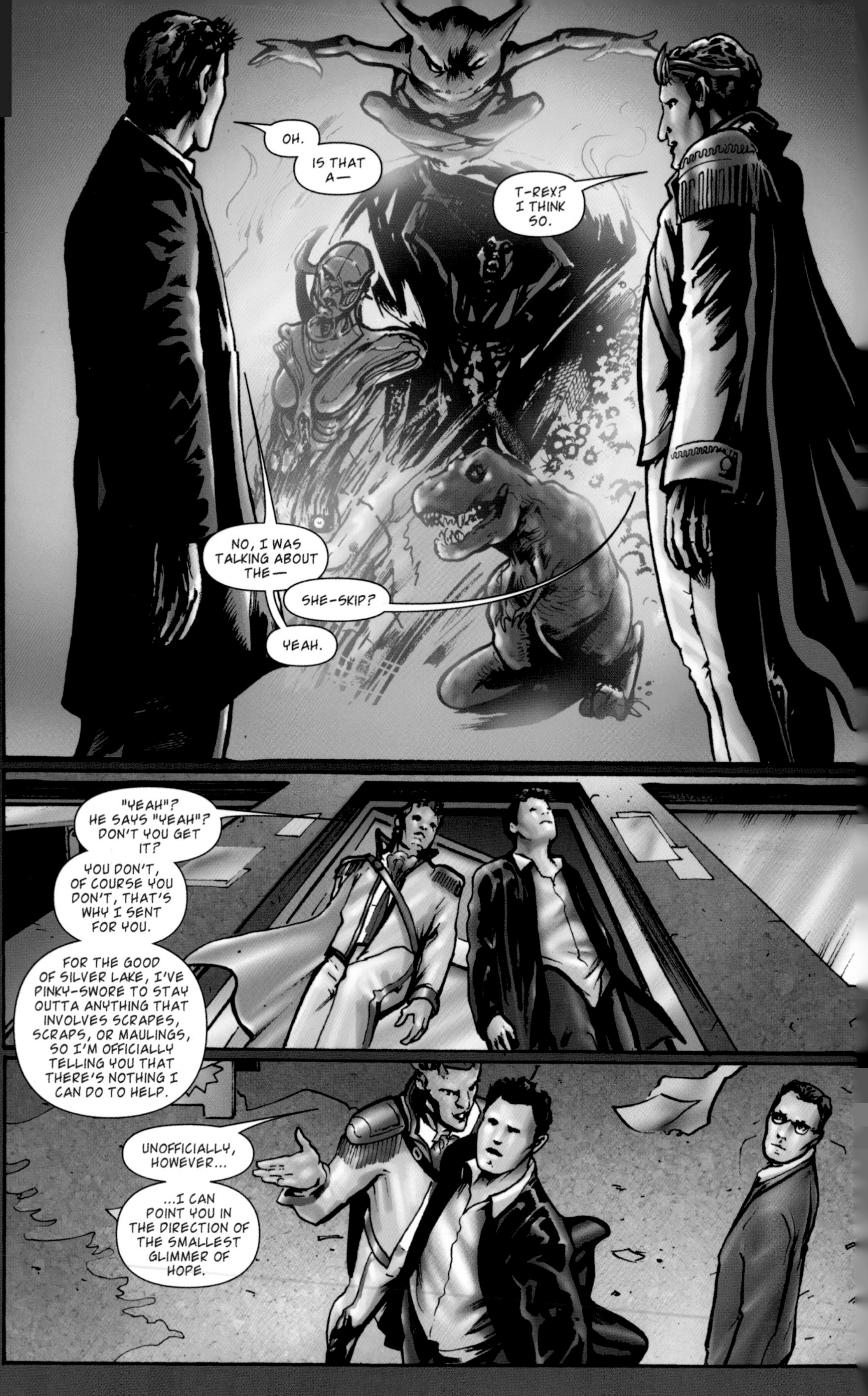
OH.
IS THAT A—
T-REX? I THINK SO.
NO, I WAS TALKING ABOUT THE—
SHE-SKIP?
YEAH.
"YEAH"? HE SAYS "YEAH"? DON'T YOU GET IT?
YOU DON'T, OF COURSE YOU DON'T, THAT'S WHY I SENT FOR YOU.
FOR THE GOOD OF SILVER LAKE, I'VE PINKY-SWORE TO STAY OUTTA ANYTHING THAT INVOLVES SCRAPES, SCRAPS, OR MAULINGS, SO I'M OFFICIALLY TELLING YOU THAT THERE'S NOTHING I CAN DO TO HELP.
UNOFFICIALLY, HOWEVER...
...I CAN POINT YOU IN THE DIRECTION OF THE SMALLEST GLIMMER OF HOPE.

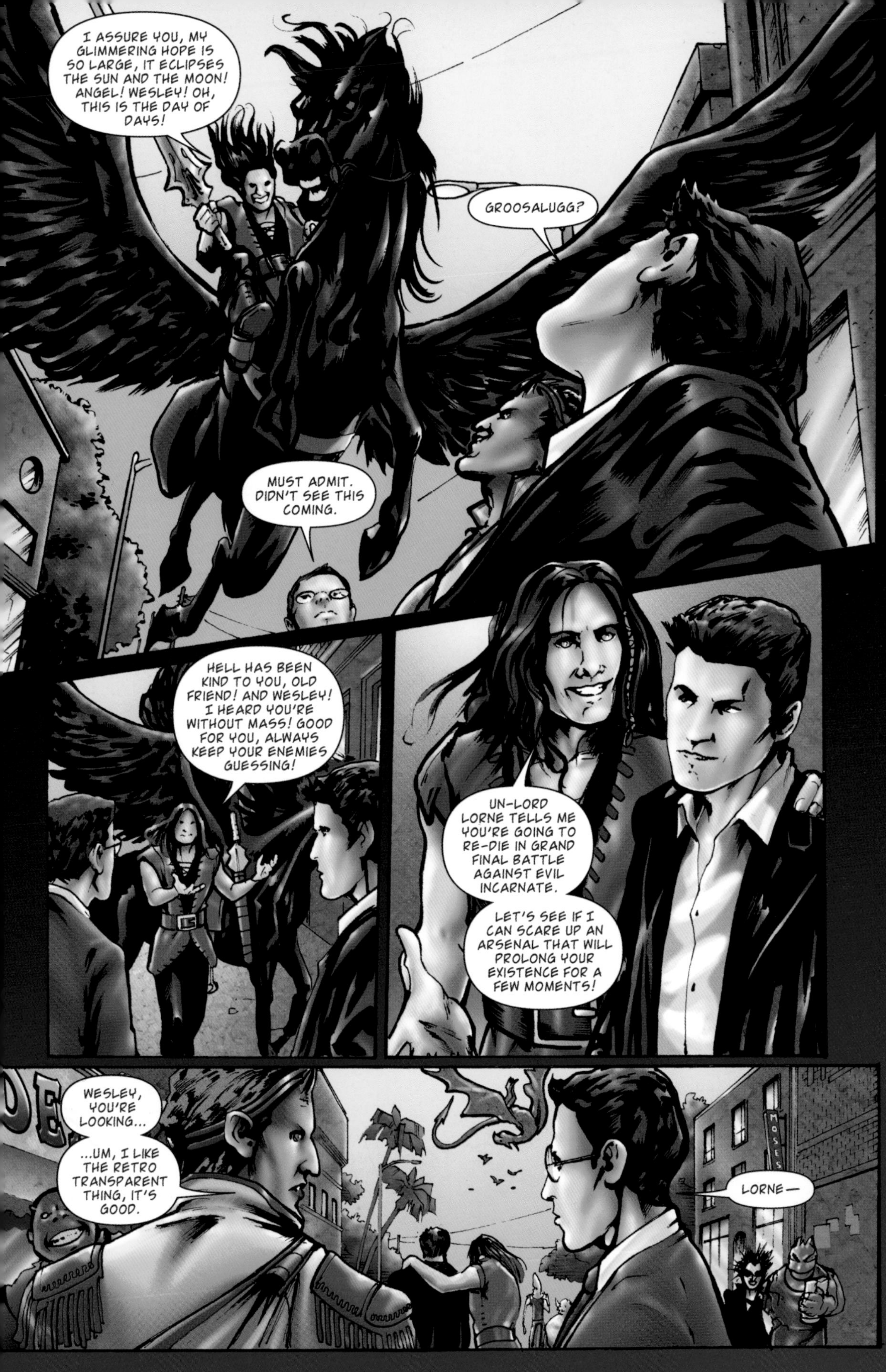
I ASSURE YOU, MY GLIMMERING HOPE IS SO LARGE, IT ECLIPSES THE SUN AND THE MOON! ANGEL! WESLEY! OH, THIS IS THE DAY OF DAYS!
GROOSALUGG?
MUST ADMIT. DIDN'T SEE THIS COMING.
HELL HAS BEEN KIND TO YOU, OLD FRIEND! AND WESLEY! I HEARD YOU'RE WITHOUT MASS! GOOD FOR YOU, ALWAYS KEEP YOUR ENEMIES GUESSING!
UN-LORD LORNE TELLS ME YOU'RE GOING TO RE-DIE IN GRAND FINAL BATTLE AGAINST EVIL INCARNATE.
LET'S SEE IF I CAN SCARE UP AN ARSENAL THAT WILL PROLONG YOUR EXISTENCE FOR A FEW MOMENTS!
WESLEY, YOU'RE LOOKING...
...UM, I LIKE THE RETRO TRANSPARENT THING, IT'S GOOD.
LORNE—

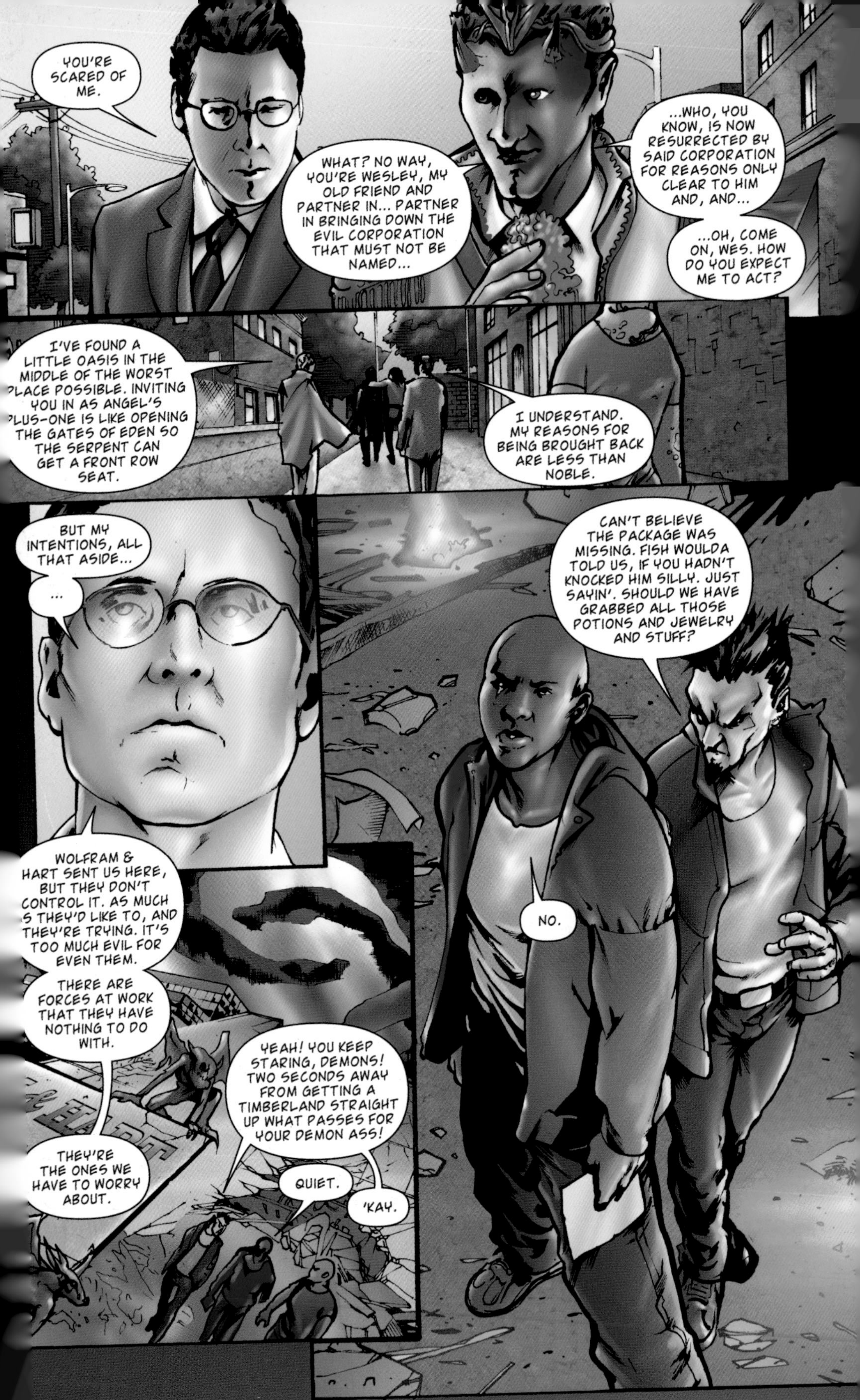
YOU'RE SCARED OF ME.
WHAT? NO WAY, YOU'RE WESLEY, MY OLD FRIEND AND PARTNER IN... PARTNER IN BRINGING DOWN THE EVIL CORPORATION THAT MUST NOT BE NAMED...
...WHO, YOU KNOW, IS NOW RESURRECTED BY SAID CORPORATION FOR REASONS ONLY CLEAR TO HIM AND, AND...
...OH, COME ON, WES. HOW DO YOU EXPECT ME TO ACT?
I'VE FOUND A LITTLE OASIS IN THE MIDDLE OF THE WORST PLACE POSSIBLE. INVITING YOU IN AS ANGEL'S PLUS-ONE IS LIKE OPENING THE GATES OF EDEN SO THE SERPENT CAN GET A FRONT ROW SEAT.
I UNDERSTAND. MY REASONS FOR BEING BROUGHT BACK ARE LESS THAN NOBLE.
BUT MY INTENTIONS, ALL THAT ASIDE...
...
WOLFRAM & HART SENT US HERE, BUT THEY DON'T CONTROL IT. AS MUCH AS THEY'D LIKE TO, AND THEY'RE TRYING. IT'S TOO MUCH EVIL FOR EVEN THEM.
THERE ARE FORCES AT WORK THAT THEY HAVE NOTHING TO DO WITH.
THEY'RE THE ONES WE HAVE TO WORRY ABOUT.
CAN'T BELIEVE THE PACKAGE WAS MISSING. FISH WOULDA TOLD US, IF YOU HADN'T KNOCKED HIM SILLY. JUST SAYIN'. SHOULD WE HAVE GRABBED ALL THOSE POTIONS AND JEWELRY AND STUFF?
NO.
YEAH! YOU KEEP STARING, DEMONS! TWO SECONDS AWAY FROM GETTING A TIMBERLAND STRAIGHT UP WHAT PASSES FOR YOUR DEMON ASS!
QUIET.
'KAY.

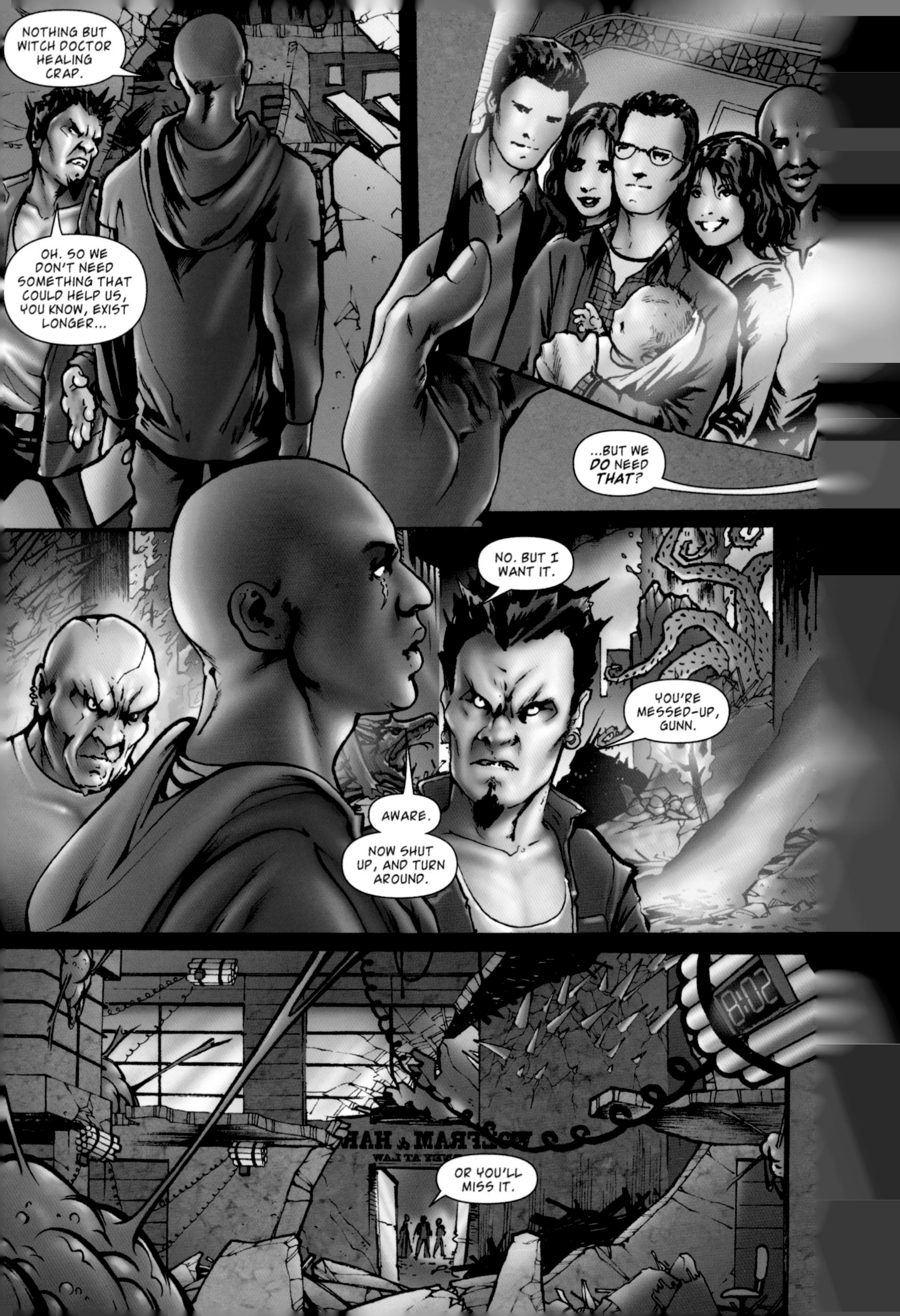
NOTHING BUT WITCH DOCTOR HEALING CRAP.
OH. SO WE DON'T NEED SOMETHING THAT COULD HELP US, YOU KNOW, EXIST LONGER...
...BUT WE DO NEED THAT?
NO. BUT I WANT IT.
YOU'RE MESSED-UP, GUNN.
AWARE.
NOW SHUT UP, AND TURN AROUND.
OR YOU'LL MISS IT.

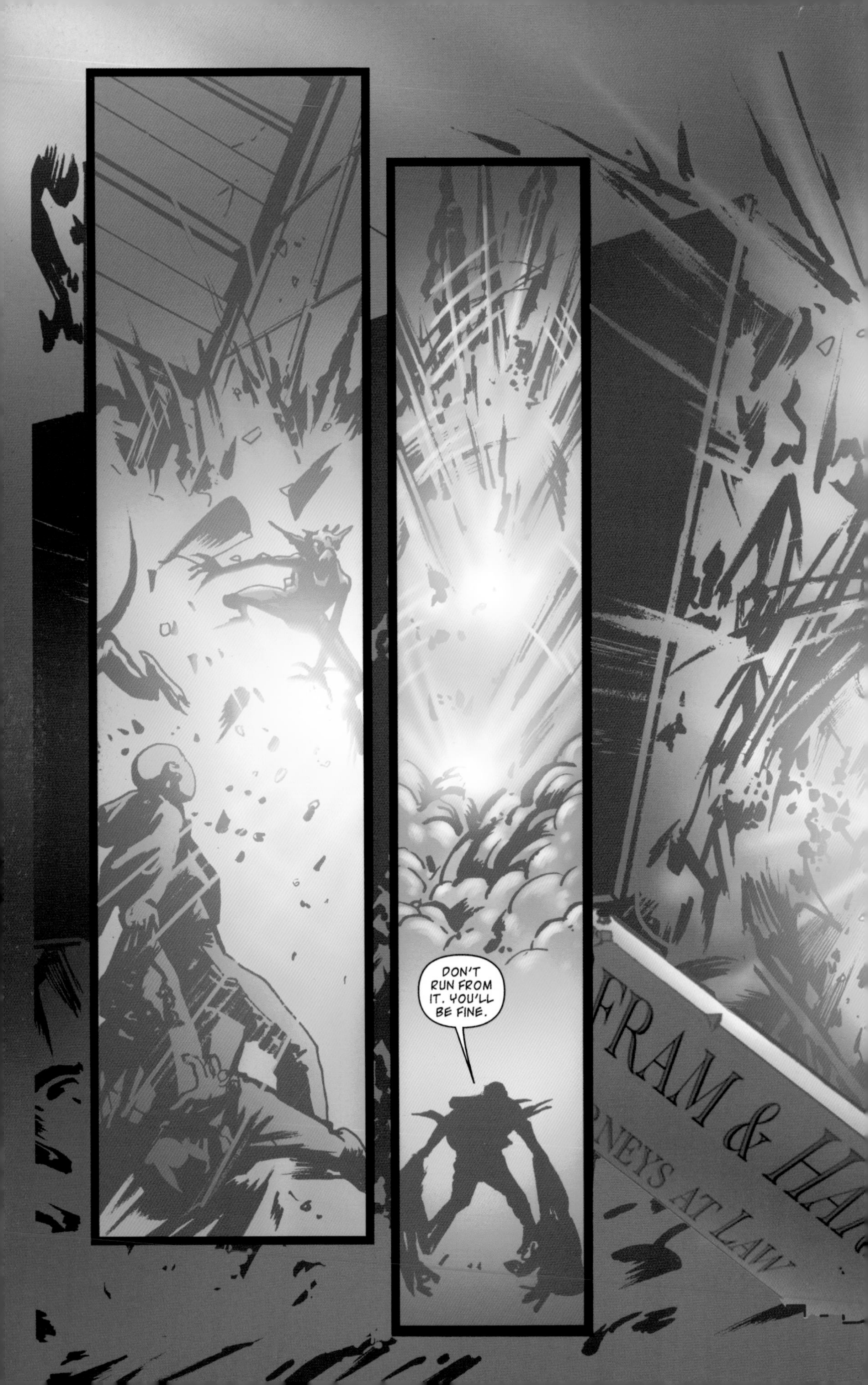
DON'T RUN FROM IT. YOU'LL BE FINE.
FRAM & HA
RNEYS AT LAW

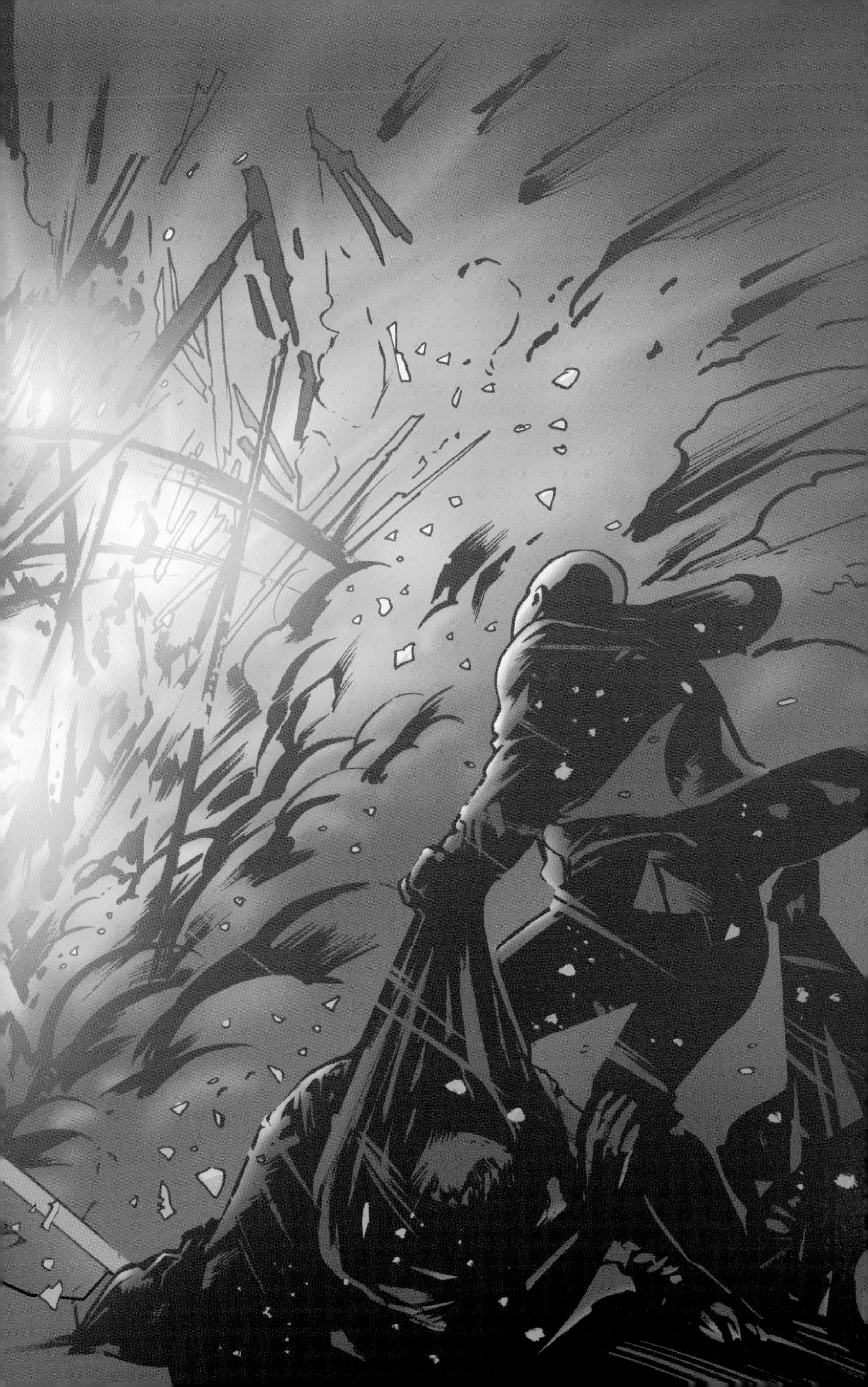

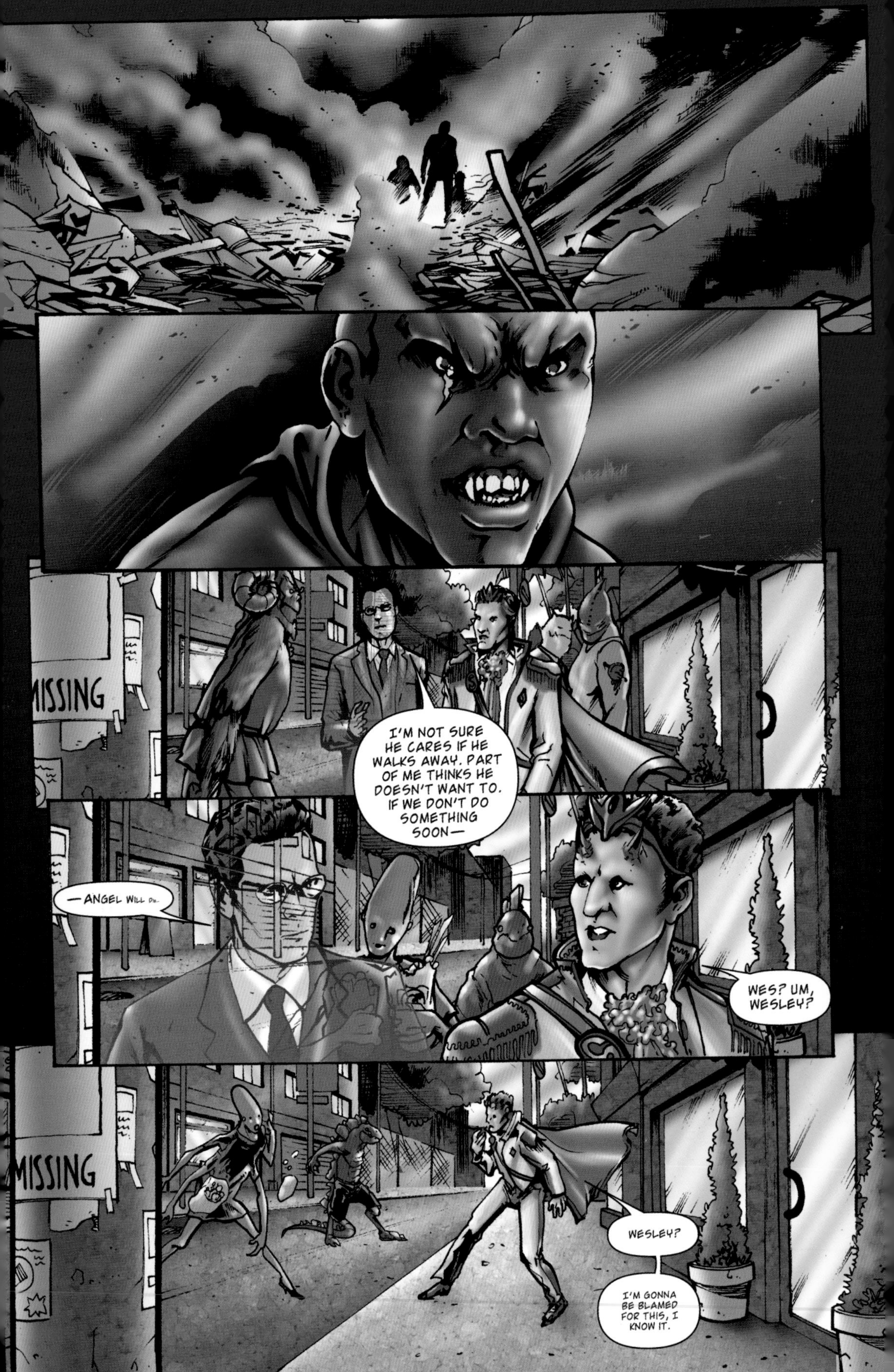
MISSING
I'M NOT SURE HE CARES IF HE WALKS AWAY. PART OF ME THINKS HE DOESN'T WANT TO. IF WE DON'T DO SOMETHING SOON—
—ANGEL WILL DIE...
WES? UM, WESLEY?
MISSING
WESLEY?
I'M GONNA BE BLAMED FOR THIS, I KNOW IT.

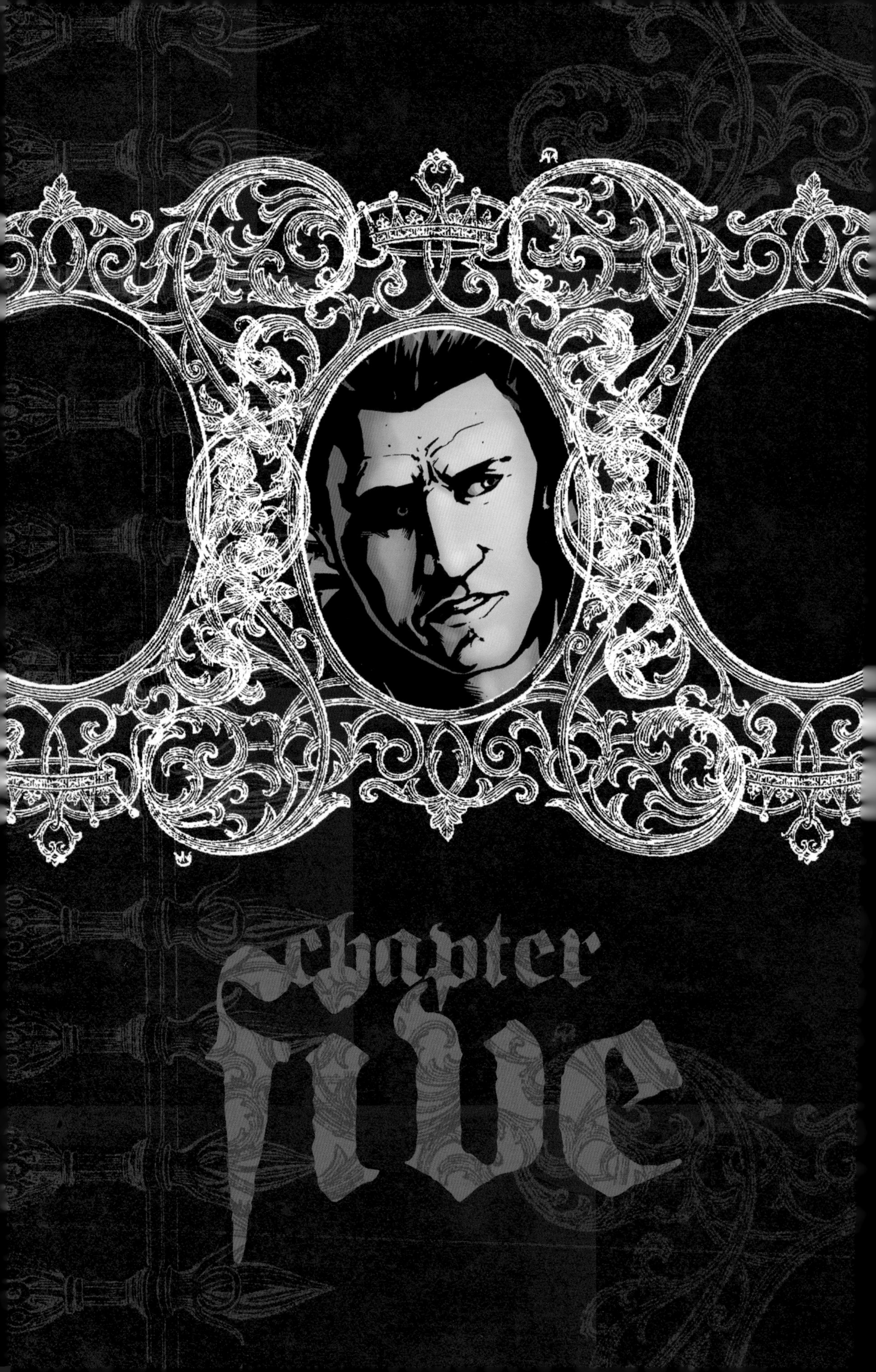

chapter five

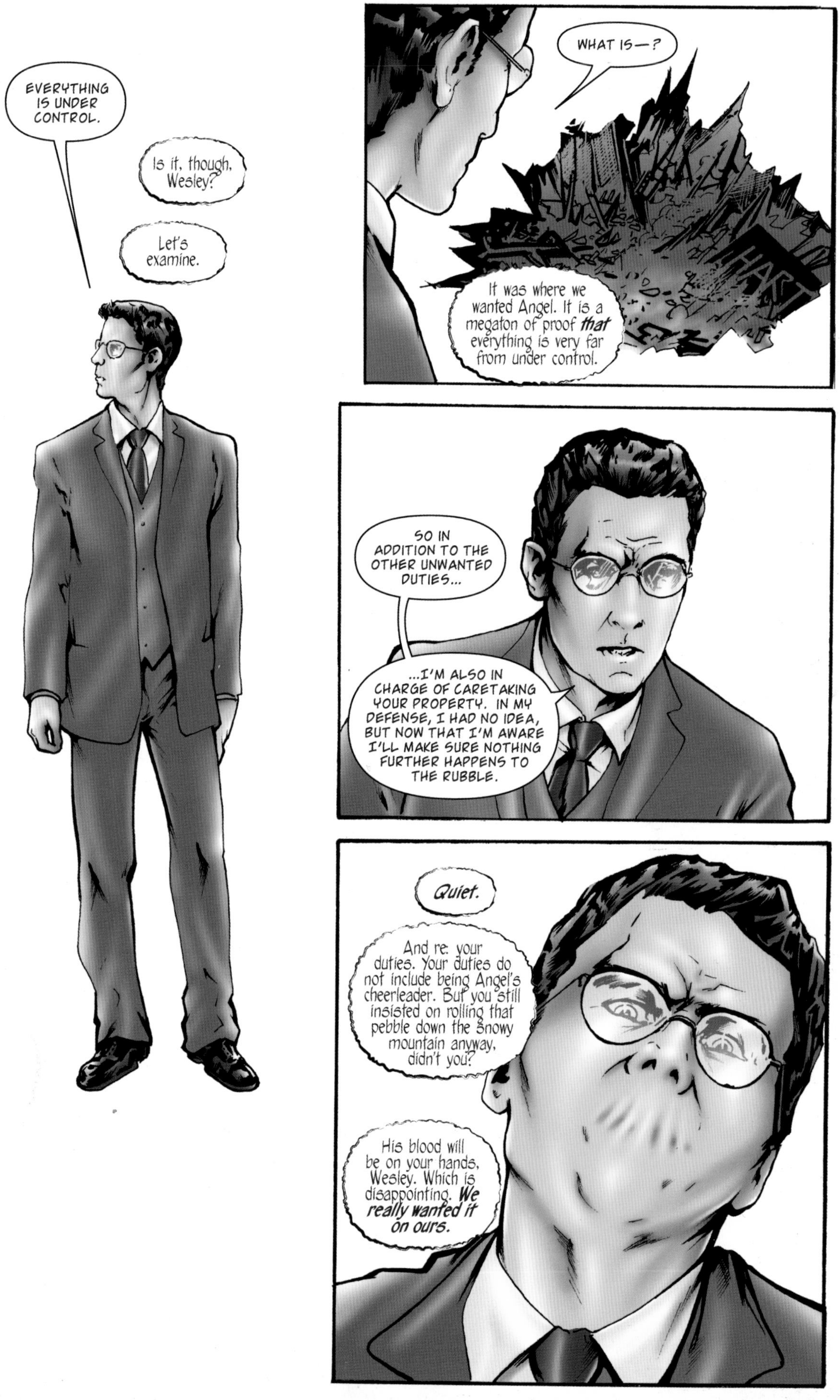
EVERYTHING IS UNDER CONTROL.
Is it, though, Wesley?
Let's examine.
WHAT IS—?
It was where we wanted Angel. It is a megaton of proof *that* everything is very far from under control.
SO IN ADDITION TO THE OTHER UNWANTED DUTIES...
...I'M ALSO IN CHARGE OF CARETAKING YOUR PROPERTY. IN MY DEFENSE, I HAD NO IDEA, BUT NOW THAT I'M AWARE I'LL MAKE SURE NOTHING FURTHER HAPPENS TO THE RUBBLE.
Quiet.
And re: your duties. Your duties do not include being Angel's cheerleader. But you still insisted on rolling that pebble down the snowy mountain anyway, didn't you?
His blood will be on your hands, Wesley. Which is disappointing. *We really wanted it on ours.*

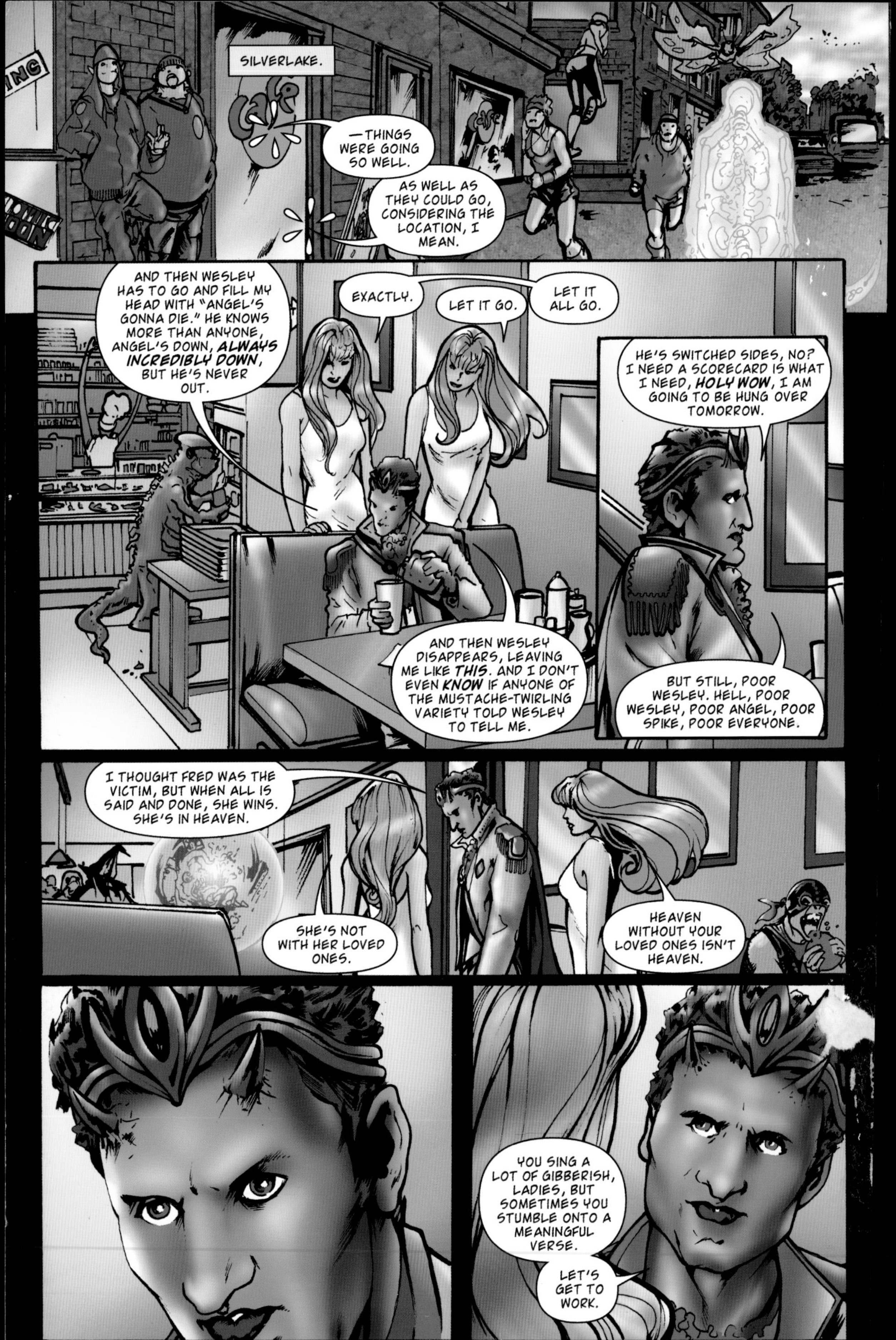
SILVERLAKE.
—THINGS WERE GOING SO WELL.
AS WELL AS THEY COULD GO, CONSIDERING THE LOCATION, I MEAN.
AND THEN WESLEY HAS TO GO AND FILL MY HEAD WITH "ANGEL'S GONNA DIE." HE KNOWS MORE THAN ANYONE, ANGEL'S DOWN, ALWAYS INCREDIBLY DOWN, BUT HE'S NEVER OUT.
EXACTLY.
LET IT GO.
LET IT ALL GO.
AND THEN WESLEY DISAPPEARS, LEAVING ME LIKE THIS. AND I DON'T EVEN KNOW IF ANYONE OF THE MUSTACHE-TWIRLING VARIETY TOLD WESLEY TO TELL ME.
HE'S SWITCHED SIDES, NO? I NEED A SCORECARD IS WHAT I NEED, HOLY WOW, I AM GOING TO BE HUNG OVER TOMORROW.
BUT STILL, POOR WESLEY. HELL, POOR WESLEY, POOR ANGEL, POOR SPIKE, POOR EVERYONE.
I THOUGHT FRED WAS THE VICTIM, BUT WHEN ALL IS SAID AND DONE, SHE WINS. SHE'S IN HEAVEN.
SHE'S NOT WITH HER LOVED ONES.
HEAVEN WITHOUT YOUR LOVED ONES ISN'T HEAVEN.
YOU SING A LOT OF GIBBERISH, LADIES, BUT SOMETIMES YOU STUMBLE ONTO A MEANINGFUL VERSE.
LET'S GET TO WORK.

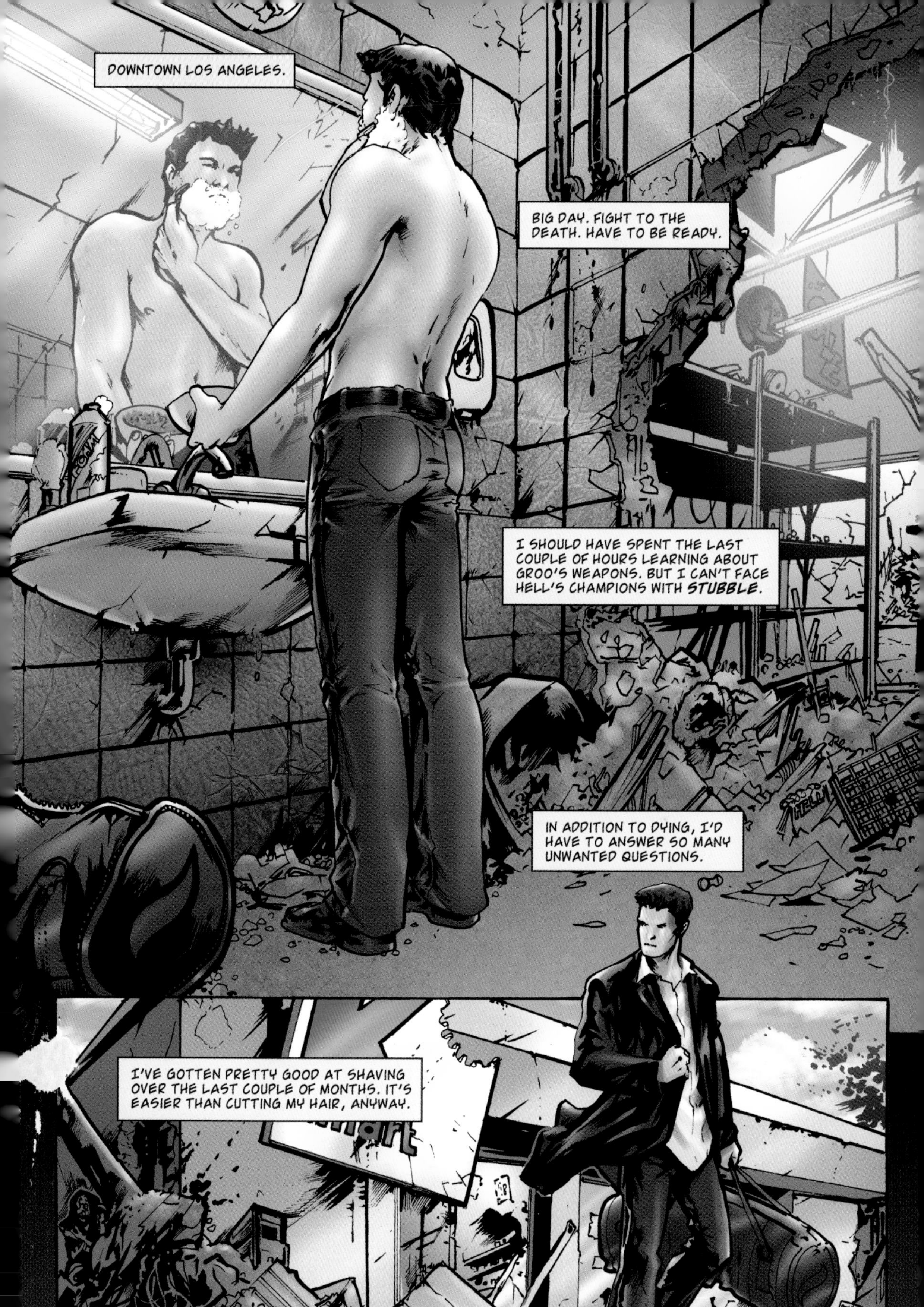
DOWNTOWN LOS ANGELES.
BIG DAY. FIGHT TO THE DEATH. HAVE TO BE READY.
I SHOULD HAVE SPENT THE LAST COUPLE OF HOURS LEARNING ABOUT GROO'S WEAPONS. BUT I CAN'T FACE HELL'S CHAMPIONS WITH *STUBBLE*.
IN ADDITION TO DYING, I'D HAVE TO ANSWER SO MANY UNWANTED QUESTIONS.
I'VE GOTTEN PRETTY GOOD AT SHAVING OVER THE LAST COUPLE OF MONTHS. IT'S EASIER THAN CUTTING MY HAIR, ANYWAY.

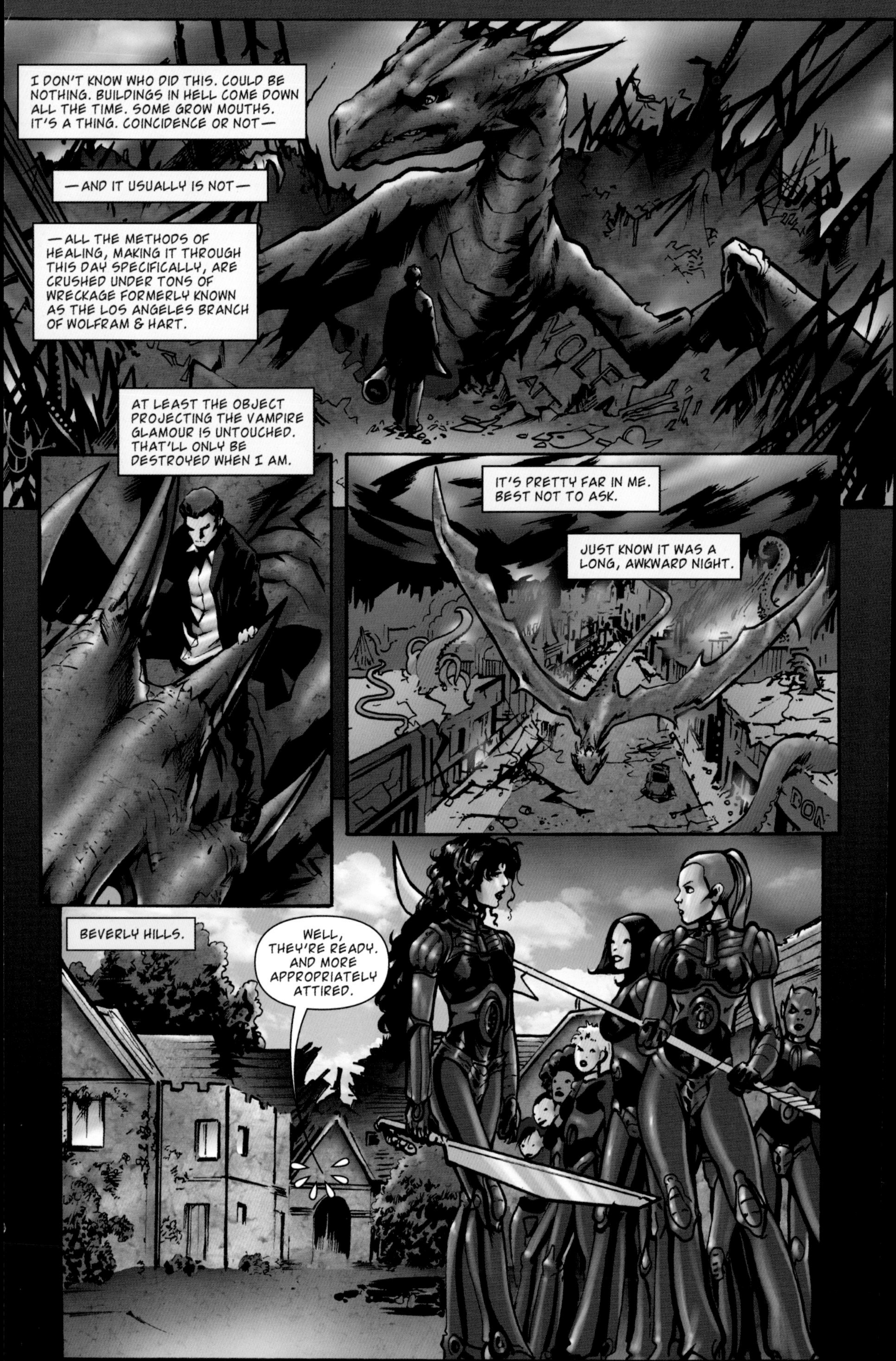
I DON'T KNOW WHO DID THIS. COULD BE NOTHING. BUILDINGS IN HELL COME DOWN ALL THE TIME. SOME GROW MOUTHS. IT'S A THING. COINCIDENCE OR NOT—
—AND IT USUALLY IS NOT—
—ALL THE METHODS OF HEALING, MAKING IT THROUGH THIS DAY SPECIFICALLY, ARE CRUSHED UNDER TONS OF WRECKAGE FORMERLY KNOWN AS THE LOS ANGELES BRANCH OF WOLFRAM & HART.
AT LEAST THE OBJECT PROJECTING THE VAMPIRE GLAMOUR IS UNTOUCHED. THAT'LL ONLY BE DESTROYED WHEN I AM.
IT'S PRETTY FAR IN ME. BEST NOT TO ASK.
JUST KNOW IT WAS A LONG, AWKWARD NIGHT.
BEVERLY HILLS.
WELL, THEY'RE READY. AND MORE APPROPRIATELY ATTIRED.

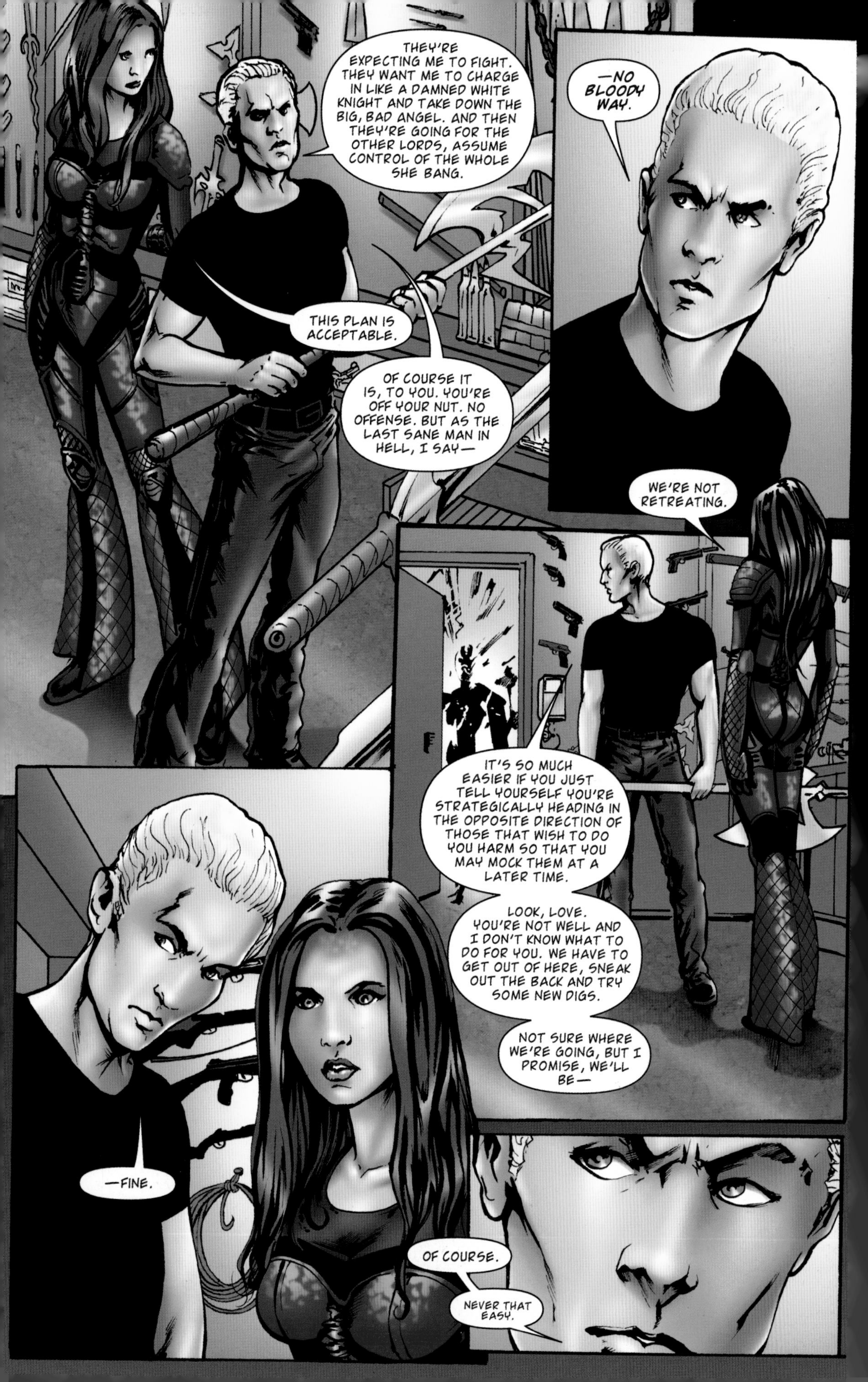
THEY'RE EXPECTING ME TO FIGHT. THEY WANT ME TO CHARGE IN LIKE A DAMNED WHITE KNIGHT AND TAKE DOWN THE BIG, BAD ANGEL. AND THEN THEY'RE GOING FOR THE OTHER LORDS, ASSUME CONTROL OF THE WHOLE SHE BANG.
THIS PLAN IS ACCEPTABLE.
OF COURSE IT IS, TO YOU. YOU'RE OFF YOUR NUT. NO OFFENSE. BUT AS THE LAST SANE MAN IN HELL, I SAY—
—NO BLOODY WAY.
WE'RE NOT RETREATING.
IT'S SO MUCH EASIER IF YOU JUST TELL YOURSELF YOU'RE STRATEGICALLY HEADING IN THE OPPOSITE DIRECTION OF THOSE THAT WISH TO DO YOU HARM SO THAT YOU MAY MOCK THEM AT A LATER TIME.
LOOK, LOVE. YOU'RE NOT WELL AND I DON'T KNOW WHAT TO DO FOR YOU. WE HAVE TO GET OUT OF HERE, SNEAK OUT THE BACK AND TRY SOME NEW DIGS.
NOT SURE WHERE WE'RE GOING, BUT I PROMISE, WE'LL BE—
—FINE.
OF COURSE.
NEVER THAT EASY.

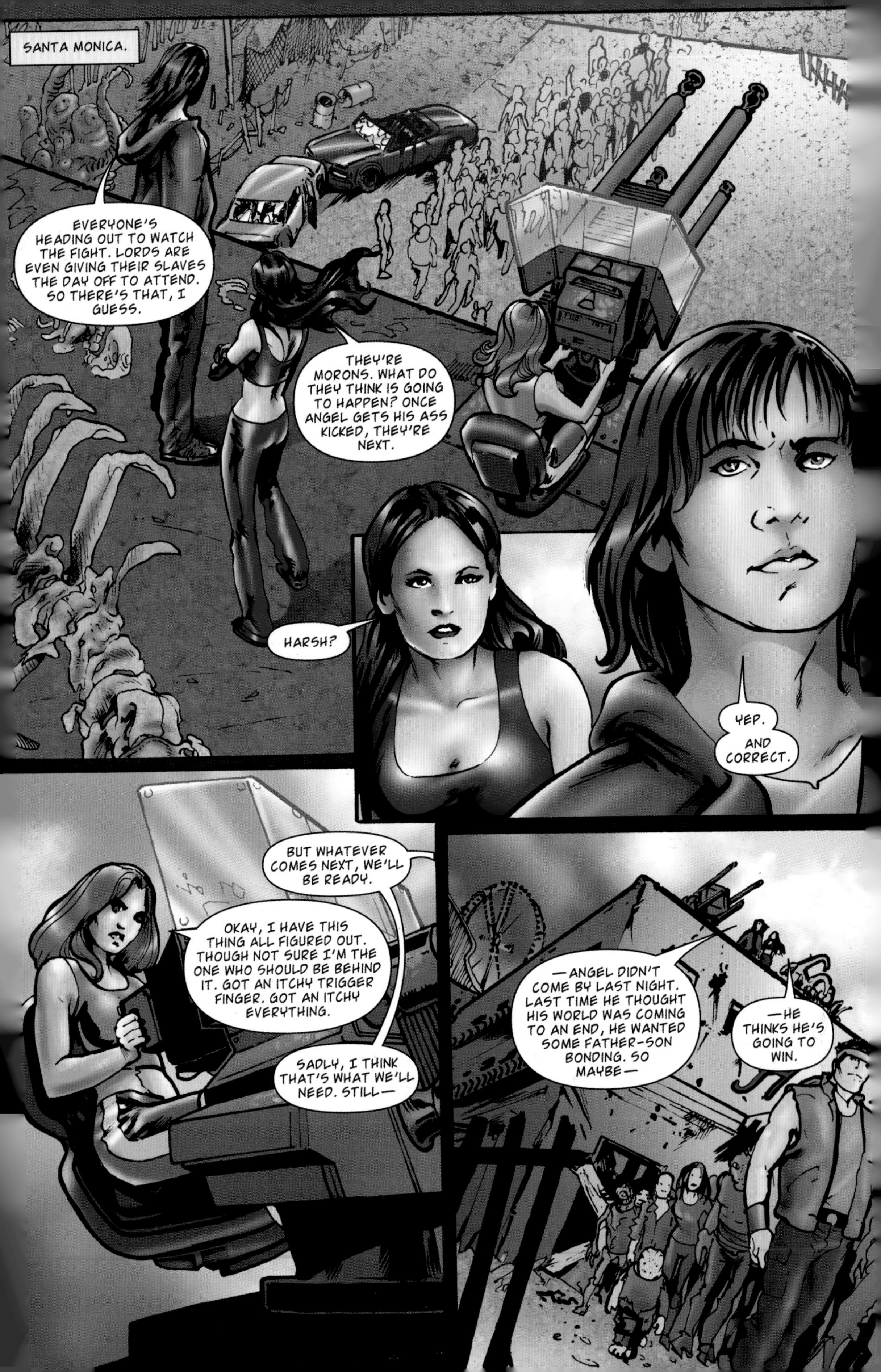
SANTA MONICA.
EVERYONE'S HEADING OUT TO WATCH THE FIGHT. LORDS ARE EVEN GIVING THEIR SLAVES THE DAY OFF TO ATTEND. SO THERE'S THAT, I GUESS.
THEY'RE MORONS. WHAT DO THEY THINK IS GOING TO HAPPEN? ONCE ANGEL GETS HIS ASS KICKED, THEY'RE NEXT.
HARSH?
YEP.
AND CORRECT.
BUT WHATEVER COMES NEXT, WE'LL BE READY.
OKAY, I HAVE THIS THING ALL FIGURED OUT. THOUGH NOT SURE I'M THE ONE WHO SHOULD BE BEHIND IT. GOT AN ITCHY TRIGGER FINGER. GOT AN ITCHY EVERYTHING.
SADLY, I THINK THAT'S WHAT WE'LL NEED. STILL—
—ANGEL DIDN'T COME BY LAST NIGHT. LAST TIME HE THOUGHT HIS WORLD WAS COMING TO AN END, HE WANTED SOME FATHER-SON BONDING. SO MAYBE—
—HE THINKS HE'S GOING TO WIN.

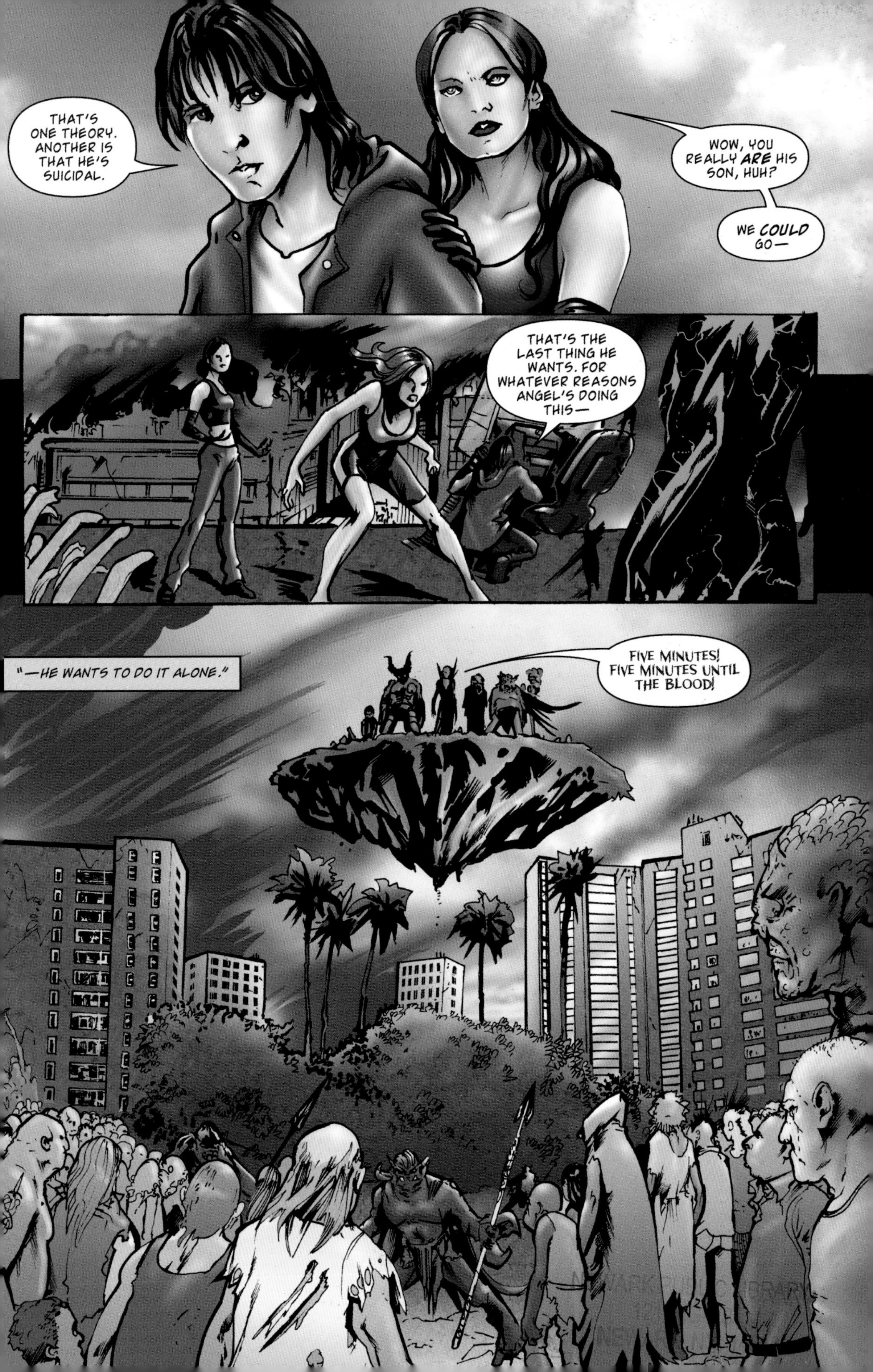
THAT'S ONE THEORY. ANOTHER IS THAT HE'S SUICIDAL.
WOW, YOU REALLY ARE HIS SON, HUH?
WE COULD GO—
THAT'S THE LAST THING HE WANTS. FOR WHATEVER REASONS ANGEL'S DOING THIS—
"—HE WANTS TO DO IT ALONE."
FIVE MINUTES! FIVE MINUTES UNTIL THE BLOOD!

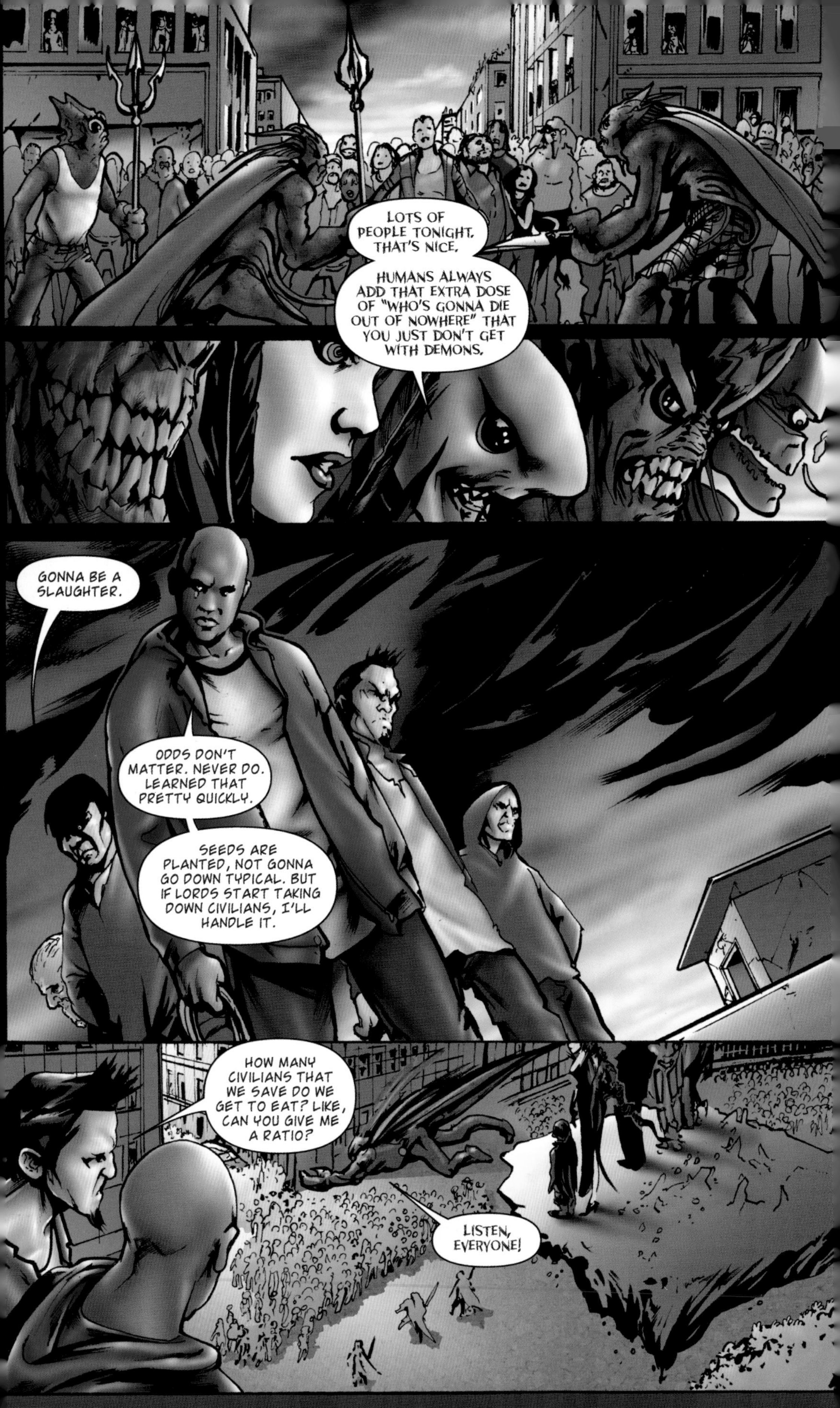
LOTS OF PEOPLE TONIGHT. THAT'S NICE.
HUMANS ALWAYS ADD THAT EXTRA DOSE OF "WHO'S GONNA DIE OUT OF NOWHERE" THAT YOU JUST DON'T GET WITH DEMONS.
GONNA BE A SLAUGHTER.
ODDS DON'T MATTER. NEVER DO. LEARNED THAT PRETTY QUICKLY.
SEEDS ARE PLANTED, NOT GONNA GO DOWN TYPICAL. BUT IF LORDS START TAKING DOWN CIVILIANS, I'LL HANDLE IT.
HOW MANY CIVILIANS THAT WE SAVE DO WE GET TO EAT? LIKE, CAN YOU GIVE ME A RATIO?
LISTEN, EVERYONE!

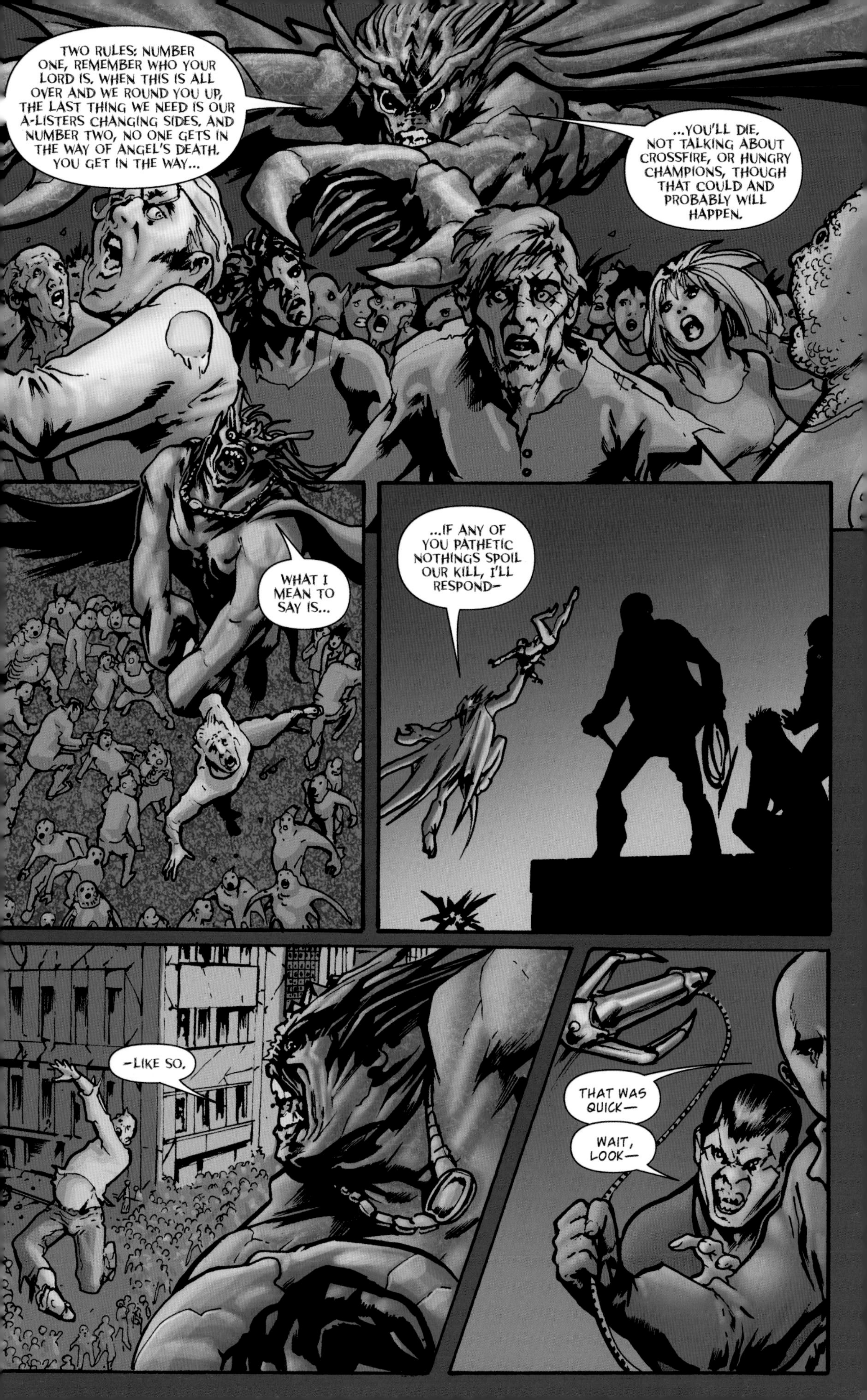
TWO RULES: NUMBER ONE, REMEMBER WHO YOUR LORD IS. WHEN THIS IS ALL OVER AND WE ROUND YOU UP, THE LAST THING WE NEED IS OUR A-LISTERS CHANGING SIDES. AND NUMBER TWO, NO ONE GETS IN THE WAY OF ANGEL'S DEATH. YOU GET IN THE WAY...
...YOU'LL DIE. NOT TALKING ABOUT CROSSFIRE, OR HUNGRY CHAMPIONS, THOUGH THAT COULD AND PROBABLY WILL HAPPEN.
WHAT I MEAN TO SAY IS...
...IF ANY OF YOU PATHETIC NOTHINGS SPOIL OUR KILL, I'LL RESPOND--
--LIKE SO.
THAT WAS QUICK--
WAIT, LOOK--

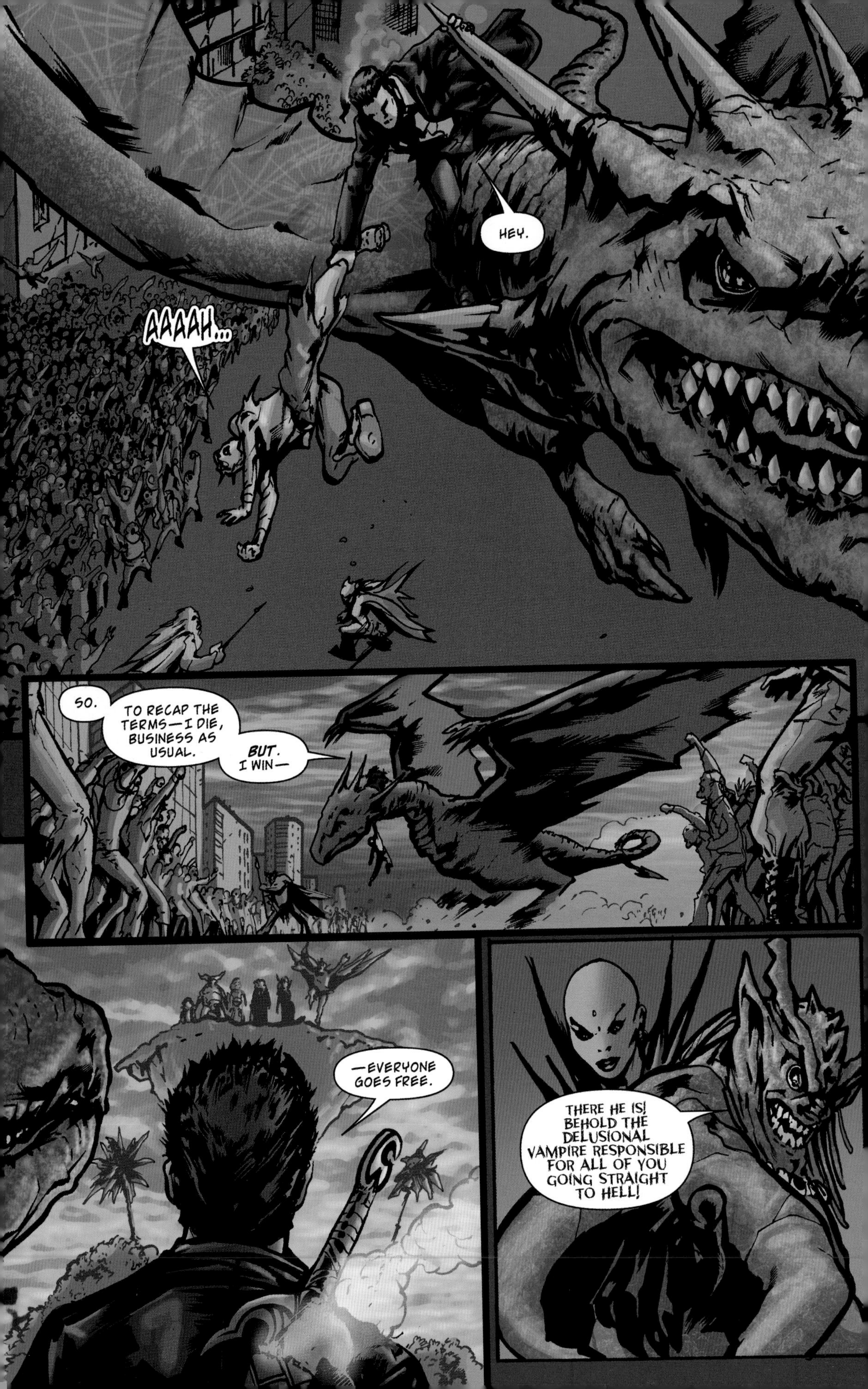
HEY.
AAAAH...
SO.
TO RECAP THE TERMS—I DIE, BUSINESS AS USUAL.
BUT. I WIN—
—EVERYONE GOES FREE.
THERE HE IS! BEHOLD THE DELUSIONAL VAMPIRE RESPONSIBLE FOR ALL OF YOU GOING STRAIGHT TO HELL!

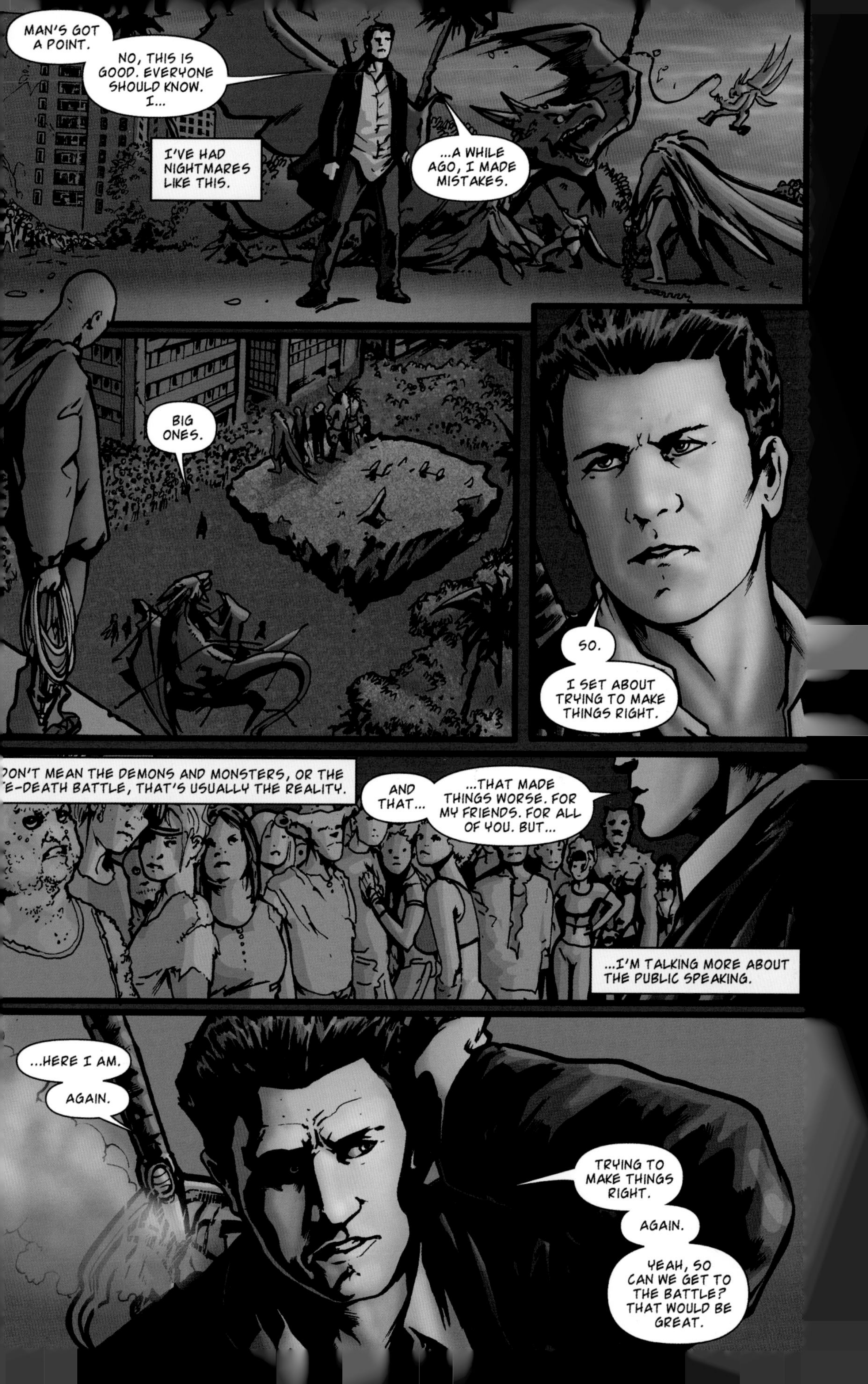
MAN'S GOT A POINT.
NO, THIS IS GOOD. EVERYONE SHOULD KNOW. I...
I'VE HAD NIGHTMARES LIKE THIS.
...A WHILE AGO, I MADE MISTAKES.
BIG ONES.
SO.
I SET ABOUT TRYING TO MAKE THINGS RIGHT.
DON'T MEAN THE DEMONS AND MONSTERS, OR THE TE-DEATH BATTLE, THAT'S USUALLY THE REALITY.
AND THAT...
...THAT MADE THINGS WORSE. FOR MY FRIENDS. FOR ALL OF YOU. BUT...
...I'M TALKING MORE ABOUT THE PUBLIC SPEAKING.
...HERE I AM.
AGAIN.
TRYING TO MAKE THINGS RIGHT.
AGAIN.
YEAH, SO CAN WE GET TO THE BATTLE? THAT WOULD BE GREAT.

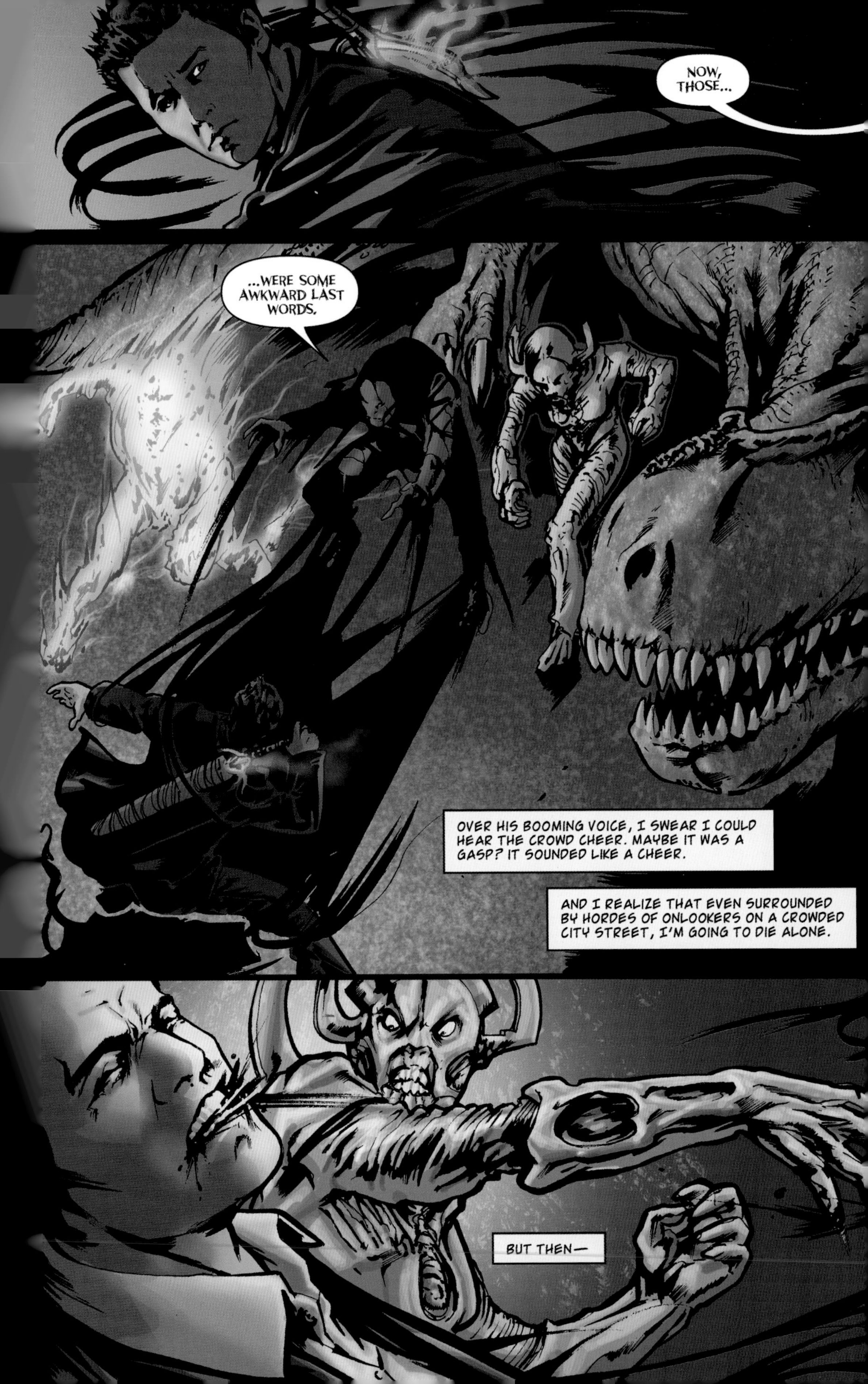
NOW, THOSE...
...WERE SOME AWKWARD LAST WORDS.
OVER HIS BOOMING VOICE, I SWEAR I COULD HEAR THE CROWD CHEER. MAYBE IT WAS A GASP? IT SOUNDED LIKE A CHEER.
AND I REALIZE THAT EVEN SURROUNDED BY HORDES OF ONLOOKERS ON A CROWDED CITY STREET, I'M GOING TO DIE ALONE.
BUT THEN—

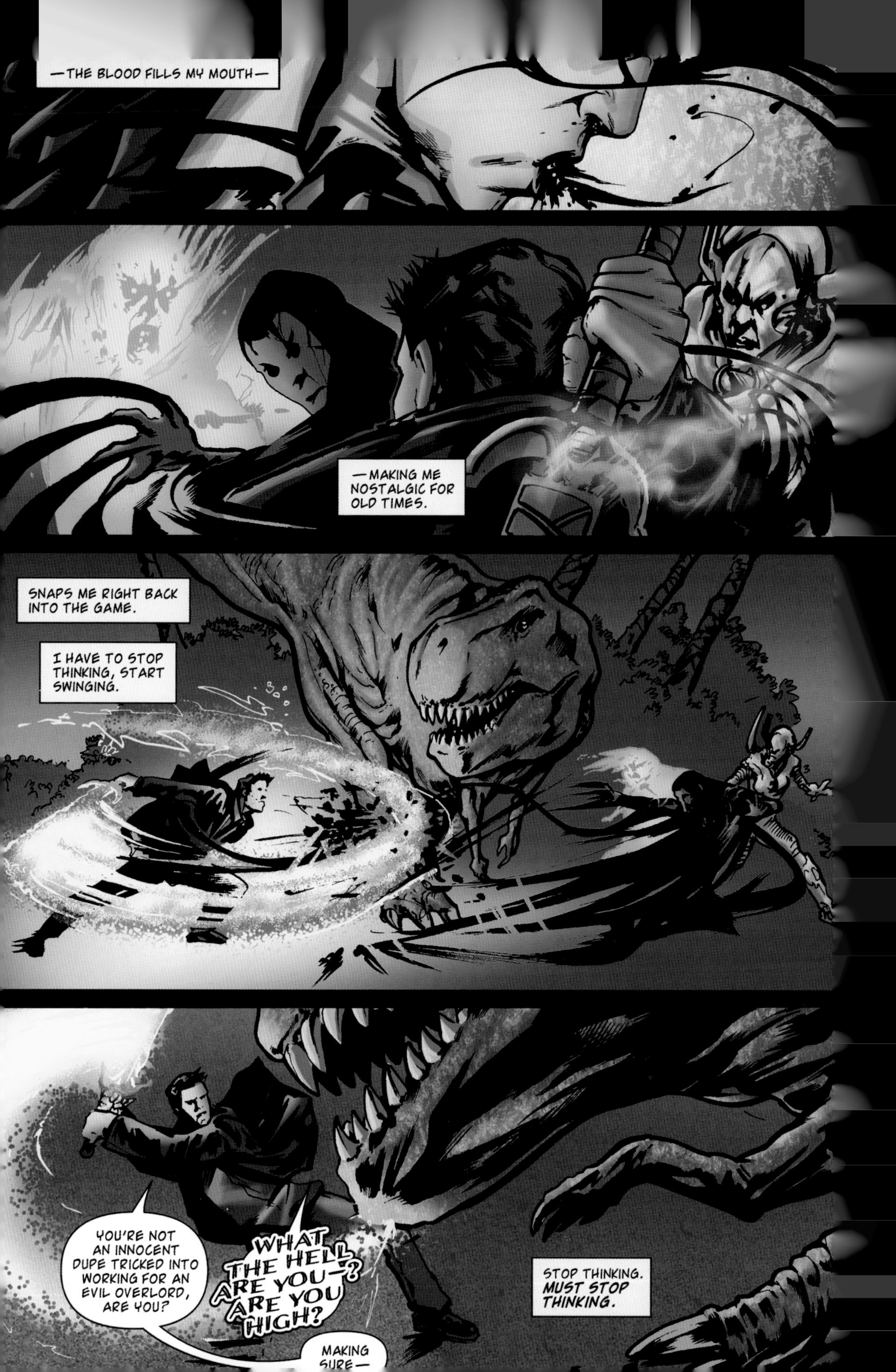
—THE BLOOD FILLS MY MOUTH—
—MAKING ME NOSTALGIC FOR OLD TIMES.
SNAPS ME RIGHT BACK INTO THE GAME.
I HAVE TO STOP THINKING, START SWINGING.
YOU'RE NOT AN INNOCENT DUPE TRICKED INTO WORKING FOR AN EVIL OVERLORD, ARE YOU?
WHAT THE HELL ARE YOU--? ARE YOU HIGH?
MAKING SURE—
STOP THINKING. MUST STOP THINKING.

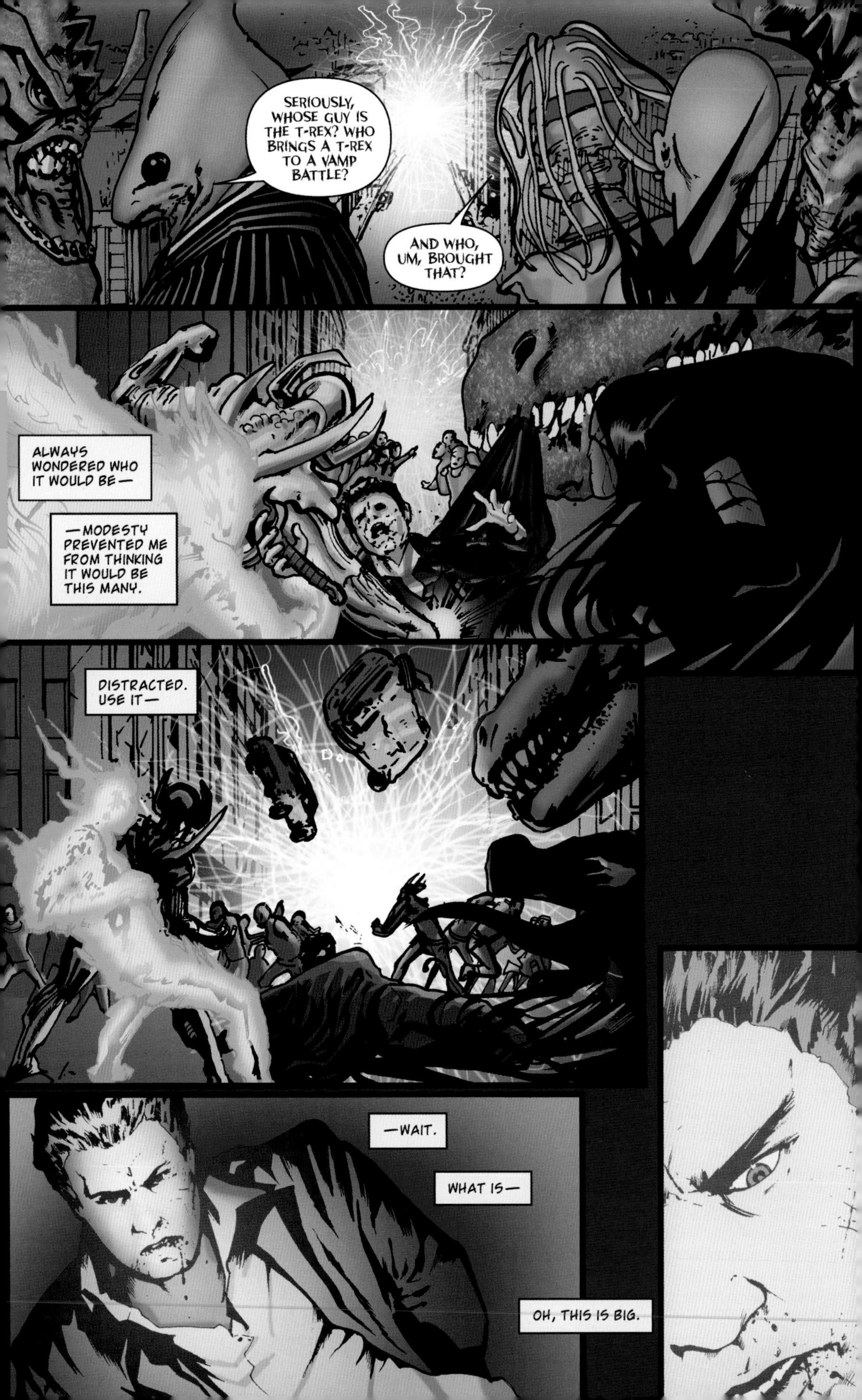
SERIOUSLY, WHOSE GUY IS THE T-REX? WHO BRINGS A T-REX TO A VAMP BATTLE?
AND WHO, UM, BROUGHT THAT?
ALWAYS WONDERED WHO IT WOULD BE—
—MODESTY PREVENTED ME FROM THINKING IT WOULD BE THIS MANY.
DISTRACTED. USE IT—
—WAIT.
WHAT IS—
OH, THIS IS BIG.

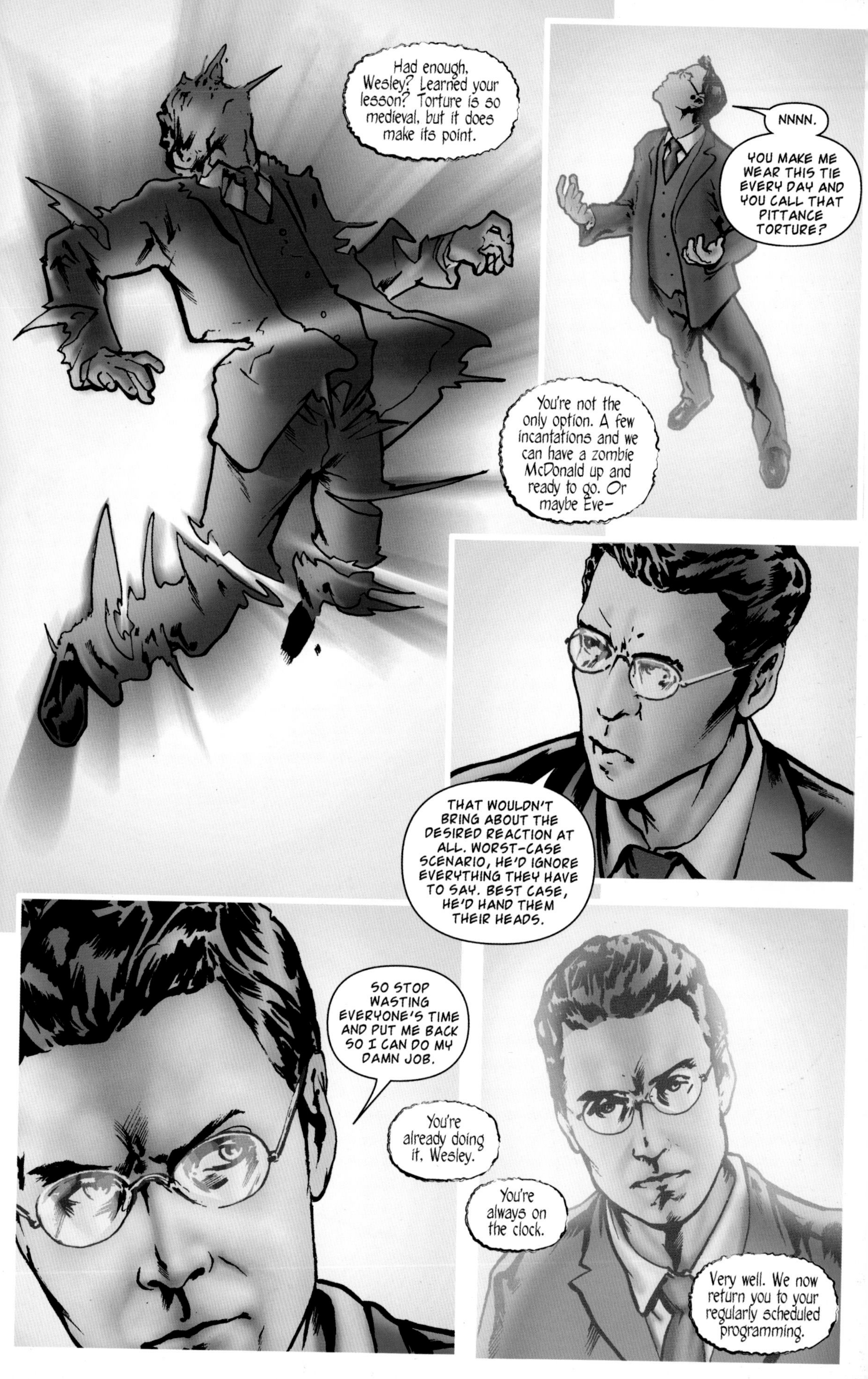
Had enough, Wesley? Learned your lesson? Torture is so medieval, but it does make its point.
NNNN.
YOU MAKE ME WEAR THIS TIE EVERY DAY AND YOU CALL THAT PITTANCE TORTURE?
You're not the only option. A few incantations and we can have a zombie McDonald up and ready to go. Or maybe Eve–
THAT WOULDN'T BRING ABOUT THE DESIRED REACTION AT ALL. WORST-CASE SCENARIO, HE'D IGNORE EVERYTHING THEY HAVE TO SAY. BEST CASE, HE'D HAND THEM THEIR HEADS.
SO STOP WASTING EVERYONE'S TIME AND PUT ME BACK SO I CAN DO MY DAMN JOB.
You're already doing it, Wesley.
You're always on the clock.
Very well. We now return you to your regularly scheduled programming.

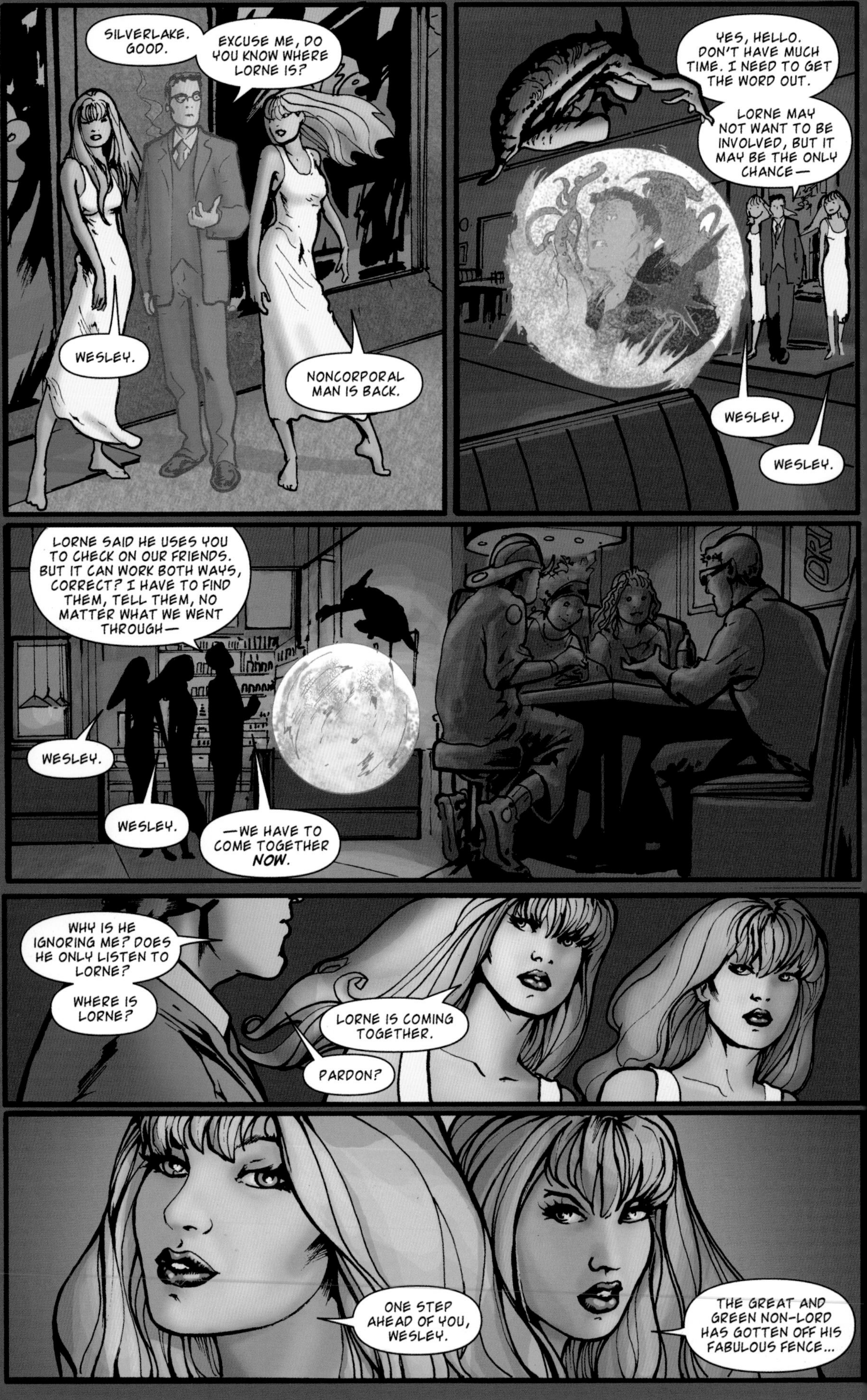
SILVERLAKE. GOOD.
EXCUSE ME, DO YOU KNOW WHERE LORNE IS?
WESLEY.
NONCORPORAL MAN IS BACK.
YES, HELLO. DON'T HAVE MUCH TIME. I NEED TO GET THE WORD OUT.
LORNE MAY NOT WANT TO BE INVOLVED, BUT IT MAY BE THE ONLY CHANCE—
WESLEY.
WESLEY.
LORNE SAID HE USES YOU TO CHECK ON OUR FRIENDS. BUT IT CAN WORK BOTH WAYS, CORRECT? I HAVE TO FIND THEM, TELL THEM, NO MATTER WHAT WE WENT THROUGH—
WESLEY.
WESLEY.
—WE HAVE TO COME TOGETHER *NOW*.
WHY IS HE IGNORING ME? DOES HE ONLY LISTEN TO LORNE?
WHERE IS LORNE?
LORNE IS COMING TOGETHER.
PARDON?
ONE STEP AHEAD OF YOU, WESLEY.
THE GREAT AND GREEN NON-LORD HAS GOTTEN OFF HIS FABULOUS FENCE...

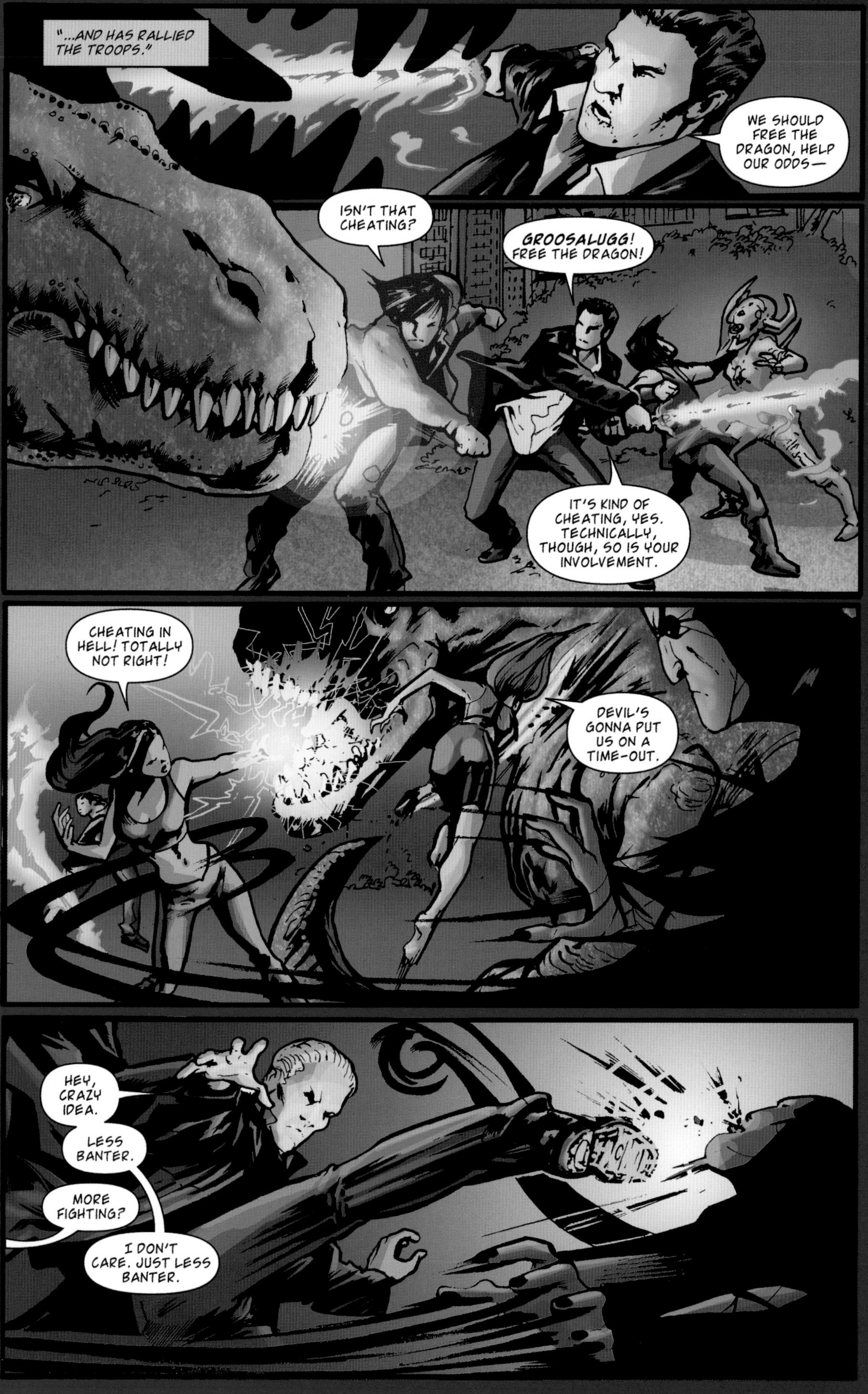
"...AND HAS RALLIED THE TROOPS."
WE SHOULD FREE THE DRAGON, HELP OUR ODDS—
ISN'T THAT CHEATING?
GROOSALUGG! FREE THE DRAGON!
IT'S KIND OF CHEATING, YES. TECHNICALLY, THOUGH, SO IS YOUR INVOLVEMENT.
CHEATING IN HELL! TOTALLY NOT RIGHT!
DEVIL'S GONNA PUT US ON A TIME-OUT.
HEY, CRAZY IDEA.
LESS BANTER.
MORE FIGHTING?
I DON'T CARE. JUST LESS BANTER.

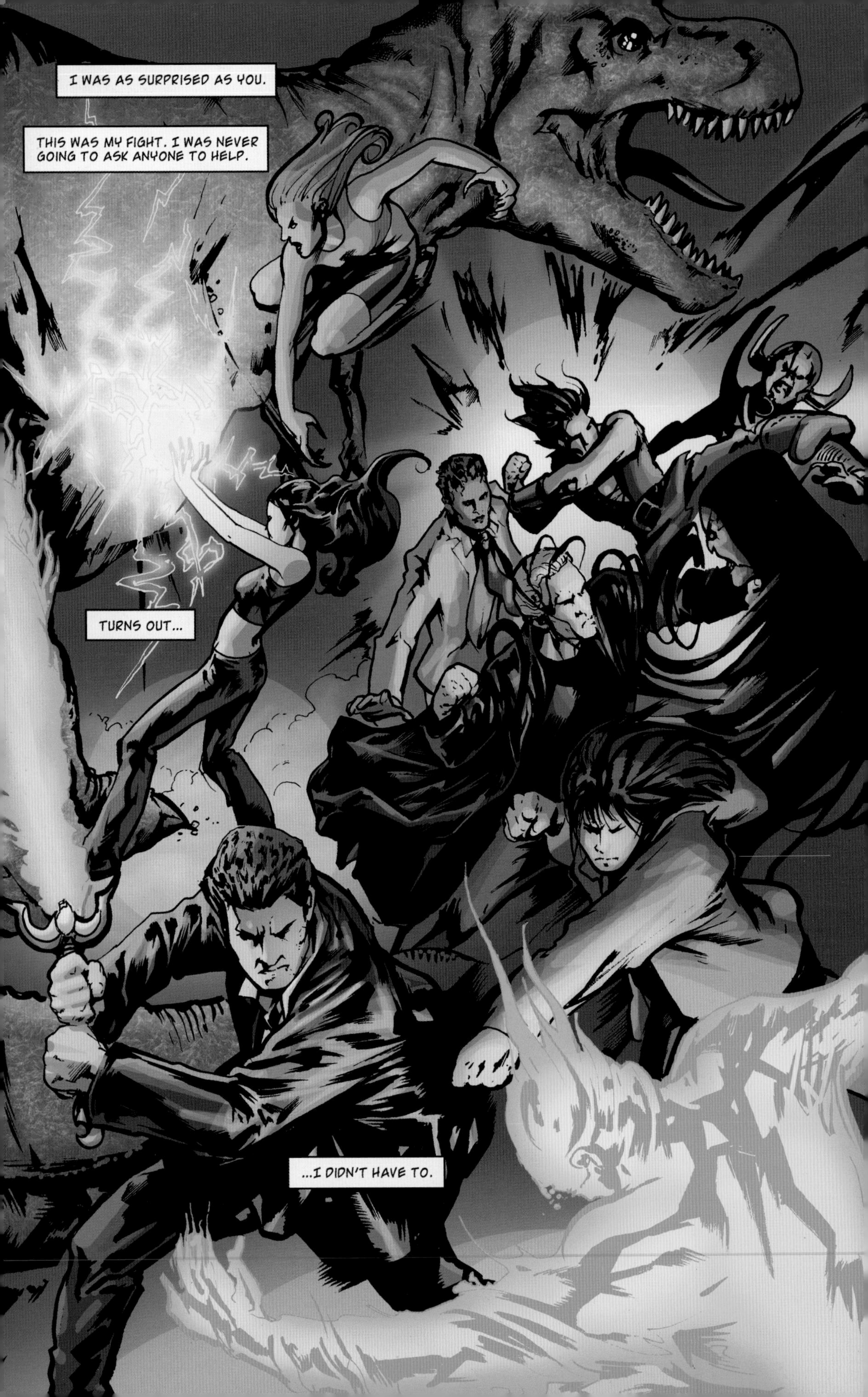
I WAS AS SURPRISED AS YOU.
THIS WAS MY FIGHT. I WAS NEVER GOING TO ASK ANYONE TO HELP.
TURNS OUT...
...I DIDN'T HAVE TO.

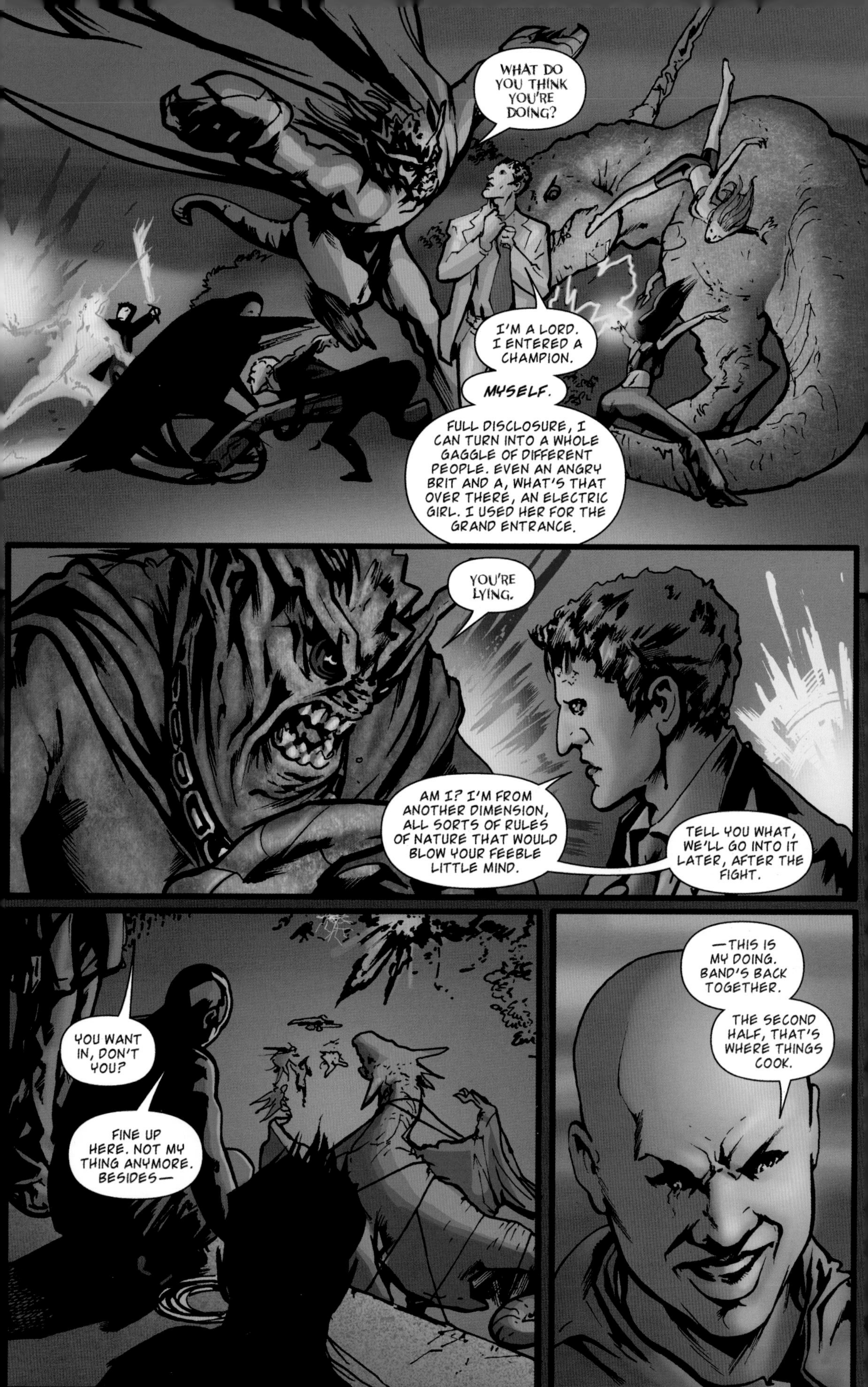
WHAT DO YOU THINK YOU'RE DOING?
I'M A LORD. I ENTERED A CHAMPION.
MYSELF.
FULL DISCLOSURE, I CAN TURN INTO A WHOLE GAGGLE OF DIFFERENT PEOPLE. EVEN AN ANGRY BRIT AND A, WHAT'S THAT OVER THERE, AN ELECTRIC GIRL. I USED HER FOR THE GRAND ENTRANCE.
YOU'RE LYING.
AM I? I'M FROM ANOTHER DIMENSION, ALL SORTS OF RULES OF NATURE THAT WOULD BLOW YOUR FEEBLE LITTLE MIND.
TELL YOU WHAT, WE'LL GO INTO IT LATER, AFTER THE FIGHT.
YOU WANT IN, DON'T YOU?
FINE UP HERE. NOT MY THING ANYMORE. BESIDES—
—THIS IS MY DOING. BAND'S BACK TOGETHER.
THE SECOND HALF, THAT'S WHERE THINGS COOK.

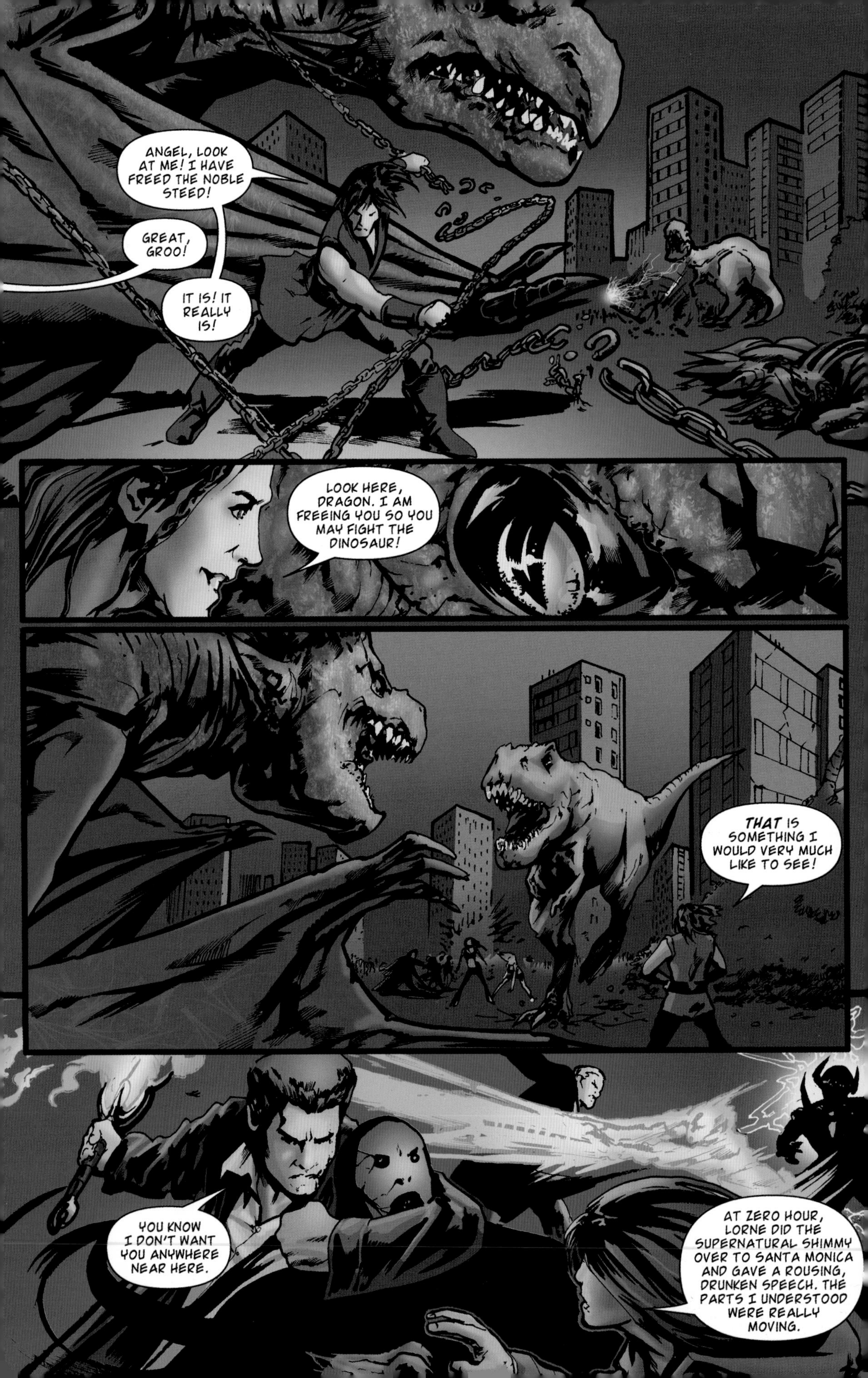
ANGEL, LOOK AT ME! I HAVE FREED THE NOBLE STEED!
GREAT, GROO!
IT IS! IT REALLY IS!
LOOK HERE, DRAGON. I AM FREEING YOU SO YOU MAY FIGHT THE DINOSAUR!
THAT IS SOMETHING I WOULD VERY MUCH LIKE TO SEE!
YOU KNOW I DON'T WANT YOU ANYWHERE NEAR HERE.
AT ZERO HOUR, LORNE DID THE SUPERNATURAL SHIMMY OVER TO SANTA MONICA AND GAVE A ROUSING, DRUNKEN SPEECH. THE PARTS I UNDERSTOOD WERE REALLY MOVING.

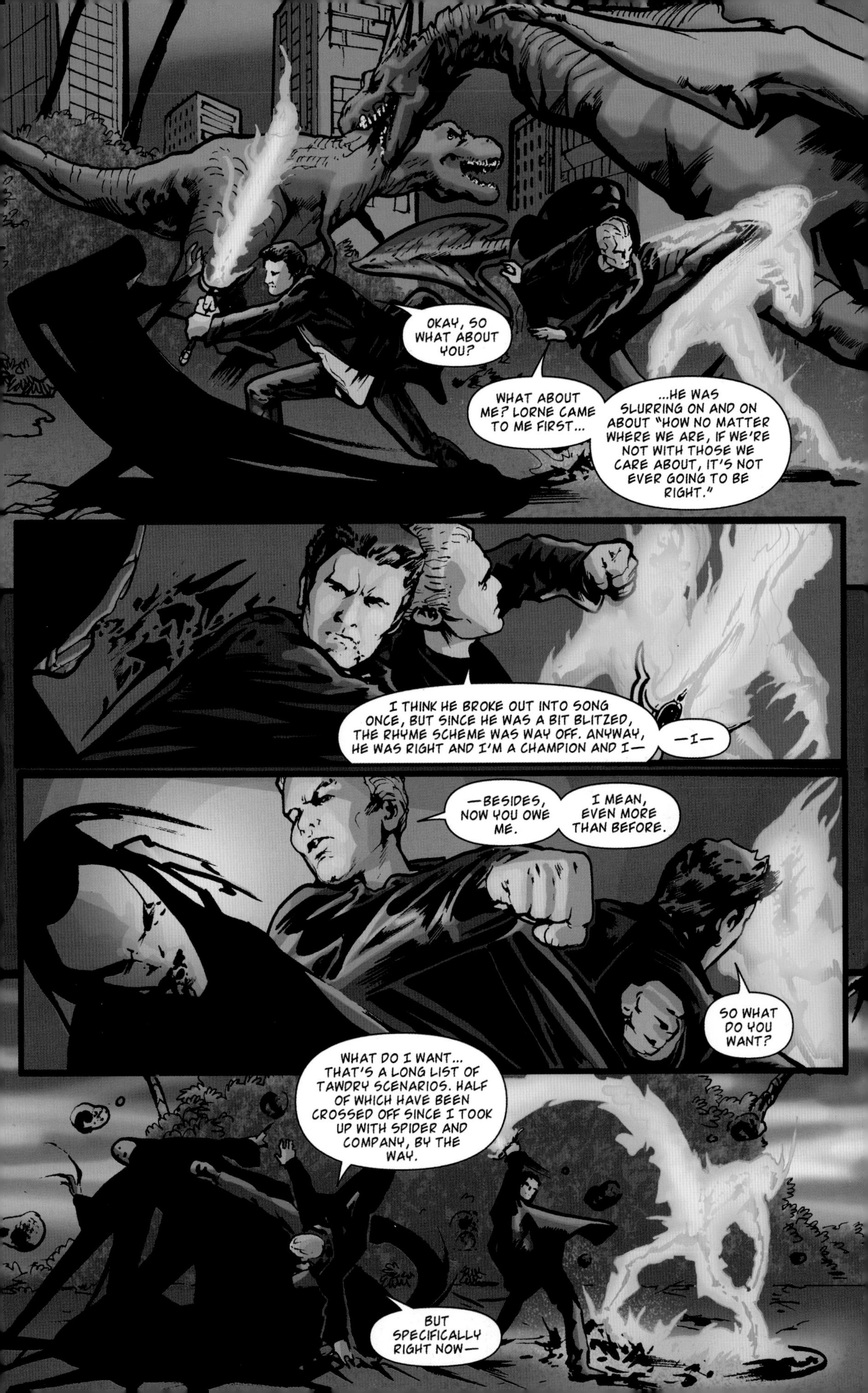
OKAY, SO WHAT ABOUT YOU?
WHAT ABOUT ME? LORNE CAME TO ME FIRST...
...HE WAS SLURRING ON AND ON ABOUT "HOW NO MATTER WHERE WE ARE, IF WE'RE NOT WITH THOSE WE CARE ABOUT, IT'S NOT EVER GOING TO BE RIGHT."
I THINK HE BROKE OUT INTO SONG ONCE, BUT SINCE HE WAS A BIT BLITZED, THE RHYME SCHEME WAS WAY OFF. ANYWAY, HE WAS RIGHT AND I'M A CHAMPION AND I—
—I—
—BESIDES, NOW YOU OWE ME.
I MEAN, EVEN MORE THAN BEFORE.
SO WHAT DO YOU WANT?
WHAT DO I WANT... THAT'S A LONG LIST OF TAWDRY SCENARIOS. HALF OF WHICH HAVE BEEN CROSSED OFF SINCE I TOOK UP WITH SPIDER AND COMPANY, BY THE WAY.
BUT SPECIFICALLY RIGHT NOW—

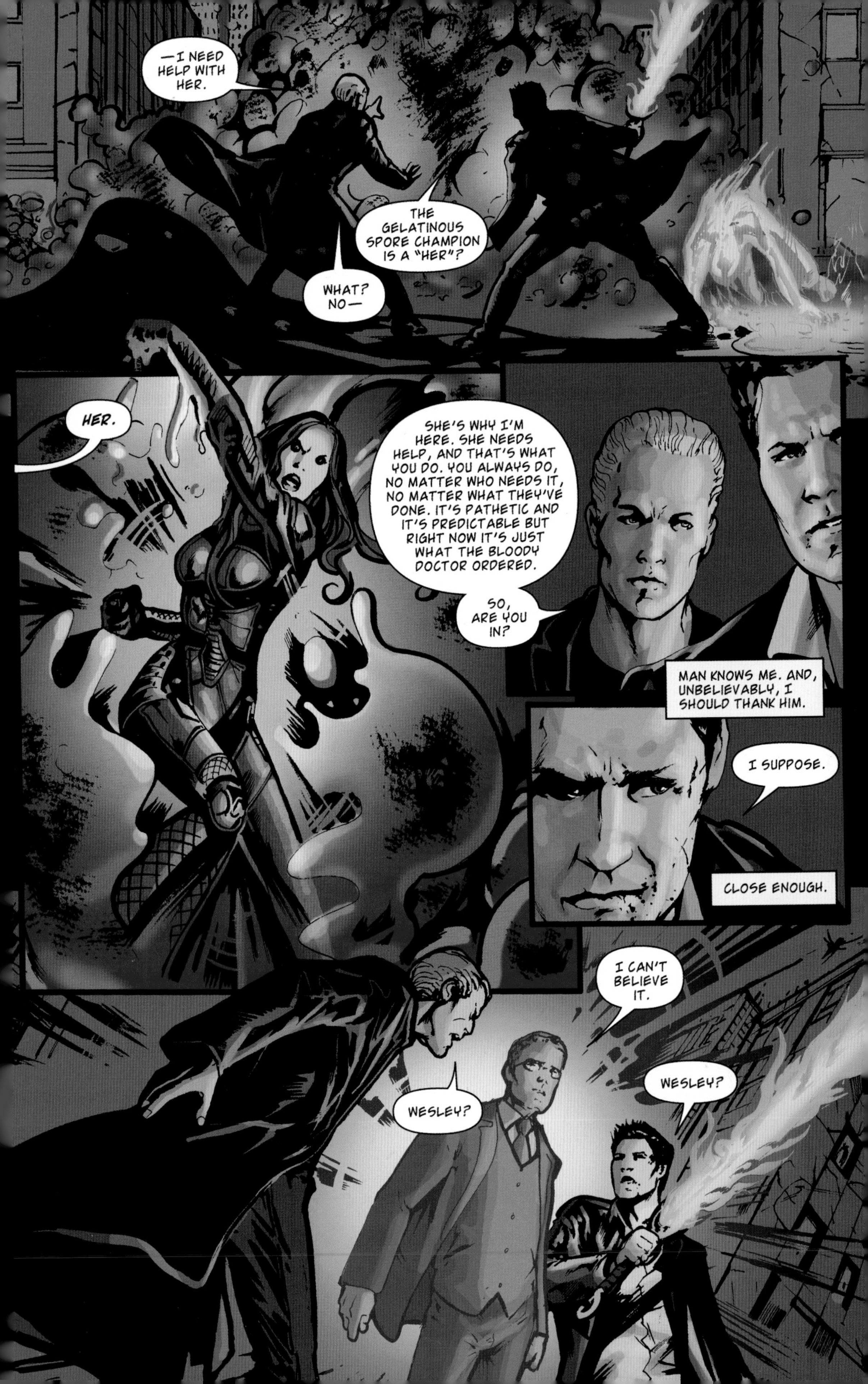
—I NEED HELP WITH HER.
THE GELATINOUS SPORE CHAMPION IS A "HER"?
WHAT? NO—
HER.
SHE'S WHY I'M HERE. SHE NEEDS HELP, AND THAT'S WHAT YOU DO. YOU ALWAYS DO, NO MATTER WHO NEEDS IT, NO MATTER WHAT THEY'VE DONE. IT'S PATHETIC AND IT'S PREDICTABLE BUT RIGHT NOW IT'S JUST WHAT THE BLOODY DOCTOR ORDERED.
SO, ARE YOU IN?
MAN KNOWS ME. AND, UNBELIEVABLY, I SHOULD THANK HIM.
I SUPPOSE.
CLOSE ENOUGH.
I CAN'T BELIEVE IT.
WESLEY?
WESLEY?

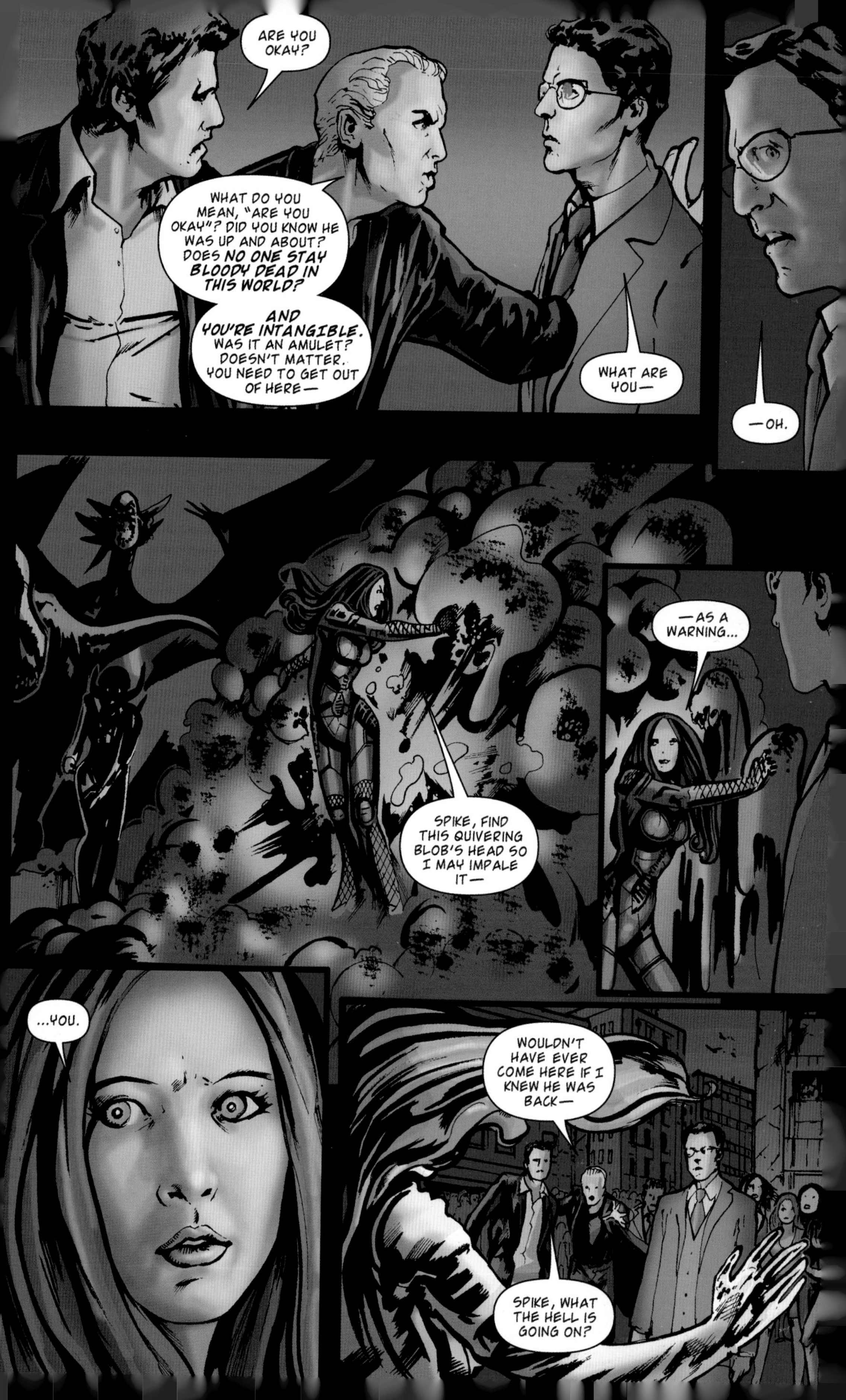
ARE YOU OKAY?
WHAT DO YOU MEAN, "ARE YOU OKAY"? DID YOU KNOW HE WAS UP AND ABOUT? DOES NO ONE STAY BLOODY DEAD IN THIS WORLD?
AND YOU'RE INTANGIBLE. WAS IT AN AMULET? DOESN'T MATTER. YOU NEED TO GET OUT OF HERE—
WHAT ARE YOU—
—OH.
SPIKE, FIND THIS QUIVERING BLOB'S HEAD SO I MAY IMPALE IT—
—AS A WARNING...
...YOU.
WOULDN'T HAVE EVER COME HERE IF I KNEW HE WAS BACK—
SPIKE, WHAT THE HELL IS GOING ON?

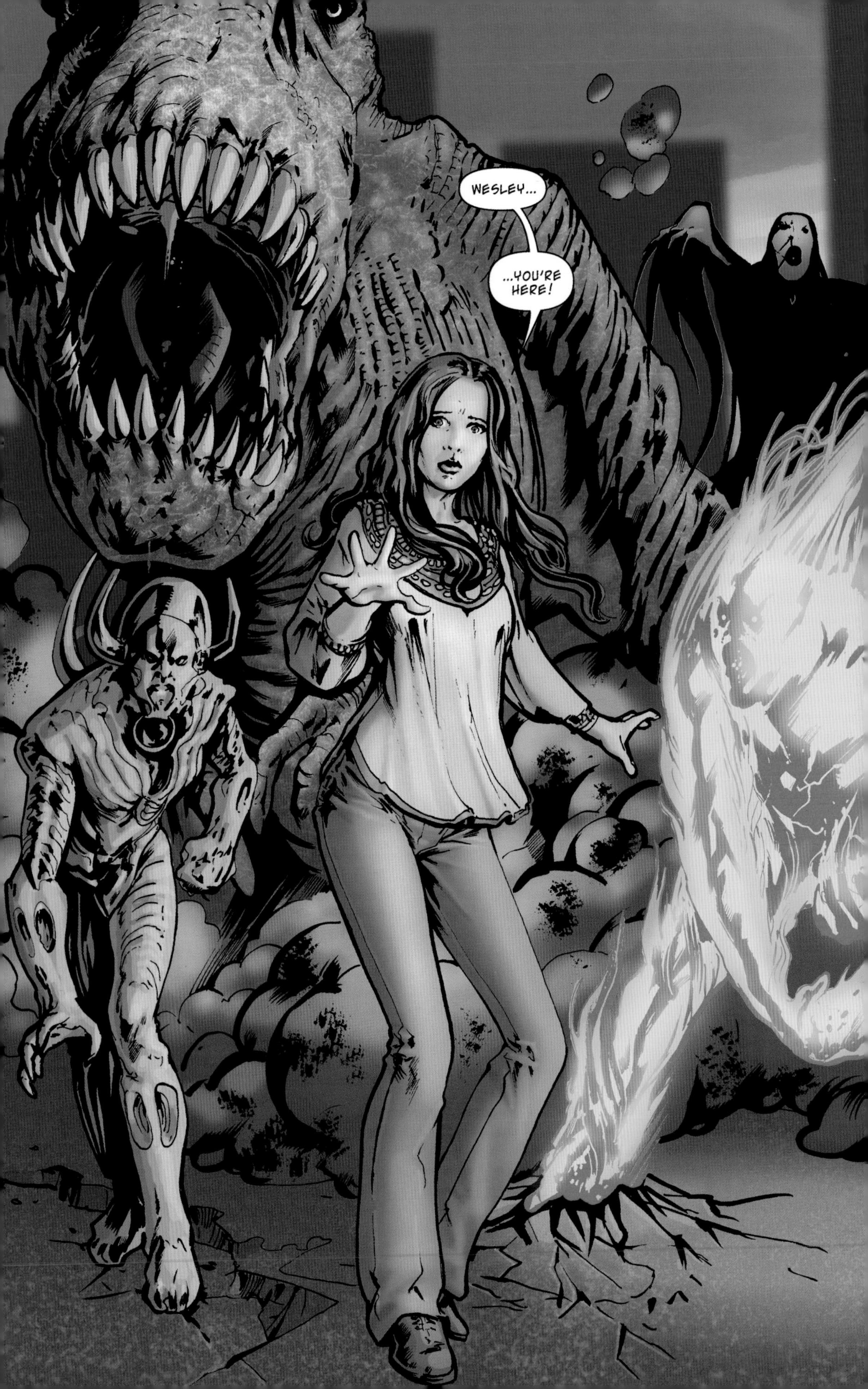
WESLEY...
...YOU'RE HERE!

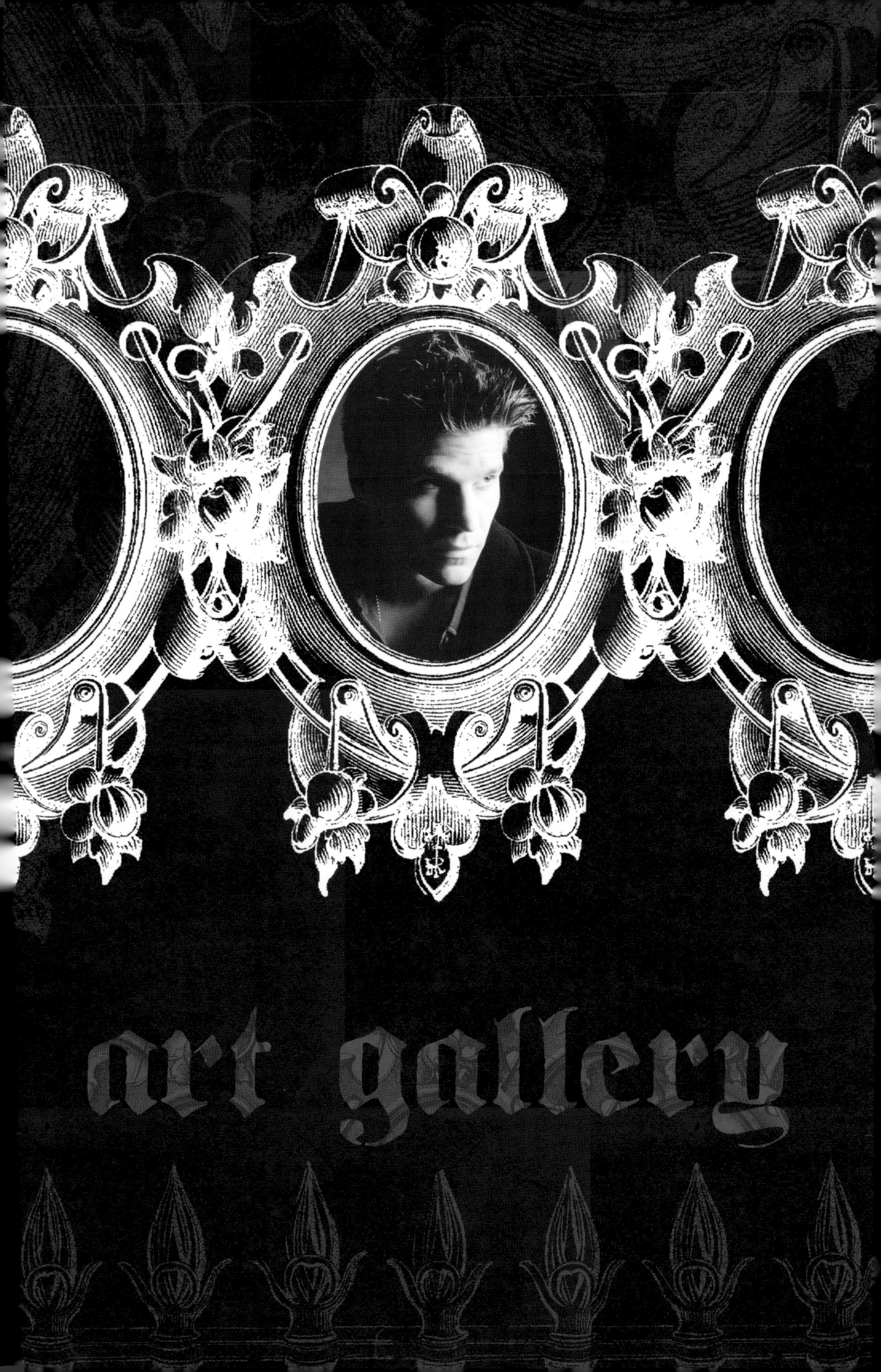

art gallery

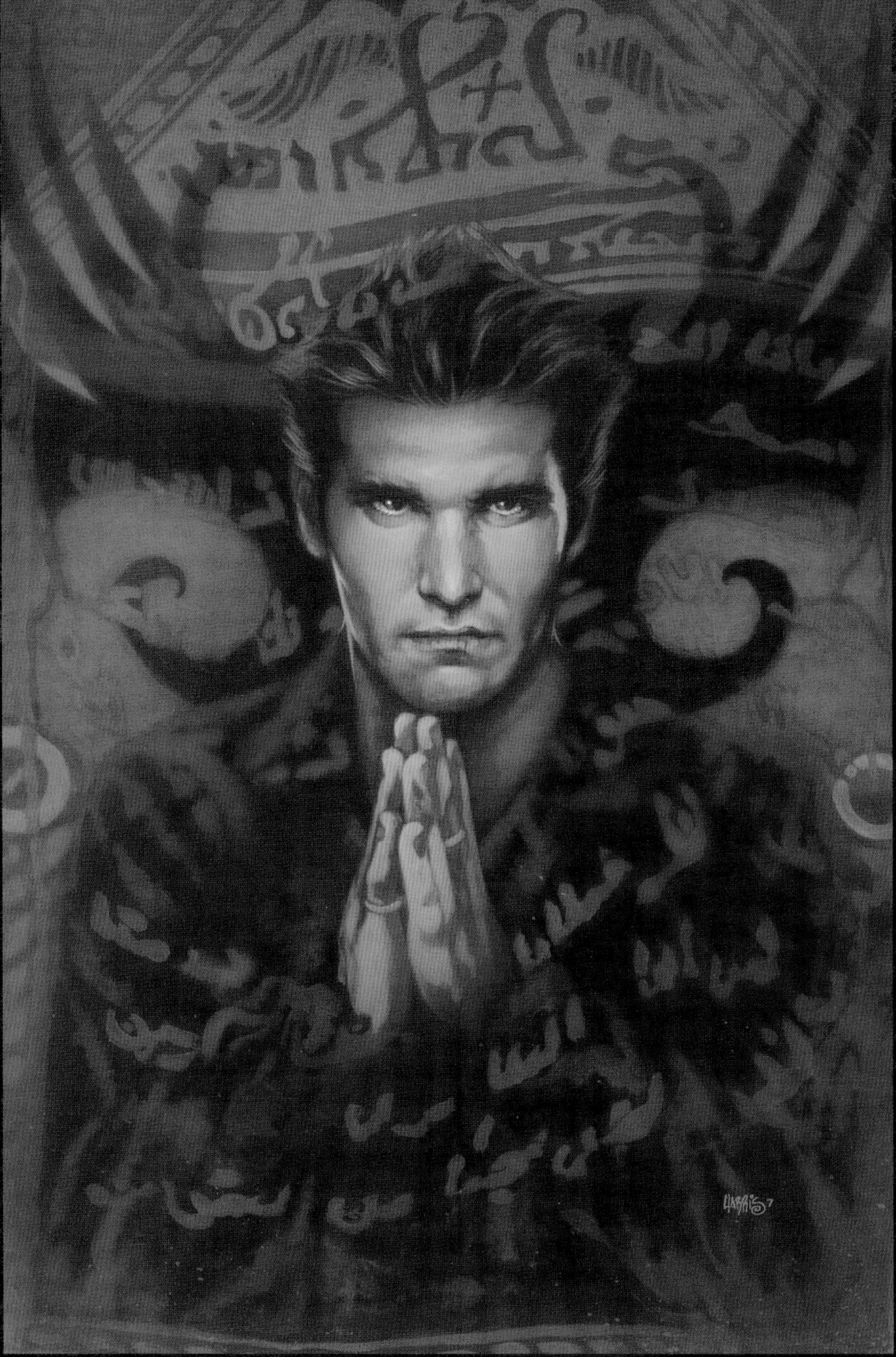
HARRIS

This Page: Art by Tony Harris

Opposite Page: Art by Franco Urru
Colors by Paolo Maddaleni

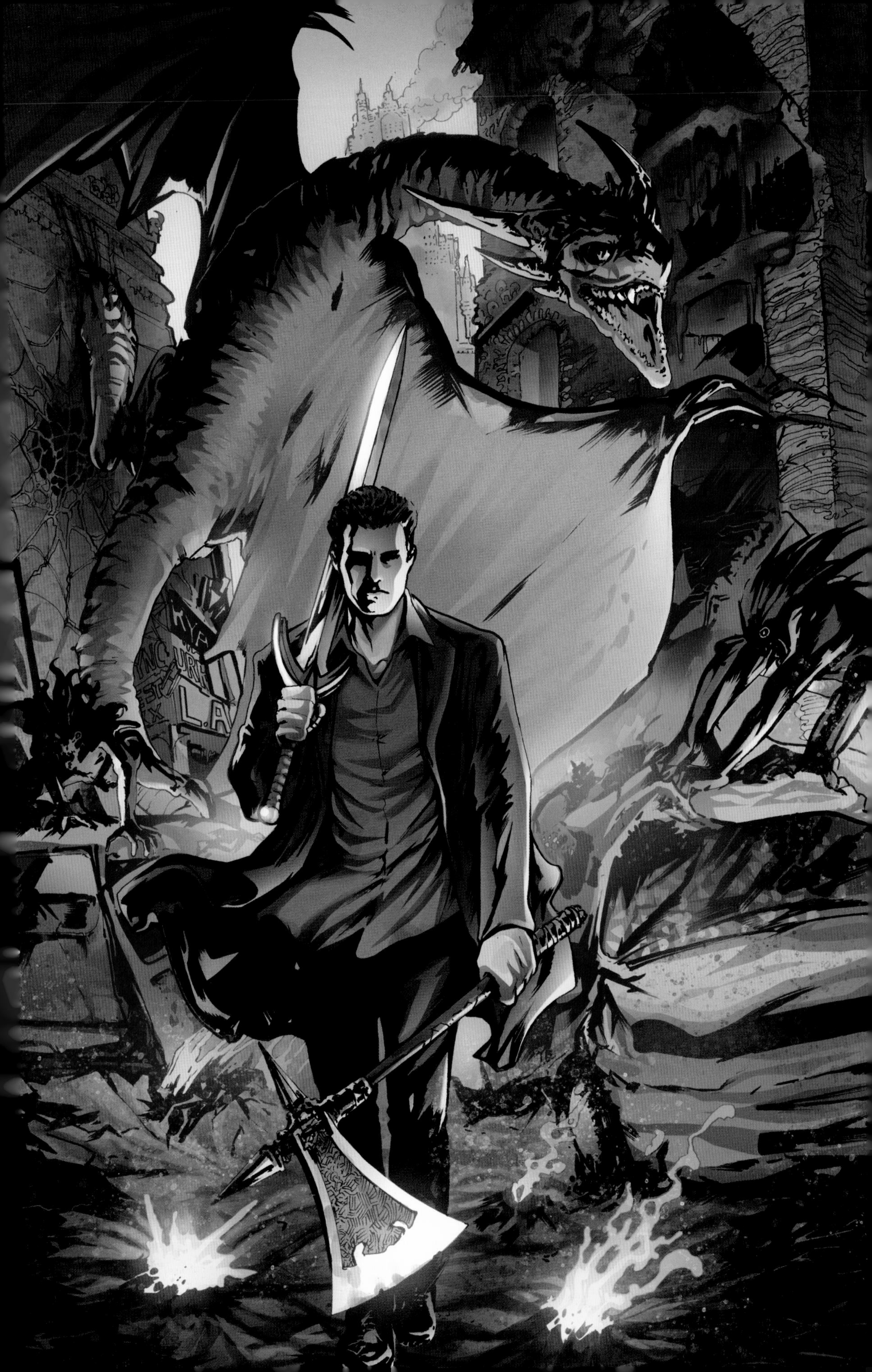

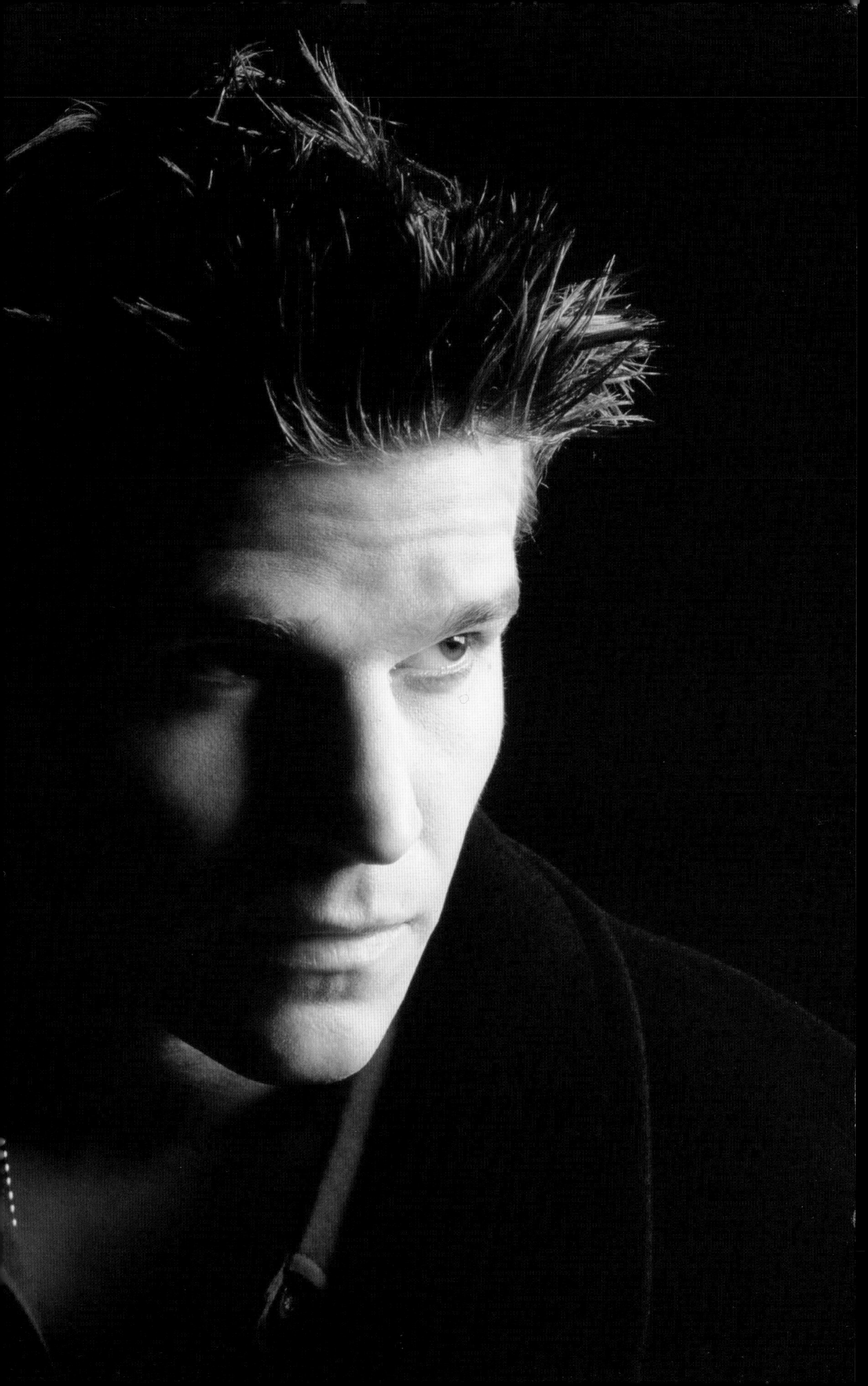

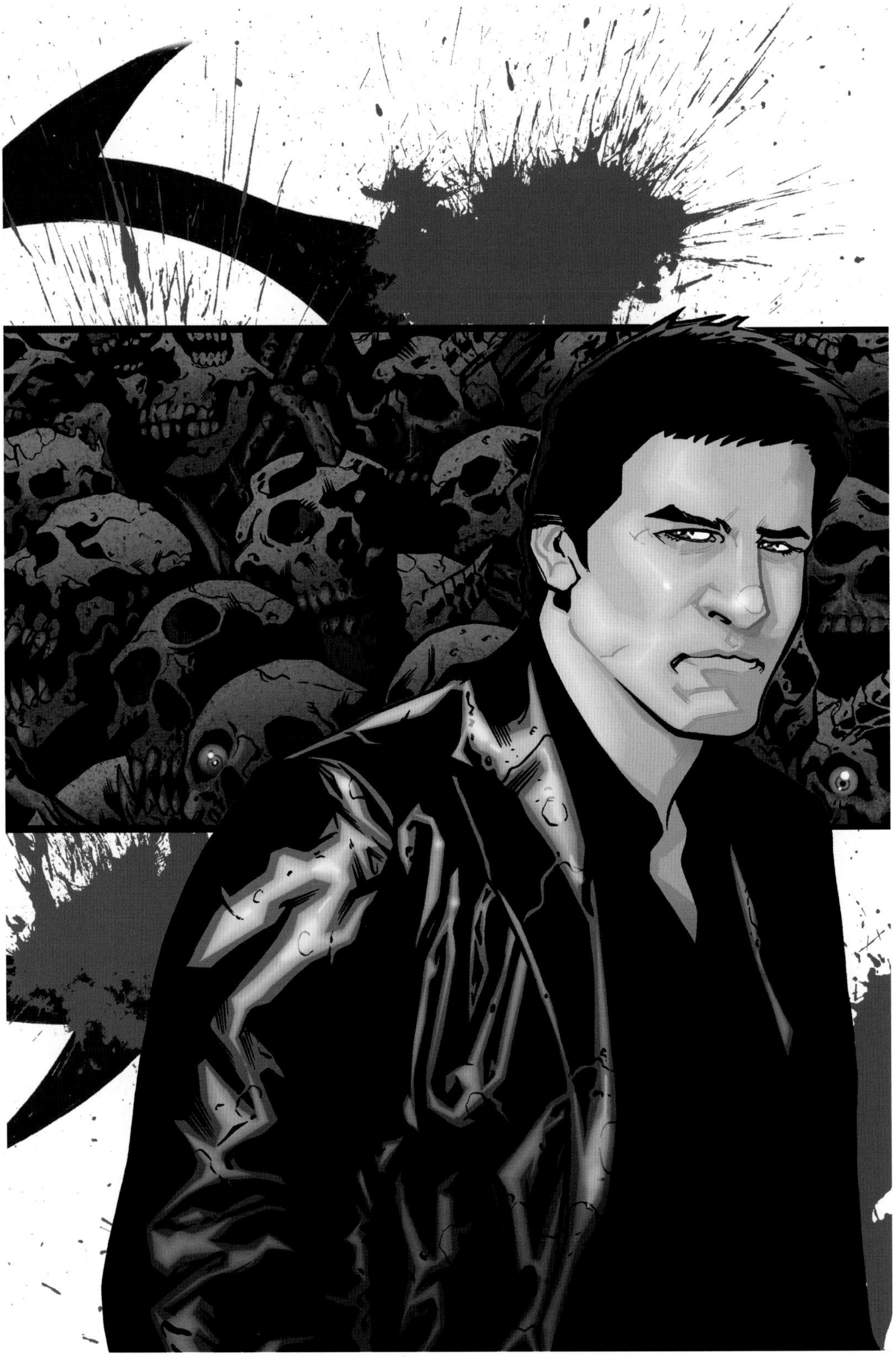

This Page: Art by David Messina and Patrick Brower

Opposite Page: Art by Franco Urru

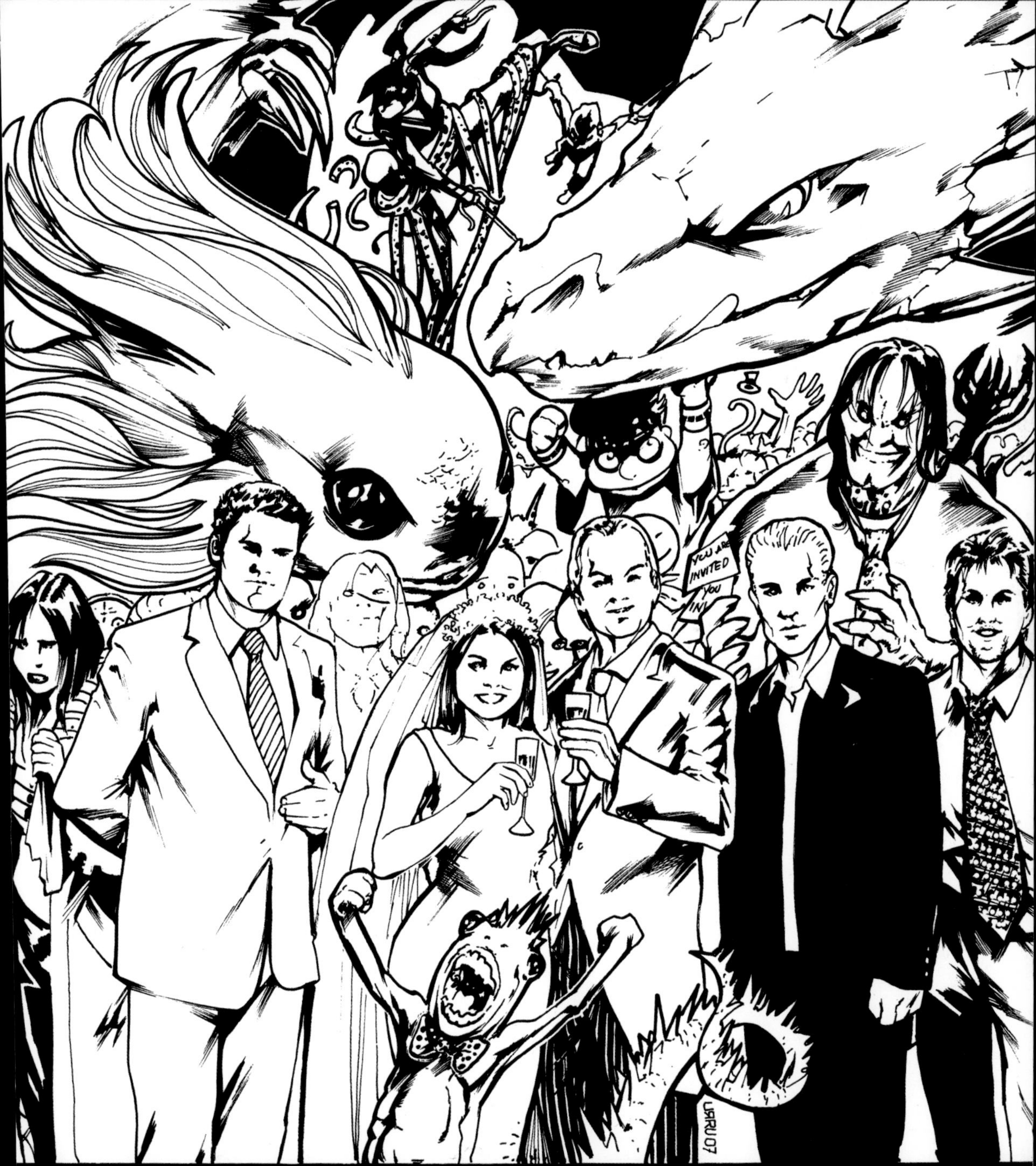
YOU ARE INVITED
YOU

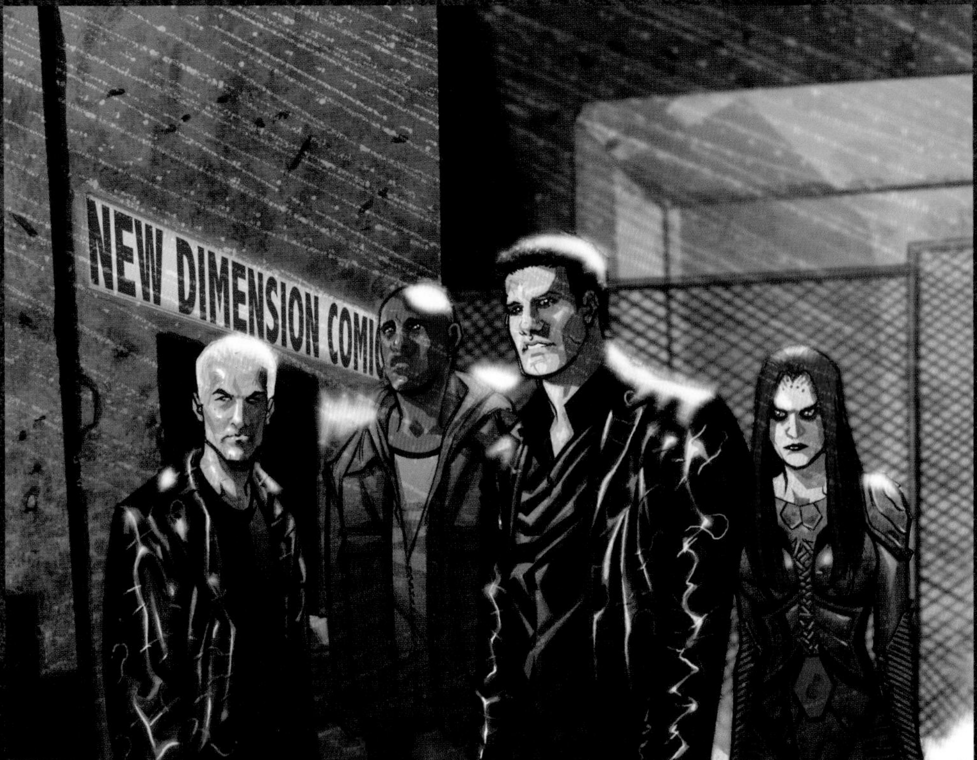
NEW DIMENSION COMI

This Page: Art by David Messina

Opposite Page: Art by Tony Harris

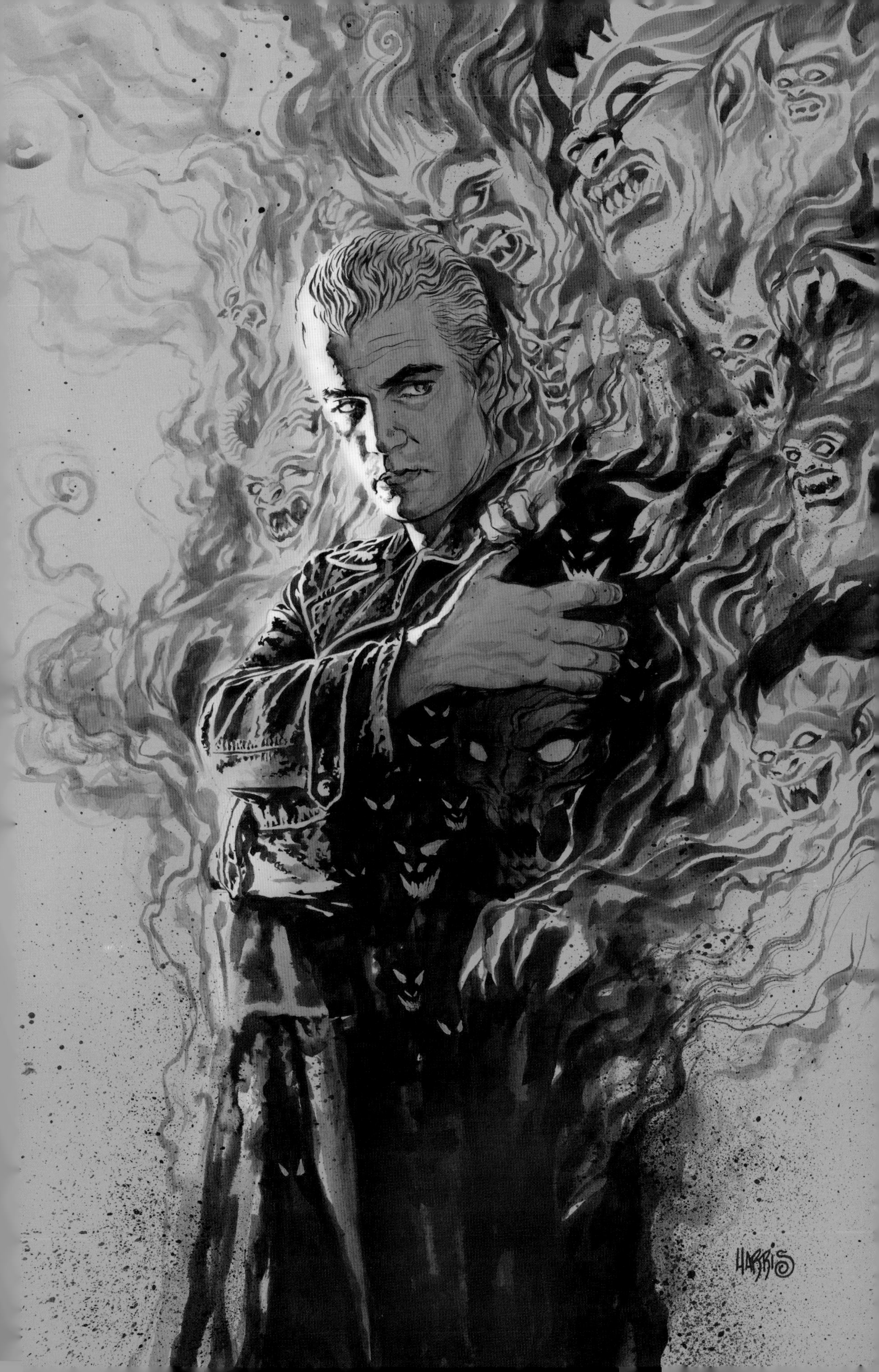
HARRIS

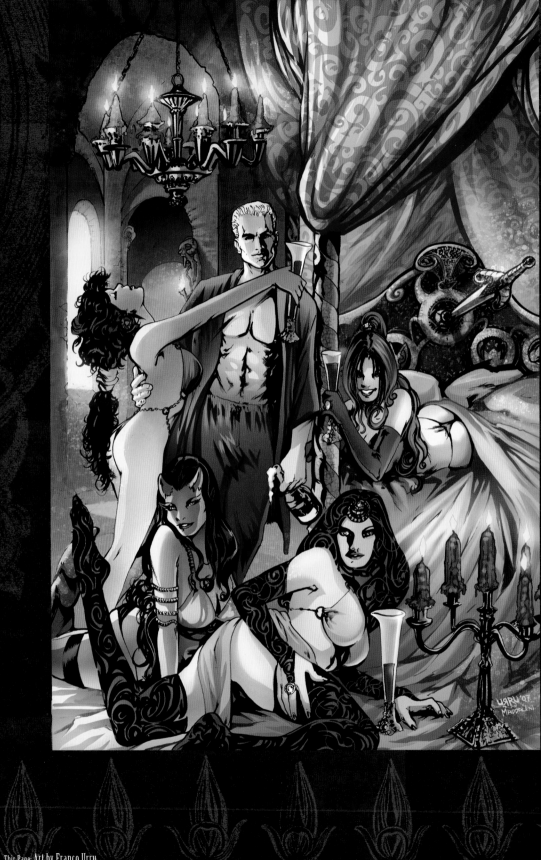

This Page: Art by Franco Urru
Colors by Paolo Maddaleni

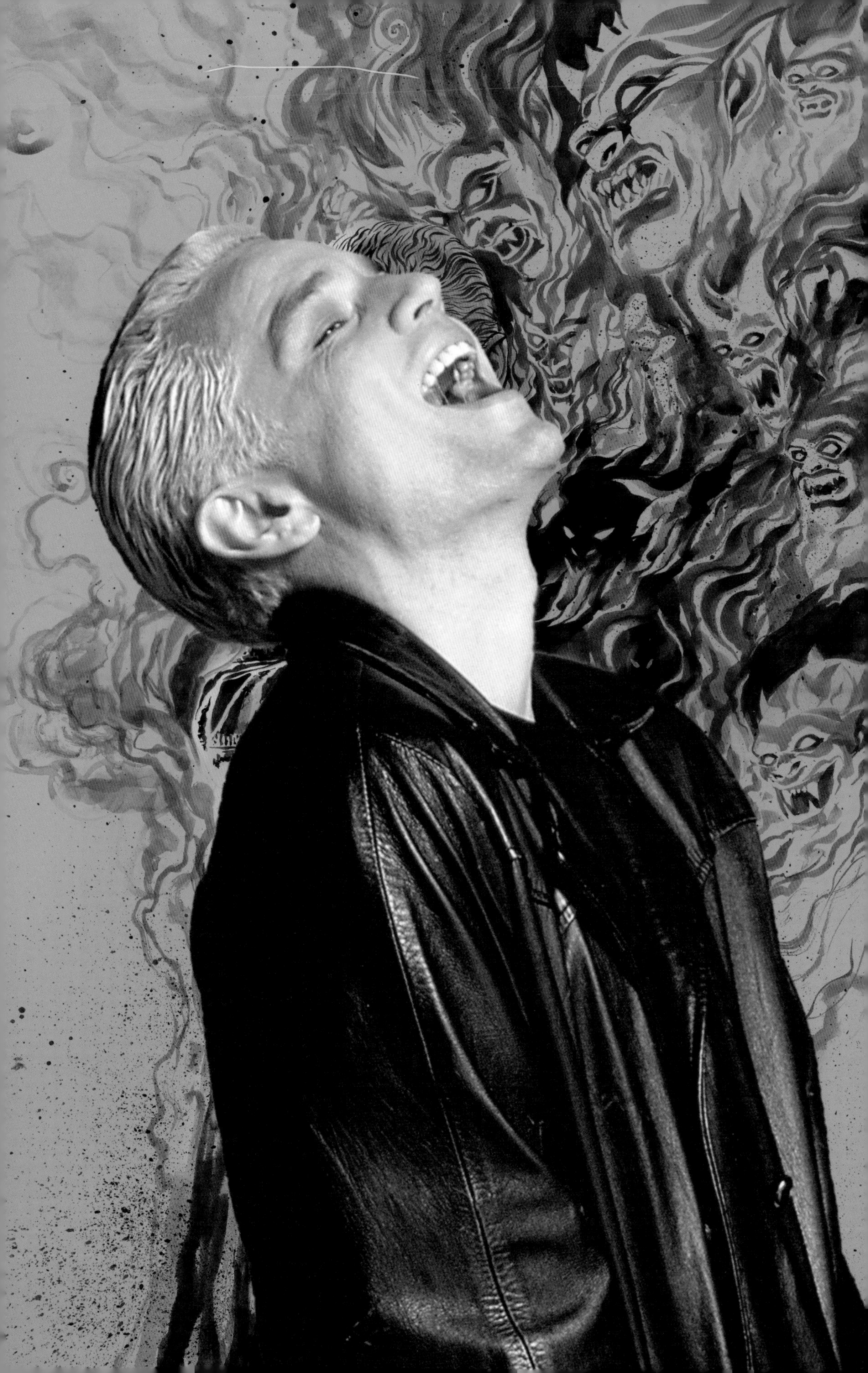

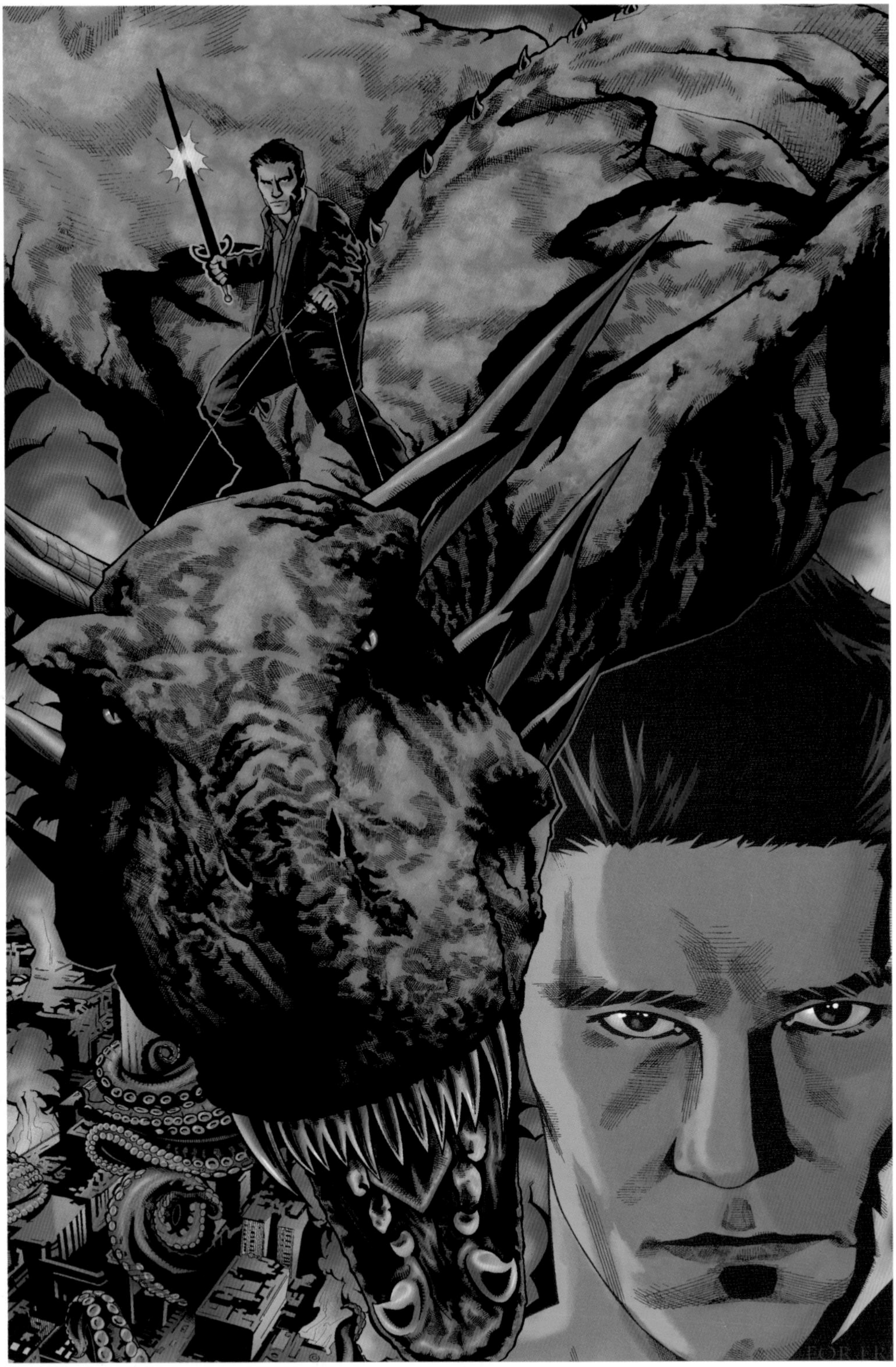

This Page: Art by Stephen Mooney
Colors by Lisa Jackson

Opposite Page: Art by Franco Urru
Colors by Paolo Maddaleni

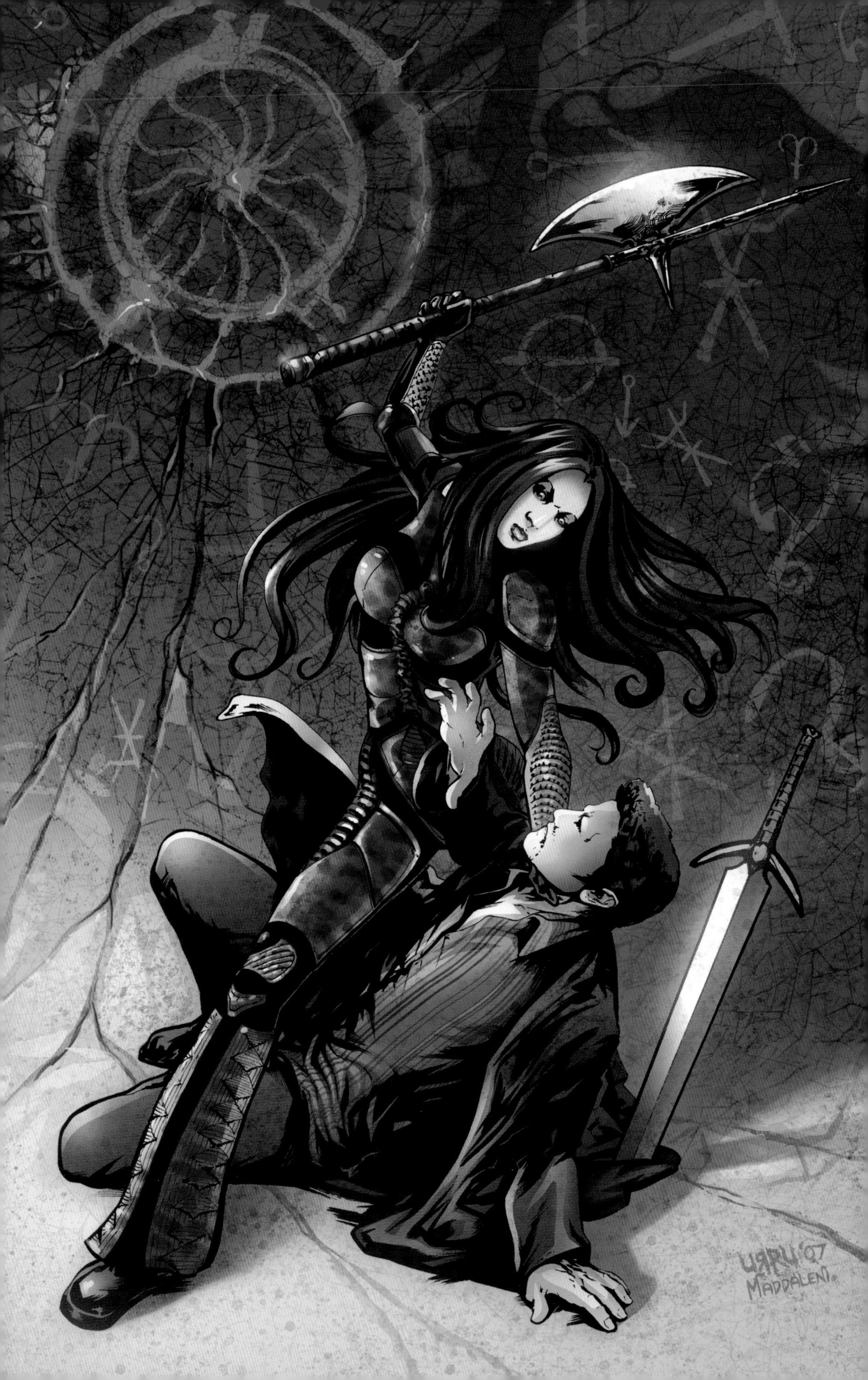

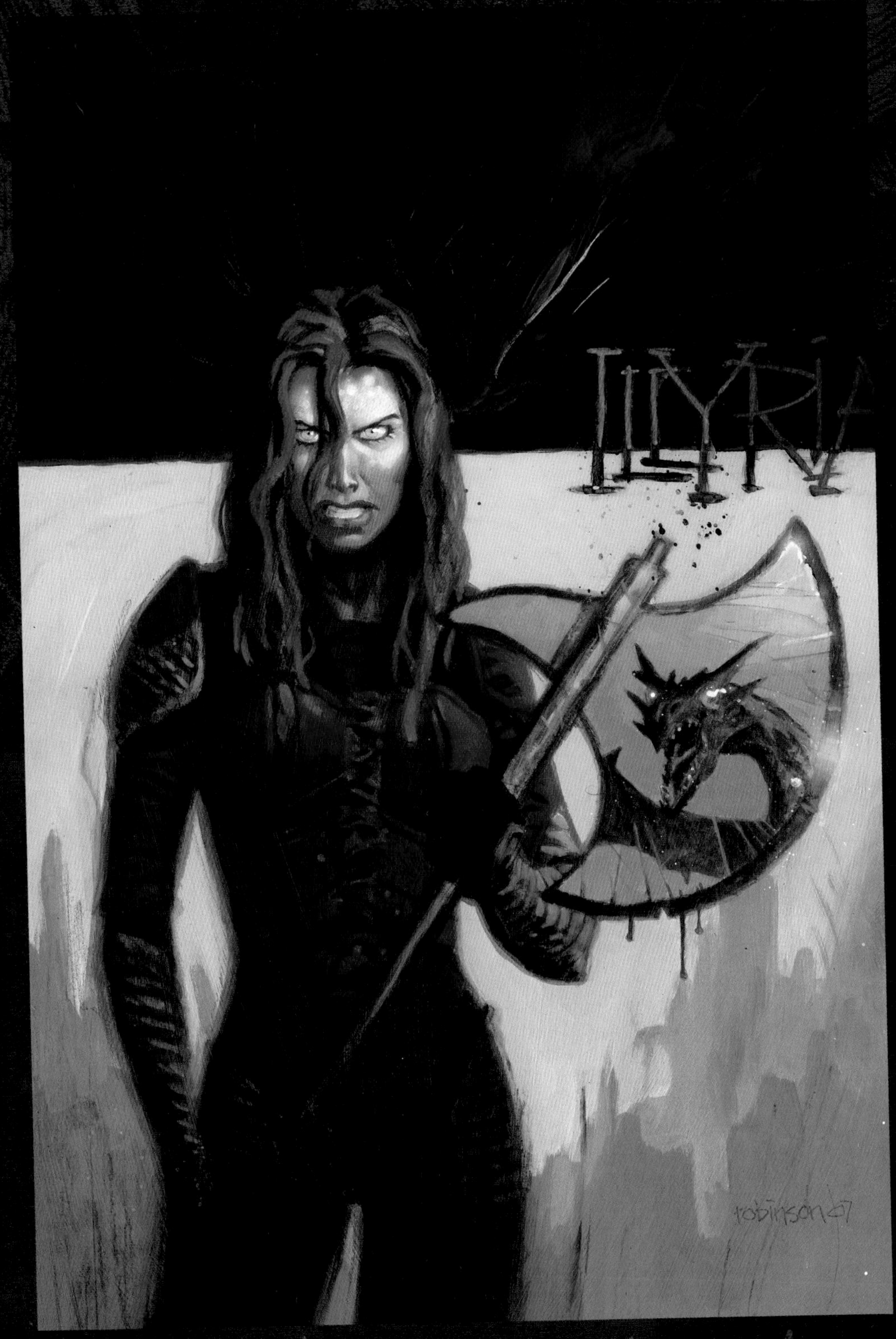
ILLYRIA
robinson 07

This Page: Art by Andrew Robinson

Opposite Page: Art by Stephen Mooney
Colors by Lisa Jackson

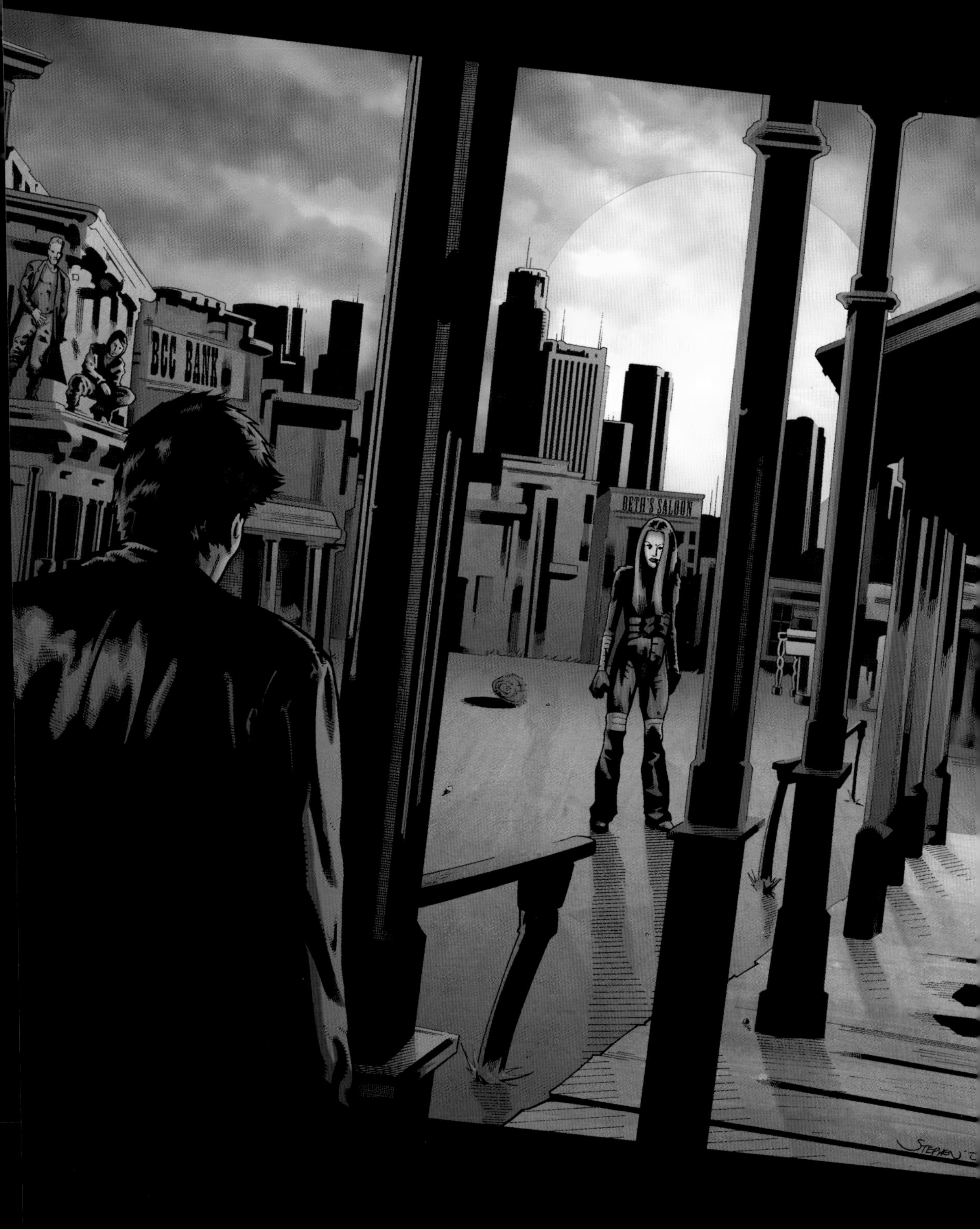
BCC BANK
BETH'S SALOON

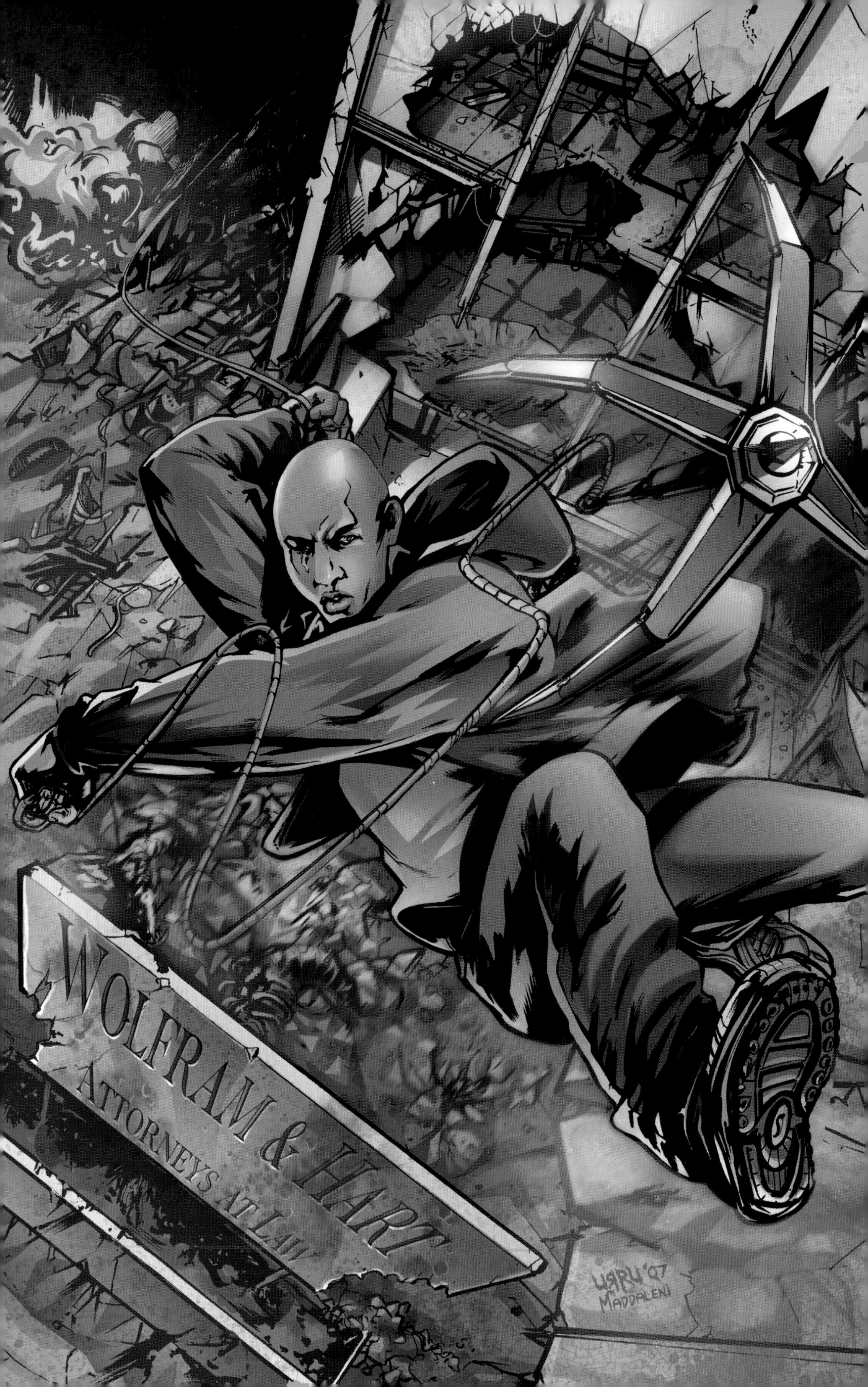
WOLFRAM & HART
ATTORNEYS AT LAW
URRU '07
MADDALENI

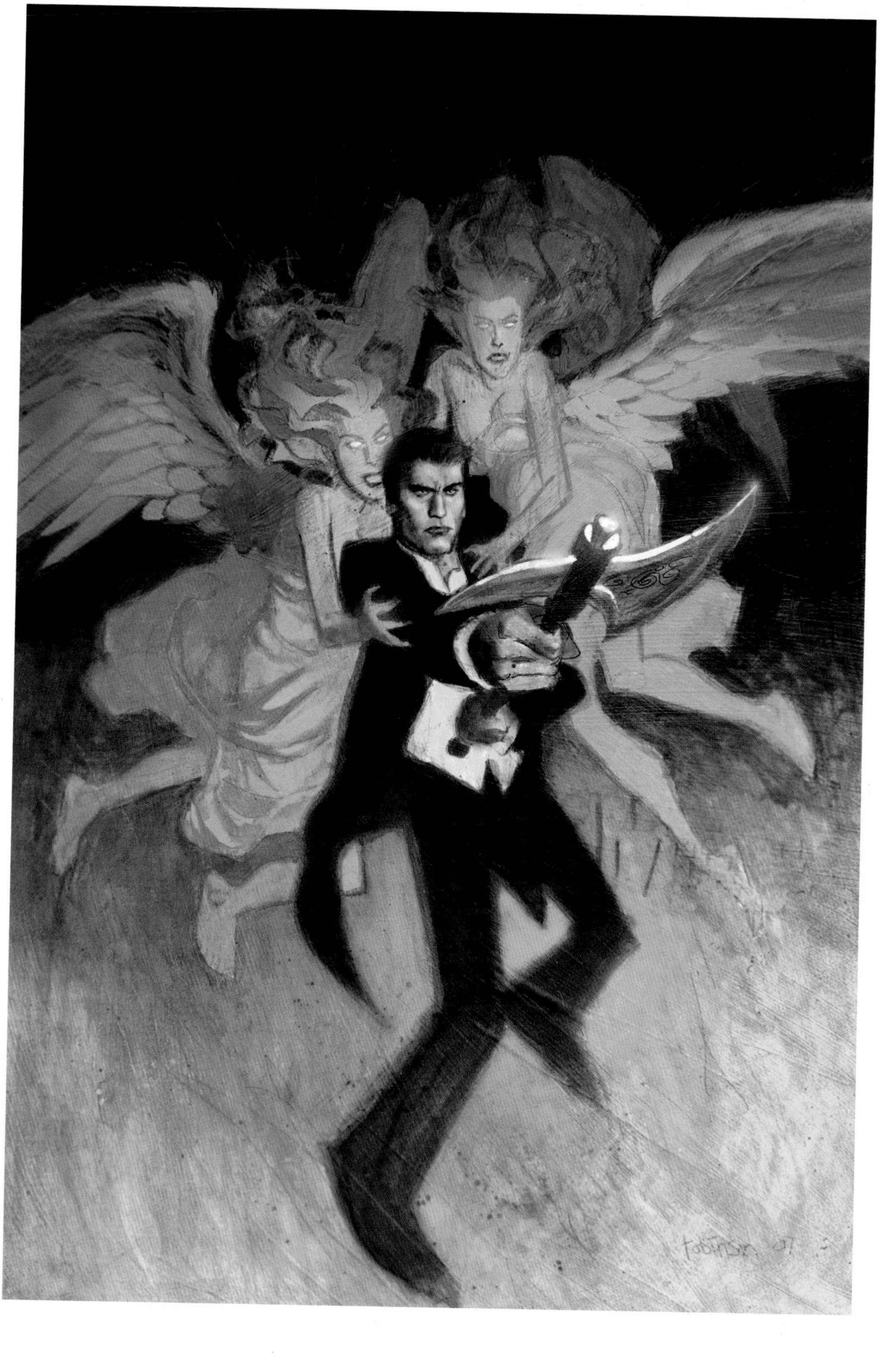

Opposite Page: Art by Franco Urru
Colors by Paolo Maddaleni

This Page: Art by Andrew Robinson

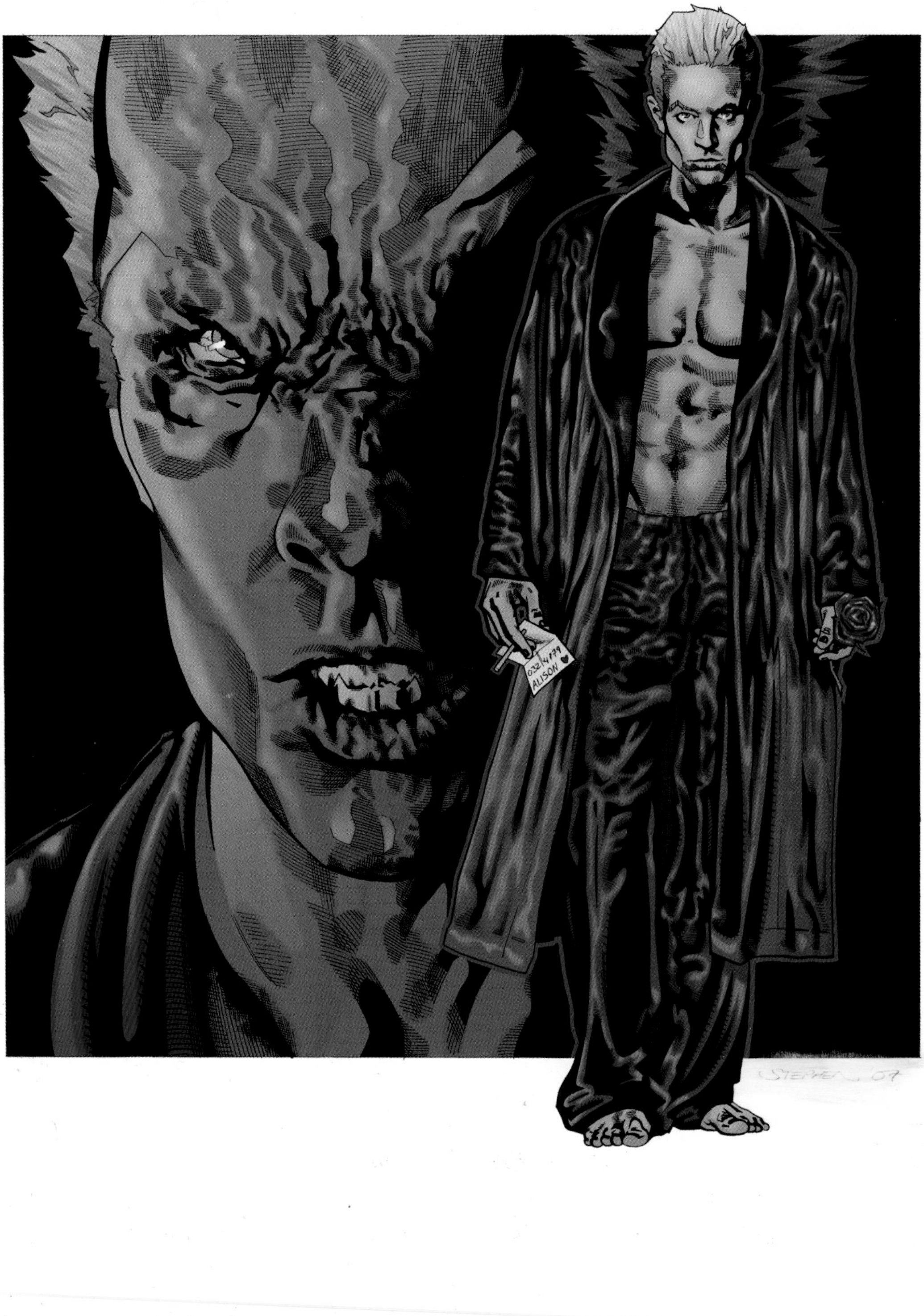
032 4179
ALISON

This Page: Art by Stephen Mooney
Colors by Lisa Jackson

Opposite Page: Art by Franco Urru
Colors by Paolo Maddaleni

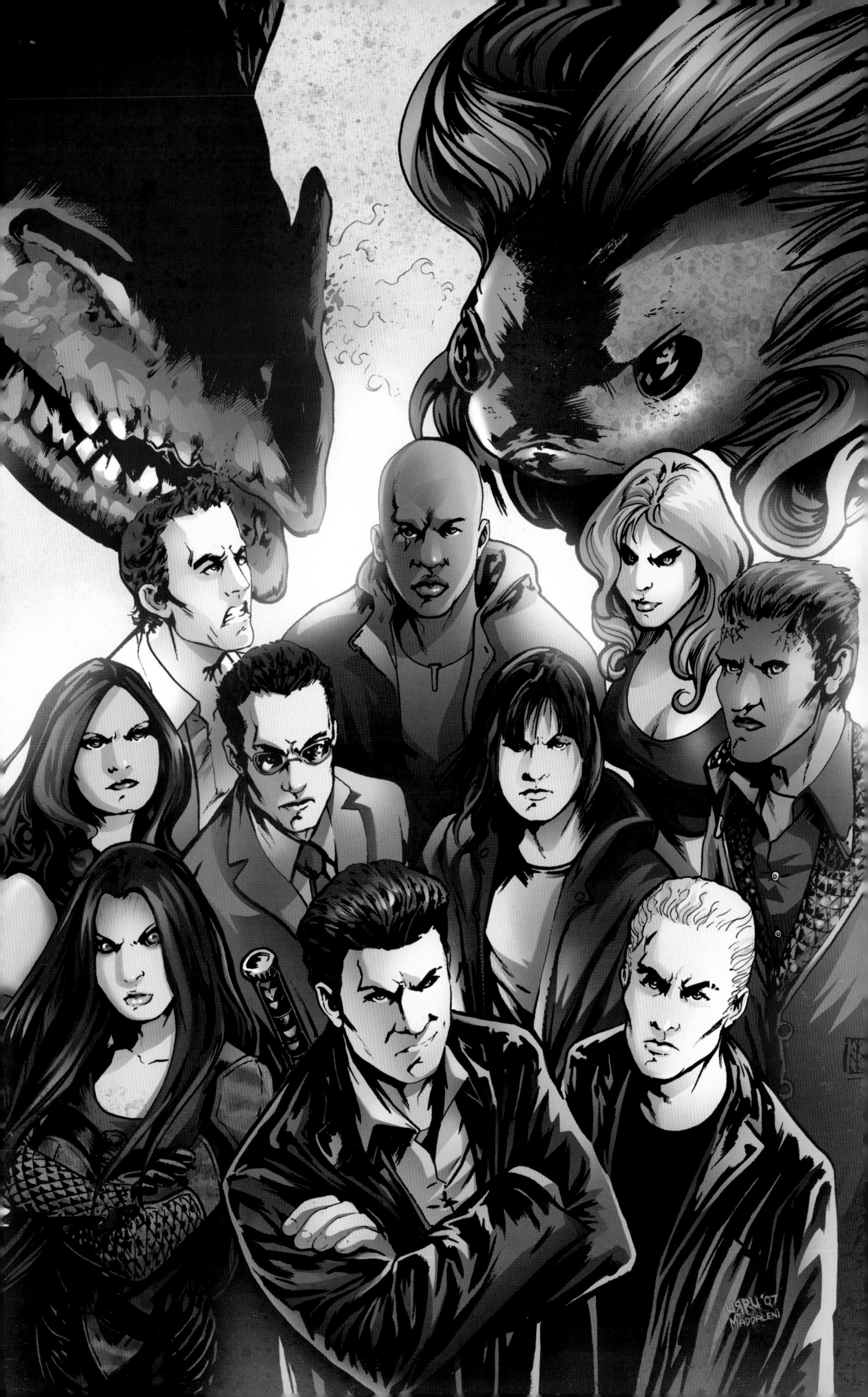
URRU '07
MADDALENI

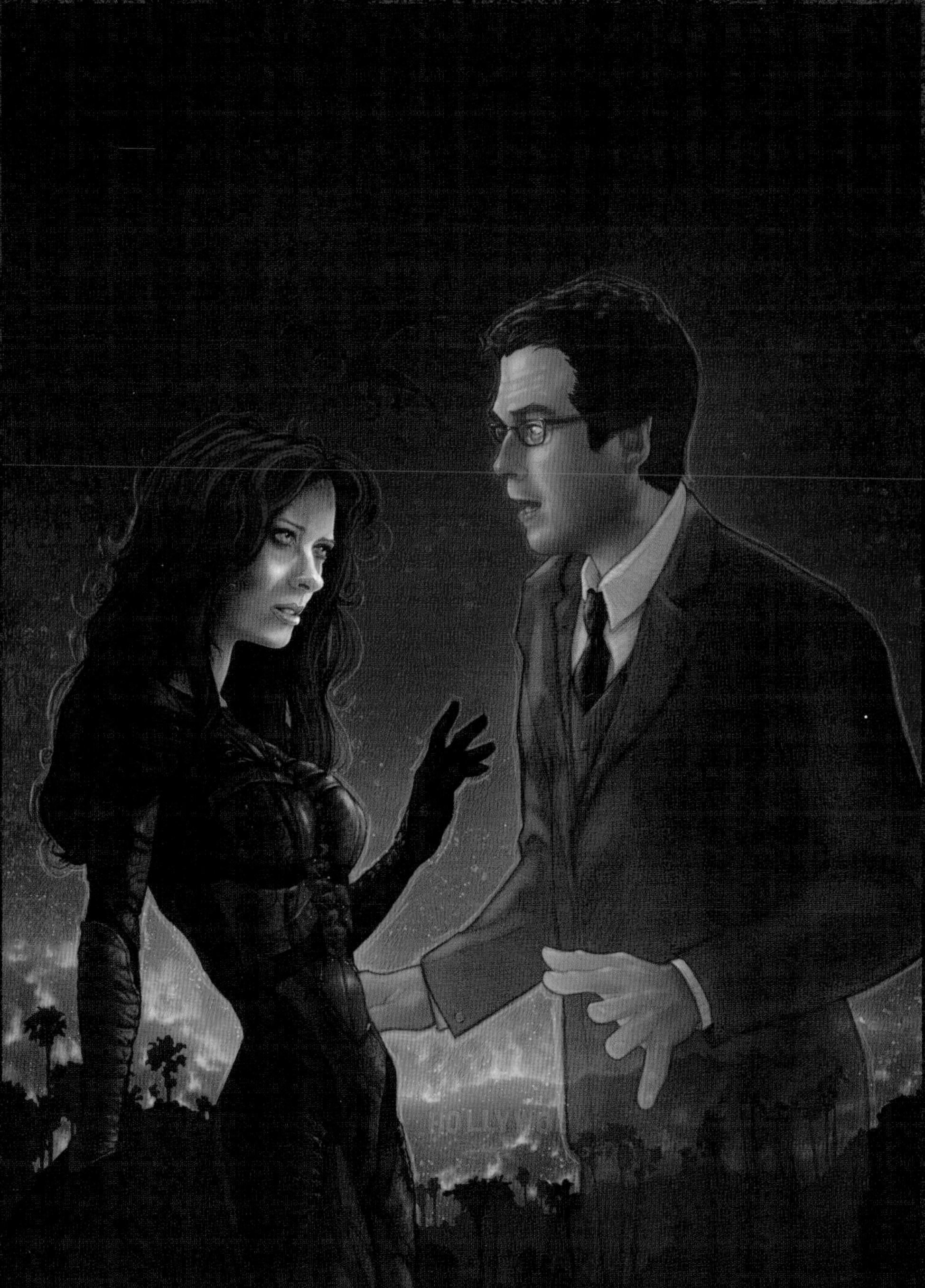

Opposite Page: Art by Andrew Robinson

This Page: Art by Rebecca A. Wrigley

Following Page: Art by Stephen Mooney
Colors by Lisa Jackson

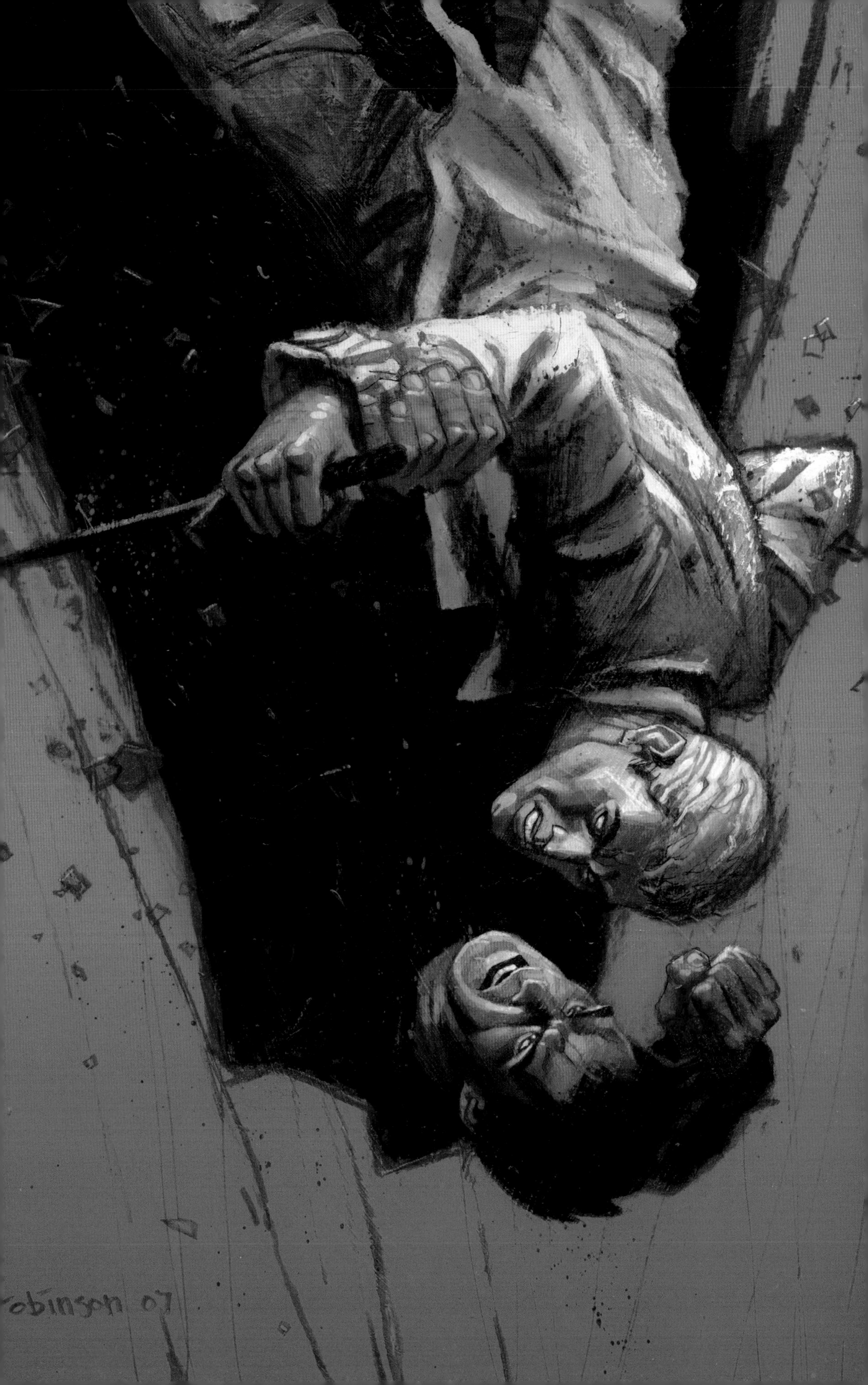
obinson 07

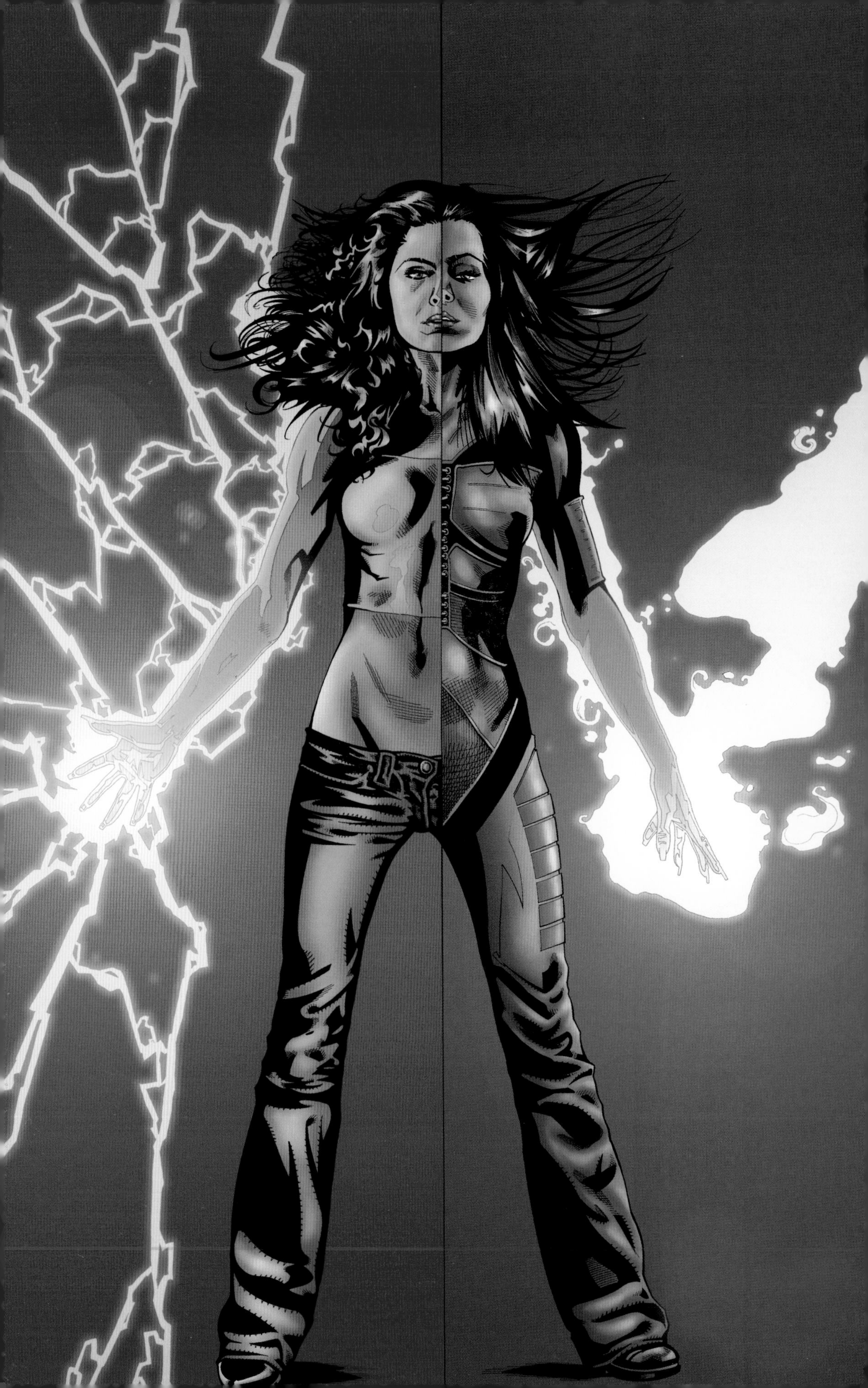

original proposal

by joss whedon and brian lynch

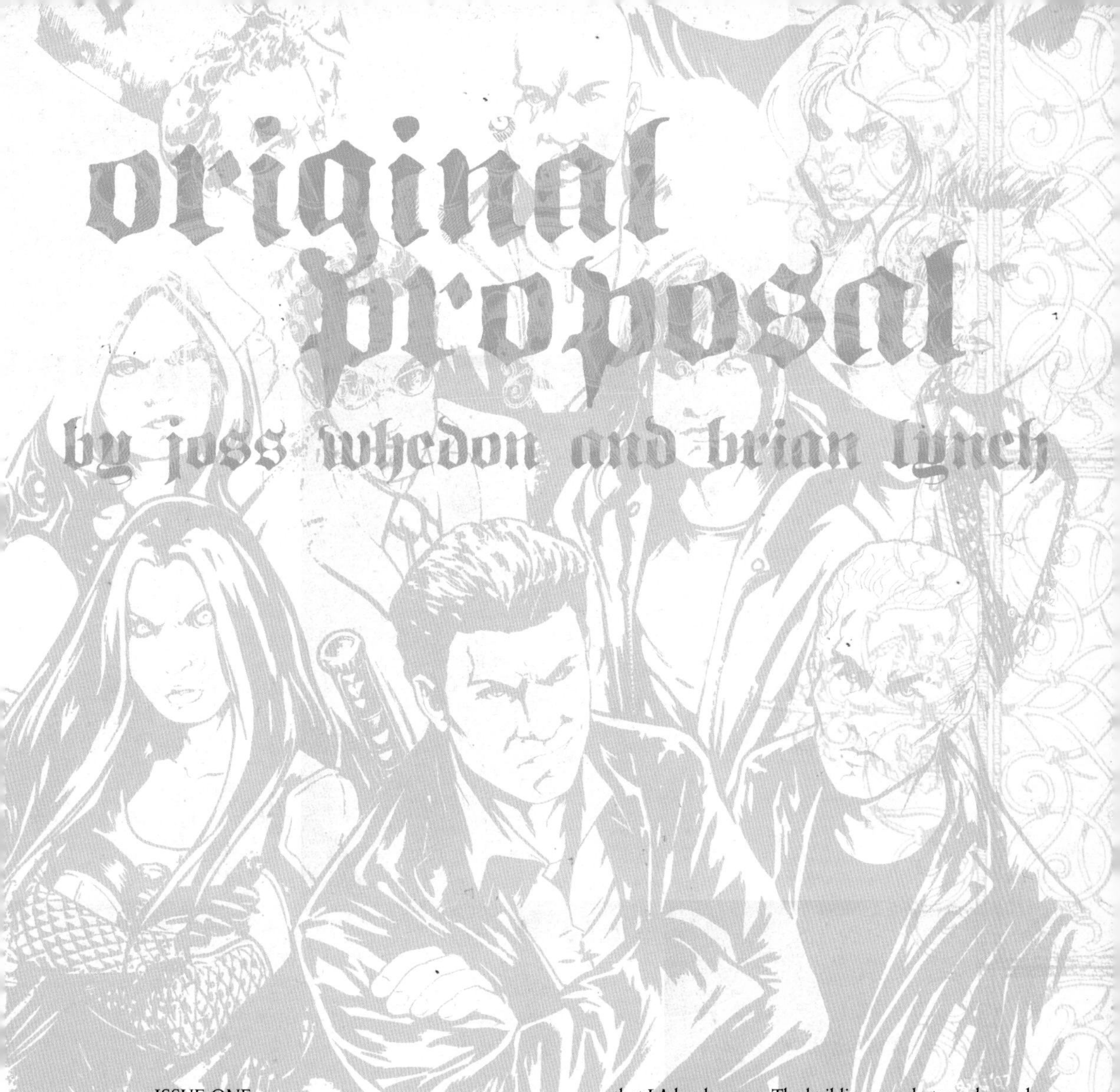

ISSUE ONE

Downtown LA. ANGEL saving a few WELL-DRESSED PEOPLE from a veritable gaggle of winged DEMONS. Angel is more heavily armed (axe, sword) than we're used to. The demons are excited to have a chance at taking him down, they've wanted to fight him for a while. Angel can identify, he always wanted to fight a dragon and a few months ago, finally got the chance. Just as a few of the remaining Demons swoop in for a choreographed attack, they're roasted alive by the Dragon. Guess Angel's plans changed.

Angel talks to the Well-Dressed People, who were looting when the Winged Demons came in for the kill. They don't usually steal, they're GOOD PEOPLE ("We're LAWYERS for God's sake!") and don't understand why the world has suddenly changed around them.

Angel gives them an address, tells them to go there, and tells them not to mention him. He gets on his dragon and takes off. The dragon takes to the air...

...at this point we see via a two page spread, the hell that LA has become. The buildings are destroyed, people are scared to leave their homes, demons and monsters roam the streets. The sky is a reddish haze, the sun AND moon out at the same time. Nightmare/fever dream scenario. Los Angeles has been sent to hell. Literally. This is the price LA paid because our hero took a stand against Wolfram & Hart.

Angel arrives at the former offices of Wolfram & Hart. Side and the roof torn off, it has been practically abandoned. Dragon lands through the building's new sunroof.

Angel hears a commotion, heads inside the reception area. WESLEY is trying to calm down BURGE, the demon who has claimed downtown LA as his own. He came here with his son, whom we shall dub SON-OF-BURGE for the sake of this treatment, a brute of a demon that tries to stare Angel down, and tosses stuff at Wesley, quite amused that objects go through his less-than-corporal body.

Burge tells Angel that every week the demons in charge of each area (LA is now a feudal society, the city is now divided into different territories, each one taken by a LORD, the most powerful demon in the area) meet, and each week, Burge keeps his mouth shut when they try to figure out Angel's location. After all, Angel takes down new demons trying to impede on his Burge's domain, and Burge feels he owes Angel, if not for him...

...none of this would ever be possible.

(NOTE: Some of the Lords don't participate in the meetings. It'll be clear who I'm typing about as this outline goes on, but there is constant reference to anyone weak or snivelling, read: not bloodthirsty, being "from Silverlake." It's a good set-up for something in issue 4. Let's continue.)

Even with Burge being SO understanding, Angel has to go and thrash a few of his men who were rounding up humans. Burge maintains they were simply looting and causing trouble, something Burge won't allow. He considers himself one of the more lenient "lords," in fact, seeing as he not only let Angel work out of the offices, he also kept the Coffee Bean down the street open, as over the years Burge has become quite addicted to their latte.

But Angel broke the rules: he killed a few of his men. Now Angel's going to have to pay: So Son-Of-Burge scours the offices for furniture they like. Burge "suggests" Angel stay in the confines of Wolfram & Hart for a while. He's grounding Angel. Next time Angel acts up, Burge is going to demand bigger recompense. He's going to take his head. And probably the big metal desk at reception.

Santa Monica. The people that Angel saved show up at the address that Angel supplied them with. They enter the building, find themselves surrounded by humans and demons alike. At first sight it's threatening, but we come to figure out Angel sent the looters to the secret location of a band of humans (and assorted docile demons) hiding out, rounded up and led by CONNOR.

Connor has blossomed as a result of recent events, fully embracing his role as leader/hero/champion. Behind him stand NINA and GWEN.

Due to the mucking up of the sun and moon, Nina's powers are flipped on their ear: she can "wolf out" at will, has extra sensory powers and claws when she needs them. She's also much more ornery than we remember, and is ready to take the newcomers down. The new arrivals practically wet their pants, panic, spilling the beans that they were sent---

Connor finishes the sentence for them, describing Angel. They tell him he swore them to secrecy. Connor smiles wearily. That sounds about right.

BACK TO WOLFRAM & HART. Angel looks at plans on the wall, asks Wesley if he's come up with anything, Wesley points out that he can't exactly do research, open books, etc.

Angel ignores this, talks about breaking the huge barrier that separates Los Angeles from the rest of the world.

Wesley tells him that Wolfram & Hart is playing with power, any magic they can conjure, certainly magic they find IN Wolfram & Hart's Los Angeles HQ, won't cut it. They need to think about defending the people that are trapped with them. And not just playing dark avenger for hours a day, they need to start taking down Lords. Starting with Burge.

Angel thinks it would be a drop in the bucket, they have to concentrate on getting everyone out.

Wesley suggest that Angel seems gun-shy to take a stand, because we all know how the last "big stand" went. But he'd like to see some kind of baby step towards rectifying the situation.

Angel is weary of Wesley. Because the Wolfram & Hart contracts don't expire when the employee does, Wesley is still on the payroll, Wolfram & Hart isn't done with him yet. Wolfram & Hart keeps him around as punishment (for both Wesley AND Angel). Either way, his old friend seems to be on Angel's side, but Angel can't fully trust Wesley yet, and neither can we. Neither. Can. We.

Besides, Angel knows that the magic they have won't cut it. He points to a page torn from a book, a sketch of what looks to be a BLACK CAT EYE. It amplifies the owner's powers. And it was plucked, not too long ago, from it's original owner, by a piece of slime named Kripp. They get the black eye, it could give them the power they need. It's just a matter of getting it from Kripp.

Westwood. A huge gladiator arena. Gladiator battle to the death among human slaves. Complete with old timey weaponry and chainmail. Problem is, his slaves are normal humans from our time, one's a cop, the other's a convenience store worker, and aren't at all familiar with the rules of gladiator style battle.

It's quite frustrating for KRIPP, Lord of Westwood. Gelatinous slop that holds (barely) human form, he's riddled with various supernatural bric a brac that is fused to the skeleton slightly visible under all that goop.

Kripp is trying desperately to turn the area into an era HE enjoyed more, he's even converted an old-timey movie theater into a full-on arena, but no one seems to know how to play by his rules. Even his bikini-clad slave girls (one's a receptionist at a talent agency, the other worked at Best Buy) aren't making him feel better, maybe it's their lackluster attitude.

So Kripp turns to BETTA GEORGE, a fish-like telepath, enslaved by and chained to Kripp. Normally George has limited telepathy, but we see the BLACK EYE from Angel's sketch, fused in Kripp's spine GLOW, amplifying George's abilities, allowing him to influence the "warriors" into doing what Kripp wants. They begin to fight...

...just as the lights in the building go out and the.

place is raided. GUNN gets a full-on hero reveal as he and his gang, a group of men who sure look human, lay waste to the Boss' henchmen and muscle. This is a Gunn we haven't seen ever. Quick, bloodthirsty, stronger. He only spares Betta George, but knocks him out quickly to avoid mind-control. They proceed to beat the many lives out of Kripp, and Gunn RIPS Kripp's spine from his body, taking the BLACK EYE with him.

Gunn's men grab Betta George. Gunn then proceeds to sweet talk the (now former) slave women. He's super cool even when dripping with demon blood. Or maybe because of it.

Back to Wolfram & Hart. Wesley, free from Angel's judging and oh-so-hunky eyes, enters the Wolfram & Hart elevator. He goes up, up, up, the doors open, bathing him in WHITE LIGHT. His eyes BURN WHITE as soon as he enters, as he begins regular communication with the higher ups at Wolfram & Hart. Definitely doing this behind Angel's back. And they are not happy with him. His job is not to rile up Angel to pick up arms again. Wesley tells them that if they don't like the job he's doing, free him of his contract and let him move on. Nope, they need him. But even in THIS form, Wesley can be hurt, as the Higher Ups make Wesley pay for going against their wishes.

(NOTE: This scene could end with Wesley simply entering the White Room and beginning his "discussion" with the Higher Ups, in case we want to leave the readers more in the dark at the end of issue one. If so, we can resume the scene, with the Higher Ups not being happy with Wesley undercutting their plans, at the beginning of issue 2.)

We INTERCUT this with two things: (1) Son-of-Burge violently rounding up human stragglers that dared escape and (2) Angel moving something QUITE BIG across the room.

These scenes have Angel's V.O. , where we are a bit more clued into his torment. All his friends stood by him when he chose to take a stand. Now, they're paying the price for it. He's not sure where they are, if they're okay. He just knows he tried to do what he thought was right, and wound up causing more damage than any of the Big Bad's he's fought.

But...

Son-of-Burge rounds up his last human, he gloats and grandstands...

...just before the metal desk from reception that Burge admired, tossed out of the giant gaping hole in the side of the building, crashing down next to him.

He looks up at Angel, standing from a window. Asks what the hell that was?

One word answer: Recompense.

Son-of-Burge's fists glow, he's ready to unleash on Angel, who calmly takes out a crossbow and shoots Son-of-Burge through the head. Burge's men run back to tell Burge (though some take longer because they're dragging the desk back to Burge).

All this was done without leaving Wolfram & Hart. So he KINDA listened to Burge.

Angel's fully aware of what this means. Burge is going to come for him, full force. But, like Wesley said, baby steps.

Back to Westwood. Gunn's gang meticulously paints symbols/Sanskrit looking markings all over the walls. They're using the blood of some of the "saved" humans to paint the symbols. Said humans are eviscerated in the corner. They're not bothering Gunn with the Sanskrit, he's in the back room with the slave girls...

...one's already dead, drained of her blood. Gunn's currently sucking the blood out of the other one. Yessir, Gunn's a vamp.

ISSUE TWO

Angel heads to Santa Monica, where he's surrounded by Nina and Gwen. He needs to see Connor, warn him about what happened the night before. Angel took down the son of a powerful Lord, and Angel fears recompense may come, directly at Connor. In reality, this is probably subconsciously Angel's very ham-fisted attempt to let Connor know he's back in action, and probably force-play a situation where Connor has to stick close to Angel.

The ladies tell Angel that Connor is in Westwood...

ALL the gangs from EVERY section of town are overriding Westwood trying to seize control.

Angel drives to Westwood, the streets are overrun with minions of all the Lords battling for control of the area. Using old fashioned weaponry, supernatural tools, astral projection, it's a six-block-wide gang fight from hell. He sees Connor is not at all in need of help, he's kicking ass so well that he puts Angel, and pretty much any super hero to shame.

Angel doesn't let Connor see him, but does his best to save the humans that are being used as weapons, shields, ammo, etc. Angel heads for the site of last issue's massacre, knowing that Kripp possesses the black eye and fearing what may have come of it.

Back to Gunn, who places the recently plucked black eye into a disturbing mesh of demon parts and skin. Gunn is building an altar/platform of sorts, but it's completely made from flayed bodies of different kinds of creatures, including a few humans.

Gunn enters Betta George's holding area, who is trying desperately to influence Gunn into letting him go. It's not having any effect, Gunn has anticipated George's plan of attack and taken the necessary precautions to guard himself from it. This Gunn guy is on the ball.

George figures out that Gunn is a vamp. Gunn violently argues the point, he may have been turned when he was dragged away and turned during the final "alley fight" with Wolfram & Hart, but he maintains he's still held onto his humanity. After all, he's working at making things right. A very messed up recently turned Vampire's version of making things right.

Back to Angel, who notices the markings all over the wall. Connor (the very one who was eyeballing him just a couple of pages ago), enters. Angel doesn't even look at him. He tells Connor that this is going to get ugly, and to go to Wolfram & Hart and get help in the form of a giant winged dragon. Connor asks him where he's going to be.

Follow the Dragon. He knows. Dragon only likes Angel, so Angel whispers the "safe word" to Connor, which is the name Angel gave the Dragon. We won't tell the readers what it is until issue 12. Start your ideas now, gentlemen!

As he heads out, we have the slightest of wonderful father/son moments: Connor smiles, tells Angel to be careful, Angel tells him the same.

No, seriously, be careful. Angel killed the son of a Lord last night, and he thinks maybe they're be payback, maybe a little "son for son" retribution.

Connor's smile falls. Wonderful father/son moment over.

Later. Angel's car rips through Beverly Hills. Filled to the brim with demons. More hellish and violent than the other sections of town we've seen so far. Must have a hell of a Lord.

And at Playboy Mansion, seemingly in charge of this section of town, is one William the Bloody, aka SPIKE.

Surrounded by beautiful women of all sorts of body type and creature breed, he's truly living an opulent lifestyle, enjoying every second of his newfound situation. Feeding him goblets of blood ("don't tell me what species it is...let me guess...")

And he's not too happy to see some of his bikini ladies are instantly smitten with Angel as he walks through the gates.

Angel wants to talk about Westwood. Spike maintains he doesn't know what he's talking about and doesn't care: after fighting the good fight for years now, Spike has more than earned his handsome reward. And whatever happened to LA (Spike assumes he finally made it to heaven), it's not his problem. He isn't harming anybody (that aren't asking to be harmed, anyway), so Angel should best leave him alone.

As they argue, the area around them BEGINS rippling, literally changing time periods around them. The people also subtly begin popping into various points in their own lifetime: becoming old, young, back to normal, so forth...

Spike is concerned by this. He REALLY wants Angel to leave. Angel wants answers.

Spike's followers, which include not just bikini ladies but ne'er do well DEMONS and other assorted monsters of all shapes and sizes, (all proclaiming Spike "the exalted thrice resurrected savior") try to remove Angel forcibly.

Spike tells them hands off. He can take it from here. You see, Spike has died quite a few times now. And that gives a man a bit of a demigod complex. Nothing can kill him. And he's going to show Angel what happens to people that ignore the wishes of the exalted thrice resurrected savior.

They square off, Spike loving every moment of it, Angel wants answers. Those markings on the wall were written in text dating back all the way from the Primordium Age. He knows Spike isn't the Lord of the Beverly Hills area. That would be ILLYRIA.

And her BOOMING VOICE and SHAKY GROUND send everyone but the two vamps running as she appears. She ain't happy Angel's there.

ISSUE THREE

Spike, surprised and worried that Illyria is making her location known, tells her to go back in, he's got this. She, of course, ignores her pet. She wants Angel to leave, now. She tried it Angel's way, she took up arms with him, and it didn't work out. Now she's back to her old ways. Angel wants answers, and, if she has it, the black eye.

She beats the ever-loving crap out of him. Tossing him through windows, beating him senseless...

...the entire time, Angel, Spike, the surrounding areas FLUCTUATE in different parts of their time stream/lifetime. Spike and Angel even fluctuate briefly to pre-vampire status, the younger, poofier, bad accent-ier Angel.

As he gets the beating of his dear sweet life, he quite annoyingly asks about the killing in Westwood. As she gets more angry, we see the area where the TIME FLUX is happening getting wider and wider, stretching out to nearby streets.

A concerned Spike tries to stop the fight, gets sent flying for his troubles.

Angel is eventually knocked into a safehouse/ holding pen full of humans. This is all Angel needs for a second wind: Illyria and her little pal Spike are enslaving humans. What should be a triumphant moment as our hero rises to the occasion is quite quickly shot down as Illyria houses him again.

He's beaten very badly. Bleeding from numerous places. As Illyria steps in for what looks to be the deathblow:

A wall of fire separates Illyria and Angel. Connor and the Dragon have arrived.

Illyria wants everyone gone. The Dragon can stay if he wants. She tells Connor to take his cattle and leave as she heads inside.

Spike heads in, he tells them he's quite certain Illyria.

didn't have anything to do with the murder. Not exactly her style. She's got enough on her plate, so to speak, and if she wanted someone dead, she wouldn't scribble Riddler-esque clues on the wall. Besides, she doesn't need any black eye, lack of power ain't really a problem lately.

Connor takes the holed up humans and loads them into some form of transportation. Angel figures out what's going on, and what he realizes wounds our hero more than any blow could...

...Spike's working with Connor. He is part of Connor's underground railroad, saving the humans. While Angel has been sitting on the sidelines (well, relatively, but the sidelines can be a dangerous place), Spike has stepped up, and TEAMED UP with Angel's own son.

Illyria has already killed a few minions, she's obviously not in a good way. She didn't want to see any more of "them." Seeing Spike is reminder enough. She heads into a ROOM with many many locks on the door. Tells Spike no one gets in for the next couple of hours. Spike locks the door after her, stands guard. He talks to one of the Demons following his lead, tells him that their location has been compromised, they're going to have to move.

Angel obviously detests that Spike is helping out Connor. It's something he should have been doing. He decides to step up his game.

Still badly wounded from his battles, he heads back to Wolfram & Hart, tells Wesley about Connor. Wesley isn't a shoulder to cry on, literally or figuratively, as he points out at least SOMEONE'S doing something. Angel agrees. And he didn't come back to Wolfram & Hart. He came to get a bigger sword.

Angel (Wesley in tow) heads right to Coffee Bean, where Burge is holding court. Burge's men rush at Angel, he takes them down.

Angel tells Burge he's no longer Lord of the area. Angel's taking over. Burge says fine... if he can stand up to Burge's champion.

Angel's down for it. But he doesn't just want Burge.

Angel wants to take control of EVERYONE'S territory. He throws down the gauntlet, everyone can pick their champion, he'll take them all, one by one.

Wesley seems to be the only guy in the room who isn't looking forward to this.

As Angel heads outside, a scared demon holds up a cross to him. He smiles at him.

They head back to Wolfram & Hart. Wesley isn't down with Angel's plan: he can't face off against someone, not in the condition he's in. Angel says he'll find a way around it. He always does. Except for that one time, when he sent LA to hell.

Still, Angel has to agree that the upcoming battle would have been a whole lot easier if he were still a vampire.

They walk away from the "camera," a trail of blood from the wounds Illyria inflicted behind him.

ISSUE FOUR

FLASHBACK. The night of the alley way battle against Wolfram & Hart. A badly beaten Angel finds himself in the Wolfram & Hart building. Hacked up, bleeding, literally watching the sky fall around him.

People are running for cover. Angel JUMPS out the window, falls for a few floors...

...and realizes he feels his heart beat rapidly.

HE SMASHES into a car, hard. He's bleeding all over, in shock, as Wesley steps forward. People running through him. As a representative of Wolfram & Hart, he tells Angel that the firm has long been working on making Angel human, either as a reward for his hard work (or, more believably, to keep him on a leash).

They figured now would be a good time to do it.

And as people are running for cover from the hellfire, demons and mass destruction, Angel has never felt so helpless.

PRESENT DAY. Angel's doing his best to conjure the right spells/create the right potions, to help speed his healing process a bit. Shirtless, we see he is a mess of bruises, stitches, and mangled flesh.

Wesley mentions he could help if they could spend a few days working on making him corporal. Angel looks at him, unsure of what to say...

...when the awkward moment is broken by the arrival of two GLOWING, ANGELIC LADIES (we're not talking Angelic features, we're talking flowing white robes, wings) who tell Angel their lord has requested audience with him. Angel looks to Wesley...

They follow these two Angelic types...

...to their SUV hybrids.

Santa Monica Beach. Sea boils red, and about a mile out, we see the BARRIER that surrounds LA from the rest of the world.

A few demons are BURNT to a crisp as GWEN steps forward. She's been saving up for quite some time, and unleashes an insanely forceful electric blast towards the barrier.

Sand kicks up, a crater is formed around her, you can see the blast from blocks away.

And it doesn't make a dent in the barrier. Gwen is spent, she's exhausted most of her energy, as DEMONS swarm around, alerted by the light show.

She's saved when Connor joins the fight. Connor is angry, such a display risks every demon in the area closing in on our their band of survivors. And after Connor's been through four or fives attempts at his family, he's not going to lose the one that seems to be working out.

Nina joins the fight, she's come with news...

BACK TO ANGEL, as he and Wesley are being taken

into Silverlake.

Silverlake is a commune. Protected from the rest of Los Angeles area, it's a safe haven for all who want to get away from the rest of the city, human, demon or otherwise. No weapons, no violence, a few HARPIES emit a soothing sound that keeps everyone calm.

The denizens all meet every night for sing-a-longs run by their leader LORNE. He refuses to use the title "Lord," as he's not "better" than anyone else, and because after Elton John got that title it was pretty much worthless (hack's been ripping him off for years).

Angel and Wesley are very much aware of Lorne's section of town, but have respected Lorne's wishes and stayed out of his area. Lorne wants to talk to Angel. He's heard of what Angel has planned, and there's no way one vampire can take down numerous "champions."

It's too late, Angel has thrown down the gauntlet, he has to do it. Lorne maintains there are better ways to handle things, as his revamped Silverlake has proven.

If Angel wants, he can hide out here. As long as he keeps to himself. Seriously, in a building by himself, away from the others. No offense, but he's got a strict "no trouble-makers" policy. Though if Connor came to him, he'd help with his problem. Lorne still feels a great deal for Connor, and thanks to a being (more of a GASEOUS ANOMALY with an attitude than a being), Lorne can astral project to keep an eye on him.

Angel points out that Connor probably wouldn't appreciate that, he prefers to do things on his own. Lorne sees the family resemblance.

If Lorne can't convince Angel otherwise, then at least he should sing for him, to see if Lorne can see how things are going to turn out. Angel refuses, and mid-sentence actually BREAKS out into song. Lorne has a demon that is the same species as SWEET from ONCE MORE WITH FEELING (or, hopefully if it's okay, IS Sweet), that he keeps around to help the riff-raff out.

He looks at Angel, confused. Clearly knowing Angel's secret. Finally, he asks "...how are you...?" Angel shows him a small jewel, providing a glamor that lets him give off the essence (mostly smell) of being a vampire.

So this is how he expects to win the battle. Maybe he's trying to get the band back together? Angel replies in the extreme negative, he's not asking anyone to fight his battles for him.

Now Lorne is somewhat concerned for Angel's well-being. He calls down the REAL reason no one is bothering the Silverlake area. It's Lorne's bouncer, keeping out the undesirables. GROOSALUG.

Back to his barbarian look, Groosalug is heavily armed, sticking out like a big Conan-esque needle in a lovely haystack. He's the protector of Lorne's commune, he keeps rabble rousers out.

Groosalug has spent much time gathering up some formidable weaponry since we've seen him. All over the globe and beyond, he's got quite an impressive stock. Lorne tells him to give Angel anything he wants. He and Angel patrol the area around Silverlake, as Groosalug displays the pros-cons of each weapon, happily giving it over to Angel if it piques his interest. "It's fine, half the fun is ripping it from the stone!"

Meanwhile, Lorne and Wesley have some catch-up time. Awkward silence at first. And then Wesley looks to him. He needs something. He'd sing to prove himself, but in his current state, he doesn't think Lorne can see anything. And if he COULD, he probably wouldn't like what he sees.

This issue also features a B (C?) story, that of Spike picking up stakes and trying to move out of his current location, only to wind up fending off some of Gunn's gang. The reasons are not clear to the reader as to WHY they're attacking, it's more alarming that the demons Spike has kept company with turn on Spike as soon as Gunn's gang offers a reward. Spike stays and fights.

Illyria could join in, or she could come at the very end, to see Spike covered in the blood of his former followers, torn up pretty bad but winning the day, telling her they have to get out of there, now.

ISSUE FIVE

Battle royale hell's-a-poppin' issue.

Wolfram & Hart. Angel is gearing up. He puts on a skin-thin layer of Groosalug-supplied armor that will prove far more effective than it looks. Groosalug doesn't like it, he prefers his armor more bulky and majestic. Wesley reminds him: the jewel used to project the vampire glamor has been kicked up a notch: it will actually provide limited bursts of vamp appearance, but if Angel is knocked unconscious or dead any point, the spell will probably wear off. Just a heads up. As Angel continues to load up on Groosalug's weapons, Wesley tells him he won't go with him. But he'll be there in spirit, which is an amazing pun.

Angel gets on his dragon and heads out. Man, I will never tire of writing that sentence, ever.

The next half of the issue is quite simple. We're intercutting between:

EVENT 1:

La Brea Tar Pits. Humans and demons alike have gathered to witness what will be known throughout the supernatural community as "the slaughter of Angel." Everyone's taking/placing bets.

Burge announces that no one is allowed to kill Angel to make a name for themselves, and to the humans in the audience that no one is allowed to kill Angel for sending them all to hell.

The Lords' champions are lined up. Some shackled, some chained, some eating nearby onlookers. And most are staying away from the REAL threat of the issue, Burge's champion:

Matthius "Reaper" Pavayne. "Hellbound." Former employee of Wolfram & Hart, blood used to desecrate the building, used to roam the halls sending souls to hell before going corporal and being sealed up for what they thought was eternity.

Burge freed him. Pavayne owes him. More than willing to pay it back fighting Angel.

Pavayne loves to torture his opponents, he's also a master of the black arts who, as a ghost, had the power to seemingly alter reality around him. Now that he's in hell, you can drop the "seemingly," as he can make hellish scenarios plucked right from the darkest recess of your brain COME TO LIFE.

Forget the other champions, who, sure, are inflicting damage. It's the stuff that Pavayne is conjuring, the images of Angel's "family" being torn from him, it's Angel having their blood on his hands, that's what's doing the most damage. Death, comparatively, would be welcome. Luckily, the way the fight is going, it looks as though it's coming soon.

All the Dragon can do is watch, held at bay by some of the Lords' armies.

EVENT 2:

The "Gaseous Anomaly" (sure to be a sought after custom figure on the ebay market) is helping Lorne (carrying out Wesley's request) to project himself, a la when he checks on Connor. Only Lorne isn't just checking in.

He's rounding up the troops. He's stating his case, first to Connor, and then to Spike.

Lorne tells them that this isn't what Angel would want. He would never ask anyone else to put their lives on the line for him, especially after what happens, but right now, Angel needs help. He's going to die if they don't help.

All of this will be done very generally and not spelled out, underlined, GO SAVE ANGEL... but that will be more apparent later in the issue...

...finally, after much trepidation and pretty much sure that he's long since killed (after all, it'll be addressed that he was dragged away during the alley fight and no one has seen him), Lorne reaches out and finds Gunn...

...who is in the room with the LARGE HUMAN/ CREATURE shrine/platform. Smart guy that he is, Lorne can tell something not quite right is up. And he quickly "leaves."

Gunn is aware he's there the whole time. He smiles, knowing he'll see Lorne soon.

EVENT 3:

Wesley is being punished by the Higher Ups for interfering. He's ENCOURAGING Angel to rise up. Wesley agrees, he's REALLY screwing up, they should

fire him and let him be on his way. No such luck.

Anyway, Lorne has done his best rallying the troops. And toward the end of the issue, after Angel takes down a number of the Lord's champions he gets overwhelmed, but at Angel's lowest moment, the cavalry arrives.

Spike. Connor. Gwen. Nina. Groo.

The band? Pretty much back together. Angel tells them to go away. Surprisingly, no one listens. And secretly, to Angel's surprise (kinda) horror and sure, relief, they fight with him.

Connor wants to know why Illyria isn't joining in the fight. Spike tells him it's for the best, lass isn't herself lately.

The dragon busts loose, ready to kick ass. But he's not needed.

Angel and company head over to the Lords. With their champions dead and Angel's gang standing before them, they back down. The humans? Freed. Their new leader...

...yeah, revealed to be the guy who's pretty much the reason they're in hell to begin with. Angel's "subjects" look at him in disbelief.

LATER, WOLFRAM & HART. Angel stands outside, talks to his new "subjects." Doing his damndest to try and find something to say. He's their new leader, but think of it as a friendly elected official type. Not that they're going to hold elections.

Spike steps forward. He tells Angel he helped beat the big bads, he deserves a spot in the monarchy and a penthouse view in the Wolfram & Hart building. Eventually, throughout the conversation, we learn that Spike is coming to Angel because he can't trust anyone he picked up arms with (as they tried to kill him last issue). He needs to be somewhere he can trust, not for his sake, he's genuinely worried about Illyria.

Who makes her presence known. She steps forward.

As does Wesley.

And for the first time since the last episode of Angel, Wesley and Illyria are reunited. Overwhelmed and confused, she THROWS A PUNCH, it goes through him. He's touched he was able to get such a reaction, but tries to calm her down.

It's not working. The "time jump" ripple effects kick in. Spike tells Wesley to go away, and then turns to Angel, tells him he needs a place to lock her up, STAT. Angel gets her into the basement at Wolfram and Hart, Spike puts her in there and locks the door.

Our heroes on the other side, unsure of the power that Illyria is unleashing. But we see what it is because we're special: Illyria isn't letting off destructive blasts or ripping the room apart: she's turning into Fred.

END OF THE FIRST ARC...

sketch gallery
by franco urru

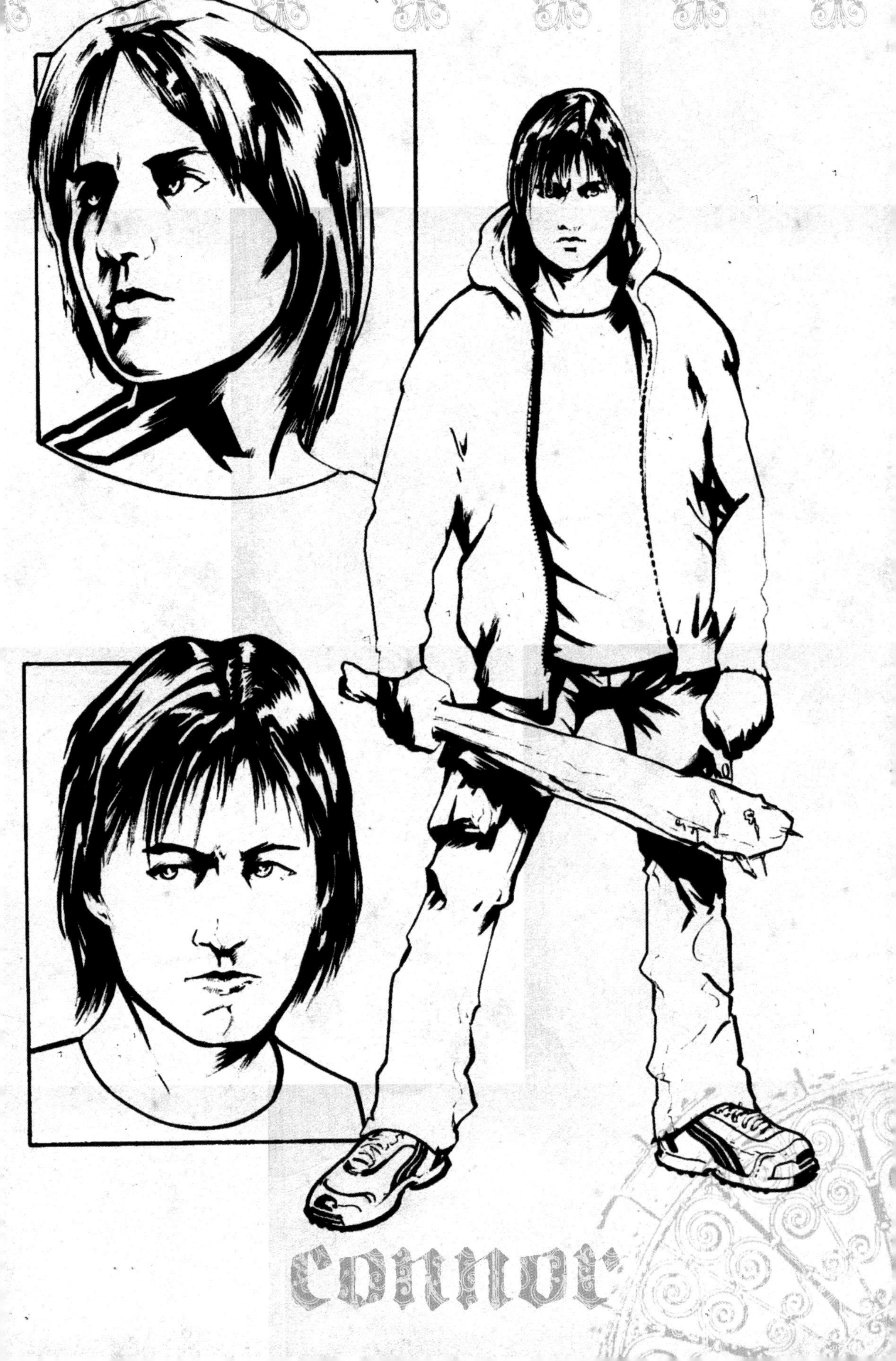

Connor

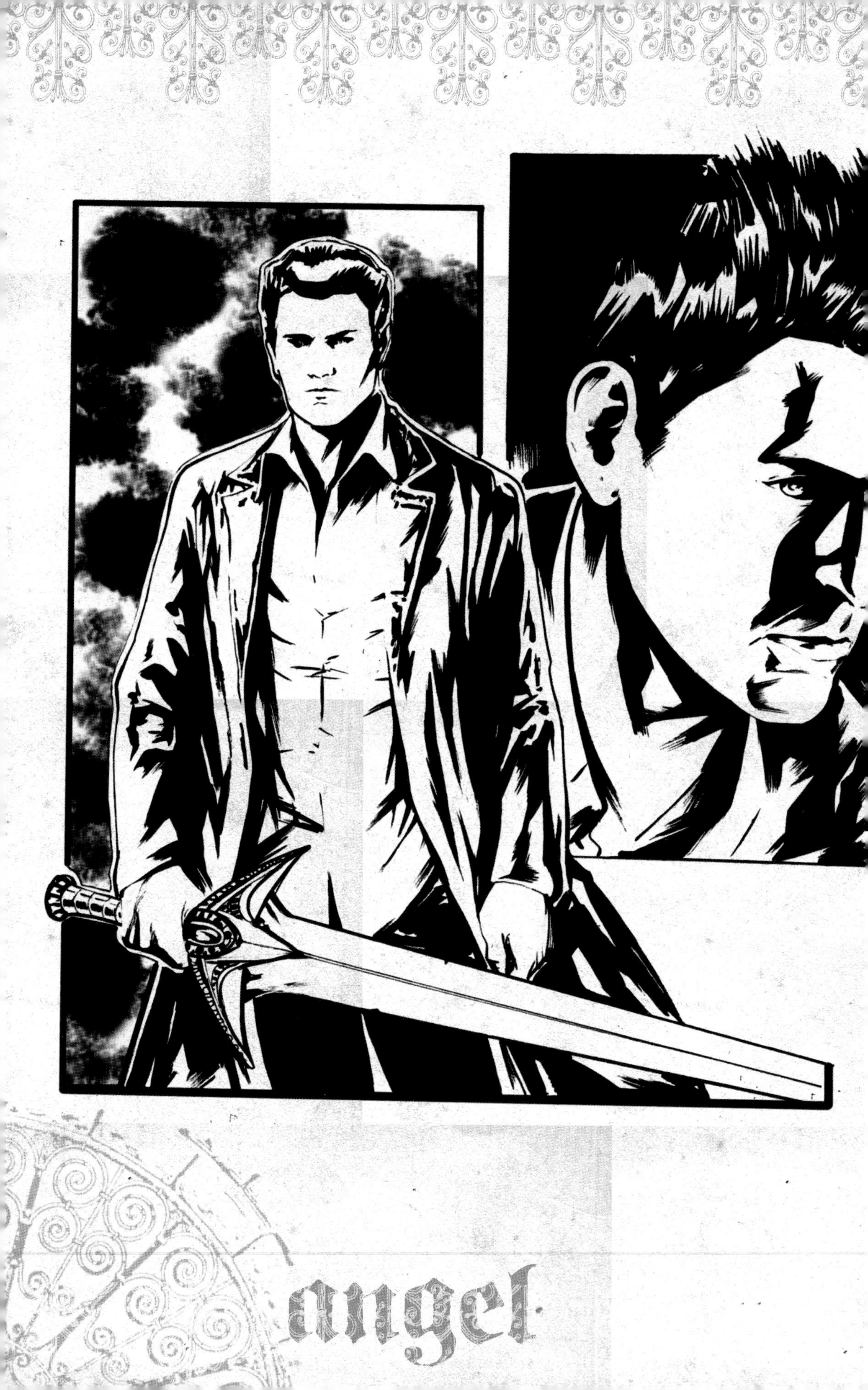
angel

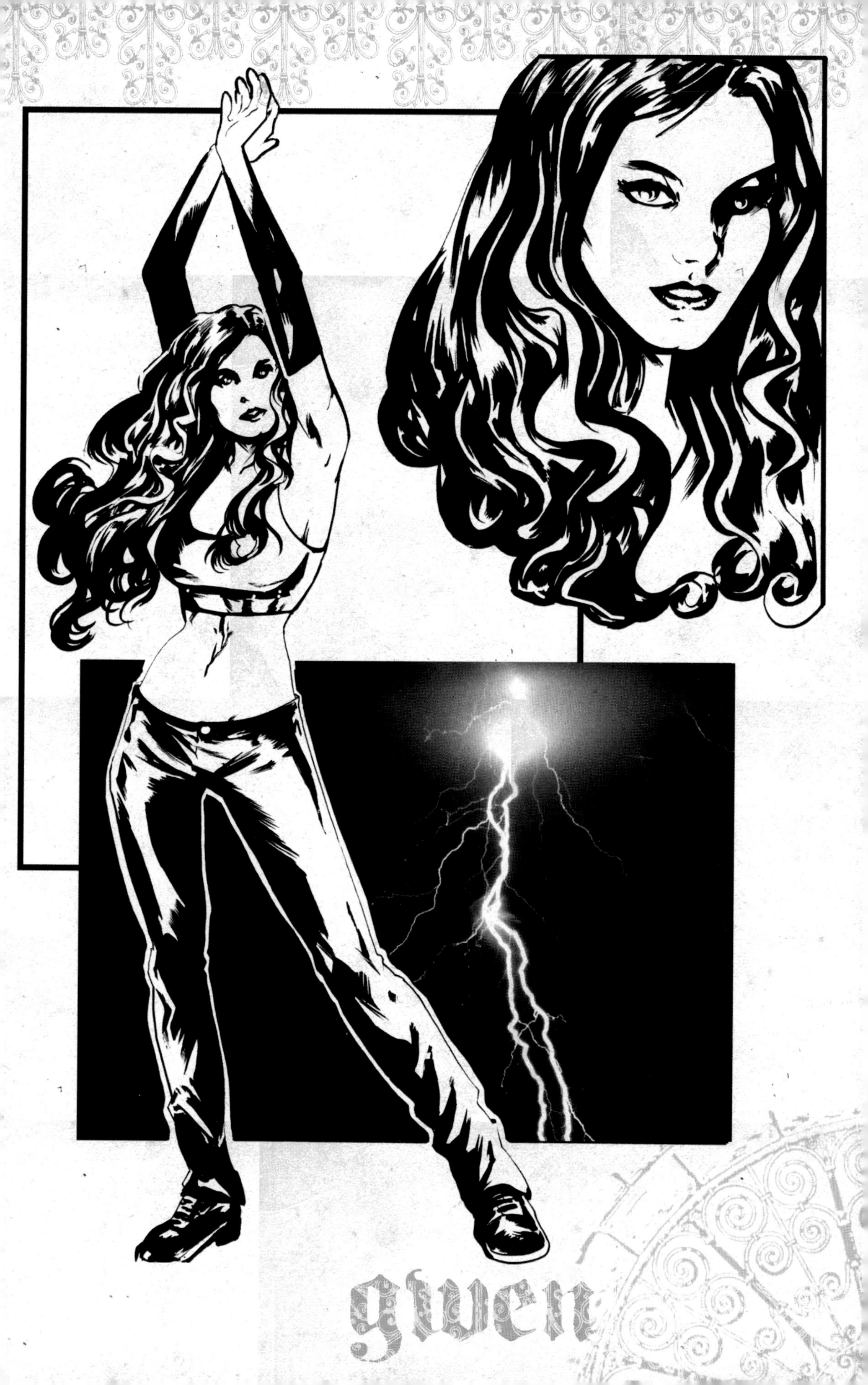
gwen

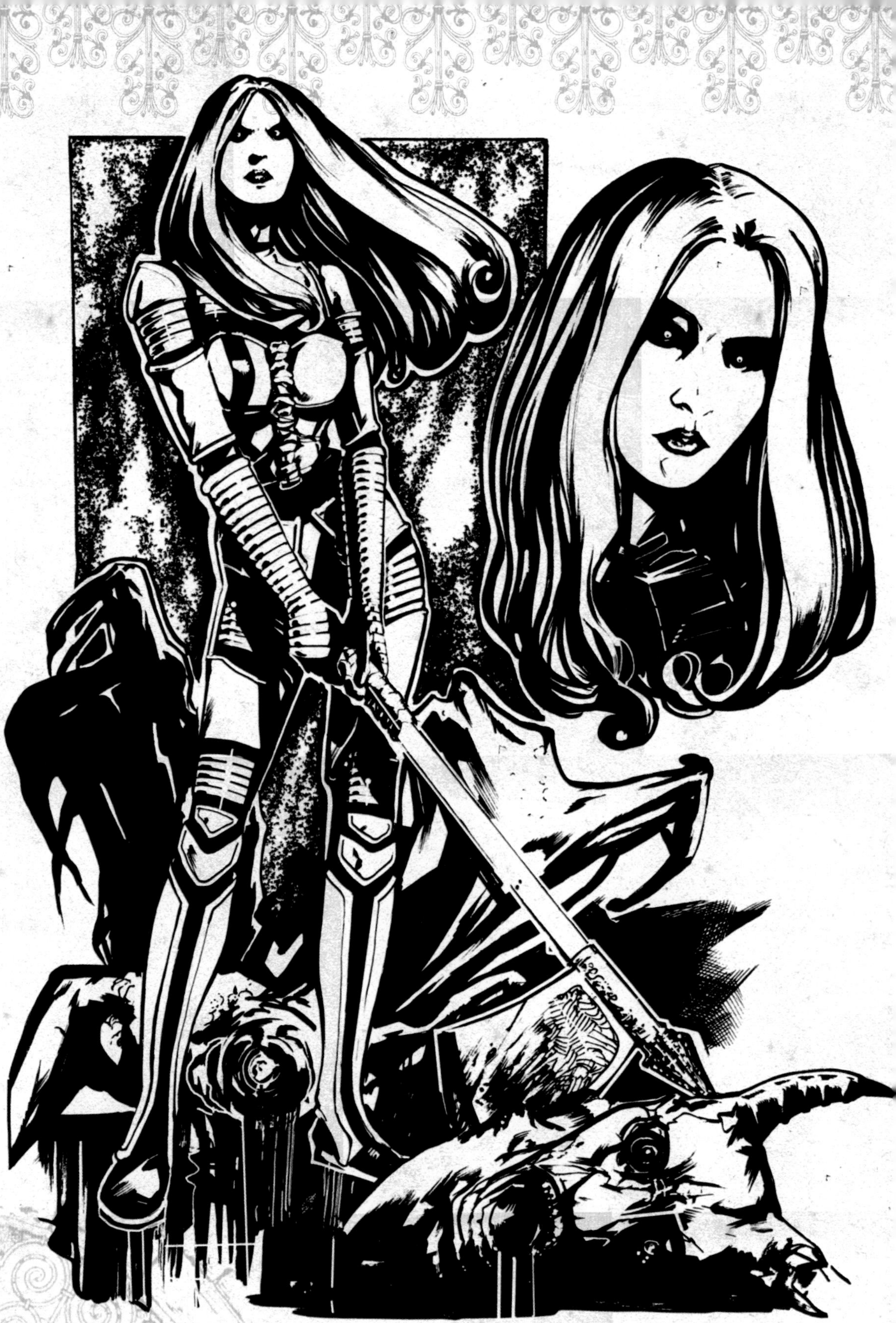

illyria

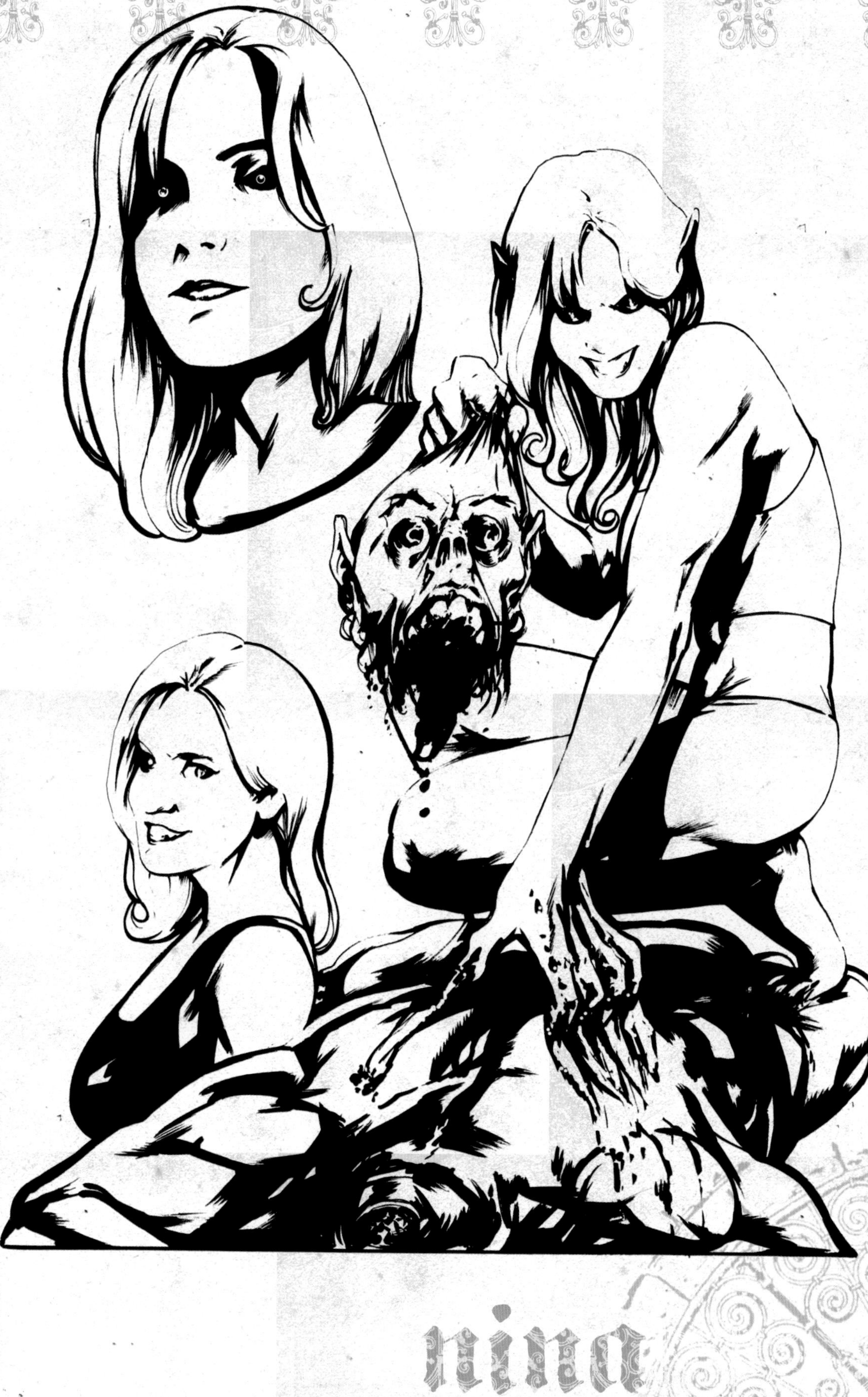
nina

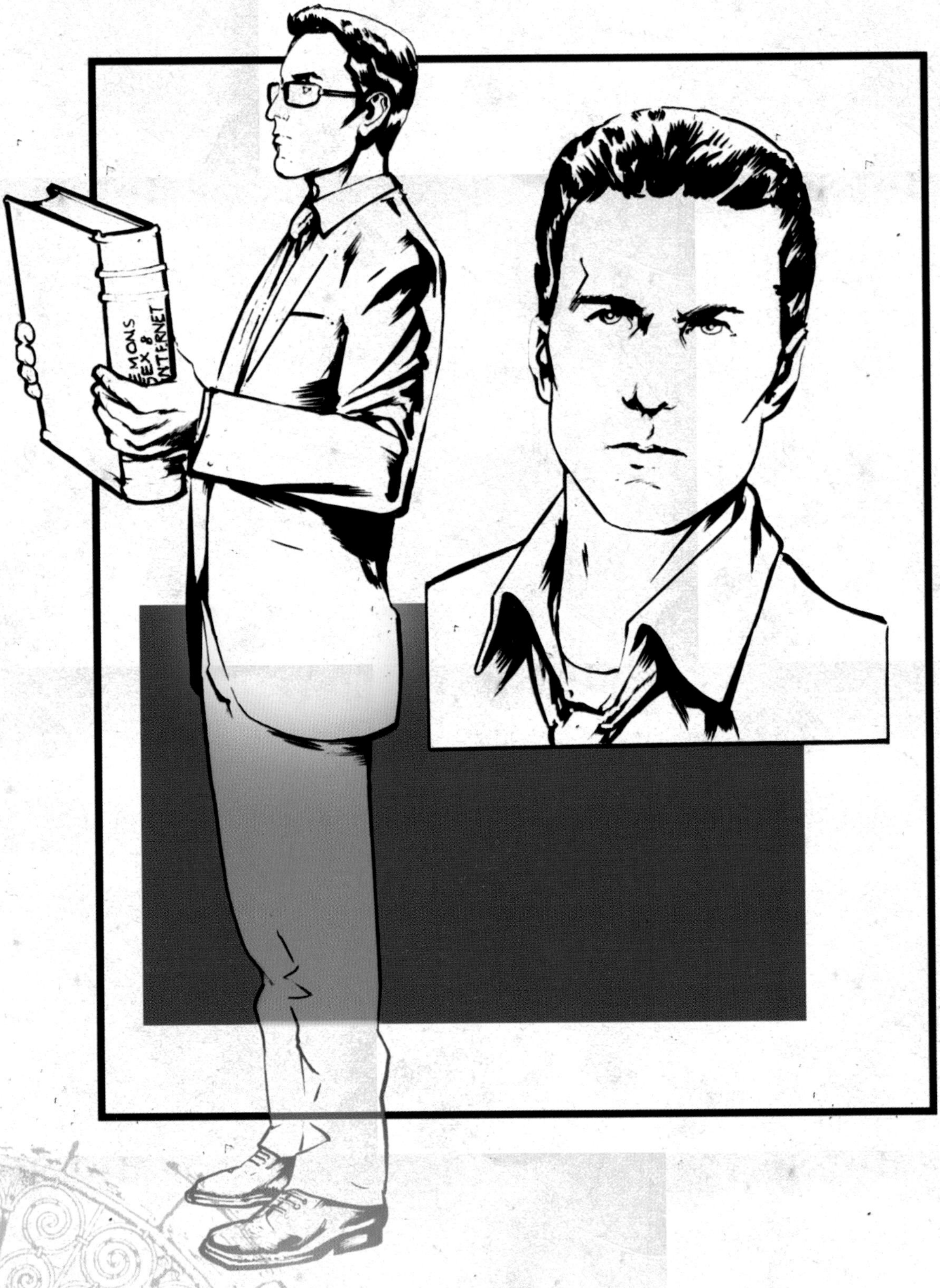
EMONS
EX &
NTERNET

ives

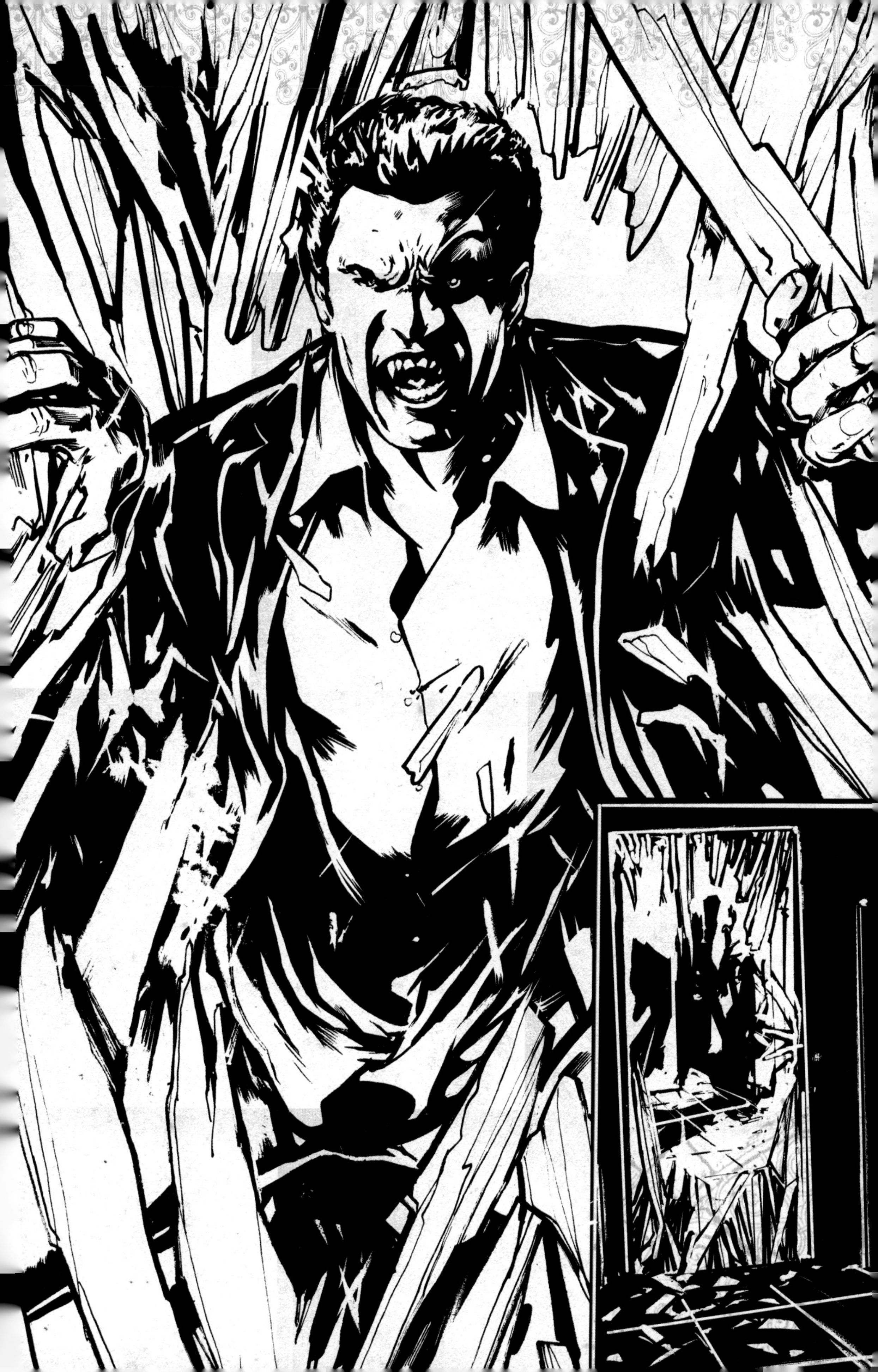

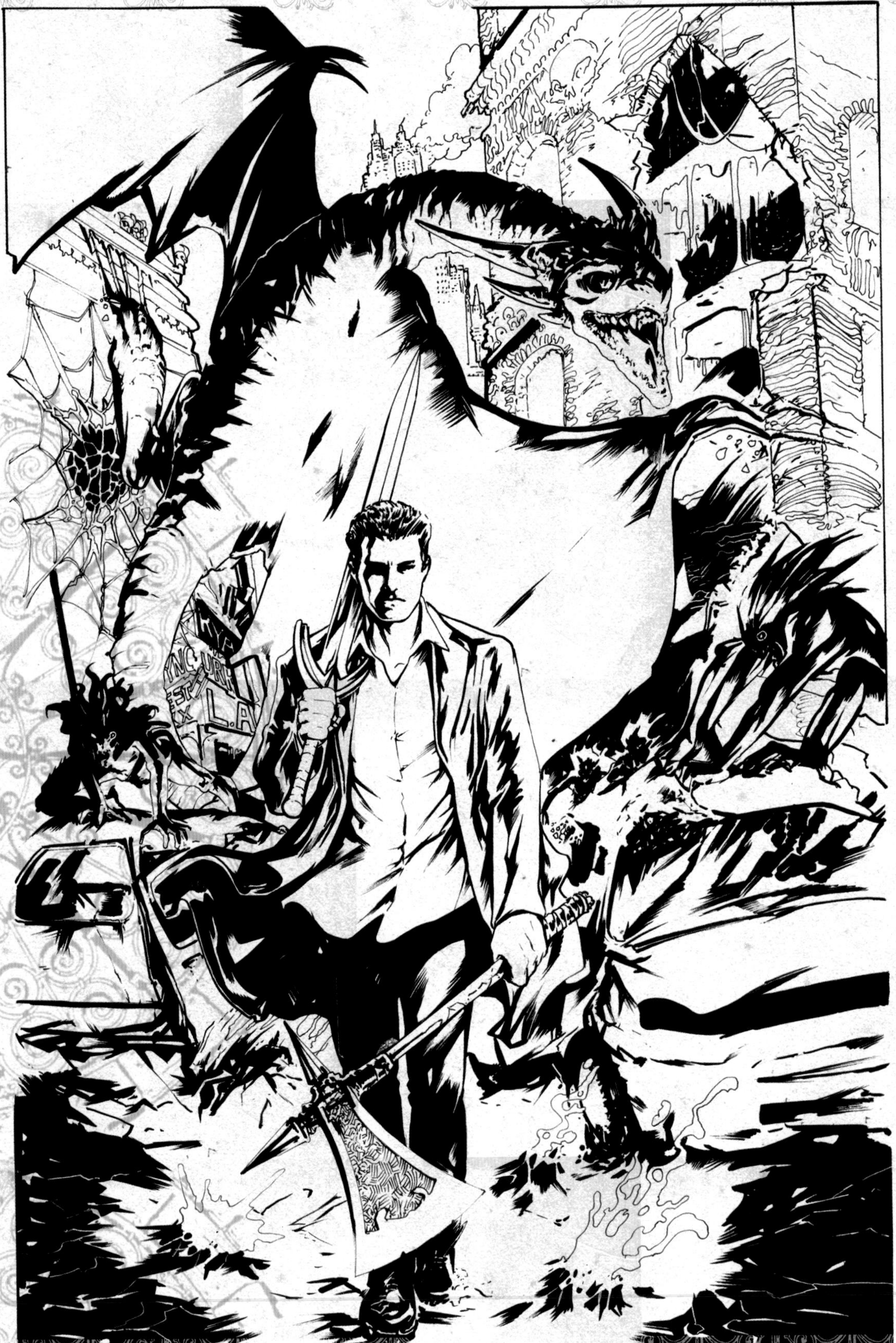

Chapter One
Script and Author Notes

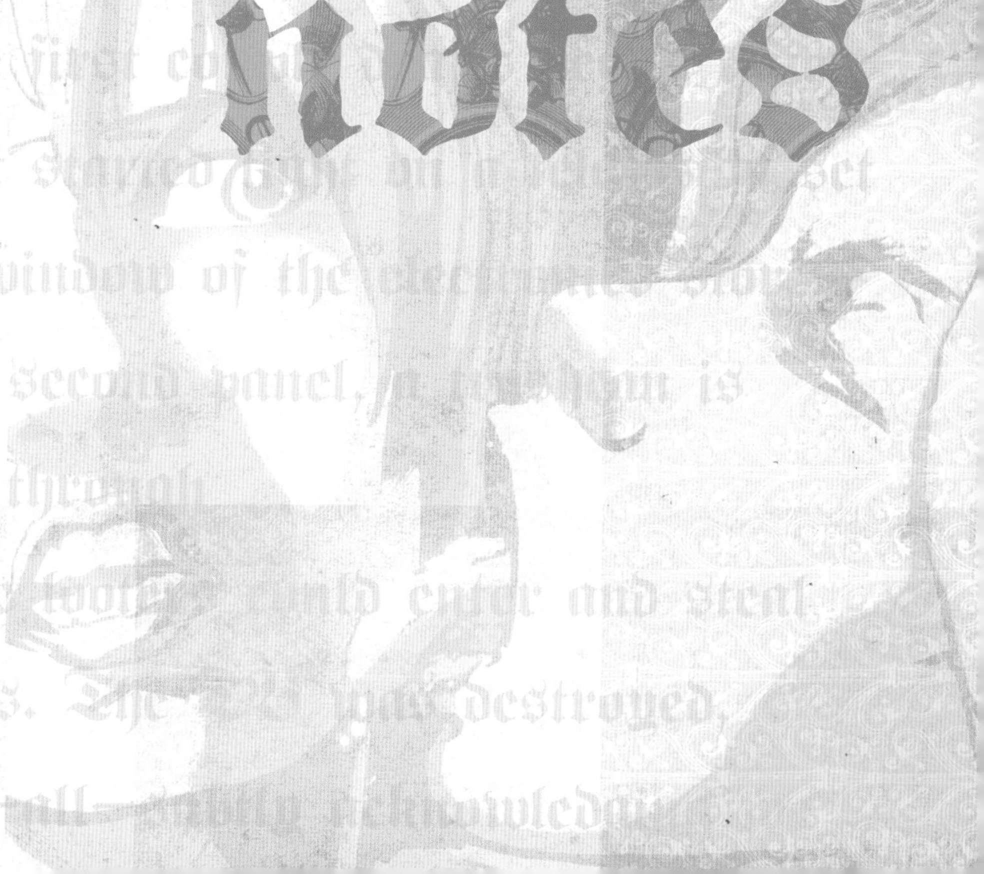

SCRIPT NOTES BY BRIAN LYNCH

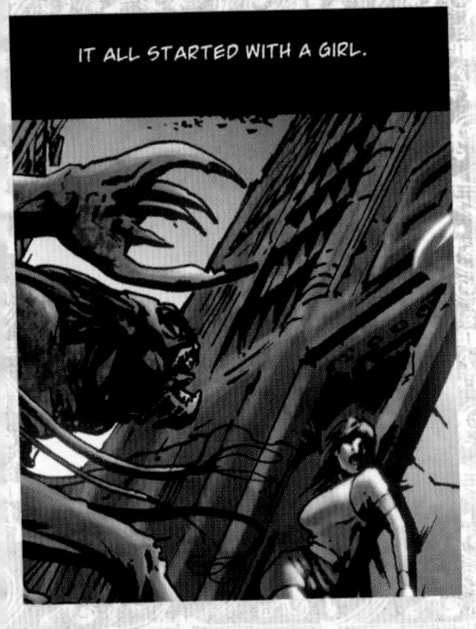
IT ALL STARTED WITH A GIRL.

PAGE ONE

"It all started with a girl."

That sparked an Internet debate the moment *Ain't It Cool* posted the preview pages. People argued over who specifically Angel was talking about. Possible suspects included Buffy, Fred and Cordy. Ryall guessed "Bruce Wayne's mother," which made me question that he actually reads my stuff.

The first couple drafts began differently: it started tight on a television set in the window of the electronics store. In the second panel, a trashcan is thrown through it so the "looters" could enter and steal supplies. The TV was destroyed, not-at-all-subtly acknowledging we were done with the TV show, and now we're in a different medium. I completely forgot that's what David Lynch did in *Twin Peaks: Fire Walk With Me* for the same reason, but a late night viewing of one of my favorite movies reminded me. I think I would have ditched it eventually anyway, as it's too on-the-nose.

Many people, by the way, figured the series would begin with the alleyway fight that occurred two seconds after the series ended. I was, indeed, one of those people. I was *so excited* that I was able to write the specifics of a scene I've wondered about for years. But as we talked about the series, we realized that it would make more sense to start some time after the fight, when everyone had gone their separate ways.

If you think about it, the alleyway fight would have been 22 pages of "look out" and "duck!" along with much slashing and fighting. It's more fun and more entertaining to reveal it in pieces.

ANGEL: AFTER THE FALL -- Issue 1
Plot by Joss Whedon and Brian Lynch • Script by Brian Lynch

PAGE ONE

Panel 1

Thin BLACK PANEL. White lettering. Enjoy the break, Franco!

CAPTION (ANGEL)
It all started with a girl.

Panel 2

A very tall, multi-tentacled DEMON closes in on a REDHEAD. Her back is against a broken WINDOW. An electronics store with a window taken out by a garbage can.

Though it's not really evident in this panel, it appears to be daytime, around dusk, as the blue sky is touched with streaks of red. (NOTE: IT WILL APPEAR TO BE DUSK PRETTY MUCH THROUGHOUT THE ENTIRE SERIES. ENJOY DUSK, READERS!)

1. CAPTION (ANGEL)
I joined an organization that was, quite literally, evil incarnate. I thought by joining them, I could change them. Channel their resources into something positive.

Panel 3

A barrel-chested individual (it's Angel, complete in Angel gear: black jacket, that kinda deal) rushes in front of her, swings the sword and TAKES out the demon. It's only a neck-to-belt kinda shot, so we can't see him yet. He DOES have a battle-worn battle axe strapped to his back.

2. CAPTION (ANGEL)
But I didn't change them. They changed me.
(connected)
3.
Distracted me.
(connected)
4.
Made me weak.

Panel 4

Angel's HERO REVEAL. He stands before the REDHEAD, as HORDES (okay, six or so) the same kind of demons swoop in. Holding the sword steady, looking all sorts of bad ass, ready for action.

5. CAPTION (ANGEL)
And then they killed her.
(connected)
6.
That opened my eyes.

Panel 5

Angel SWINGS a fist off-panel, as DEMON BLOOD sprays a bit.

7. CAPTION (ANGEL)
I took a stand.

PAGE TWO

Panel 1

Demons tackle Angel to the ground. They are joined by 10 or so other demons, flying in. One CLAWS him through the shirt. A bit of blood streaks out.

1. CAPTION (ANGEL)
That was a while ago. And ever since then...

Panel 2

The demons LOOK UP from their attack as something BIG SHADOWS them from above. Maybe even a bit of GREEN DRAGON WING DIPS into frame. Angel smiles slyly as a sound F/X says:

2. SOUND F/X
Snurt

3. CAPTION (ANGEL)
...I've been trying to make up for it. But I'm only one man.
(connected)
4.
One man...

Panel 3

DRAGON REVEAL. He's hovering above them. Giant face about ten feet from theirs. The Dragon is clutching a RED SPORTS CAR (one of the many Wolfram & Hart gave Angel when he joined up) in his feet. STREAM OF FIRE from his mouth evaporating the demons surrounding Angel, turning them to ash from the knees up. Angel takes out the REMAINING two demons with ONE SWORD swipe. He's not even getting up to do it.

5. CAPTION (ANGEL)
...with a very large dragon on his side.

Bottom of panel:

6. CAPTION (ANGEL)
He was part of the same organization. Two minutes into fighting him, I realized he was as mislead I was.
(connected)
7.
Since then we have an understanding.

PAGE THREE

Panel 1

Smoking demon legs all about, Angel grabs one of the Demons' weapons from the ground as the Redhead walks over, YELLING. Behind her, two MEN (one blonde, the other BALD) resume going through the broken window to grab some electronics: radios, flashlights, etc. This can be shown throughout the page.

1. REDHEAD
What the hell is going on?

2. ANGEL
Everything's fine. Resume your looting.

3. REDHEAD
We weren't looting!

Panel 2

Angel, not checking to see if she's alright, not even really acknowledging her, hands her a card. Behind them, we see the CAR dragon was holding DROP to the ground. Still drivable, though it has big dragon-claw-marks on the top of it.

4. REDHEAD
We were stealing what we need to survive! Is that looting?

PAGE TWO

The Dragon being Angel's best new pal was Joss' idea. I wanted Spike to run in and kill the Dragon seconds after Angel declared that HE wanted to. Joss had the better idea. This is not the last time this would be the case.

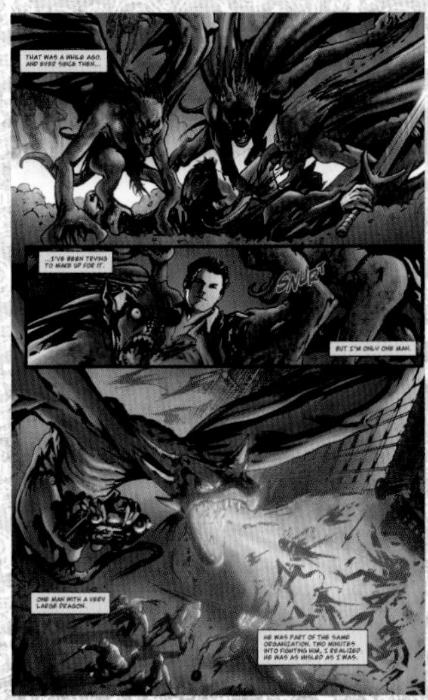

THAT WAS A WHILE AGO, AND EVER SINCE THEN...
...I'VE BEEN TRYING TO MAKE UP FOR IT.
SNURT
BUT I'M ONLY ONE MAN.
ONE MAN WITH A VERY LARGE DRAGON.
HE WAS PART OF THE SAME ORGANIZATION. TWO MINUTES INTO FIGHTING HIM, I REALIZED HE WAS AS MISLED AS I WAS.

PAGE THREE

Angel's at his most interesting when he is burdened with massive amounts of guilt, or when he's forced to "reach out" and engage people. The guilt came easy (sending an entire city to hell will do that), and you'll notice we've forced Angel into situations where he has to let his guard down, or talk to people (be it strangers or his own son, or in issue 5, a huge crowd).

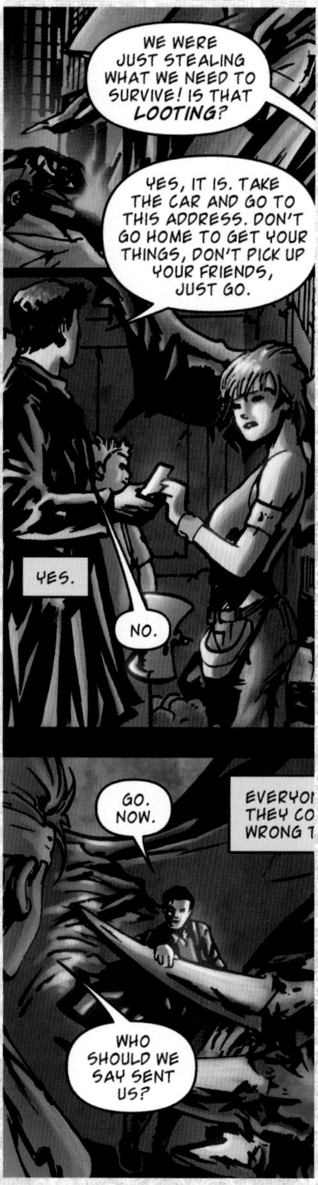
WE WERE JUST STEALING WHAT WE NEED TO SURVIVE! IS THAT LOOTING?
YES, IT IS. TAKE THE CAR AND GO TO THIS ADDRESS. DON'T GO HOME TO GET YOUR THINGS, DON'T PICK UP YOUR FRIENDS, JUST GO.
YES.
NO.
GO. NOW.
WHO SHOULD WE SAY SENT US?

5. ANGEL
Kind of. Take the car and go to this address. Don't go home to get your things, don't pick up your friends, just go.

6. REDHEAD
Do you know what's going on?

7. CAPTION (ANGEL)
Yes.

8. ANGEL
No.

Panel 3

Angel hands one of the weapons from the demon to the Redhead. The Bald Guy hands the Blonde Guy a bunch of flashlights from the electronics store behind him.

9. REDHEAD
One minute everything was fine, and then...
10.
(little letters)
...I don't deserve this! I'm a good person! I'm a lawyer!

11. CAPTION (ANGEL)
All night.
(connected)
12.
Hell, for the last few months, it's the same story.

Panel 4

The Dragon lowers so Angel can walk onto his back.

13. ANGEL
Just go. Now.

14. CAPTION (ANGEL)
Everyone wants to know what they could have possibly done wrong to be in this situation.

15. REDHEAD
Who should we say sent us?

Panel 5

The Dragon takes off. Angel rides away, leaving the humans below.

16. ANGEL
You shouldn't.

17. CAPTION (ANGEL)
Each time. Every time, I leave them in the dark.

PAGES FOUR-FIVE

Double page spread! Somewhat!

Panels 1 and 2 are small panels, positioned, jagged, on the top left of the page, one staggered below the other.

Panel 1

A shot of the Dragon flying higher and higher above the city. The "camera" is below.

1. CAPTION (ANGEL)
I can't tell them that they're here because I took a stand. My friends stood by me. Wolfram & Hart sent an army.

Panel 2

Closer still, we can see more of Angel. Grim face.

2. CAPTION (ANGEL)
There were losses on both sides.

Panel 3

THIS IS THE BIG PANEL! TWO PAGES WORTH! The camera is just above Dragon and Angel. Dragon is flying over Los Angeles, allowing us to see blocks and blocks of it. And it's gone to hell.

The skyscraper buildings are in various states of destruction: either completely destroyed, or halfway (sides ripped off, or "demon" additions added on, with levels added (comprised of organic tissue, or bone, or shadows, or all three, LA is a big place), or smoking. Demons and monsters of all shapes and sizes roam the streets. The sky is a reddish haze, the sun AND moon out at the same time. Nightmare/fever dream scenario. Los Angeles has been sent to hell. Literally.

3. CAPTION (ANGEL)
And then Wolfram & Hart sent Los Angeles to hell.

PAGES FOUR-FIVE

Franco is amazing. Let's continue.

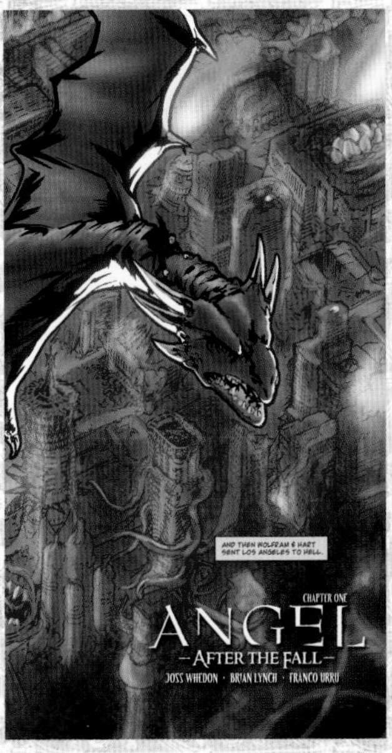
AND THEN WOLFRAM & HART SENT LOS ANGELES TO HELL.
CHAPTER ONE
ANGEL
—AFTER THE FALL—
JOSS WHEDON · BRIAN LYNCH · FRANCO URRU

PAGE SIX

Panel 1

High above the city, we center in on a city street. Desolate, torn apart. Ahead of ANGEL is the barrier. Wrapped around the city, it's a clear, almost invisible barrier that extends at the city limits into the sky. We wouldn't even notice it's there but for a plasma-esque sheen to the foreground. Basically, use your artistic wiles to demonstrate that there's no leaving Los Angeles. They could be in a dimension made to look like LA that simply ENDS where the LA city limits ends, they could have a barrier around the real LA. Anyone IN the city has no idea. But we will. And I will tell you, just call me and we'll chat.

1. CAPTION (ANGEL)
It took the citizens a few hours to realize it wasn't a temporary situation.
(connected)
2.
They figured it out roughly when the demons did.

Panel 2

Still above the city, we see a LARGE DEMON MONSTER trudging down the block, picking up cars, looking for humans.

3. CAPTION (ANGEL)
The more powerful creatures conquered and divided the town.
(connected)
4.
They hunted any human that wasn't going along with their game plan.

Panel 3

Angel is fast approaching the Wolfram & Hart building. Just as we remember it, only sans a side and a roof.

5. CAPTION (ANGEL)
And Wolfram & Hart, always a fan of irony...
(connected)
6.
...in addition to torture...
(connected)
7.
....dropped me where it all began.

Panel 4

Dragon hovers next to the aforementioned hole in the side of a building. The room is the Research and Development Department, filled with many half-finished inventions, creepy old books, and walls of blueprints. Angel gets off the Dragon, heads out of the room, looking back at Dragon.

8. CAPTION (ANGEL)
I abide for now.

9. ANGEL
Go to the parking garage, grab a few more cars for the night rounds. Leave the black ones.

10. CAPTION (ANGEL)
Go against their rules, the punishment would be worse. Not sure how, but they're Wolfram & Hart, they not only know of places worse than hell, they have timeshares there.

Panel 5

Angel heads into another room as he HEARS SOMETHING...he takes a STAKE from his inside jacket pocket. SOMETHING IS COMING UP AT HIM FROM THE SHADOWS.

11. CAPTION (ANGEL)
Place is kinda dead lately.

PAGE SEVEN

Panel 1

Biggest panel on the page. Angel is SLAMMED AGAINST A WALL, so hard he's knocking pictures and whatnot off of the wall. It's painful for him.

Behind him, is BURGE. An overweight pudge of a demon with massive wings, impressive in stature. Older. Clearly the boss. OFFSPRING OF BURGE is the guy slamming Angel against the wall. He's the same species of Demon, but is all rippling muscle. Big thick imposing meathead of a creature.

1. CAPTION (ANGEL)
But we do have the occasional walk-in.

2. BURGE
So, Angel.
(connected)
3.
How was your work?

4. CAPTION (ANGEL)
Burge. Lord of Downtown LA. And his son. Moron offspring of the Lord of Downtown LA.

Panel 2

CAMERA ANGEL: Close up on Offspring of Burge snarling at Angel, spittle dropping from the corners of his fangs. Behind them, in the background, Burge calmly examines a lamp. Angel's face is in pain, he's trying his best to not show it—

5. BURGE
Bring down lots of big bad monsters?

6. ANGEL
It's not work when you love what you do. Always a pleasure, Burge.

7. OFFSPRING
I want to pop his head off, poppa. I want to wear his skin as a spawning cloak.

PAGE SIX

"Leave the black ones" was changed to "leave the Viper" after someone e-mailed me and asked if Angel's Viper would be making any appearances.

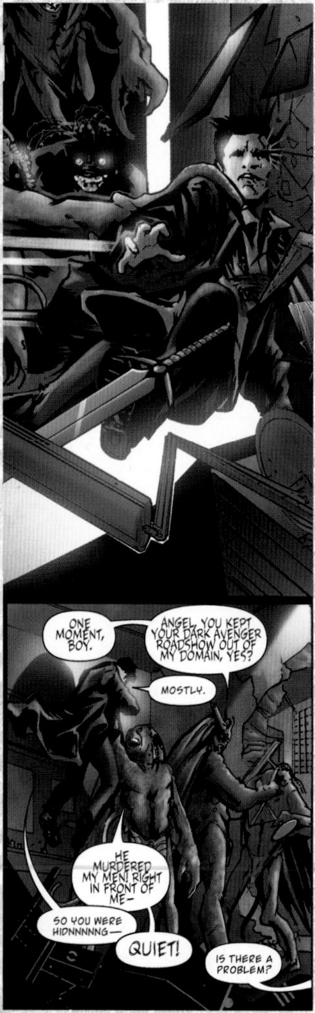
ONE MOMENT, BOY.
ANGEL, YOU KEPT YOUR DARK AVENGER ROADSHOW OUT OF MY DOMAIN, YES?
MOSTLY.
HE MURDERED MY MEN! RIGHT IN FRONT OF ME–
SO YOU WERE HIDNNNNG—
QUIET!
IS THERE A PROBLEM?

Panel 3

Offspring of Burge HOISTS Angel into the air. He YELLS at him, gets spittle on Angel's face. Burge hands the lamp to a Helper Demon (same kind of demon as Burge and his son, but lesser in stature). Burge is clearly taking stuff from Wolfram & Hart as payment for Angel killing his men.

8. BURGE
Ah, youth. You kept the demon slaying to locations strictly outside my domain, yes, yes?

9. ANGEL
For the most part...

10. WESLEY (off-panel)
Is there a problem?

PAGE EIGHT

Panel 1

BIG PANEL, BIG, BIG CROWD PLEASING REVEAL. WESLEY. Standing in the forefront, turning around to face "us", he's wearing his old suit, with a RED TIE. As the scene goes on, it will be quite clear that Wesley is non-corporal, but that shouldn't be obvious yet. His arrival has surprised everyone in the room, the workers drop their office supplies and protect Burge.

Angel is in-panel, still being manhandled.

1. ANGEL
Where were you?

2. WESLEY
I was out. I'm back.

3. OFFSPRING
He took down six of my men!

Panel 2

Wesley calmly steps forward, as Offspring gets irate. He TIGHTENS HIS GRIP on Angel.

4. ANGEL (words get smaller in last sentence)
They were trying to kill humans. Right under my nose can't help but notice your grip is getting tighter—

5. WESLEY
Now Angel, I'm sure they weren't trying to KILL the humans. They were trying to enslave them.

6. OFFSPRING
Exactly!

Panel 3

Burge steps up to Wesley. Wesley doesn't back down. Burge's Men provide back-up, aim their (human bone-made) SPEARS at Wesley.

7. BURGE
You have to keep your boy on a leash, Price.

8. WESLEY
Has that worked with your son?

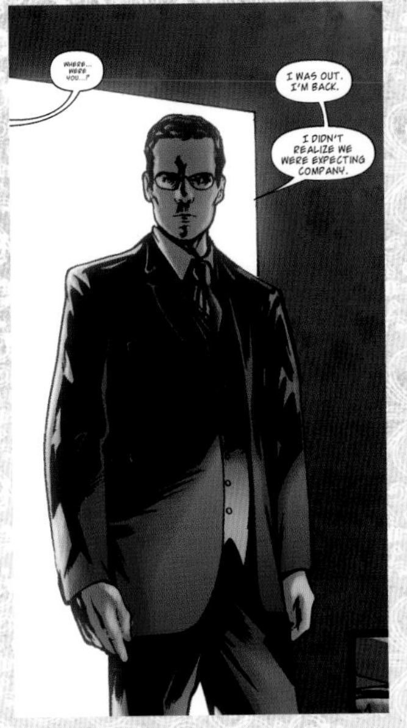
WHERE... WERE YOU...?
I WAS OUT. I'M BACK.
I DIDN'T REALIZE WE WERE EXPECTING COMPANY.

PAGE EIGHT

I think Wesley's return was the most dividing event in the book. Half of the people wanted Wesley to stay resting in peace (his story over), the other half argued it wouldn't be *Angel* without Wesley.

As for me? Joss said "let's bring Wesley back" and I said "okay." And then I asked him if he would be a ghost or up and about, and Joss said "a ghost" and I said "you're so smart" and he said "leave me alone, I have to get back to *Dollhouse*" and I said "oh, Joss, you're so funny, what's a dolls house?"

The reason Wesley's story is officially over is the best reason to bring him back, actually. Wesley earned his rest and it's still taken away from him.

As for Wesley's return to suit-and-tie? Well, Lorne explained it best in issue 4: Wolfram & Hart is cruel. They know Wesley's evolved beyond the person he was when he sported this look, so they slap him back down and force him to wear it 24/7.

9. BURGE
The other lords, we talk. They all want to know where Angel is. I keep my mouth shut because I appreciate what Angel does. His little jaunts on the outside give the humans some kind of false hope and that keeps them placated.

PAGE NINE

Panel 1

CLOSE-UP on Angel's face. Even as he's having the lifeforce STRANGLED out of him, Burge's words hurt even more.

1. BURGE
Plus, you know, I owe him.
(connected)
2.
If not for Angel, none of this would be possible.

Panel 2

Over the shoulder shot of Burge, who points at Angel, annoyed and yelling. Wesley, standing before him, is front and center in the panel.

3. BURGE
But then he goes and—

4. WESLEY
I know, he's a loose cannon. Always has been. And, as the last official representative of this branch of Wolfram & Hart, I can assure you that we do not condone Angel's actions in the least.

5. BURGE
Well, good—

Panel 3

Match shot of the last panel, but this time it moves in a bit, so we get a CLOSE UP of Wesley. He means business. Firm, cool.

6. WESLEY
I can also assure you that Angel's fate isn't up to you.
(connected)
7.
We kept him around, even after a fairly alarming indiscretion. So I ask you to tell your steroid-ridden child to step down lest he kills Angel before we get a chance.

Panel 4

On Angel and Offspring.

Panel 5

Burge heads out. His underlings, armfulls of office supplies.

8. BURGE
Son, let's go.

9. OFFSPRING
Father...

10. BURGE
Stay in tonight, Angel. You're grounded.

11. WESLEY
And no dessert for a week.

HE SPENDS TONIGHT INSIDE. LET HIM THINK ABOUT WHAT HE'S DONE.

I'M ALSO SERIOUSLY CONSIDERING TAKING AWAY HIS TV PRIVILEGES, BELIEVE-YOU-ME.

PAGE NINE
Almost every panel of Wesley's dialog in the final comic is tweaked from the original script. I really played with it until it sounded right. Annoying to the letterer, absolutely, but I wanted it to be perfect. For instance, the "no dessert for a week" line was changed to the "TV privileges" line, which isn't all that different, but I think the final line is much stronger and funnier.

PAGE TEN

Panel 1

Burge still doesn't loosen his grip. Wesley steps up to him. Burge, back to us, points to a pretty impressive STEEL DESK as he walks out the door.

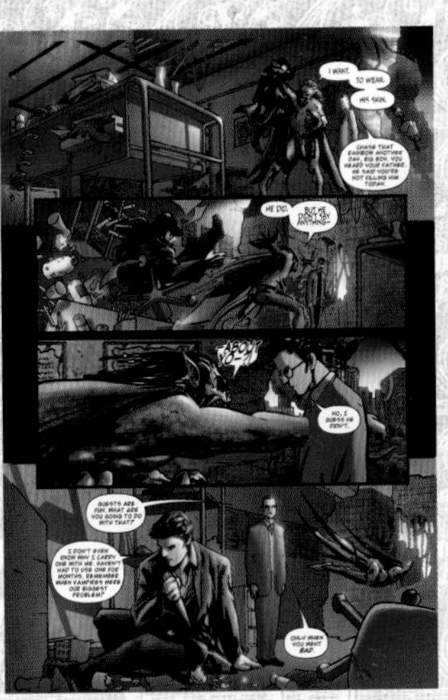

1. BURGE
And you take down any of my men again, I'm coming back for your head as recompense.
(connected)
2.
And that desk, I love that desk.

3. WESLEY
You heard Daddy. Let the vampire go. You're not killing him today.

Panel 2

Burge TOSSES Angel aside, into a row of desks. He turns to Wesley, who looks at him, calmly. Burge is ready to take down Wesley...

4. OFFSPRING
I know. But he didn't say anything—

Panel 3

Big panel. Offspring SENDS A FIST FLYING TOWARDS Wesley. Who, we reveal in this moment, is non-corporal. The fist GOES THROUGH Wesley (their point of contact is shown by Wesley's body whisping away a bit). Offspring takes out a wall, however.

5. OFFSPRING
—about—?!

6. WESLEY
No, I guess he didn't.

Panel 4

Offspring heads out. Angel picks himself, holds up his stake as up Wes heads over.

7. OFFSPRING (little letters)
I'm killing six in his name.

8. WESLEY
Guests are fun. What were you going to do with that?

9. ANGEL
Haven't used one in a while, but it's still a reflex. Remember the good old days, when Vampires were our biggest problem?

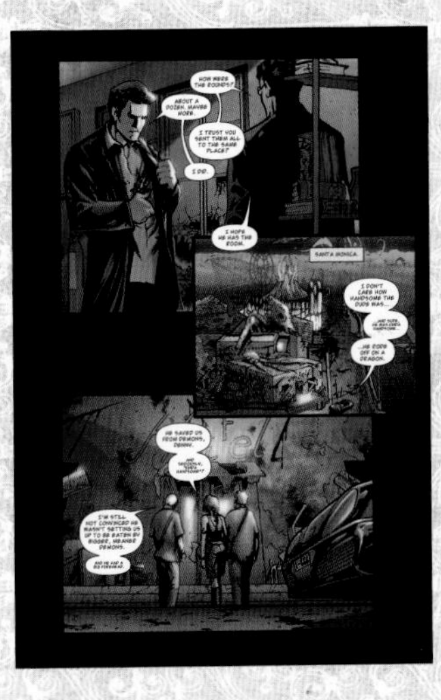

10. WESLEY
Only when you went bad.

PAGE ELEVEN

Panel 1

Angel looks at the wound in his belly. Some blood on his shirt. Wesley stands before him. We see he's standing amidst the broken desk, standing through it. Our boy is definitely a ghost.

1. WESLEY
How were rounds?

2. ANGEL
About a dozen. Maybe more.

3. WESLEY

I miss rounds. But I guess aside from the occasional popping through walls and freaking out the evil-dooers with a heartfelt booga booga I'd be quite inconsequential.
(connected)

4.

I trust you sent them all to the same place?

5. ANGEL

I did.

Panel 2

Big panel. SANTA MONICA. The car Angel gave the Redhead and company is parked outside a BIG ABANDONED HOTEL. The ocean is nearby, it's BOILING and RED. The door is opened.

6. CAPTION (WESLEY)

"I just hope he has the room."

7. BALD MAN

I don't care how handsome the dude was...
(connected)

8.

...and sure he was kinda handsome...
(connected)

9.

...he rode off on a dragon.

Panel 3

They make their way through a door.

10. REDHEAD

He saved us, Denny.
(connected)

11.

And seriously, come on, he was very handsome.

12. BALD MAN

He had a big head, and I'm still not convinced he wasn't setting us up to be eaten by bigger, meaner demons.

PAGE TWELVE

Panel 1

Over their shoulders as they look out. There are a ton of people in the waiting room. All a bit scared. Some have guns, rifles at their side. You can throw a couple of (non-threatening) demons in there too, not all of them are bad, you know. Don't be a speciesist. The Bald Guy whispers to the Redhead.

1. REDHEAD

Oh, hi.

2. BALD MAN

(small letters)
See? Our chances were better on the outside. THESE demons can assume human form.

3. REDHEAD

So, yeah. We were—

Panel 2

Match shot of 1. Only every single person AIMS a gun/knife/sword/ tentacle at them.

CHILL OUT, HOTSHOT.

PAGE TWELVE

Gwen and Nina didn't really get a chance to shine on the TV show, and we quickly decided how much fun it would be to spotlight them, especially in this medium. A werewolf girl and an electric lady suit comic books so well.

Connor obviously had a lot of face-time in the show, but this is a completely new role for him. Everyone in the book is going through some form of insane change, but Connor being this well-adjusted is as big a change as Angel no longer being a vampire. Our boy is all grown up. He's become his father's son in the best sense of the word.

At one point, when I realized that the issue was running long, we were going to drop this scene into the beginning of issue two, leaving the audience to wonder WHO Angel sent the looters to. But we needed some time away from Angel and Wesley before jumping into Gunn's current situation. It also helped to show the scope of what Wolfram & Hart had done.

I think it's kinda cool that, coming off of *Spike: Asylum* and *Spike: Shadow Puppets* (available in trade paperback now!), people were expecting me to favor Spike at the expense of Angel. It wasn't on purpose, but the fact that Spike's intro doesn't happen in the first issue kinda let people know that the series wasn't going to be *Spike and His Little Pal Angel: After the Fall*.

4. REDHEAD
Oh.

Panel 3

All the electricity in the room (from all the lights) JUMPS from the lamps and becomes a curved BOLT OF ELECTRICITY that surrounds all three of them.

5. BALD MAN
This is so much better than being on our own and NOT dying.

Panel 4

The light bulbs pop as GWEN RAIDEN steps forward. Exactly as we remember her, same outfit and everything. She's manipulating the electricity, it's emanating from her hands, and she's enjoying every second of it. Give her an awesome first panel.

6. GWEN
Relax, hotshot.
(connected)
7.
We just need to see if you're on the up and up.

PAGE THIRTEEN

Panels 1-4 are match shots. Redhead from the waist up, surrounded by darkness...

Panel 1

1. NINA (off panel)
Their hearts are racing.

Panel 2

NINA leans in from the darkness, SNIFFS the Redhead. Nina also looks the same, only she's phasing a bit in werewolf mode, a bit more bestial than she should be. Not necessarily in appearance, more in stance and attitude.

2. REDHEAD
We're not, I'm not...

3. NINA
And their scents...

4. REDHEAD
Oh...?

5. NINA
Pure fear.

Panel 3

She LICKS the Redhead up the cheek.

Panel 4

Match shot. Nina is HORRIFIED. Redhead is scared?

6. NINA
Did I...?

7. REDHEAD
She's tenderizing me she's tenderizing me she's tenderizing me

8. NINA
No! It's the sun/moon situation! They're both out at once, do you have any idea what that does to a werewolf?

9. REDHEAD
Makes you hungry?!

10. NINA
No!

11. REDHEAD
Makes you bi-curious?!

Panel 5

Someone steps forward. The crowd parts when he arrives. It's an over the shoulder shot of CONNOR. Everyone's in awe of him in the room, he's clearly in charge.

12. CONNOR
Relax, Nina, Gwen.
(connected)
13.
Angel sent them.

14. GWEN
How can you be sure?

PAGE FOURTEEN

Panel 1

AWESOME AWESOME shot of Connor. We see the Redhead and company from behind, but definitely the FOCUS of the shot is Connor.

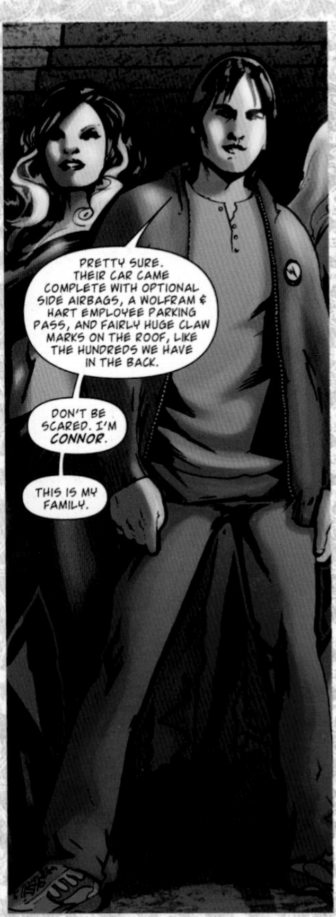
PRETTY SURE. THEIR CAR CAME COMPLETE WITH OPTIONAL SIDE AIRBAGS, A WOLFRAM & HART EMPLOYEE PARKING PASS, AND FAIRLY HUGE CLAW MARKS ON THE ROOF, LIKE THE HUNDREDS WE HAVE IN THE BACK.
DON'T BE SCARED. I'M CONNOR.
THIS IS MY FAMILY.

Hooded sweatshirt unzipped over a t-shirt, jeans, sneakers. Warm, friendly smile on his face. A bit war-torn but he's not at all grim. He's embraced his role of champion. He's kick-ass and cool. Gwen and Nina stand behind him. The crowd stands behind them.

1. CONNOR
Because they came in a Wolfram & Hart company car completete with optional dragon claw marks on the hood, like the hundreds we have in the back.
(connected)
2.
Don't be scared. I'm Connor.
(connected)
3.
This is my family.

Panel 2

Small panel. Back to Wolfram & Hart building.

4. ANGEL (from inside)
Damn it...

Panel 3

Small panel. We're in the the lab at Wolfram & Hart. Angel is trying to heal his belly wound. This entails putting what looks to be a small LEACH LIKE CREATURE on the wound.

5. ANGEL
This is supposed to heal?

6. WESLEY (off-panel)
I think so. Do you feel it biting—

7. ANGEL
Do I feel "it"? This is alive?

PAGE FIFTEEN

Panel 1

Wesley is looking over all the shelves of potions and such. Angel is doing his best not to look like a crybaby in the background. The creature on his belly is SMOKING a bit.

1. WESLEY
Something in the room should be. It's not capable of emotion or anything.

2. ANGEL
Oh, good. I'd hate to think I'm bumming the parasite out. Don't we have anything better?

3. WESLEY
I'm sure.

Panel 2

Angel tries to PULL the creature off, but it has planted suction tentacles into his wound. Angel is pulling it about a foot from his belly, but it's still sucking to the wound.

4. WESLEY
If it was ever used to heal, destroy, mutate, murder or conjure, it's somewhere within these walls.

5. ANGEL
Gotta hand it to them. Wolfram & Hart is prepared for anything. Most likely because they're also the cause of it.
(connected)
6.
So. You went out.

Panel 3

Head and shoulder shot of Angel, who tosses the leech-thing away.

7. WESLEY (off-panel)
When?

8. ANGEL
When Burge was here. You said you went out.

9. WESLEY
I didn't. I was watching you.

Panel 4

Angel buttons his shirt back up. Wes walks over.

10. ANGEL
Were you waiting for Burge's son to put my head through a wall before you intervened?

11. WESLEY
No.
(connected)
12.
I was waiting for you to do that to him.

13. ANGEL
I take out Burge's son, Burge and his men come after me. I take them out, and every demon in hell rises up to become Lord of this area, using their humans slaves as weapons, shields and projectiles. What am I supposed to do then?

14. WESLEY
Kill them all.

PAGES FIFTEEN-SIXTEEN

Thus begins the scene that went through infinite drafts. This was so important to me to get just right. This is the moment that motivates Angel to get back on his horse and try again. It was also the scene that I kept rewriting and sending Chris, even after it was drawn.

You'll notice that Angel and Wesley mention they don't know where their former teammates are. That's how it was in the original outline: the group had gone their separate ways and definitely kept more of a distance. This didn't ring true, though. Angel would know. He'd seek everyone out. He might not send them a basket of oranges and a birthday card, but he'd want to know where they are and how they were, for various reasons.

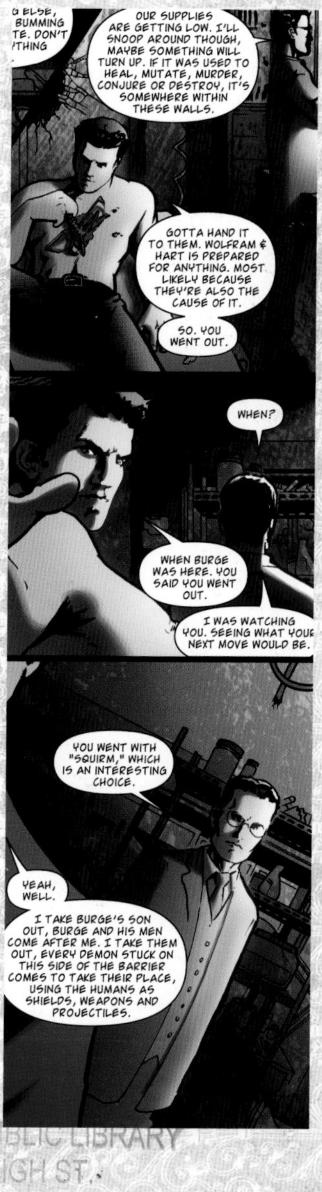

OUR SUPPLIES ARE GETTING LOW. I'LL SNOOP AROUND THOUGH, MAYBE SOMETHING WILL TURN UP. IF IT WAS USED TO HEAL, MUTATE, MURDER, CONJURE OR DESTROY, IT'S SOMEWHERE WITHIN THESE WALLS.
GOTTA HAND IT TO THEM. WOLFRAM & HART IS PREPARED FOR ANYTHING. MOST LIKELY BECAUSE THEY'RE ALSO THE CAUSE OF IT.
SO. YOU WENT OUT.
WHEN?
WHEN BURGE WAS HERE. YOU SAID YOU WENT OUT.
I WAS WATCHING YOU. SEEING WHAT YOUR NEXT MOVE WOULD BE.
YOU WENT WITH "SQUIRM," WHICH IS AN INTERESTING CHOICE.
YEAH, WELL.
I TAKE BURGE'S SON OUT, BURGE AND HIS MEN COME AFTER ME. I TAKE THEM OUT, EVERY DEMON STUCK ON THIS SIDE OF THE BARRIER COMES TO TAKE THEIR PLACE, USING THE HUMANS AS SHIELDS, WEAPONS AND PROJECTILES.

PAGE SIXTEEN

Panel 1

Angel puts the jacket on, heads for the door.

1. ANGEL
Is that what your bosses want me to do?

2. CAPTION (ANGEL)
Okay, that was low.

3. WESLEY
No.
(connected)
4.
My "bosses" won't be happy I said it. To be quite honest, I'm hoping it convinces them to break my contract and let me move on but that's not why I'm suggesting it.

Panel 2

Angel walks down the hallway. Wesley follows, passing through walls.

5. ANGEL
Do you remember what happened last time I rose up, Wesley?

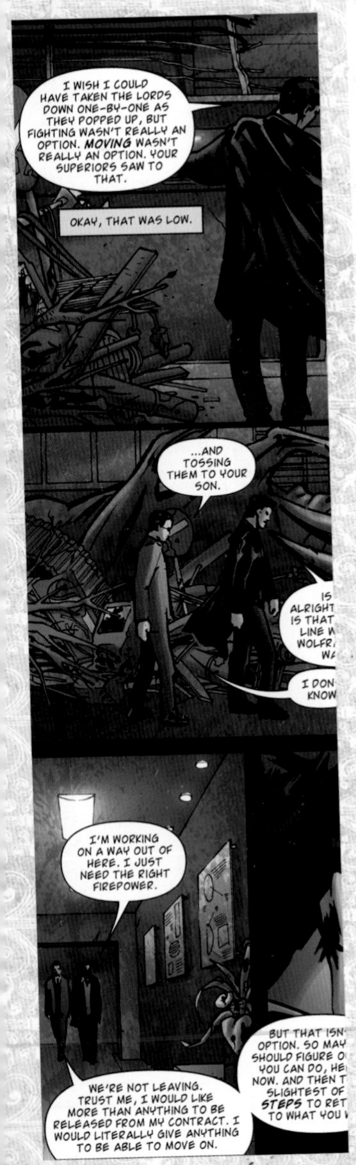

I WISH I COULD HAVE TAKEN THE LORDS DOWN ONE-BY-ONE AS THEY POPPED UP, BUT FIGHTING WASN'T REALLY AN OPTION. MOVING WASN'T REALLY AN OPTION. YOUR SUPERIORS SAW TO THAT.
OKAY, THAT WAS LOW.
...AND TOSSING THEM TO YOUR SON.
I'M WORKING ON A WAY OUT OF HERE. I JUST NEED THE RIGHT FIREPOWER.
WE'RE NOT LEAVING. TRUST ME, I WOULD LIKE MORE THAN ANYTHING TO BE RELEASED FROM MY CONTRACT. I WOULD LITERALLY GIVE ANYTHING TO BE ABLE TO MOVE ON.

(connected)
6.
I got you killed. And, as a bonus, sent everyone straight to hell. We still don't know what happened to—

7. WESLEY
You looked for them. They're most likely dead.
(small letters)
8.
That didn't help the argument at all, did it?

Panel 3

Angel passes by the Dragon, who is sleeping. He is hording cards in a makeshift nest of desks, cabinets, full trees, light posts, stop signs, etc. Wesley continues.

9. ANGEL
And I'm working on a way out. But we're going to need firepower.

10. WESLEY
And you're going to get it?

11. ANGEL
Working on it.

12. WESLEY
Building up to it?

13. ANGEL
WORKING ON IT.

Panel 4

Angel looks at the BLUEPRINTS on the walls. One, which we will zero in on later, is a big OPAL LOOKING CAT'S EYE. Go nuts, make it look awesome. About the size of someone's hand, definitely powerful and of mystical origin. Don't worry for this panel, though, just know we're going to have to zoom in on it.

14. ANGEL
I wish I could have taken the lords down as they popped up, but I...
(connected)
15.
...well, you were there. Fighting wasn't really an option. Moving wasn't really an

option. But now I'm healed, and I'm trying my best. But I won't risk anyone else's safety—

                    16. WESLEY
Other than yourself.

                    17. ANGEL
And Spike, if we can find him.

Panel 5

CLOSE UP of Angel who looks at the blue prints.

                    18. ANGEL
I'll get us out of here.
(connected)
                    19.
I'll get everyone out.

PAGE SEVENTEEN

Panel 1

Establishing shot of Kr'ph and Betta George. Sitting in the stands, some of the seats cleared out for the throne. He has a bunch of well-armed DEMONS (with a few HUMANS too) around him and the football field.

                    1. KR'PH (Demon-y font)
You're all breaking my stride! I am Kr'ph, Lord of Westwood! Dark Overseer of everything West of Beverly Hills!

Panel 2

Establishing shot of the newly converted football field.

                    2. KR'PH
THIS is my domain! YOU are my monkeys! I have converted Uk-La sporting field into great gladiator arena!

Panel 3

Shot of the "warriors". Normal Human Men, forced to hold big weapons. All of which stand casually on the football field, unsure of what to do.

                    3. KR'PH
And yet you warriors stand there and stare at me with mongrel cocked heads and your fifth digit housed in your sit-down spots!

                    4. Gladiator 1
(small letters)
"Warriors"? I was a cop.

                    5. Gladiator 2
(small letters)
I was a bouncer. That's kinda like a warrior, I guess.

Panel 4

KR'PH turns to Betta George.

                    6. KR'PH
Splenden Beast, brain-yell at the warrior monkeys! Make them stab!

                    7. BETTA GEORGE
"Brain-yell"? Dude, I am a telepath. But if you think I have the power to force anyone to do anything, let alone, you know, stab—

                    8. KR'PH
The fish wants power?

PAGE SEVENTEEN

Had to be careful to not make Kr'ph too Yakov Smirnoff ("hell, what a country!"). Whereas Burge favored modern-day stuff (like the desk and Angel's office supplies), Kr'ph is desperately trying to go back to what he remembers as "the glory days." Gladiator arena, big throne, guys forced to be gladiators, girls forced into a harem.

More importantly, the introduction of Betta George into official Angel continuity. A character from *Asylum* and *Shadow Puppets* (have I mentioned anything about their availability?), he proved popular among the fans and Joss himself, who wanted to find a place for him in the book.

Originally he was just going to be Spike's sidekick from the get-go, but it seemed awkward. Kr'ph is a "brittle-boned" guy with translucent skin and it just clicked that Betta George could do anything that character was going to do and more. Poor George. As Spike's sidekick he would have had fun, but as Gunn's prisoner, he gets tied up and his fish ass kicked. He's got something big coming, I can't wait…

Someone on this thing called "the Internet" called George the "Jar Jar" of *After the Fall*, which is weird because George is, despite appearances, the most normal and well-adjusted of the characters (save for maybe Connor). It was cool to see a bunch of people come to George's defense.

I'm kinda proud and surprised "your fifth digit housed in your sit-down spots" got by everyone. I thought someone at IDW or Fox would have a problem with Kr'ph saying "your thumbs up your asses" but no one did. Hooray!

Kr'ph occasionally referred to humans as "monkeys" in addition to "mongrels." However, upon seeing the issue with lettering for the first time, I was absolutely horrified to see Gunn being called a "monkey." Of course, Kr'ph meant "monkey" in the sense that humans are lower life-forms and it didn't occur to me that it could be taken a far worse way until it was laid out in front of me. So out came all the monkeys. Thank God.

PAGE EIGHTEEN

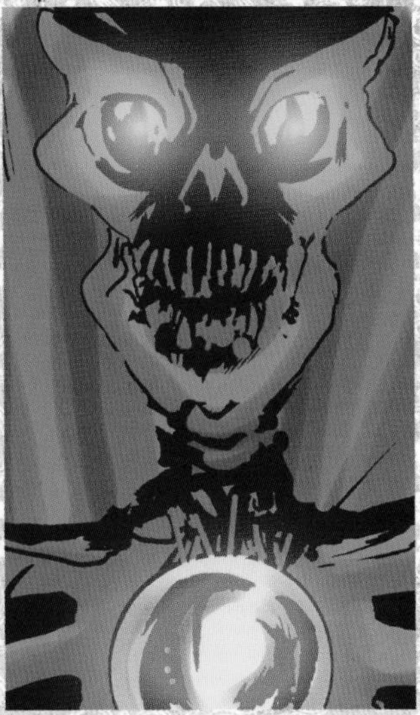

Panel 1

Kr'ph's "cats eye" glows a bit within his belly. It triggers a chain reaction that makes George's EYES glow the same color.

1. KR'PH
Now you play with power, yes?

2. BETTA GEORGE
Whoa... what is...? Whoa...
3.
...man, does everyone hate you.

4. KR'PH
A gaggle of monkeys die for every second you don't brain-yell.

Panel 2

The "warriors" mindlessly start hacking each other as George's "thoughts" fill their heads.

5. BETTA GEORGE
(BIG LETTERS)
Warriors... I need you...
6.
...and I am so sorry...
7.
...I need you to FIGHT.

Panel 3

All THE LIGHTS GO OUT at once. Kr'ph looks around, confused and annoyed.

8. KR'PH
What now? Fish, tell the lights to go back on.

9. BETTA GEORGE
Um.

10.
You should get out of here, Kr'ph.

Panel 4

Kr'ph yells at George. We see SHADOWY INDIVIDUALS coming closer in the distance.

11. BETTA GEORGE
I'm picking up some new voices. They're SCREAMING so loud it's drowning everything else out.

12. KR'PH
Ha! They are scared because they know I am Kr'ph!

13. BETTA GEORGE
They're not screaming because they're scared.

Panel 5

Small panel, of CLOSE UP on Kr'Ph's face. He's a tad alarmed.

14. BETTA GEORGE
These guys are angry.

PAGE NINETEEN

Panel 1

SHUK! An arrow HITS Betta George square in the head. It IMBEDS into his head. Not a kill shot by any means, but it takes him down.

1. KR'PH
...

2.
SOMEONE ISN'T AWARE OF MY STATUS!

Panel 2

Absolute chaos! Arrange the panels during the fight to display that: the attack is all over the place, no real rhythm to it, and the layout should reflect that.

Betta George is out. Kr'ph forces some of the remaining guards around him, to form a protective circle.

Other Guards head out towards a gang of about FIVE humans, in hoodies, carrying crossbows, knives, swords. The leader, still in shadow, carries Gunn's hubcap-axe deal. We can just kinda make it out.

3. GUARD
Protect Kr'ph!

4. KR'PH
My life for yours! My life for yours!

Panel 3

ON THE FIELD, the "Warriors" are already snapped out of it, and watching as the five figures in HOODIES take out the remaining Guards.

5. GUARD 1
DEFEND KR'PH! DEFEND OUR LORD!

6. GUNN (off-panel)
Gotta admire their loyalty.

Panel 4

SHUK! The hubcap AXE lands in one of the Guard's heads.

7. GUNN
Their fighting style? Not so much.

PAGE TWENTY

Panel 1

Kr'ph is so surrounded by Guards that he can't see the attack. But he's scared and he's crouched down low. He SMACKS the unconscious Betta George, but our boy ain't waking up today.

The "cats eye" glows. The Guards around him also kinda glow, their powers boosted by the trinket.

1. KR'PH
Lazy Fish! Wake up and yell at their heads to go! Fight well, Guards! Your love for me is unboundful!

Panel 2

One Guard gets TAKEN OUT by an arrow.

PAGE NINETEEN

Gunn! Gunn's story was something that Joss and company planned to do for a while. I was honored to be asked to carry it out, but it was also, obviously, daunting. Turning one of the show's leading characters into the "villain" is beyond intimidating. But, the best villains are those that you can identify with and have a point of view that isn't necessarily wrong, just twisted to the point of being dangerous. Gunn fits that criteria. For the record, I'd be mad at Angel, too. Angel better thank his lucky stars that I didn't get turned into a vampire, I'd show him what-for.

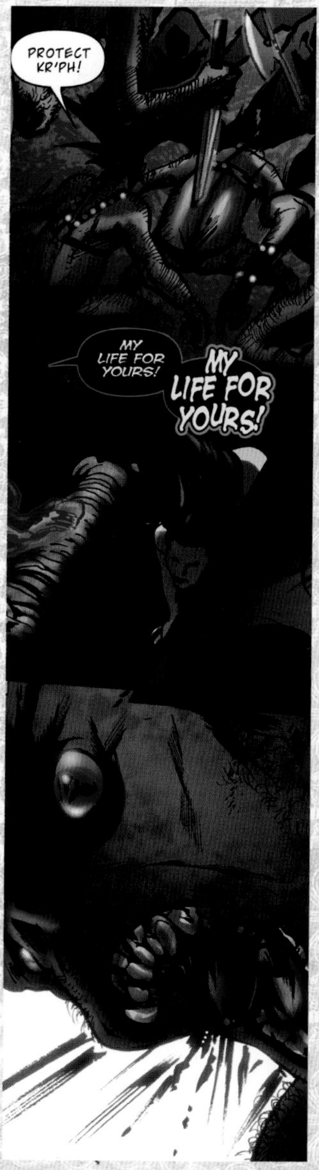
PROTECT KR'PH!
MY LIFE FOR YOURS!
MY LIFE FOR YOURS!

2. KR'PH (no tail)

...

3. KR'PH (no tail)
WHOEVER THIS IS, I AM ANGERED BUT NOT TURNING A BACKSIDE TO BARGAINING!

Panel 3

The "camera" is just below Kr'ph, looking up. Kr'ph's view of the field is blocked by three Guards. One of them ANOTHER GUARD goes down...

4. KR'PH (no tail)
YOU ARE MIGHTY AND NOBLE MONKEYS! A HANDSHAKING CAN HAPPEN!

Panel 4

Match shot of panel 1. A tiny SPLIT, a streak of blood SLICES the two remaining Guards just above the waist from someone directly behind them.

5. KR'PH (no tail)
Tell me what you want! I can help you get it!

PAGE TWENTY-ONE

Panel 1

Big panel. The Guards's halves fall off, revealing who is standing behind them. It'S GUNN'S HERO REVEAL. Hoodie on, pants, weapons at his side, bloody hubcap axe in his hand. He's got a scar near his right eye. A bit war-torn, but otherwise, looking good.

1. GUNN
I know you can.

Panel 2

Gunn SWINGS his fist down. The gelatin covering of Kr'ph flies into frame a bit as we hear a sickening sound effect of fist plowing through muck. The background goes RED behind him.

2. GUNN
You're just not gonna be the biggest fan of how.

Panel 3

Gunn THROWS HIS HAND IN THE AIR (Kr'ph's ooze arcing from Gunn's hand into the air), it's now clutching the CAT'S EYE, yanked out of the spine of Kr'ph. Kr'ph is dead, a big pile of gelatine corpse with a scared looked permanently on his mug. The slave girls are shaken up a bit. Gunn's GANG throws their hands up, triumphant! The warriors on the field are relieved and happy!

3. GUNN
WE GOT IT! ONE FIGHT, ONE LORD DOWN!
4.
CHALK THAT UP TO A WIN FOR TEAM GUNN!

PAGE TWENTY-TWO

Panel 1

On the gang. They are all around Gunn's age of various ethnic backgrounds. Among them is save one OLDER MAN with a thick grey beard. A look of confused and hurt looks on their all their faces.

1. GANG MEMBER 1
Wait, dude. Did you say "Team Gunn"?

PAGE TWENTY-ONE
Kr'ph was originally going to be captured. Idea was to allow him to live so he could be killed later by Illyria (which would have been a fine comeuppance for the harem), but Gunn killing him so swiftly was much more powerful.

2. GUNN
You may have been together before I joined, but I trained you. Plus I coordinated the outfits.

3. GANG MEMBER 2
You made us wear these.

Panel 2

Gunn points to the knocked out Betta George. He notices the SLAVE GIRLS are scared.

4. GUNN
Can we hash this out later? Get up here and wrap up the fish. Don't let him wake up until we get back, that's a whole bag of trouble we don't need.
5.
One second...

Panel 3

He caresses one of the slave girls chins. She smiles. Even with ooze dripping from Gunn's hand, he's charming as hell. This is a new Gunn. A leader. A champion. A ladies' man.

6. GUNN
It's okay, you're fine now. Think of the last couple of months as a bad, bad dream. That's all they were.
7.
I tell you what, though. You play your cards right and this dream could suddenly turn downright erotic.

Panel Four and Five

Angel puts the sword back on the wall and walks towards something in the two panels in question.

SON OF BURGE (off-panel, yelling from below)
SIX FOR SIX! SIX FOR SIX!

PAGE TWENTY-THREE

Panel 1

Angel watches as Burge has the humans lined up for the kill.

1. SON OF BURGE
Angel killed six of my men!
(connected)
2.
I kill six of his humans!

3. CAPTION (ANGEL)
I was told not to leave the building. Not one step.

Panel 2

On Wesley, in the elevator.

4. CAPTION (ANGEL)
I was also told that everything I was doing was wrong.
5.
A friend said it, face to transparent face.

Panel 3

6. CAPTION (ANGEL)
Thing is...

PAGE TWENTY-TWO

Gunn's dialog when talking to the "slave girls" is very un-Gunn like, which should have been the first clue that he's not the same old Gunn. He's a bit pushy/creepy with the dames, no?

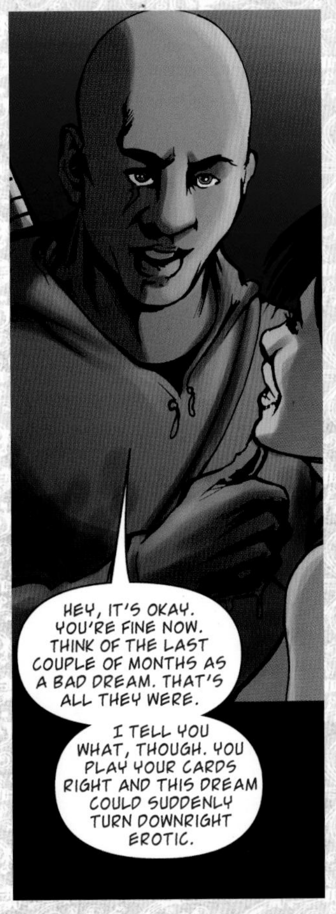
HEY, IT'S OKAY. YOU'RE FINE NOW. THINK OF THE LAST COUPLE OF MONTHS AS A BAD DREAM. THAT'S ALL THEY WERE.
I TELL YOU WHAT, THOUGH. YOU PLAY YOUR CARDS RIGHT AND THIS DREAM COULD SUDDENLY TURN DOWNRIGHT EROTIC.

Panel 4

Wesley in the white room.

7. CAPTION (ANGEL)
...everything's different.

8. CAPTION (ANGEL)
And I don't know who told him to say it.

PAGE TWENTY-FOUR

The "recompense" line was what the entire issue was building towards. The original idea was to have the heavy metal desk be the thing that kills Burge's son. However, it would have required Burge's son to be in JUST the right spot to be Wile E. Coyote'd. Too convenient. The next idea was to have a play on Angel's old wrist-stake-gauntlets, but they'd actually EJECT at high speeds, but the set-up for that earlier in the issue took up too much time.

We wound up with Angel hurling a stake into the demon's eye. On one hand, it would be revealed two issues later that he was human and, speaking as a human, I couldn't hurl a stake into a demon's eye. But the demon was racing towards him so fast that he provided the momentum himself. Basically, Angel could have just held the stake out and the Burge Jr. could have run into it. That would have been kinda funny.

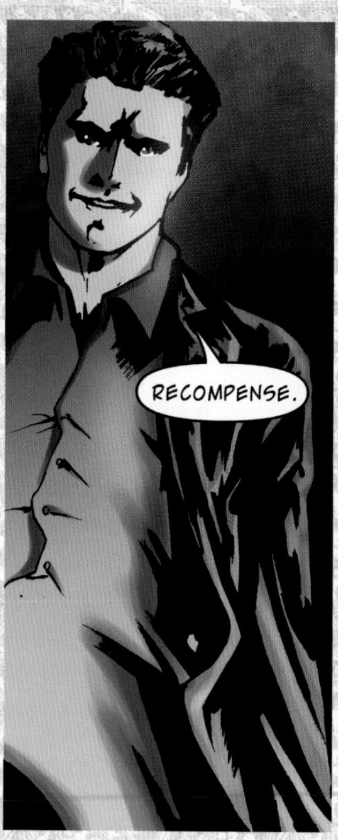
RECOMPENSE.

PAGE TWENTY-FOUR

Panel 1

Son of Burge is about to kill the humans.

1. CAPTION (ANGEL)
But...

Panel 2

The desk drops.

At the bottom of the picture:

2. CAPTION (ANGEL)
It doesn't mean he was wrong.

3. SOUND F/X:
Klllllang

4. SON OF BURGE
What—?

Panel 3

They look up, see Angel.

5. SON OF BURGE
What the hell was THAT?

Panel 4

Shot of Angel, triumphant.

6. ANGEL
Recompense.

PAGE TWENTY-FIVE

This page could almost be a collage of pictures. Very frantic, very epic, and Panel 1 should be big! Panels 2-4 are smaller, not as important, obviously.

Panel 1

BIG PANEL. BIG CROWD-PLEASING PANEL. Maybe even harried and cock-eyed in its panel borders. This is the moment Angel fans have wanted for the whole issue, Angel's stepping up and taking action.

Angel HURLS a stake at him. Angel doesn't even have to be dead center, hero-reveal type shot. In fact, it might be cool if the STAKE is really close to the "camera," and Angel is far behind it. We could even make everything out of focus EXCEPT the stake. Basically, we are Offspring and the stake is about to hit us right in the eye.

Panel 2

Faraway, side shot of the lackeys looking up.

SOUND F/X

Squitch

Panel 3

Match shot of 3. Maybe even the same panel. They're still looking up.

PAGE TWENTY-SIX

Panel 1

Camera is over Offspring's body. Stake firmly driven through his right eye. That demon is dead. Some lackeys stare up at Angel, yelling. Still others are walking off with the desk (Burge wanted it).

>   1. LACKEY
> You have declared war, vampire! You have no idea what you've done!

>   2. ANGEL
> I've declared war. You just said.

Panel 2

On Angel who smiles to himself slightly. The "camera" is below him, looking up at Angel. He looks heroic.

>   3. CAPTION (ANGEL)
> Can't take that back, can I?
> (continued)
>   4.
> Good.
> (continued)
>   5.
> It all begins with a stake to the eye.

Panel 3

Wesley stands in the elevator. The doors open, flooding the elevator with WHITE LIGHT from outside.

>   6. CAPTION (ANGEL)
> Of course, this might be exactly what they wanted.

Panel 4

THE WHITE ROOM. Wesley steps off the elevator. His eyes GLOW WHITE to match the room.

>   7. CAPTION (ANGEL)
> That's fine.
> (continued)
>   8.
> Let them think they're in charge.

PAGE TWENTY-SEVEN

Panel 1

Small panel, stretching across the page. We're at the end of a corridor, leading to where the football players run out onto the field. The field is visible behind us. And it's covered, as are the hallway walls, in what looks like SANSKRIT.

In the interest of full disclosure, all the little letters are written in the blood of Kr'ph's warriors and are made to look like the writings of the OLD ONES (Illyria's people).

I don't think this lettering was ever shown, but you can look on Illyria's esophagus for how to do it. It COULD look like Tony Harris' lettering on one of the covers

PAGE TWENTY-SEVEN
Yep, Gunn's a vampire. I swear, that's him. Some readers were confused as to whether or not it was Gunn or one of his new gang. That's the problem with giving Gunn and the Gunnlings matching hoodies. My bad, readers. Not Franco's, mine.

PAGE TWENTY-SEVEN

I actually wanted to end the first issue with the reveal that Angel was human, because (A) I thought hiding that he was human would interfere with the story, (B) I thought it was a hell of a way to sucker-punch the audience and (C) I thought Gunn's reveal wouldn't be much of a surprise, as it was generally known that this was a possible storyline if *Angel* continued or if they made a *Spike* movie. I believe Amy Acker mentioned it. I forgive her.

In the end, though, it was always in Joss' plan to end with Gunn being a vampire, so of course I wasn't about to muck with it. He was absolutely right. To begin with Wesley being dead and forced to work for Wolfram & Hart, and then end with Angel's *other* close friend being turned into the very thing he hates the most, that was a bookend of misery (in other words, that was *Angel*).

Those be my notes. I hope it shed some light on the process. I know I learned a heck of a lot. I just want to thank you guys for your interest. It has been and continues to be a thrill. Back to work on *Angel: After the Fall*. I'm currently scripting issue 10, or as I like to call it "the issue wherein we reveal Angel has been a werewolf the entire time."

—Brian

for ANGEL: AFTER THE FALL issue 1. Just for a little cover-inside story synchronicity.

The Slave Girl's screams trail off into nothing.

> 1. SLAVE GIRL (off-panel)
Aaaaaaaarg---...

> 2. CAPTION (ANGEL)
Wolfram & Hart has taken away everything I've had.

Panel 2

CLOSER STILL. Up on the dead bodies of the SLAVE GIRLS. Vamp marks in their necks. A crouched figure kills of the last one.

> 3. CAPTION (ANGEL)
Everything I was.

Panel 3

BIG BIG PANEL.

Gunn, VAMPED OUT. The last Slave Girl dead. He's holding onto her body, bringing his face up from her neck. She's dangling lifeless in his arms. A look of fear on her face. And a look of pure ANGER on his. He's SCREAMING, blood running from his mouth.

> 4. CAPTION (ANGEL)
But that's how I'm going to win.

> 5. CAPTION (ANGEL)
(Bottom of Panel)
They think they've changed me.

> 6. CAPTION:
To be continued!

[illegible] all tarted with a girl [illegible]

That sparked an Internet de[illegible] moment Aint It Cool poste[illegible] preview pages. People argued over [illegible] specifically Angel was talking about. Possible sus[illegible] included Buffy, Fred and Cordy. Ryall guessed Bruce Wayne[illegible] which made me question tha[illegible] reads my stuff.

The first couple dra[illegible] differ-ently: it start[illegible] in the window [illegible] store. On the secon[illegible] thrown throu[illegible] so the toppe[illegible] supplies. The [illegible] was destroyed, not-at-all-subtly acknowled[illegible] me

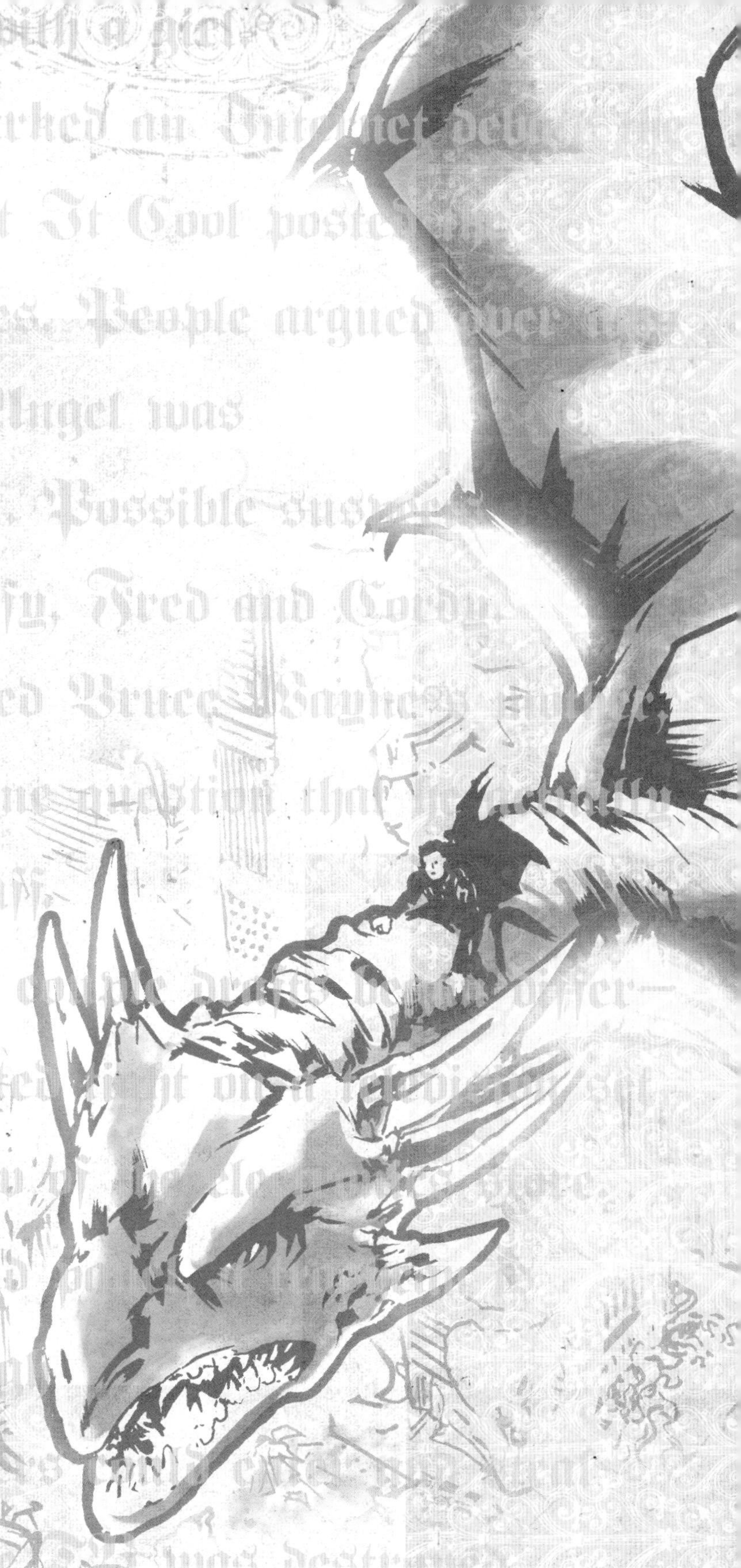

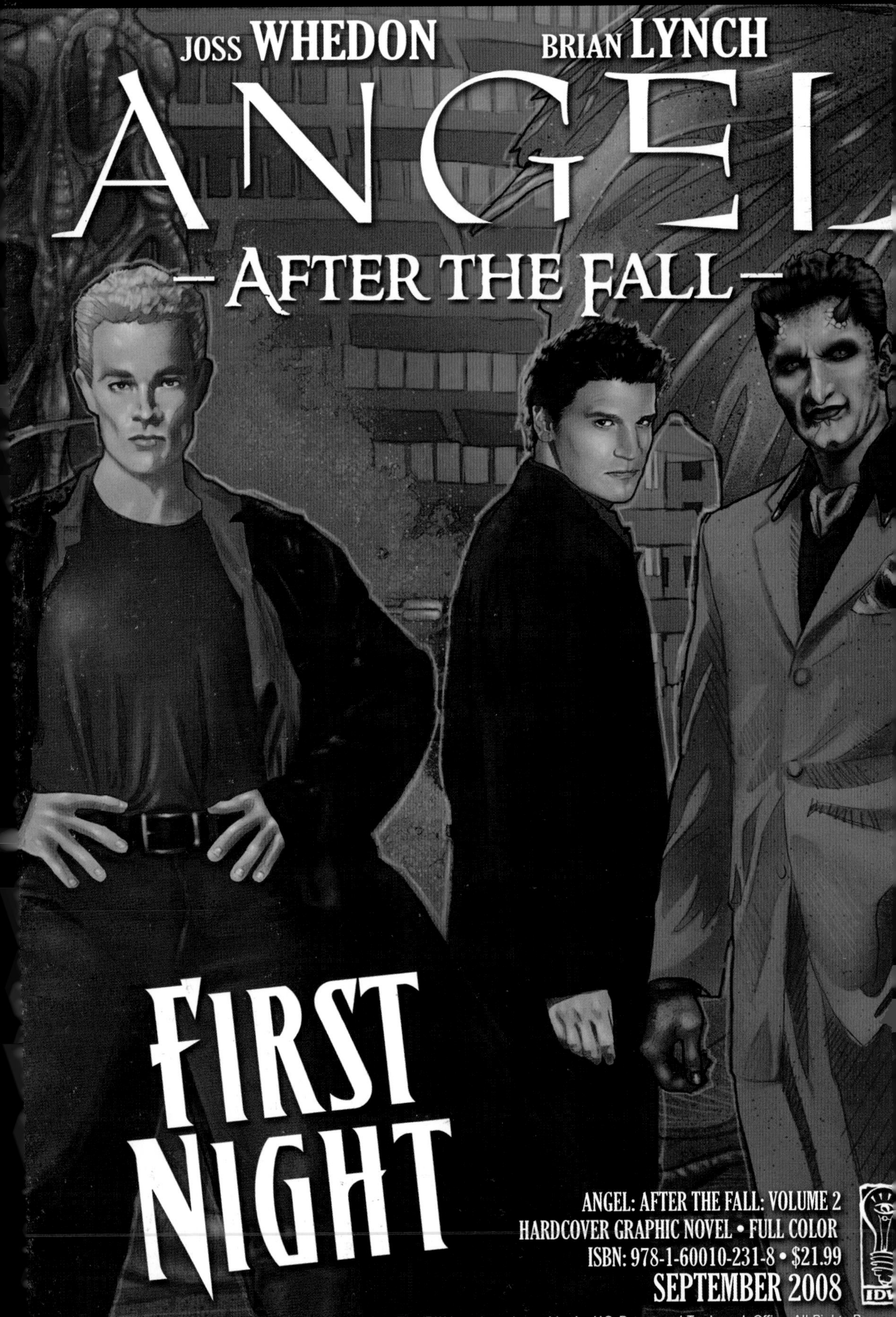
JOSS WHEDON
BRIAN LYNCH
ANGEL
-AFTER THE FALL-
FIRST NIGHT
ANGEL: AFTER THE FALL: VOLUME 2
HARDCOVER GRAPHIC NOVEL • FULL COLOR
ISBN: 978-1-60010-231-8 • $21.99
SEPTEMBER 2008

ANGEL AND SPIKE GRAPHIC NOVELS FROM IDW PUBLISHING

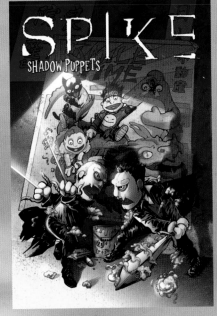

ANGEL
AULD LANG SYNE

ANGEL: AULD LANG SYNE
Scott Tipton (w), David Messina (a)

While tracking a mysterious cult in Los Angeles in hopes of solving a kidnapping, Angel finds himself face to face with some familiar faces–faces he shouldn't be seeing!

ISBN: 978-1-60010-063-5 • $19.99

SPIKE
SHADOW PUPPETS

SPIKE: SHADOW PUPPETS
Brian Lynch (w), Franco Urru (a)

Spike and Lorne head off to Japan to stop the latest Japanese kids' show... *Smile Time*! Will they become "puppetized" themselves?

ISBN: 978-1-60010-112-0 • $17.99

ANGEL
The Curse

ANGEL: THE CURSE
Jeff Mariotte (w), David Messina (a)

Joss Whedon's classic vampire character, Angel, returns to comics and begins a search for the Gypsy tribe that cursed him so many years ago.

ISBN: 978-1-933239-79-8 • $19.99

ANGEL
OLD FRIENDS

ANGEL: OLD FRIENDS
Jeff Mariotte (w), David Messina (a)

When a strangely familiar, seemingly vampiric figure is spotted killing victims in Los Angeles, Angel is lured back to the city to put a stop to the string of slayings.

ISBN: 978-1-933239-76-7 • $19.99

ANGEL

ANGEL: SPOTLIGHT
Peter David, Dan Jolley, Scott Tipton, Jeff Mariotte, Jay Faerber (w), Nicoloa Scott, Mark Pennington, Mike Norton, David Messina, Bob Gill (a)

A collection of stories starring *Angel's* cast by all-star comic talent, featured characters include Illyria, Gunn, Wesley, Doyle, and Connor.

ISBN: 978-1-60010-023-9 • $19.99

ANGEL
SCRIPTBOOK, Volume 1

ANGEL SCRIPTBOOK, VOL. 1
Joss Whedon, David Greenwalt, Jim Kouf (w)

A collection of five complete shooting scripts from the very best episodes of *Angel's* five-season run.

ISBN: 978-1-60010-020-8 • $19.99

ANGEL

ANGEL SCRIPTBOOK, VOL. 2
Jeffrey Bell, Ben Edlund, David Greenwalt, Douglas Petrie, Jeannine Renshaw, Joss Whedon (w)

This collection of five scripts includes the fan-favorite "Smile Time" and the series finale, "Not Fade Away" written by Jeffrey Bell and series creator Joss Whedon.

ISBN: 978-1-60010-049-9 • $19.99

SPIKE

SPIKE
Peter David, Scott Tipton (w), Fernando Goni (a)

Joss Whedon's fan-favorite character Spike goes solo in three tales featuring appearances by the vengeance demon Halfrek, Los Hermanos Numeros, The Gem of Amarra, and more.

ISBN: 978-1-60010-030-7 • $19.99

SPIKE
vs.
Dracula

SPIKE VS. DRACULA
Peter David (w), Joe Corroney (a)

When Spike destroys the tribe of gypsies that cursed Angel, he outraged Count Dracula and began a rivalry that spans decades.

ISBN: 978-1-60010-012-3 • $19.99

SPIKE
ASYLUM

SPIKE: ASYLUM
Bryan Lynch (w), Franco Urru (a)

Spike checks himself in as a patient at Mosaic Wellness Center. But there's a big problem–the hundreds of super-powered, supernatural patients at Mosaic know Spike, and want him dead.

ISBN: 978-1-60010-061-1 • $19.99

JOSS WHEDON: THE WATCHER.

BRIAN LYNCH: is a screenwriter who started his career writing and directing the independent film *Big Helium Dog*, and followed it up by selling an original *Muppets* script to the Jim Henson Company. He wrote *Nightcrawlers* for Warner Brothers, currently in production for a 2008 release, directed by McG. He has done uncredited rewrites for Dimension Films and Twentieth Century Fox, and is currently writing the movie *The Sims* for Fox.

Lynch is the creator of the comedy site angrynakedpat.com. He also wrote a story for the first issue of *Spider-Man Unlimited*. His work on *Spike: Asylum* caught the attention of Joss Whedon, who sought him out to co-plot and write *Angel: After the Fall*. In between *Asylum* and *After the Fall*, Lynch wrote a series about Spike fighting evil puppets, which, oddly—but if you think about it, quite predictably—won him an Academy Award.

FRANCO URRU: used to do different jobs a long time ago, but kept coming back to the comic biz. It must have been the rough beginning at Giolitti Studio in Italy that made him more stubborn than most people. He worked for several publishers—Italians and foreign—on various genres. He even had some professional experience in graphic design, commercials, and illustrations for children books. After another pause of a few years which he spent working for a company that was the farthest thing to creativity, he got back to the comics world with IDW, where he's illustrated *Spike: Asylum* and *Spike: Shadow Puppets* before being hand-picked by Joss Whedon for *After the Fall*. Franco and Brian paired up again on *Spike: After the Fall*, which takes place in the months leading up to the story in this volume.

biographies